CHICANO STUDIES

CHICANO STUDIES

THE GENESIS OF A DISCIPLINE

MICHAEL SOLDATENKO

The University of Arizona Press
Tucson

To my granddaughters, Graciela and Angela

The University of Arizona Press
© 2009 The Arizona Board of Regents
All rights reserved

www.uapress.arizona.edu

Library of Congress Cataloging-in-Publication Data
Soldatenko, Michael.
Chicano studies : the genesis of a discipline / Michael Soldatenko.
p. cm.
Includes bibliographical references and index.
ISBN 978-0-8165-1275-1 (alk. paper)
1. Mexican Americans—Study and teaching. 2. Ethnology—
Study and teaching. 3. Minorities—Study and teaching. I. Title.
E184.M5S611   2009
305.868'72073—dc22   2009024369

Manufactured in the United States of America on acid-free,
archival-quality paper and processed chlorine-free.

16   15   14   13   12   11   6   5   4   3   2

Contents

Acknowledgments   vii

Introduction   1

1. The Genesis of Academic Chicano Studies, 1967–1970:
Utopia and the Emergence of Chicano Studies   12

2. Empirics and Chicano Studies: The Formation of
Empirical Chicano Studies, 1970–1975   38

3. Perspectivist Chicano Studies, 1967–1982   67

4. Chicano Studies as an Academic Discipline, 1975–1982   94

5. Chicanas, the Chicano Student Movements,
and Chicana Thought, 1967–1982   130

Conclusion   168

Notes   189

Bibliography   231

Index   271

Acknowledgments

Like most acknowledgments, mine are tied to my life.

As part of an attempt to bring my wife to the Department of Women's Studies at Arizona State University (ASU), in the fall of 1995 the Hispanic Research Center offered me a postdoctoral fellowship so that I could change the direction of my research agenda and become part of the Department of Chicano(a) Studies. I had received my doctorate in European history in 1987. Unfortunately, my attempts to link my dissertation work on British economic thought with ethnic studies had been unsuccessful. One journal reviewer found my attempt to look at eighteenth-century Scottish thought through the lens of ethnic studies and Chicano(a) Studies "barbaric." At ASU's Hispanic Research Center I began the transition to becoming a scholar in the field of Chicano(a) and Latino(a) Studies. This book is part of the result of that transformation. I thank the center, especially its director, Felipe Castro, for their support. I would also like to thank my colleagues at ASU: Mary Romero, Eric Margolis, and (in a bizarre way) Ray Padilla.

Sadly, the Department of Chicano(a) Studies at Arizona State decided that I did not fit their needs. We returned to southern California, where I reestablished my relationship with Chicano(a) and Latino(a) Studies scholars in the area. With their help I was able to continue my exploration of Chicano(a) Studies as a discipline. In particular, I would like to thank Ray Rocco, Bill de la Torre, Mary Pardo, Adolfo Bermeo, Rudy Acuña, Tony Hernandez, Raoul Contreras, Jose Calderon, Marta Lopez-Garza, David Hayes-Bautista, and the Chabráns (Angie Chabram-Desnersesian, Richard, and Rafael Chabrán). I found that many of my questions could not be answered through printed sources alone. I turned to archivists and librarians, who guided me to materials that helped me discover ever more questions. Richard Chabrán, who at that time was the UCLA Chicano Studies Research Center (CSRC)

Acknowledgments

librarian, played the role of Virgil, as he led me through the confusing history of Chicano(a) Studies. I spent many hours exploring the UCLA CRSC archives and having Richard clarify what I was reading. When he was too busy, his well-trained assistants (such as Romelia Salinas) came to the rescue. I would also like to thank the folks at UCLA's University Archives, in particular Dennis Bitterlich.

At the University of California–Berkeley, I would like to thank the many individuals at the Bancroft and Ethnic Studies Library, in particular, Lillian Castillo-Speed. I would also like to thank Christine Marin, who worked in Special Collections at the Hayden Library at Arizona State University. I would like to thank the editors of *Latino Studies Journal, Latin American Perspectives,* and *Ethnic Studies Review* for publishing earlier versions of my ideas. For their support and friendship, I would like to thank my colleagues at Santa Monica College and now at the Department of Chicano Studies at California State University–Los Angeles.

I would like to thank a few scholars who set me on this path. While I am now a different type of historian, my intellectual development arose from my discourse with their positions and ideas. I wish to thank Jasper Blystone at Loyola Marymount University. In the history department at UCLA, I want to recognize Amos Funkenstein, Norton Wise, Russell Jacoby, and Robert Brenner, who chaired my dissertation committee.

This book would not have been possible without the critical eyes of Maria Angelina Soldatenko and our two sons, Gabriel and Adrian, as well as our daughter, Rosie Salazar. I want to thank Adrian, for interrupting his work on his doctorate in physics to read this manuscript; Gabriel, for spirited discussions about my particular readings of Foucault given his philosophical training; and Rosie, who kept us going with fine sustenance. Of course, Gela has always been there to point out when my gender, heterosexual, and race privileges have bubbled to the surface. I would like to thank the University of Arizona Press for their editorial assistance, in particular freelance editor Amy Smith Bell. Last but not least, gratitude must be given to our *juguetones* pugs that always alerted us when we became too serious.

Although many people have helped me work through my ideas, I alone am at fault for any inaccuracies and errors. I hope that this book results in a spirited debate about the future of Chicano and Chicana Studies.

Chicano Studies

Introduction

My interest with Chicano Studies as an academic discipline originated with the struggle at the University of California at Los Angeles for a department of Chicana and Chicano Studies in the spring of 1993.[1] While I had done some research in the area, I had never really thought out the assumptions, models, theories, and practices of the field. Chicano Studies as a discipline did not seem to differ from my own field of training (history). I had not thought about the formation and genesis of Chicano Studies. Just like history, its characteristics, terminology, and methods were assumed to be "neutral." Chicano Studies appeared as an oppositional discipline that could coexist, albeit in tension, with other fields. While Chicano Studies had problems (what discipline did not?), they were resolvable. I expected that with effort Chicano Studies could be restored to a healthier manifestation. I was naïve.

The 1993 struggle woke me from my intellectual slumber. The protest at the university made me realize that Chicano Studies could not be a singular subject, although many students, scholars, and activists acted as if there had always been a single Chicano Studies. During the protest, however, multiple articulations of Chicano studies appeared.[2] The central questions that emerged were the following: Why was there only one acceptable Chicano Studies? Why did the field demand such compliance? How did it become singular? I came to appreciate that just as this homogenized Chicano Studies had silenced many at the 1993 protest, it was possible that other Chicano studies had existed in the past, different from the current orthodoxy. What happened to these other expressions? I was curious to explore and unpack the discursive formation of Chicano studies with its multiple dissensions, elisions, erasures, and silences that eventually resulted in Chicano Studies. The UCLA struggle made me concede that the Chicano Studies I had been practicing had a particular history with a set agenda. It had intentionally excluded (and continues to exclude) other visions and readings of the Mexican American experience and denied its institutional relationship with the academic world.

Motivated by this protest, I decided to diagnose how and why Chicano Studies had become the practice that I had observed. The patriarchal practices and the politics of nationalism that occurred throughout the 1993 protest were not new. Yet why, after twenty-some years of teaching and practicing Chicano Studies, did Chicanos(as) still find themselves grappling with patriarchy, nationalism, and homophobia, together with *chingón* politics?[3] Was the facile transformation of the protest into Chingón Studies inevitable? More disturbing, possibly reflecting the continued oppressive power of Chicano politics, the protesters did not question these exclusionary, antifeminist, and homophobic practices. These practices appeared as second nature. All of this was made even more troublesome by the apparent ignorance over the production, control, and distribution of academic knowledge. Could this be the nature of Chicano Studies, at least as practiced at UCLA?

These concerns led me to this book, which interrogates the genesis, formation, and development of academic Chicano studies from 1967 to 1982. Throughout this fifteen-year period, I trace the maturation of Chicano studies from its initial equivocal and fluid character to its construction into a unitary academic discipline. My story delineates a multiplicity of Chicano studies, exemplifying a diversity of intellectual and political positions.[4] Like most intellectual enterprises, these early Chicano studies pushed particularity over homogenizing endeavors and theoretical constructs. Within this multiplicity, some Chicanos(as) wanted to corral the anarchy of particularism by creating a unitary theme and practice. They sought to construct, whether they stated it or not, a discipline as defined by U.S. higher education. As Chicano studies established itself in the academy, scholars' intellectual production became regulated and defined by the discipline's methods, methodology, and epistemology as well as by the institutional procedures and the system of academic hierarchy.[5] Chicano studies, whether independently or as part of some type of inter- or transdisciplinary program, operated as a social science or humanities discipline.

I explore the association between Chicano studies and certain nondiscursive domains—in particular, Chicano(a) student politics and academic institution building. Chicano studies appeared during a period of campus struggles that reflected personal agendas, ideological beliefs, societal pressures, as well as institutional procedures. Some scholars have argued that there is a determinant relationship between the origins of Chicano studies and both campus politics and the larger Chicano movement. A few have suggested that effective programs retained this connection with nondiscursive practices. To avoid this position, I trace the emergence of Chicano studies without situating it within a particular political or institutional oeuvre. Therefore, besides laying out a discursive archeology of Chicano studies, my goal is to trace a genealogy that explores the nondiscursive tracts of Chicano studies and its development from a nonacademic though intellectual oppositional epistemology into a traditional, albeit alternative, academic discipline: Chicano Studies.[6]

The accepted narrative of Chicano studies begins with the social and political struggles of the 1960s, collectively referred to as *el movimiento*. As self-identified Chicano(a) students arrived on campus, many became active in their educational institutions, initially working with white organizations but eventually establishing organizations that challenged their campus's policies on admissions, retention, and funding. They began to organize actions to "transform" their home communities. For these students, commitment to a more equitable world for Mexican Americans was central. Chicanos(as) were also concerned with curricular issues. If students were planning to change the world, they had to comprehend it. For many Chicanos(as), the explanations provided by higher education were wanting. Like white and black radicals, Chicanos(as) began to explore the meaning of education and the academic knowledge that resulted from the compact among faculty, academic institutions, and a selective intellectual tradition. They were critical of the academic culture and its institutional apparatus that provided neatly packaged knowledge—assembled by fields, disciplines, departments, schools and the like—to its consumers. They hesitated before an academic knowledge that privileged scientism and empirical methods and sought to establish the laws of nature and society—using a masculinist language. They suspected that this knowledge was part of the continuous reconstruction and defense of American exceptionalism.[7] Chicanos(as) understood that the Mexican American had little space within this intellectual dynamic.

In the late 1960s, for most Chicanos(as), their conceptualization of knowledge had ensued from the culture of academic life and its "hidden curriculum."[8] Knowledge was produced through academic disciplines and fields with their corresponding methods, methodologies, and perspectives. The division among social science, humanities, science, professional programs, arts, applied science, public programs, and so on shaped their view of how knowledge was assembled and reproduced. Thus academic knowledge revealed itself in the curricular programs that fostered a selective intellectual tradition and canon. It therefore became impossible to detach concepts like "knowledge," "discipline," "social science," and "humanities"—they were all involved in the building of the institution of higher education. The simultaneous connection among academic culture, knowledge, and the university system left limited possibilities for the germination of alternative (much less oppositional) perspectives or to conceive of knowledge outside the bounds of the academy.[9]

At the center of American academic knowledge was a scientific and masculinist discourse. The social sciences and humanities privileged empirical and realist methods to ascertain the fundamental laws that operate in nature and society. This language was built on a gendered speech of hard facts, science, and power.[10] This version of knowledge, as the historian Dorothy Ross has described, emerged in defense of American exceptionalism that had been challenged by the possibilities of change at the turn of the twentieth century. Furthermore, as historian and journalist Ruth Rosen has advanced, "Cold War culture and its ideas about gender patrolled the boundaries between men and women, gay and straight, patriotic and subversive."[11]

To avert this crisis, Ross explained, academic practices redrew the uniqueness of "America" and turned natural law and historical principle into the unchanging bases for American civilization.[12] The faith in scientism was reinforced by an academic professionalism that provided an authoritative understanding of the world. As the university system in the United States flourished, its decentralization nurtured the separation among the disciplines, reinforcing the antihistorical and antiphilosophical tendencies in American academic knowledge. Moreover the American university experience consecrated a covenant among professional instructors, a canon, and a group of young affiliates that reproduced the disciplines and legitimized American knowledge.[13] The augmenting specialization and professionalization of the social sciences and humanities, bounded by academic cultural dogma and procedures, created a particular knowledge whose purpose was social control and empire building.

Firmly conjoined to American exceptionalism was race. Many public intellectuals had written the United States as the central figure in the universalist commitment to civil and human rights. In particular, U.S. history had become the mythic tale of a nonethnic national ideology, where ancestral (and racial) affinities meant little. As the historian Nikhil Pal Singh explained: "Civic myths about the triumph over racial injustice have become central to the resuscitation of a vigorous and strident form of American exceptionalism—the idea of the United States as both a unique and universal nation."[14] But he questioned this performance: "What if there is a recurring oscillation between universalizing abstractions of liberal democracy, in which individuals are considered equal with respect to nationality, and a persistent regression, in which the actual individuals and communities who benefit from national belonging are implicitly or explicitly constituted in white supremacist terms?"[15]

In American academic practices, race is erased while simultaneously being at the center of intellectual production. In much of the public intellectuals' engagement with "America," the issue of race was envisioned as always being at the point of resolution and therefore no longer (or ever, for that matter) a concern. Singh, following on the work of others, has added that both American liberalism and race are connected to American imperial expansion. Imperial expansionism and Jim Crow at the turn of the twentieth century "gave new life to racist schemas of thought already deposited in the American past."[16] When higher education fostered the tale of "America," it also asserted a racialized view of the United States and the world.[17]

In the 1960s, students of color, following radical whites, contested American academic knowledge and laid siege to the pact among professors, their acolytes, and a selective intellectual tradition. Furthermore, they questioned the association among knowledge, American exceptionalism, and empire (though less clearly regarding race and often not at all looking at gender or sexuality). To undermine this bond, students sought to subvert the university as a political institution. Given the generation of this mythic universalism, students of color initially sought to disrupt academic knowledge. In its place, they wanted to design a new body of knowledge. They required a knowledge that could more honestly and truthfully explain the condition of people of color. For Mexican American activists, this often meant that a space had to be carved out of higher education—a space that would be controlled by Mexican Americans and driven by Mexican American social and political concerns. This could only be accomplished by direct confrontation with the academic institution. This occupied territory of higher education would deal with student services, teaching, and research. This was to be Chicano studies—a liberated zone within the oppressor's institution. From this liberated terrain, activists could then direct their attention to transforming the community. The political scientist Rick Olguin has asserted that ethnic studies was to have a distinct discourse from all academic models; it was to be grounded in its community orientation, its historical and social perspective, and self-reflexivity.[18]

As el movimiento progressed and the Chicano(a) student movements flourished, students and faculty constructed several formulations of Chicano studies. These perspectives reflected sundry regional, political, and intellectual currents. Nonetheless, all of these constructions sought to disrupt academic knowledge that had denied space to the Mexican American experience.[19] In the process, Chicano studies produced a variety of intellectual tools required to express and analyze the experience of Chicanos(as). Many Chicano(a) students felt that institutional control was central to this intellectual revolution and the struggle for self-determination and liberation. In the academy, Chicanos(as) conflated political with intellectual concerns. What was left unclear was how their perceived need to separate Chicano studies (or ethnic studies) from academic work was due solely to the quest for autonomy or the inadequacy of academic practices as a way of knowing.[20]

To explore these various issues, I examine two expressions of early Chicano studies. Although other vistas existed, I believe what I have termed Empirical Chicano Studies and Perspectivist Chicano Studies were the most common. By examining the intellectual expressions of each thread, I show distinct practices of Chicano studies. To understand how these came about, I examine the intense intellectual discourse that took place in the late 1960s. From the first essays in *El Grito: A Journal of Contemporary Mexican-American Thought* (1967) to the appearance of *El Plan de Santa Bárbara* (1969) and the initial issues of *Aztlán: Chicano Journal of the Social Sciences and the Arts* (1970), this era reflected a maelstrom of academic Chicano studies. Through these writings, several expressions of Chicano studies appeared with various possible options of bringing Chicano studies to (and not *only* into) the academy. No univocal version of Chicano studies existed. Although these versions of Chicano studies overlapped, they expressed radically distinct meanings and approaches.

When I discuss Perspectivist Chicano Studies and Empirical Chicano Studies, I do not imply any necessary relationship to a particular philosophical orientation; my use of these terms is merely descriptive. When I use "perspectivist," I want to point out the tendency of these scholars to center their research on a Chicano standpoint that arises from their particular, often cultural, experience in the United States. I contrast this with those intellectuals who center their analysis on the institutional mechanisms that result in inequality. Because of this latter perspective, these scholars saw the battle for Chicano studies as one of institutionalization of programs. This group I call the "empirics." Of course to assume any clear-cut separation is to ignore the massive overlapping of these expressions and to miss the chaotic and complex history of the making of a discipline—especially one created in a hostile and turbulent environment. Nevertheless, only one of these visions would eventually become "official."[21]

The most successful expression of adapting to institutional control and intellectual production came from the empiric scholars, who molded Empirical Chicano Studies. They saw the battle for Chicano studies in two stages. The first and most important stage was the institutionalization of all programs that dealt with Chicanos(as) under Chicano control. The empirics visualized these programs as part of the overall political struggle for Chicano self-determination. Their second concern was to develop objective methods that could provide students with a structural knowledge of their historical and cultural inheritance. These curricular concerns supplemented the institution-building process. Empirics successfully replaced other potential versions of Chicano studies. By 1975, Empirical Chicano Studies had become the only legitimate vision of Chicano Studies and simultaneously matured into part of the American academic project.

It is more difficult to provide a thumbnail sketch of Perspectivist Chicano Studies, however. This vision failed to become a successful and legitimate interpretation of Chicano studies. By the mid- to late 1970s, Perspectivist Chicano Studies had become a fragmented intellectual agenda, surviving in the periphery of teaching institutions, alternative educational institutions, the arts, and certain community organizations. As victorious Empirical Chicano Studies dominated the field, perspectivist writers were progressively pushed toward peripheral journals or self-publication. Because of this, Perspectivist Chicano Studies never matured into a concise intellectual style, and its practitioners

were often isolated. Their lack of success allowed much differentia-
tion among perspectivists. Given these caveats, however, we can still
provide a working definition for this intellectual style. Perspectivist
scholars centered their work on formulating a Chicano standpoint that
grew out of Chicano(a) experiences in the United States. Critical of
social-science research and questioning academic work, these thinkers
sought to establish an oppositional epistemology rooted in the process
of Chicano(a) identity formation.

Empirical Chicano Studies progressively transformed itself into Chicano Studies by exorcizing all possible competitors and critics. After
1975, Chicano Studies had become a singular subject and began to
accommodate itself within the academy, increasingly mimicking the
behavior of traditional academic disciplines. While some scholars and
campus activists have argued that the weakening of Chicano Studies
was due to the demise of el movimiento, it can be argued that the incorporation of Chicano Studies resulted from the participants' inability (or
unwillingness) to understand the process by which the academy controls, produces, and distributes knowledge. In short, Chicano Studies
was mainstreamed and its research depoliticized.

African Americans, Chicanos(as), feminists, Asian Americans,
Native Americans, and Latinos(as) expected that the assault on the academy would rupture the compact and initiate a transformation of knowledge and its production. What most did not comprehend, though, was
how the academy composed knowledge. By drawing attention toward
the various aspects of the university structure (such as "disciplines" and
"fields" or "admissions" and "services"), these student activists uncon-
sciously affirmed the process by which knowledge was assembled and
distributed. In the end, the challenge to academic knowledge became
incorporated and served to strengthen the very institutions that had
manipulated knowledge production. Like the formation of ethnic studies, Chicano studies was incorporated into the academic institution.
In the struggle for institutional power, many activists ignored how the
academy composed and distributed knowledge. The initial desire to
establish a discussion between various knowledges and life-situations
was transformed into curricular objectives through which the academic
institution reproduced itself. In effect, the community was replaced by
the institution. Moreover, theories came to the fore that reduced thinking to the methods and epistemologies of academic knowledge.

Much like the narrative the cultural critic Raymond Williams has told about cultural studies in Britain, the various manifestations of ethnic and racial studies were incorporated into the academic institution. In comparing the formulation of Chicano studies with British cultural studies, we can discern a similar zeal to establish a discussion of literature and writing in relation to "life-situations . . . outside the established educational system."[22] Once in the university, however, curricular interests soon supplanted this bond; knowledge began to reproduce itself in the image of the institution. Cultural studies became disassociated from its community (adult education, in the case of cultural studies), and its development was reduced to textual analysis—expressed in academic jargon. "At the very moment when that adventurous syllabus became a syllabus that had to be examined," Williams wrote, "it ceased to be exciting."[23]

Success was transformed into institutionalization. The same transpired in most ethnic studies programs in the United States. The rebelliousness and anarchy between students and discipline gave way to management (that is, the need to be "professional" and "organized"). Williams has remarked that at this point of institutionalization, "a body of theory came through which rationalized the situation of this formation on its way to becoming bureaucratized and the home of specialist intellectuals."[24] For him, this meant the arrival of theories that "tended to regard the practical encounters of people in society as having relatively little effect on its general progress."[25] For the case of ethnic studies, and in particular Chicano studies, it meant an initial return to academic liberal arts methods and principles, later followed by acceptable academic alternatives (such as colonial theory and Marxism).

Was this unavoidable? Was Chicano studies destined to incorporation just like Marxism, women's studies, and cultural studies? I am not certain. I believe that the life of Chicano studies as oppositional could have been extended by the continuation of a multiplicity of voices within Chicano studies itself. Contradiction and conflict kept various manifestations of Chicano studies from simply following some teleological or set pattern. The oppositional quality of the variety of early Chicano studies rested in their rhizomic character and in the belief that utopia was possible. The tension between Empirical Chicano Studies, Perspectivist Chicano Studies, and other Chicano studies was essential for its autonomy; this made it more difficult for academic incorporation and allowed a necessary academic unruliness. However, with the dominance of the empiricists, Chicano Studies soon began its negotiation with the academy.

Yet there was an undercurrent that bared the weaknesses and contradictions in Chicano studies. Chicana critics of el movimiento questioned the patriarchal practices they were forced to accept—especially in its nationalist garb. Their political rebellion challenged the narrow vision of both el movimiento and the student movements, generating a potential alternative insight. This Chicana perspective established a foundation for a critique of Chicano studies and eventually an alternative Chicano(a) studies that would provide the hope of a new Chicana(o) academic project. In the groundbreaking collection *This Bridge Called My Back,* women of color, drawing on their political activism, provided the tools to disrupt Chicano Studies as an academic discipline. *This Bridge* echoed philosopher María Lugones's use of *mestizaje* "as a central name for impure resistance to interlocked, intermeshed oppressions" by complicating notions of identity, especially sexuality.[26]

In chapters 1, 2, and 3, I establish the core of the book: the genesis of academic Chicano Studies. Chapter 1 details the initial Chicano works that emerged and sought to understand the Mexican American experience. Many of these endeavors started from a rejection of scholarly assumptions, methods, and theories. By examining some of these writings, I introduce two potentially conflicting expressions of Chicano studies: Empirical and Perspectivist. Chapter 2 develops Empirical Chicano Studies with particular emphasis on the attempt to develop the internal colonial model as the research method for understanding the Mexican American experience. The endeavor to push this model as the academic method in Chicano studies was assisted by the rise of the journal *Aztlán.* In contrast, chapter 3 traces the contradictory evolution of Perspectivist Chicano Studies. Given its inability to hold off the success of Empirical Chicano Studies, perspectivists never formulated an academic camp with a particular methodology. Rather, we encounter a myriad of individual expressions of Perspectivist Chicano Studies, often centered on personal standpoint, cultural nationalism, and artistic expression.

Chapter 4 focuses on the success of the empirical camp in the 1970s. In addition to tracing the various new intellectual layers of Empirical Chicano Studies, I examine the institutional grafting of Chicano Studies onto the academy. By acknowledging the subordination of

Chicano Studies to academic practices, Chicano Studies legitimated its position within the academy. We turn to the case of UCLA to understand this process. Ironically, as an academic expression of the "loyal opposition," Empirical Chicano Studies provided legitimacy to American exceptionalism.

The last chapter heralds the demise of Chicano Studies by examining the rise of a gender critique and its transformation into a feminist epistemology. Women, as participants in both expressions of Chicano Studies (Empirical and Perspectivist), found themselves physically and intellectually excluded. Female scholars drew attention to the central contradiction: How could Chicanos talk about a Mexican American experience without speaking about women? Some of these scholars further complicated the Chicano(a) understanding of women, resulting in a two-level critique. On the one side, women, even as participants in either view, wanted to draw attention to the Chicana-story that had been excluded. Female empirics and perspectivists rejected how these vistas framed their analysis within a masculinist language and set of assumptions that had subordinated women and excluded any gender analysis. On the other side were women who rejected both outlooks as simply yet another example of academic patriarchy; they too called for Chicana-story.

Hidden in herstory was the ground for an oppositional feminist epistemology. The story of Chicana experiences threw light on the one-dimensionality of any struggle for unity; rather, the Chicana narrative drew out the multiplicity of lived experiences and identities. Thus at the same time that Empirical Chicano Studies was establishing its singular definition of the discipline, some Chicanas were preparing the ground for a feminist epistemology that would lead the charge against Chicano Studies in the 1980s and create the conditions for a renewed multiplicity of Chicano, Chicana, and Chicana(o) Studies.

The Genesis of Academic Chicano Studies, 1967-1970

Utopia and the Emergence of Chicano Studies

As Chicanos and Chicanas protested social, political, and economic inequalities, Chicanos(as) on university and college campuses demanded the introduction of courses and eventually programs that examined the Mexican American experience. By the late 1960s, the first programs in Chicano studies appeared on a variety of campuses. Faculty, who only a semester before might have been student activists, faced the task of constructing a curriculum and the more thorny undertaking of developing the procedures of an academic program. In the process, they sought to flesh out a Chicano pedagogy and specify the content for these courses. Unfortunately, most Chicano(a) faculty were unclear about their understanding of the intellectual meaning of Chicano studies. Some accepted the rhetoric of white radicals and African Americans about the need of a relevant education. Yet Chicano(a) activists did not offer any explanation of what this relevant education might be—aside from the general endeavor to uncover the historical, social, economic, political, and psychological experiences of the Mexican American. At the same time, for many participants in nascent Chicano studies programs, a central concern was the establishment of cultural programs that highlighted an often mythical past and present. The establishment of Chicano studies was made more difficult by the desire to couple academic programs with the political struggle over control of academic institutions that, the Chicano(a) faculty hoped, would advance the transformation of the Mexican American community.

In this chapter, I explore Mexican American writings within the academy (1967–1970), tracing the genesis of Chicano studies as an academic program. These writings were in opposition to an American academic epistemological constellation that denied Mexican American ontological and epistemological autonomy. Hidden among these Chicano(a) writings and their equivocation with the typical American university were a myriad of Chicano epistemological gazes that held the totalizing U.S. academic epistemological field in tension. To understand these developing intellectual alternatives, I assert the importance of campus political behavior without suggesting a one-to-one relationship between el movimiento or campus protests and Chicano studies. Political action in the Mexican American community created a utopian spirit that provided a space for the construction of Chicano studies and a questioning of traditional U.S. academic practices and American exceptionalism.

In these temporary decolonized spaces, Chicanos(as) accomplished two goals. The first was to start to explain the Mexican American condition. Chicanos(as) began to reexamine materials on Mexican Americans, disseminate information on this community, and research and ascertain new materials to replace deficient or nonexistent data. In the process, Chicanos(as) challenged the assumptions concerning the Mexican American. The second aim was to utilize this new information to transform their communities. This proposed transformation ran the gamut from individual self-discovery through cultural rebirth to radical political change. To achieve both goals, Chicanos(as) had to deal with university institutional procedures and the American academic epistemological field. Chicano(a) academics equivocated before this abyss.

Some Chicanos(as) proposed a radical mutation of academic practices; others projected the creation of a Chicano space in the U.S. university system without any fundamental change of intellectual practices. This distinction could only be read after the fact, however. Even those concerned with overturning the academic framework appeared to accept Chicano studies as part of higher education. For their academic survival, Chicano(a) academics had to present cogent arguments using a particular methodology that fit academic definitions of knowledge. In looking over this early Chicano literature, I discern at least two trends in negotiating this intellectual revolution. From one direction came the work of the Quinto Sol collective, in particular the essays of the anthropologist Octavio Romano in *El Grito: A Journal of Contemporary Mexican-American Thought*. From a different direction, Chicano(a) activists presented another manner of engaging in Chicano studies. This perspective found its initial expression in *El Plan de Santa Bárbara* and was further developed in *Aztlán: Chicano Journal of the Social Sciences and the Arts*. This chapter traces the roots of these distinct visions of Chicano studies.[1]

Utopia and the California Chicano(a) Student Movements

Most Chicano(a) scholars have argued that Chicano studies was the product of the 1960s and 1970s Chicano and Chicana student movements.[2] Despite the fact that not every campus in California had Chicano(a) student protests, all benefited from Chicano(a) student activism and the wider *movimiento*. The Los Angeles "blowouts" in March of 1968 and the ensuing months of conflict, together with the university strikes at San Francisco State and the University of California at Berkeley (1968–1969), generated campus mobilizations that were fundamental to the genesis of Chicano studies throughout the state. To achieve their immediate campus goals, students used a variety of political positions that later formed the background for institutionalizing Chicano studies at California universities and colleges. A partial explanation of the diverse styles of Chicano studies stemmed from these different tactics, ideologies, and practices. These activists sought an academic program that would serve to prepare the next generation of activists and provide students with the proper political and organizational orientation. Therefore these activists saw Chicano studies as an extension of Chicano politics.

Most histories of this period accept this narrative as the starting point for any dialogue about Chicano studies. The usual argument is part of a Chicano studies creation myth with a teleology that creates a continuous story linking past, present, and future.[3] This origin myth, often summarized in departmental mission statements, homogenizes the student movement and el movimiento by asserting that control of academic institutions would assist in the transformation of the Mexican American community. The creation myth proposed that Chicano studies was to offer an oppositional practice of intellectual investigation that would explain Mexican American inequality and provide a radical pedagogy, a continuous involvement with the community, and a transformative political practice. This story erased the conflict among political ideologies as well as the gendered behavior of activists in their creation of a singular masculine identity, with its assumed association to a particular Mexican and Mexican American historical pageantry. Even today, however, this myth provides meaning and unity to contemporary Chicano(a) awareness of the discipline and its role in the American academic project.

In *Youth, Identity, Power,* political scientist Carlos Muñoz Jr. has asserted a variation of the creation myth. He establishes a continuum of Mexican American politics in the second half of the twentieth century. Chicano power politics, while distinct from post–World War II political action, formed part of a larger Chicano political project. He homogenizes Chicano power around the movements of César Chávez, Rodolfo "Corky" Gonzáles, and Reies López Tijerina, and eventually around a variety of student organizations. Muñoz's chronology allows nationalism, Marxism, or a hybrid of the two to provide an ideological cover to this particular periodization and its historiography. His origin myth constructs a series of connected causes and effects that creates a lineage from 1945 to 1975, and in the process, it dismisses assorted ideological perspectives and potentially disparate events. The second element of Muñoz's origin myth is to connect this historical and political chronology with the formation of Chicano studies. Thus he briefly traces the institutionalization of Chicano studies programs and attempts to bridge these efforts with an academic framework through *El Plan*. He argues that Chicano(a) scholars were searching for a paradigm of Chicano studies as part of the long-term battle of Chicanos(as) with dominant society. This narrative, with major variations, resonates with most Chicano(a) scholarship.[4]

Yet I hesitate to accept this Chicano studies creation myth, especially as it relates to the genesis of Chicano studies. Instead, I explore the emergence of Chicano studies by examining the written dialogue among Chicanos(as) from 1967 to 1970 in their endeavors to sketch the Mexican American experience, their elucidations of those experiences, and the politics of change. Although Chicano politics forms a background to the discipline, it is not vital to the intellectual origins and development of the discipline—no matter what the creation myth insists. Therefore I look at the Chicano(a) student movements as a series of events that were not necessarily linked or directed but nonetheless disruptive of the "institutional imaginary."

One way to minimize the creation myth and evade any dependent relationship between student protests and Chicano studies is to emphasize the particularity of each campus protest. Thus Chicano(a) movement scholars need to highlight the differences among campus protests, like those at UCLA, University of California at Berkeley, San Francisco State College, San Fernando State College, Merritt Community College, or University of California at San Diego, to name just a few in California, in order to avoid a standardized story to these protests and

Chicano studies. These disparate protests, however, did serve to make hope possible. The particular political positions, ideologies, or goals of the actors became secondary to the anarchical practices that disrupted the institutional imaginary. Thus descriptions of campus protests do not center on the political hopes of the actors; rather, focus is placed on how peoples' actions—whatever they might have thought—disrupted the American imaginary and presented a contrarian possibility, an oppositional imaginary, a utopia. Only by accepting these events, without their imposed chronology and narrative, can we turn to a discussion of Chicano studies without some guiding narrative. In this way, we avoid the privileging of some works and events over others. My goal is to acknowledge campus politics as a central backdrop without reproducing a narrative that links these events and then privileges them as foundational to Chicano studies.

I begin by acknowledging the chaotic rupture that el movimiento and campus protests caused on typical political and social activity. Their query to American exceptionalism and the colonial condition was the result of a community's struggle for autonomy and self-determination, an expression of participatory democracy. The Chicano(a) community's quest for self-management questioned the legitimacy of the system and created the possibility of solutions to problems that had earlier seemed irredeemable. In other words, what happened among people of color, in particular Chicanos(as), was the creation of hope that utopia was indeed possible.[5] The "American dream," always postponed for Mexican Americans and people of color, was thus exchanged for a utopia constructed by Chicanos(as) and people of color. In the academy this suggested a new knowledge, study, and pedagogy that would provide a better understanding of the Mexican American and the conditions in which they found themselves. Chicano studies programs were a by-product, not of student protests as a movement but of the rupture of the institutional imaginary that Chicanos(as) (as well as other disenfranchised communities) created.

The concept of utopia has multiple meanings and uses—from early Christian thought to contemporary discussions of dystopia.[6] Its long history has laden utopia with layers of meanings. The intellectual and art historians Frank and Fritzie Manuel have written that utopia is "shrouded in ambiguity" and therefore "acquires plural meanings." Given this, I have avoided any rigid definition for utopia.[7] One solution is to follow the historian and critical theorist Russell Jacoby's usage: "Utopia here refers not only to a vision of a future society, but a vision pure and simple, an ability, perhaps willingness, to use expansive concepts to see reality and its possibility."[8] Utopia becomes present when individuals challenge official life, formulating community and laying claim to other possible, albeit temporary, worlds. Utopia turns into a possibility when people subvert the day-to-day practices that uphold usual social and political operations. Utopia is about hope. Hope becomes possible when alienated people engage in unhindered dialogue, debate, and activity, fostering a temporary though unstable unity that results in a provisional but real democracy. Utopia is unique, irreproducible, and momentary; it is the product of its historical location and therefore reproduces aspects of established power differences.[9]

There is a tendency to think of utopia as fantasy and unrealistic. This results from the structures that society constructs around us. The Mexican scholar César Gilabert has written that in order to understand utopia, we need to recognize that societies create imaginary relations to comprehend and control real conditions: "La sociedad, para mantener las condiciones de su reproducción, construye conjuntos de imágenes, representaciones, símbolos, signos, con las cuales los individuos se comunican, establecen metas y posibilidades, valores y esperanzas, puede decirse entonces que la producción imaginaria, 'en última instancia,' corresponde a lo que se han dado en llamar estructura o base de la sociedad." (Society, in order to maintain its conditions for reproduction, constructs constellations of images, representations, symbols, signs, by which individuals communicate, establish goals and possibilities, values and hope; it can be said then that imaginary production, "in the final instance," corresponds to what has been called structure or base.[10]) We might add, following the critical pedagogue Peter McLaren's discussion on schooling, that society implants a "ritual rhythm" in our nervous system. "We are ontogenetically constituted by ritual and cosmologically informed by it as well," he says. "All of us are under ritual's sway; absolutely none of us stands outside of ritual's symbolic jurisdiction. In fact, humanity has no option against ritual."[11] Ritual or the imaginary is thus reinforced by an activist state in its defense of society's economic, political, social, psychological, and ideological structures. This institutional imaginary, however, can be challenged by alternative imaginaries that typically remain wishful and unrealistic.[12]

How can the unreal and fanciful become possible and thereby

challenge patterns and rituals that are fundamental to our lives? The Marxist philosopher Ernst Bloch's concept of "not yet" can help us answer this query.[13] The "not yet" is a hope based on possible futures that lie dormant in the remnants of the past.[14] In this way, hope is an expression of what is really possible.[15] Utopia is therefore as real as any presently unfolding possibility, since it is grounded in the many possibilities of the past. Interpreters of Bloch have written about "remembering the future," which is possible because "reality" is not what is but includes what is *becoming* and what might *become*. This propensity-to-something is not the result of material conditions alone. Of course in our day-to-day practices, we reproduce and acknowledge only a given static objective world; in this world, the utopic is repressed and hidden.[16] Hope must be understood as a cognitive act.[17] For Bloch, "concrete utopia" flows from a willful thinking that interacts with reality. "Reality, in this view," the coauthors Henry Giroux and McLaren have written, "is engaged as both a subjective and objective experience, and due to its unfinished nature it is seen as something that is always in a state of becoming."[18]

Human activity thus chooses which possible futures may become real. Utopia is not some abstract fanciful thinking about the future. Since hope permeates everyday consciousness, it is human action that draws out these unrealized dreams, lost possibilities, and abortive hopes buried in reality.[19] Different futures depend on tapping this repository of possibilities. The political philosopher Stephen Eric Bronner said it this way: "The future is thus no mechanical elaboration of the present; nor does it emerge from a series of 'steps' or 'stages' deriving in linear fashion from the past."[20] This depends on the degree of consciousness generated in the present. Utopian possibilities begin with the subjects' awareness of the complexity and ambiguity of reality.[21]

Yet we should not underestimate the power of the institutional imaginary to replace hope with tolerance. The Marxist philosopher Herbert Marcuse has claimed that in contemporary capitalist society "[t]olerance toward what is radically evil now appears as good because it serves the coherence of the whole on the road to affluence or more affluence."[22] We come to accept things as they are as the only way they can be.[23] In another essay, Marcuse contends that once a specific morality is firmly established as a norm of social behavior, like McLaren's "ritual rhythm," it becomes second nature managing our "voluntary servitude."[24] For this reason, the institutional imaginary denies hope and utopia. The second nature that comes from capitalism and the authoritarian state burdens us with its inescapable regulations and rituals. In the process, utopia is maligned because no one really can or wants to visualize, much less actualize, possibilities.[25] Hope is brushed aside and replaced by continuous discussions about the necessary or proper conditions for change.

For the Marxist critical theorist Max Horkheimer, the only real possible choice, recalling Bloch's notion of the "not yet," is to accept that the time for utopia is always now. He writes: "Present talk of inadequate conditions is a cover for the tolerance of oppression. For the revolutionary, conditions have always been ripe."[26] Horkheimer proposes that the first step in resistance is "to keep oneself from being deceived any longer."[27] Utopia is the time/place when self-deceit is recognized and laughed away. In "remembering the future," Marcuse suggests we can open the space for real and universal tolerance. The ability to determine one's own life, together with the capability of being free with others, creates "the society in which man is no longer enslaved by institutions which vitiate self-determination from the beginning."[28] This radical change must reach into people's "biological dimension" to bring out a new sensibility. Here the imagination, drawing on the "not yet," becomes the grinding force in the reconstitution of reality. Only then can second nature, with its self-perpetuating majority, be recognized for what it is—rationalization of the status quo.

Simiotician and literary critic Mikhail Bakhtin's discussion of the carnival adds to this conversation on utopia. He allows us to see the construction of a second world and second life outside officialdom.[29] This oppositional world supplants official institutional rituals by bringing change, freedom, and disorder. At carnival, for instance, popular behavior overthrows normal social operations. Through these endeavors, new forms of speech and new meanings to old forms appear. Profanities as well as sexual and bodily innuendos become part of political discourse. As Bakhtin has pointed out, there is a transfer to the material level. This freedom, of course, is possible "only in [a] completely fearless world." Only then is laughter positive, regenerative, and creative: "Laughter create[s] no dogmas and could not become authoritarian; it [does] not convey fear but a feeling of strength."[30] Student political action parallels carnival.

Bakhtin's analysis allows us to understand how official political culture asserts that all is stable, unchanging, and perennial. Seriousness and authoritarianism are coestablished with liberty. The activist and philosopher Cornelius Castoriadis has suggested that politics becomes technique and bureaucratic manipulation.[31] In the second world, however, politics is "carnavalized" and democracy appears.[32] Bakhtin writes: "As opposed to the official feast, one might say that carnival celebrate[s] temporary liberation from the prevailing truth and from the established order."[33] Here participants suspend hierarchy, rank, privilege, norms, and prohibition. In this politics-as-carnival becoming, change and renewal manifest the merging of utopia and the real. In this freedom, "reckless" laughter disrupts official seriousness and fear. In the fearless world of utopia, laughter purifies and completes seriousness. "It is a temporary transfer to the utopian world."[34] In Los Angeles and the Bay Area, Chicanos(as) created the conditions for this second world through political action.

The Chicano student movements and el movimiento unveiled a variety of possible futures. Hope was not simply a projection of an "abstract utopia," born of only wishful thinking, but a willful expression of what could be possible. As the ethicist Ze'ev Levy has written: "Reality holds within itself the anticipation of a possible future."[35] The student rallies, marches, demonstrations, and innumerable meetings manifested the hope and recognition of possibilities that might lead to an alternative future. Self-determination and participatory democracy were the passageway to this different utopic possibility.[36] Chicano(a) protests delegitimated the institutional imaginary and subverted ritual. In particular, the Los Angeles Chicano(a) high school walkouts ruptured the cultural ether that made all hope utopic and revealed real emancipatory qualities allowing a new social imaginary to emerge.[37] For Chicanos(as) who participated in the protest, utopia was the only viable option. Utopia cohabited with an epistemological tremor that contested the American epistemological constellation. Chicanos and Chicanas defied officialdom and its multiple social, economic, psychological, and political practices. The historical structures of control and management were challenged, making possible a world driven by autonomous action. Although this was not the stated goal of activists or participants, the very enactment of a different set of practices, not their conditioned second nature, made possible the "not yet." The utopic moment was not reducible to particular leaders, organizations, statements, or actions during the walkouts or the various campus protests; these succumbed to passive tolerance, reproducing officialdom.[38] What mattered were those moments when people actualized a different set of rules that existed outside the static and given world.

Intellectually this suggested an alternative curricular and institutional world. Again, we need to distinguish between what activists and their organizations might have said and the unintended consequence that resulted from their actions. To suggest curricular transformation and a reinterpretation of the academy's vision of community service as the promise of the utopic world, misses the point. In fact, these choices did not challenge the official world. The production, distribution, and legitimization of knowledge remained undemocratic. However, within the utopic moment, to question admission procedures, curricular definitions, teaching methods, and the like—all driven by student practices outside the limits of tolerance—suggested a possible new intellectual/academic world. That this world was temporary did not take away its radical and transformative quality. Thus the demand for Chicano studies or Ethnic studies should be read as this contradictory "not yet." At one level, these programs were simply possible alternatives within curricular practices, in the end reproducing the university. At the same time, they were at the center of a different conception of knowledge and the university. Chicano studies at the utopic moment articulated an oppositional possibility that vitiated the university by creating it anew. Chicano studies allowed the practitioner to ask and answer traditional and new questions without the inquisitorial fear exercised by the academic sacerdotal class.

Unfortunately, the utopic moment did not survive, and with its demise went the intellectual quake initiated by the questions of excluded communities. Without the hope of a future, the curricular revolution found its home within the American epistemological framework. Although the new programs retained their hope of community transformation and self-determination, Chicano studies' language was a balance of the normative instrumentalism of the academy with naïve anti-intellectualism.[39] Chicano studies was reduced to another tool in the Chicano(a) battle against oppression.[40] Chicano studies programs and Chicano(a) student organizations pushed this instrumentalist vision. This was reflected in their use of terms like "community," "activism," and "organization." Whether successful or not, these programs and organizations presented themselves as activist programs whose links with the community allowed new community organizations necessary for the struggle of justice and self-determination. Real transformation was long forgotten as some utopian dream. What happened to the campus activists' desire for a curricular revolution?

El Grito, Octavio Romano, and the Emergence of Chicano Studies

With *El Grito,* an oppositional academic Chicano studies, not as social sciences or humanities, was made possible. As the editors pointed out in the initial issue, Chicano(a) intellectuals have to wage war against the "intellectual mercenaries," the social scientists who create and propagate a language that erases the Mexican American. Therefore the task of Chicanos(as) is to destroy these rhetorical structures that subvert the Mexican American.[41] In this battle, Chicanos(as) would have to fashion an intellectual perspective that situated itself on the border between the academy and society. What this meant was not clear. In most cases, the articles in the journal saw their intellectual responsibility to criticize the university and society from the vantage of a minority community.[42]

Although the voice of Octavio I. Romano dominated *El Grito,* we should not forsake the many intellectuals that gave rise to the vision present in the journal and the construction of this expression of Chicano studies. Even though internal conflicts would fracture the Quinto Sol collective and eventually *El Grito,* their intellectual work provoked an epistemological quake. This intellectual movement was the product of an intense dialogue among members of the Quinto Sol/ Mexican American Student Organization at University of California at Berkeley and later in the editorial staff of *El Grito.* This is not a denial of the important role Romano played; I simply would like to acknowledge that this early expression of Chicano thought, like other intellectual formations, came out of collective work. As the art critic Tomás Ybarra-Frausto observed: "The earliest and most historically significant group which functioned as purveyor of the new Chicano aesthetic was 'El Grupo Quinto Sol' established in Berkeley, California, in 1967. In a series of 'Mexican American Liberation Papers' distributed at meetings, street corners, and community gatherings, they called for a recognition that the Mexican American ferment of the time was not the result of new consciousness, but rather a continuation of a long struggle for human dignity."[43]

Aside from their endeavor to help students succeed academically, Quinto Sol also engaged in an examination of the Chicano(a)'s relationship with the university and the academy's construction of the Mexican American. An example of this work was Nick Vaca's essay, which can be read as the "call" of the Quinto Sol collective. It serves as an introduction to his and Romano's later pieces in *El Grito*. "Mexican-Americans have never been passive or docile," Vaca emphasized in the first line of his essay.[44] He contended, using the recent UCLA Mexican American Project as his starting point, that social scientists had stereotyped Mexican Americans into a passive population. Social scientists' discovery of the Mexican American movement led them to conclude that the Mexican American was only now "emerging" or "changing." These social scientists argued that this provided evidence that Mexican Americans' passivity, fatalism, and docility had come to an end. Vaca responded that the Mexican American has never been docile, passive, or fatalistic. Rather, the attempt to depict the Mexican American in such a manner is an instrument of control. He wrote: "To tell them such is to try to prevent them from ever thinking of themselves as accomplished."[45] Vaca's essay called into question the relative ease with which the American epistemological totalizing project had created a Mexican American fantasy. As the anthropologist Karen Mary Davalos has written, "Vaca's most significant contribution to the conversation is his suggestion that the power and politics of racism and nationalism, which in turn can disguise the sources of oppression, mediate research."[46]

Romano's various essays exemplified *El Grito*'s program allowing us to discern the evolution of this Chicano(a) critical perspective at the periphery of the academy.[47] In both "Minorities, History, and the Cultural Mystique" and "The Anthropology and Sociology of the Mexican Americans: The Distortion of Mexican American History," Romano depicted social scientists as scholars who have translated the Mexican American into a masochistic, passive, irrational, fatalistic, and questionable American. Social scientists, Romano noted, use concepts, such as "traditional culture," that distort the realities of these communities by presenting them as ahistorical peoples.[48] Social scientists, the "high priests of modern society," he went on to say, engage in creating a "social science fiction."[49] In fact, contemporary social scientists view Mexican Americans in the same fashion as did those "westward pioneers" of more than a hundred years ago.[50] In "Goodbye Revolution—Hello Slum," Romano reminds us that the social scientists have erased Mexican American history: "This amputation is professionally performed by social scientists wielding the scalpel of sociological and anthropological semantics."[51] In "Mugre de la canción—A Play (Sin Fin) En Tres Actos," Romano pokes fun at social scientists and their eternal quest for funding to research the "chai-cay-nose."[52]

As Romano lashed out at social scientists in these essays, he initiated his critique of social science research and its failure to investigate knowledge and truth. He built an intellectual framework to overturn social scientists' myths and began an exploration of the *real* Mexican American experience.[53] This approach had to start with the restoration of Mexican American history, given that academic practices had denied any claims of a rigorous self-reflexivity.[54] In "Goodbye Revolution— Hello Slum," Romano recovered a portion of this history to reconstruct the Mexican American: "a vivid reinterpretation of Twentieth Century Chicano history."[55]

In "The Historical and Intellectual Presence of Mexican Americans," Romano provided the guidelines for encountering the Mexican Americans' intellectual roots. Reacting to the Mexican author Octavio Paz's "quixotic quest for the Mexican," Romano proposed that Paz's work instead revealed a multiplicity of lifestyles and therefore many Mexicans.[56] The Mexican American inherited at least four distinct ideological trends tied to historical experiences: Indianist philosophy, historical confrontationism, mestizo philosophy, and the immigrant experience.[57] Indianism, Romano explained, permeates Mexican American life, for it provides a "timeless symbol of opposition to cultural imperialism."[58] Historical confrontation, secondly, manifests the long history of Mexican American resistance. Romano further observed that this "confrontationist philosophy" had multiple expressions: it could be self-deterministic, protectionist, nationalist, reactive, and existential.[59] The experience and philosophy of the mestizo manifests a reconceptualization of nature and man that leads toward humanistic universalism, behavioral relativism, and a recurrent form of existentialism. Romano linked the "transcendent idea of the Mestizo" with a "form of Cultural Nationalism."[60] Thus for Romano, cultural nationalism is "unlike the rampant ethnocentrism with its traditional xenophobia . . . that has been so characteristic of ethnic groups in the United States."[61] These three trends, together with the immigrant experience, undercut any idea of a "pure" Mexican American and destabilized the work of social scientists.

Here we have to note Romano's use of cultural nationalism. He noted a connection between *Aztlán*, Mexico, and chicanismo as articulated in *El Plan,* but he did not limit its expression. Romano rejected an empirical view of independent and autonomous historical and cultural traditions. He emphasized the mutual interdependence of histories and cultures. Chicanos(as) needed to move toward a politics that postulates "that duplicity, complicity, coalitions, and social networks are much more fundamental to the historical process than are ethnicity, skin color, group history, tradition, and religious affiliation."[62] Given this formulation, Romano's use of cultural nationalism brought his ideas closer to the politics of the Bay Area Third World strikes that occurred as the first issues of *El Grito* appeared. How then can we come to know these Mexican American experiences? In a review of Carey McWilliams's *North from Mexico,* Romano continued his endeavor to construct his framework. To know if something is true, one has to converse "with los viejos in the barrios."[63] The need to turn to the community, in particular the elders, was already present in his dissertation.[64] From the elders, he suggested, Chicanos(as) could learn that Mexican Americans have been both participants and generators of the historical process: "The picture that emerged from the dialogue with the viejitos was one of constant struggle."[65] These stories, together with McWilliams's text, exposed "how 'social' 'science' 'studies' have prostituted and distorted the history of Mexican-Americans."[66]

In these pieces, Romano worked in two directions. First, he criticized the work of social scientists on the Mexican American. He saw himself as the Socratic gadfly irritating and confounding the academy and its claims to veracity, asserting that academic knowledge was not the truth that the institution claimed. His second concern was to validate and present the Mexican American as an active historical agent. Romano wanted us to reflect on the complex nature of the Mexican American that social scientists had distorted. But his thinking did not stop here; he moved beyond critique and a simple return to history.

In "Social Science, Objectivity and the Chicanos," we encounter a refinement of Romano's critique. Where initially he attacked individual works, scholars, and disciplinary models, Romano now problematizes the field of social science and reveals the assumptions behind academic knowledge. He begins by tracing the intellectual origins of objectivity to dehistoricize the concept, subvert its meaning, and more important, undercut its utility.

Romano wrote: "[T]he concept of objectivity is impossible without a corresponding belief in man's ability to separate his mind not only from his body, but also from all of his ecological surroundings."[67] The Western European quest, he maintained, for objectivity and objective reality demands the separation of events, phenomena, and ideas from personal self-consciousness.[68] This empirical project is at the center of academic knowledge. Moreover, this dualism grants methodological and conceptual legitimacy to social science, since an assumed unity exists between the laws governing the physical universe and those that govern human behavior.[69] For this reason, social science is presented as value-free, culture-free, and tradition-free. Romano, as the activist and political scientist Raoul Contreras has pointed out, extended "the ideological critique of social science on the Mexican American to a critique of the ideology of social science."[70]

At this point in his argument, Romano took a crucial step beyond his earlier work and many of those who had recognized that the work of social scientists was not objective, since it was influenced by time, place, and culture.[71] For Romano, the very nature of objectivity, based on the separation of mind and body, had to be rejected. Thus social science studies about the Chicano must also be set aside. Instead, Romano proposed to initiate Chicano(a) research from the perspective of the Chicano(a) subject. Chicano studies must begin from the "self-image" of the Chicano(a). Given the deception of objectivity and social science, Chicanos(as) needed to reclaim and rewrite themselves. "If this self-image is rejected by non-Chicano social scientists," he wrote, "then, in effect, they will have rejected summarily the rationality of the Chicano."[72] As the Chicano(a) became subject, social science and academic knowledge would be tossed out. Romano thus altered the relationship between Chicano(a) scholarship and the academy. From this point, Chicano(a) research had to start from the standpoint of the Chicano(a) and his/her position in U.S. society and not from assumed social science or humanities-based academic practices.

Romano proposed a form of standpoint epistemology in contrast to the empiricism of the social sciences and other fields. This provided a radically new starting point for Chicano(a) intellectuals who sought an oppositional stance to myths created by academic intellectual practices. Furthermore, it afforded an argument that rooted knowledge in the multiplicity of Mexican American experiences. Unfortunately, Romano himself did not follow up on this epistemological break. In subsequent pieces in *El Grito,* he either returned to his criticism of social scientists' work, to issues of identity and history, or he delved into policy.[73] More important, his work moved increasingly toward the arts. In his evaluation of the publishing record of *El Grito* and Quinto Sol Publications, while noting the need to "analyze the fallacious and educationally detrimental content of social science studies of Mexican Americans," his main concern was to provide an open space for alternative literary voices.[74] He saw his various enterprises as providing a necessary outlet for Chicano(a) talent, to "forge new ground in literary publications."[75] Thus in his anthology *El Espejo The Mirror,* he wrote that he saw his role to provide "the Chicano community [with] works by *Chicano authors* which reflect *Chicano experiences* from a *Chicano perspective.*"[76] By the appearance of *El Grito del Sol* in 1976, Romano saw Tonatiuh's role to "leave the narrow horizons of the immediate past behind, and to publish literature which is more representative of the rich, varied, and infinite universe that is the Chicano world."[77] Romano's standpoint position led him away from a rupture of academic knowledge to the production of another knowledge through the arts.[78]

Though Romano did not build toward an epistemic break, his essays, together with the work of the Quinto Sol collective and *El Grito,* provided Chicanos and Chicanas with a radical weapon in their battle with the academy and knowledge.[79] Their recognition of the Chicano(a) scholar as an engaged intellectual opened up new intellectual possibilities for Chicanos(as) in the academy. This vision allowed a radical repositioning of Chicanos(as) in relation to the engrossing academic project; a Chicano(a) perspective that made possible a Chicano(a) studies that could avoid the pitfalls of university-based knowledge. If Chicano studies accepted the assumptions of the academy, as Romano had noted, it was doomed to incorporation.[80] Thus he articulated, though not as clearly as he could have, a nondisciplinary, nonsocial-science Chicano studies that could survive, albeit always peripheral and questionable, in the university. This epistemic framework would remain ambiguous, tethered to a utopian hope. Unfortunately, Romano did not pursue this discussion; he remained a critic of social science without forcing an oppositional epistemological and methodological break.

El Plan de Santa Bárbara

El Grito provided one approach to explicate the relationship of Chicanos(as) with the academy. However, for some, the critique in *El Grito* seemed disconnected from the political and social needs in the

Mexican American communities and lacked a program for change. As the Chicano student movements unfolded, the growing number of Chicanos(as) in higher education demanded some response to their concerns about the political relevance of education and its examination of the Mexican American experience. For campus activists, political, social, and economic problems in their home communities had to be dealt with through Chicano studies programs. Drawing on el movimiento, university activists—many having participated in the Los Angeles "blowouts," Bay Area Third World strikes, or United Farm Workers struggles—pushed for the creation of Chicano studies programs (centers, departments, support programs) throughout California and the Southwest. As students extracted these programs from reticent institutions, many conceded that some structure and system of ideas were necessary to implement and direct these Chicano programs if they were to achieve their political goals. Chicano(a) activist Rene Nuñez played a pivotal role in bringing together a select group of students, faculty, staff, and administrators to devise a plan. The result was *El Plan de Santa Bárbara*.[81]

The Santa Barbara conference can be read as an extension of the first national Chicano youth conference, organized by the Crusade for Justice in Denver in March 1969. Among the Crusade participants were California students from organizations like United Mexican American Students, Third World Liberation Front, Brown Berets, and others. The three-day Denver conference dealt with unity, identity, culture, and revolution. For the first time, it offered "a clear demonstration of the growing concept of ethnic nationalism and self-determination among Chicanos in the entire Southwest."[82] All this was reflected in the key document of the conference, *El Plan Espiritual de Aztlán*. Of course not everyone was happy with the spirit of the Denver conference.[83] The split between Chicanos(as) from the Bay Area who were Marxists and the nationalists at the Denver youth conference were not resolved; rhetorical statements that "Marx was just another *gabacho*" were made.[84]

The authors of *El Plan* wrote that the Chicano struggle for self-determination and self-liberation could be assisted by a "strategic use of education."[85] This strategic plan rested on building institutions within the academy that would be under Chicano control and provide them relative autonomy. In this way, Chicano power could be realized on campus and university services could be redirected to the Mexican

American community.[86] For the authors of *El Plan,* the university could serve as an institutional base in the struggle for Chicano equality.[87] *El Plan* proposed that the "resources [not only academic] of the university be harnessed to enrich and develop the Chicano community."[88] The historian Juan Gómez-Quiñones commented: "The major thrust of the plan was to stimulate the growth and operation of Chicano studies programs along movement premises and to coordinate politically and organizationally local programs statewide in an effort to further a particular vision of education and one with a particular purpose, both of which the plan provided for the first time."[89]

The Chicano(a) student and community were central to building Chicano studies institutionally. Carlos Muñoz Jr. has recalled that the hope was to develop "organic intellectuals of Mexican descent within the university—that is, the kind of academic who would be an integral part of his community and actively participate in the Chicano Movement, do research critical of society, and simultaneously contribute to the shaping of a Chicano consciousness"—and in the end be part of the transformation of the Mexican American communities.[90] *El Plan* supported the formation of an organization that acknowledged the reality of a hostile and oppressive environment; the various constituencies were to develop a junta or *mesa directiva* to provide leadership and direction to Chicanos(as) at the university.[91]

El Plan further examined the role of Chicano studies as an academic program in their political agenda. It stated: "Chicano Studies . . . thus represent[s] an over-all university program for the Chicano and his community. As such, the academic aspect of Chicano Studies is but one dimension, albeit a major one, of a broad and multi-component program."[92] Chicano students demanded a relevant curriculum that led to an activist program. Chicano(a) intellectuals, therefore, must engage in research that would establish a compendium of data useful to the community. This information could foster a well-developed political agenda. As the document stated: "[S]olid research becomes the basis for Chicano political strategy and action."[93]

Contemporaneous with this view on research was the need to prepare and organize Chicano(a) students for political battle. Chicano studies would "socialize the Chicano student by providing him with the intellectual tools necessary for him to deal with the reality of his experience" and help him/her engage the world at large.[94] Thus the academic side of *El Plan* proposed a Chicano studies that would provide the manpower and resources for the struggles with dominant society. To achieve this curricular goal, lower-division courses would affirm identity through an appreciation of the Chicano cultural heritage. Upper-division classes would examine the Chicano(a) experience from the angles of history, economics, psychology, sociology, literature, political science, and education. The end result would be "to provide a coherent and socially relevant education, humanistic and pragmatic, which prepares Chicanos for service to the Chicano community and enriches the total society."[95]

Unfortunately *El Plan*'s intellectual program was underdeveloped. It remained unclear what exactly *El Plan* did offer epistemologically speaking, aside from a collection of courses on the Mexican and Mexican American experiences with special attention to culture. This weakness allowed Chicano studies academic programs to be framed within traditional university practices, muting *El Plan*'s radical hope. Although many who followed the political vision of *El Plan* also acknowledged *El Grito*'s critique of social science, they did not see a possible contradiction between institutional building and the limits of American academic practices. In fact, the battle for institutionalization further justified minimizing academic concerns as secondary if not divisive.

For many researchers tied to the Chicano studies creation myth, the decline in student activism compounded the curricular limitations of the new programs.[96] The educator Raymond Padilla, for example, has explained the failure to develop a radical curriculum in Chicano studies as the result of the de-emphasis of an activist agenda.[97] Thus in his study of the Ethnic Studies department at University of California at Berkeley, he concluded that the decline of activism left only one "route to curricular legitimacy . . . the liberal arts model."[98] With this shift, Chicanos brought traditional and workable technologies to bear on Chicano studies. On the one hand, Padilla believed that activists could manipulate the university for the purpose of changing the Mexican American community. Yet, on the other, he wondered how could they utilize the university if it was an inhospitable and alienating place. "Viewed in its most extreme manifestation," he wrote, "some campus Chicanos sought to address community problems by using campus resources but maintaining an adversary relationship with the very same campus."[99]

For Padilla, this inconsistency was acceptable and resolvable so long as activism was present. As student and community politics declined, however, this contradiction led to a transformation of the goals for Chicano studies from community transformation to self-preservation in the academy. "What began as a Chicano Studies goal of people-community development based on the use of university resources," Padilla wrote, "changed to sheltering students from an alien and inhospitable university environment."[100] At this point, the degree and discipline had taken precedence. Chicano studies conflated administrative control with intellectual production.[101] Padilla's assumption that the vitality of Chicano studies relied on activism was simply an expression of the origin myth. He was unable to escape *El Plan*'s equivocation about the university. Although Padilla criticized the shift, he believed that this acceptance of the liberal model could have been averted. He agreed with the authors of *El Plan* that it was the existence of an organized and activist student body that would had given Chicano studies the autonomy it needed to survive as an oppositional site in the academy. Even though he was close to Romano and others in *El Grito*, Padilla did not seem to fully grasp the depth of the epistemological critique they had offered. His work became an early articulation of the Chicano studies creation myth.

Two Traditions Emerge

The language of *El Grito* and *El Plan* should be read as a bifurcation in the development of Chicano studies. Although the differences were not as keen as I make them out to be, there clearly existed at least two potential directions for the growth of Chicano studies after 1969. On one side was the vision, albeit imprecise, that Romano had presented through his essays and leadership at *El Grito*. His use of the Chicano self-image, as his point of departure for the production of knowledge, turned research away from social science empirical models toward a "perspectivist epistemology." By questioning the dualism inherent in Western thought and reversing the traditional epistemology-ontology dynamic, Romano's work pointed Chicanos(as) toward a "Perspectivist Chicano Studies."

This contrasted with the vision presented in *El Plan*. For activists, the struggle was to capture the academy, or at least some of its resources, to continue the fight to transform the barrio. Their interest was to use the institution as a political tool. Simultaneously, the thinkers behind *El Plan,* while agreeing with the critique of the social sciences and the humanities, held on to a traditional outlook on knowledge and the academy. Academic work was ancillary to political work. For this reason, they had no vision for intellectual work and could easily accept social science models for academic work. The problem with Anglo research was that they allowed their research to be tainted by their assumptions and stereotypes of race and therefore resulted in "serious distortions." [102] To counter this problem, Chicanos had to engage in correct empirical work to draw a more accurate image of the Mexican American. This outlook led to "Empirical Chicano Studies."

Certain intellectuals and essays reveal the differences in perspectives, but I do not want to suggest that they were necessarily aware of the implications of their work. Intellectual production is always more complicated. We could say that the various social, political, cultural, as well as intellectual activities wrote these very pieces. Let's borrow the language of the biologist Ludwik Fleck, when he wrote about "scientific facts" to stress the autonomy of the epistemological configuration: "Cognition is therefore not an individual process of any theoretical 'particular consciousness.' Rather it is the result of a social activity, since the existing stock of knowledge exceeds the range available to any one individual." [103] Fleck uses the concept of "thought collective" to denote the community of people who maintain an intellectual interchange, sharing a special "carrier" that facilitates the development of a field of thought. This intellectual facilitator, Fleck terms the "thought style." For him, the individual in the collective is hardly aware of the prevailing thought style, "which almost always exerts an absolutely compulsive force upon his thinking and with which it is not possible to be at variance." [104]

Following Fleck, Chicano(a) early writings manifested particular thought collectives and styles. Thus Romano's writings told us much about the Quinto Sol/*El Grito* collective and their thought style (a burgeoning critique of knowledge and academic politics). The multiple versions of Chicano studies were not about personalities and biographies; these styles were more than the sum of a set of writings and individuals. The difference between a perspectivist and empirical thought style can be illustrated in their view of UCLA's Mexican American Study Project. [105] The project, conducted in 1963–1968 and partially funded by the Ford Foundation, aimed at depicting the realities of life for Mexican Americans. They questioned the notion that this community was unassimilable by demonstrating changes in the community. The

Mexican American population was "showing a growing potential for participation in the larger society."[106] The authors concluded that, even though there were many obstacles, the basic policies needed to meet the concerns of Mexican Americans were already present or under development.[107] At the same time, Mexican American leaders made clear the weaknesses and failures of the system by their presentations and boycott of the 1967 Cabinet Committee Hearings on Mexican American Affairs.

El Plan's authors were unhappy with the research by Leo Grebler, Joan W. Moore, and Ralph C. Guzman. They wrote: "the study is subject to controversy as to its validity." Yet they also believed that "these works [the various reports that form the study] should be consulted."[108] They acknowledged that only an examination of structural inequality was the path to understanding the Mexican American condition. In other words, the problem with the project was not fundamental; there were facts that could still be salvaged from the project. For the thinkers of *El Plan,* facts were not theory laden. In contrast, however, Nick Vaca saw the same "liturgical repetition" in the Mexican American Study Project of social science's myths about Mexican Americans.[109] The political scientist Charles Ornelas launched a similar critique. The study suffers, he argued, from an assimilationist perspective. It had an Anglo perspective toward integration and cultural pluralism.[110]

By exploring two key essays of the period, a better understanding of these two styles of Chicano studies can be explored. Padilla's essay on the work of Leonard Pitt ("A Critique of Pittian History") resonated with Romano's criticism of social science as the best epistemological device. Padilla concurred with Romano that social science could not offer Chicano(a) intellectuals an instrument for understanding their condition. The intellectual had to start from his/her own reality, unobstructed by social science appurtenances. In contrast, Deluvina Hernández's essay (a criticism of Audrey J. Schwartz and C. Wayne Gordon) did not explore the epistemological shift that Romano's work implied. Instead, she rejected "bad" social science but accepted the possibility of doing "good" social science, though reconstituted through a Chicano perspective. Hernández's work pointed to the need for a Chicano social science.

Padilla's "A Critique of Pittian History" works within *El Grito*'s vision of Chicano studies. In a critique of Pitt's California history, Padilla epitomizes how cultural and attitudinal biases affect historical thinking and writing. At the same time, he sharpens Romano's appraisal of academic work. He interrogates the meaning and relevance of social science research for Chicanos(as): "I also want to challenge the Chicano to examine critically the generic concept of research and its implications for the Chicano."[111] Padilla rejects social science research, not because it is incorrectly applied or not fully developed, but because its very nature cannot allow the Chicano(a) to exist as subject. Therefore the Chicano(a) cannot operate by the rules of academic research because he/she becomes victim of the logic of rationalism and objectivism. The Chicano(a) response, Padilla emphasizes, must come from the existential level: "His response is fundamentally an act of self-assertion where the Chicano refuses to negotiate the authenticity of his own reality."[112] Again, we encounter a form of standpoint epistemology to challenge and, more important, to overturn empiricist discourse. But like Romano's work, Padilla did not complete the epistemological rupture.[113]

Hernández's criticism in *Mexican American Challenge to a Sacred Cow* initially draws from Romano's criticism of the work of social scientists. Social science thinking, she stresses, is founded on fixed stereotypes and ignorance.[114] Social science cannot be a science in the same way as physical science; rather, social science, Hernández emphasizes, hides its prejudice behind the image or myth of science. "The mask of physical science," she wrote, "gives to social science researchers the image of objectivity in social matters, in politics and in the ethics of the individuals they observe. This image carry-over is false."[115] Hernández asks Chicano(a) scholars to be wary of social science: "A fact is not the end truth. It itself is not science. Scholars therefore cannot and must not continue to unquestioningly offer observance to the sacred cow of social science. They must continue the quest for relevance and truth—elusive and illusive as they are."[116]

Up to this point, much resonance exists between Padilla's and Hernández's pieces. Hernández, however, is not clear why social science has this style of thinking. Is this an epistemological issue, or merely one of bad social science? Unlike Romano or Padilla, she is unable to visualize an adequate response. Her uncertainty results in an unintended return to social science and academic knowledge. This regress is reinforced by her belief in the existence of objective science; her dichotomy between social and physical science reflects this vision. Thus Hernández hopes and believes social science can still be done: "Research which is founded, as much as is humanly feasible, upon a reliable knowledge base combined with the researcher's personal perspective, which is both introspective and humanistic (or compassionate), will tend to produce meaningful observations and relationships and, in turn, create the circumstances for understanding the social phenomenon at hand and its needs."[117] She suggests a perspectivist reading of Chicano research, but in the end turns back to social science. Her essay cannot find a balance between a "reliable knowledge base" and a "researcher's personal perspective."[118]

Padilla and Hernández exemplified the emerging traditions within Chicano studies. Although their views overlapped at key points, they manifested two styles of thinking about academic research, intellectuals, and Chicanos(as). After 1970, the initial bifurcation present in the work of Romano and *El Plan* began to impact the intellectual development of Chicano studies.

Chicano Studies Curriculum

The protests in the Mexican American communities and college campuses disrupted the institutional imaginary that up to this point had guided their perceptions of American society. Mexican American's political behavior questioned the daily practices of tolerance that made the myth of American democracy and justice viable; they upset the ritual rhythm of their voluntary servitude. At that point, they drew from the well of remembrances, forgotten possibilities. Mexican Americans mobilized a range of latent choices that days before were considered impossible and utopian. In this truly democratic activity, they became real subjects (self-determinant) who could create an identity and an oppositional world outside officialdom—they became Chicanos and Chicanas. Although some contemporary scholars would like to link this temporary freedom to particular struggles, organizations, individuals, or ideologies, the reverse was closer to the truth. It was the disruption of the imaginary that allowed organizations, individuals, and ideologies to flourish as so many alternative imaginaries. I therefore disassociate particular political events from the utopian moment; the whole was greater than the sum of the parts.

Given the constitution of utopia, Chicano studies became possible. Up to this point, academic practices had shrouded the Mexican American experience by the epistemologies, methodologies, and methods of the social sciences and humanities. With the possibilities of alternative imaginaries, however, Mexican Americans who reclaimed their identity also sought to replace the social sciences and the humanities with Chicano studies. By 1970, one could count about sixty-five campuses (in the state of California) with some form of Chicano studies. A survey by the Summer Institute for Chicano Studies noted sixteen programs in the California state college system, eight in the University of California, thirty-one in the community colleges, and thirteen in private institutes.[119] In 1972, a study observed forty-three programs in the community college system in California.[120]

Nonetheless, there was little agreement on the meaning of the programs. The poet, activist, and scholar Alurista (Alberto Urista Heredia) recalled: "Chicano Studies was created by students, by Chicano students, and as students we had no concrete idea of what it was that a department of Chicano Studies would accomplish in view of our recognition of the corruption and decadence of the American educational system."[121] What could make Chicano studies different from other programs, Alurista pointed out, was Chicano(a) practices. "[I]t is our practice that will differentiate us from other academic studies detached from the corrupt American reality which they practice everyday, deodorant, suit and ties, monthly paycheck, dinning, winning ph.d. and all."[122] For most activists, Chicano studies was about carving spaces within the institution that would be for Chicanos(as) and under the control of Chicanos(as). Chicanos(as) had to direct these programs whose purpose was to use the university "as a vital institutional instrument of change."[123] Thus control of student services was at the top of their list. For a few, possibly influenced by various forms of experimental colleges and courses in the community, Chicano studies would also deal with curricular issues. Most accepted that these courses were "to acquaint all students . . . with the values and culture of the Mexican American, and to expose the values in the culture of the Anglo American that affect negatively the participation of the Mexican Americans in the 'American way of life.'"[124]

Not all campuses moved equally in the construction of a Chicano studies curriculum. Ahead of the curve, for example, was Chicano studies at California State University at San Diego. By just looking at their list of classes offered at the time, one can see a developed curriculum that sought a space between nationalism and Third World studies. These courses were consistent with *El Plan*. As the activist and scholar Rodolfo Acuña observed: "Chicano Studies address itself directly to the creation of the best possible intellectual and practical environment in which an active student of critical mind and scientific approach can develop and flourish and then apply his or her knowledge and expertise toward the eradication of the socio-political and economic bases of the realities of oppressed peoples."[125]

I do not want to give the impression that the Chicano studies curriculum at San Diego was ready-made. It unfolded in conjunction with the political activism on the campus. Thus in the fall 1969 catalog, the Chicano studies curriculum was defined as providing the history and way of life of the Chicano people through a Chicano point of view.[126] Compare this with four years later, when the purpose of Chicano studies was defined there as developing students with the skills of "objective critical analysis," preparing them to enter the struggle to transform everyday realities for the benefit of the many.[127] Yet most of these early curricula lacked an explanation of their relationship to the American university system. They assumed an instrumentalist relationship with knowledge, and therefore their academic practices flowed from the nature of the academic institution—no matter the rhetoric of its speakers. Chicano(a) scholars did not ask how they could research and teach about the Mexican American without reproducing the biased information present in the vast majority of scholarly works on the community.

Empirics and Chicano Studies

The Formation of Empirical Chicano Studies,

1970-1975

Most Chicanos(as) visualized an academic program that could serve and transform the Mexican American community. University activists, of course, differed in their interpretation of how to serve their communities and who the communities might be. Among some university activists, it could be simply dealing with issues of admissions and retention; to others, it was a transformation of the political, social, and economic reality of Mexican Americans throughout the Southwest. To most, one way to achieve these goals was the construction of Chicano studies programs. The university therefore would be the place to battle for self-determination and Chicano liberation. The way to achieve these goals was through the building of Chicano programs that would be under Chicano(a) control. Once these institutions were established, Chicanos(as) could turn to curricular concerns.[1]

Scholars who accepted this view and devoted themselves to institution building followed by curriculum construction, I call "empirics." Chicano(a) empirics saw the process of organizing and institution building as central to their intellectual work. The establishment of a program, department, center, and so on was at the heart of their vision. They saw program construction as a central step in the struggle for Chicano liberation, in which Chicanos(as) would gain control of academic structures with the goal of servicing the community. In this manner, Chicanos(as) would assert their freedom and express their self-determination. Empirics expressed a variety of political stands. While at the beginning most would have considered themselves nationalists, later many could have labeled themselves as liberal, progressive, or Marxist. From whatever political orientation they started, they believed that political issues were subject to fixed final solutions that always worked.[2]

Chicano(a) empirics also expressed a particular intellectual perspective as they built a curriculum. Empiric scholars conceived of the Mexican American condition as the result of oppressive structures. These structures might arise from colonialism, internal colonialism, class oppression, or the simple failings of the American system. They agreed that once the Chicano(a) figured out the system of oppression, he/she would devise a political plan to challenge and then change this situation. For empirics, this understanding reinforced the need for organization and institution building. The earliest expression of this empiric vision was *El Plan de Santa Bárbara*. While *El Plan* furnished a political conception of using the academy in the battle for self-determination, it was weak in providing an intellectual vision. *El Plan* did not provide an adequate intellectual response to understanding Mexican American oppression. This intellectual vision would be developed in the meetings of El Concilio Nacional de Estudios Chicanos, the essays in *Aztlán: Chicano Journal of the Social Sciences and the Arts,* and presentations at the National Association for Chicano Studies. As the result of these projects, by 1975 Empirical Chicano Studies would become the only acceptable expression of Chicano studies.

El Plan de Santa Bárbara and Discipline Formation

Chapter 1 provided a particular reading of the political and intellectual implications of *El Plan*. I emphasized activists' construction of academic institutions that would serve as an autonomous space in the university to transform the condition of the Mexican American in the university and society at large. The university was presented as "a vital institutional instrument of change."[3] Chicano power could be achieved through a political application of university resources—channeled through Chicano studies programs.[4] *El Plan* influenced the majority of Chicano studies programs; "[n]early all of the programs today are formulated on the basis set forth in *El Plan de Santa Barbara.*"[5]

At the heart of *El Plan*'s political vision was "chicanismo." According to the historian Juan Gómez-Quiñones, "'Chicanismo' referred to a set of beliefs; in particular, a political practice. The emphasis of 'Chicanismo' upon dignity, self-worth, pride, uniqueness, and a feeling of cultural rebirth made it attractive to many Mexicans in a way that cut across class, regional, and generational lines."[6] This ideology served to link activists in their struggle for self-determination and the push for institution building. "The Movement was driven by profound political and cultural ideas on being Chicano," wrote the historian Ignacio García. "This activist philosophy came to be known as *chicanismo*."[7] Yet chicanismo was an amorphous term that lent itself to much ambiguity. For some, chicanismo was a political tool necessary to bring Chicanos(as) together to push for a political goal. For others, chicanismo was a poetic voice, harking back to pre-Columbian times, affirming a metaphysical spirit uniting all Chicanos(as). A few tried to retain both readings.[8] The difficulty for Chicanos(as) was to navigate among these conflicting notions of chicanismo while actualizing *El Plan*.[9]

El Plan also suggested an articulation of a Chicano intellectual academic project. The authors of *El Plan* hoped to establish a curriculum that examined the Chicano heritage; in this way, students would learn and affirm their identity and begin to act politically. With this knowledge and responsibility, Chicano(a) students could begin to emancipate their communities. *El Plan* proposed Chicano studies programs that would provide the intellectual and moral resources for the struggle with dominant society. Two problems, however, confronted the endeavor to implement this project. First, institutional resistance altered the activists' radical hopes. For instance, the resolution of the Third World strike in Berkeley and the development of an Ethnic Studies College led to a compromise that displaced the goal of community transformation for academic self-preservation. Instead of creating autonomous institutional regions within the academy, Chicano student programs became practitioners of traditional university administrative procedures.

The second problem resulted from the activists' own confusion over intellectual production. The scholars Ronald Lopez and Darryl Enos recognized this issue: "There has been no major effort to deal with curricular development or refinement in a philosophical or academic sense."[10] Besides conflating intellectual production with administrative control, *El Plan* never offered an authentic oppositional intellectual vision. Instead, *El Plan* activists felt satisfied with institutional control. Their vision of Chicano studies did not challenge academic epistemology; it did not offer any break with the traditional practice of knowledge. As Carlos Muñoz Jr. wrote: "What the Plan did not do was to define or redefine Chicano Studies curricula as outlined in earlier proposals in concrete terms or in terms that could be interpreted as an authentic alternative to traditional academic curricula."[11] Muñoz added that Chicano studies was simply defined as curricula on "the Chicano experience," with an overriding focus on culture. A decade later, the scholar Carlos Ortega characterized *El Plan*'s vision of Chicano studies as a restatement of the functions of any academic program. "It was to be an institutionalized discipline," he wrote, "it would create a body of critical and empirical knowledge, there would be multi-disciplinary approaches, and there would be a group of working practitioners in working relation with one another."[12]

El Plan scholars developed little to contest academic practices. As Muñoz pointed out: "[T]he plan did not spell out how the university could be compelled to produce knowledge in the interest of Mexican Americans—in fact the plan did not go beyond the question of access to higher education."[13] For this reason, Chicanos(as) ended up accepting traditional and workable technologies, like the liberal arts model, for Chicano studies.[14] In this fashion, the empirical approach, so prevalent in U.S. social science and humanities, was quietly constituted in Chicano studies.[15] Thus the battle for institutionalization suffocated the intellectual struggle necessary to establish an oppositional and critical perspective and knowledge. In the end, *El Plan*'s visions of Chicano studies could result in simply another program within the university. Gómez-Quiñones concluded: "The framers of the plan were not actually concerned with changing the university so much as they were with redirecting its resources to meet the needs of the Mexican American community."[16]

The progressive subordination of Chicano studies to the logic of the administration bounded the elaboration of curriculum and the academic program. *El Plan* had left unclear the responsibility of the academic in relationship to Chicano(a) intellectual production. Although *El Plan* depicted student-to-student, student-to-faculty and/or -administrator, and student-to-community relations, it was, at best, vague when it came to the production and distribution of knowledge.[17] As more Chicano studies programs appeared, intellectuals (now as academics) accepted the established dynamic among Chicano knowledge, Anglo knowledge, and the social sciences or humanities. Franco Alejandro highlighted: "As a result of this phenomenal growth in Chicano Studies programs, a lack of any definite coordinated effort to develop a common pattern of program offerings has developed."[18]

The writers of *El Plan* left scholars with no alternative philosophical position except an uncritical return to a variety of empiricist models to explain the Mexican American condition. This was more than simply "Chicano youth . . . moved from Romano's idealism to a radical nationalism."[19] As Chicano studies elaborated its institutional niche, the epistemological issues, ignored by El Plan, succumbed to the traditional logic of research centers and departments. This is not to say that all Chicano scholars used the same methods and methodologies; they did, however, operate with the same epistemological gaze. Unfortunately, most Chicano(a) activists felt that their demand for control of academic institutions and/or institutional procedures was a radical stance and sufficient in and of itself. Their success in achieving institutional power further justified minimizing academic concerns as secondary or possibly divisive. Scholars had embarked, whether they intended to or not, on the building of a traditional discipline.[20] The scholar Jesse Contreras understood the endeavor was to "construe Chicano Studies as an emerging discipline or area of academic study."[21]

The historian Ronald Lopez is less sanguine about the establishment of Chicano studies programs. He recognizes that the politics that led to the creation of Chicano studies programs could not help run these programs. "I think that there is more than ample evidence to demonstrate that the political power moves that brought many of these programs into existence are not the same kind of moves that can effectively be utilized to give those programs the kind of quality and enduring characteristics that most of [them want] to have."[22] He reveals the problems that emerged at campuses like San Francisco State, Fresno State, and Long Beach State. A new politics of transition is necessary to legitimate Chicano studies. Unfortunately, he left unclear what this different politics might be and thereby accepted institutionalization as the answer.

Following the Santa Bárbara conference in 1969, the Chicano Council in Higher Education (CCHE) tried to follow up on the plans and ideals of El Plan, possibly in recognition of its limits on academic intellectual production. Unfortunately, the CCHE was unable to continue its work. A second conference to critique El Plan never came to fruition. When the CCHE was funded anew in 1973, it attempted to link various California college and university systems together. "It was expressed that statements pertaining to recruitment and admissions, support programs, Mecha organizations, etc., which are contained within the plan must be adopted and institutionalized by all Chicanos in higher education."[23] At the base of this new endeavor was El Plan. By this time, University of California faculty had formed a statewide organization and would not participate with the CCHE.[24] The end result was that issues left unresolved in *El Plan* were never fully dealt with; rather, Chicanos(as) turned to organization and institution building.

El Concilio Nacional de Estudios Chicanos: Birthing a Discipline

Resolving deficiencies in *El Plan*'s curricular vision, Chicano(a) scholars wrote a series of papers for the Chicano Studies Institute in 1970 that were later published in *Epoca*. Although this summer institute was organized at California State College at Long Beach, there were also institutes at Arizona State University, University of Colorado at Boulder, and possibly in Texas.[25] These institutes led to the formation of El Concilio Nacional de Estudios Chicanos, which provided a response to the practical problems that had resulted from the growth of Chicano studies programs and the limitation with *El Plan*.[26] While these various institutes were not the first attempt to work out some of the underdeveloped points in *El Plan,* the institute papers and El Concilio Nacional de Estudios Chicanos make a nice starting point to understand the formulation of Empirical Chicano Studies.[27]

The Concilio's purpose was to advocate for Chicano educational programs and to provide resources for the Mexican American community and government agencies. Frank Sánchez with his fellow editorial committee wrote: "The goal for Chicano Studies is to provide a relevant education. This learning is preparing the Chicano student with a different political, social, and cultural perspective than the society at large has traditionally imposed so that he can be prepared to work and live for the purpose of changing established institutions that have failed to meet the needs of the Chicano community."[28]

Some of the essays endeavored to structure the curricular side of Chicano studies. The educator Manuel Guerra, for instance, has written that Chicano studies belonged in its own specialization and categorization. This was due, he continues, to the unique nature of the subject, the interdisciplinary study of the Mexican American, the "White Anglo-Saxon Protestant value systems" that determined the current curriculum, and finally the need to "create an entirely new philosophy and approach to the problems of the barrio."[29] The scholar Julius Rivera has said that the goal of Mexican American programs was to educate Anglos, correct social science distortions, achieve academic recognition, link up with the community, become a magnet for activists, and apply an interdisciplinary model.[30] The writer and critic Sergio Elizondo has inserted his opinion: "The main point made here is that we, as Mexican American, can no longer tolerate anyone to pretend that the study of Mexican Americans is an object of curiosity any longer."[31]

Chicano studies, these authors would agree, needed to develop alternative approaches to the problems of the barrio and the students' relationship to the community, since the goal of Chicano studies had to be the transformation of the barrio.

> [I]n higher education the academic world has not intellectualized the problems of the barrio and the nature of these problems and their possible solutions have remained outside the current of thought of American life.[32]

> The emergence of Mexican American studies as a distinct, legitimate and transcendental academic and scholarly discipline is more important to the Mexican American for its philosophical import.[33]

For most of the Concilio writers, the current philosophy of U.S. education was inconsistent with the values of the Chicano movement: "We must recognize that that which we seek in Chicano Studies call[s] for radical change in the university."[34] Underlying this perspective was the assumption that the Chicano(a) could not leave the barrio or Raza.[35] For this reason, Chicano studies had to focus on community action; Chicano studies needed to provide techniques to resolve community concerns.[36] Elizondo felt that "we need that information [new type of research] to be used by us in the implementation of programs to solve specific programs by *us*."[37] When dealing with the objectives of Chicano studies, these writers had not moved much beyond *El Plan*. The Concilio essays did not engage the issue of academic knowledge. Most papers were concerned with the university's link to the barrio and the need to deal with community concerns—at times acknowledging social scientists' distortions.[38]

Among the Concilio pieces, an essay by Reynaldo Macías, Juan Gómez-Quiñones, and Raymond Castro was an exception and furnished the most thought-out program to structure Chicano studies. Their essay, "Objectives of Chicano Studies," epitomized the search for a discipline.[39] These authors indicate that Chicano studies was present when one could verify its administrative independence and therefore autonomous interactions with the academy. Chicano studies had to be institutionalized under Chicano control; only then could Chicano studies have sufficient latitude to achieve self-determination and self-definition. With this control, activists might recruit Chicano(a) students, faculty, and staff; develop a formal program on Chicano culture and history; as well as expand support programs, research programs, publication programs, and cultural/social centers in the community.[40] Once this was achieved, the Chicano(a) scholar could turn to academic work. The authors added: "Chicano Studies, then, in all disciplines and in all areas involve, re-definition, re-interpretation, and most importantly, a premise for the above two, it involves a change of framework. It in effect affirms a counter culture that is authentically Chicano and universal."[41] Once the program had established its autonomous base in the institution, they argued, Chicano studies could be an academic space controlled by Chicanos(as) for Chicanos(as). From this liberated zone, Chicanos(as) could challenge academic frameworks that had erased or stereotyped the Mexican American.

To construct an alternative intellectual space, Macías, Gómez-Quiñones, and Castro called for a different philosophy of education. The current framework of cultural pluralism resulted in an ethnocentric education, completely ignoring the needs of Mexican Americans.[42] Students therefore needed a Chicano philosophy of education; this alternative framework would provide students with a relevant education that would prepare them for community service resulting in needed political, social, and economic change.[43] The Chicano philosophy of education, based on the institutionalization of Chicano studies, would generate students who could partake in the "reformulation of knowledge in relation to the Chicano" and the transformation of the Chicanos(as)' position relative to the "gabacho system."[44] Macías, Gómez-Quiñones, and Castro's definition of Chicano studies as an academic discipline emerged from the activist institutionalizing efforts as proposed in El Plan.

What Macías, Gómez-Quiñones, and Castro and other Concilio scholars left unclear was their characterization of knowledge. What would knowledge production mean within the newly institutionalized Chicano studies? Would it be any different from any other field? How would it compare to academic knowledge? Their response—"A Chicano student must know how to locate the knowledge that he may need for pursuing action"—left much to be desired.[45] They assumed a neutral objective process in knowledge formation; they accepted an empiric and instrumentalist perspective of American academic knowledge with its acknowledgment of objectivity.[46] They believed that institutional control would have direct impact on the production of knowledge.[47]

Aztlán and the Formulation of Chicano Studies

The maturation of Empirical Chicano Studies corresponded to the appearance of *Aztlán*.[48] *Aztlán* continued the Concilio's response to *El Plan*'s intellectual vacuum.[49] With the first issue in 1970, we encountered an initial effort to think out Empirical Chicano Studies as a research program. Unlike the earlier *El Grito*'s critique of social science, the authors in the first issue of *Aztlán,* while critical of social scientists, retained an ambivalent relationship with social science logic and academic knowledge. This link with social science and the humanities was already present when the UCLA Mexican American Cultural Center first proposed a Chicano journal. The authors of the proposal noted that no Mexican American journal had been published in any university in the United States. The Center wanted to publish such a journal. The objectives would be (1) to publish articles in the social sciences, humanities, and the arts; (2) to inform readers of issues that relate to the Mexican American; (3) to present abstracts of theses and dissertations; and (4) to offer students the opportunity to learn editing. Aside from the content, the journal had little to distinguish it from other academic journals. There was little exertion to present a critical approach to academic research, writing, and publishing.[50]

An illustration of the new scholarly Chicano research example was the two lead articles in the opening issue by sociologists Fernando Peñalosa and Deluvina Hernández. These empiric scholars retained an equivocal relationship with social science discourse. While they acknowledged that academic research had created a distorted image of the Mexican American, they still found their methods and epistemologies acceptable. Often the difference among empirics was the balance between their criticism of their discipline and use of academic practices. Empirical Chicano Studies scholarship therefore formed a continuum between liberal empirics (who muted their criticism of social sciences or the humanities in favor of disciplinary practices) and radical empirics (who questioned their discipline though negotiated with their discipline's methods and epistemologies). Although Peñalosa and Hernández both operated from the field of sociology, each had a different relationship with their discipline representing these liberal and radical variants.

Peñalosa asserted that a new period of research was at hand that "should certainly produce more fruitful, more realistic, more relevant data and conclusions" than prior work.[51] Why was this the case? The difference from earlier social science was that the Chicano scholar would ask the "right questions" and therefore avoid the search for the "typical" or "true" Mexican American. Chicano research, Hernández differed, sought the range of variation without surrendering to the discipline. In this manner, their work provided insight into the diverse nature of the contemporary Chicano.[52] Jaime Sena-Rivera's essay in the same issue, placed somewhere between Peñalosa's and Hernández's articles, followed up on this reconstitution of "critical" social science research by saving the methods of social science. Possibly all three of these scholars would have agreed with Julius Rivera's statement: "One's discomfort with the literature, to speak only of it, is increased by the knowledge . . . that the essential tools do exist, at least in sociology, for perception and measurement of the truer reality."[53] Peñalosa, Hernández, and Sena-Rivera defined Chicano scholarship and research within social science. Their work remained grounded in the dominant theories of their disciplines. They used their disciplines to explain the Mexican American condition. While these scholars were critical of how Mexican Americans had been treated by society, their analyses flowed from the use of the traditional tools of the fields. They suggested that Chicanos(as) needed to engage in "good" social science.

Although one could distinguish Peñalosa's liberal approach from the radical position taken by Hernández, both scholars represented variants within Empirical Chicano Studies.[54] In most cases, liberal empirics created space within their disciplines' epistemologies and methodologies. While they recognized the weakness of their field, in the final instance they saw their scholarship rooted in their discipline. They explained the Mexican American experience through a correct or more profound use of their discipline's tools, often with a view that assimilation was the goal. They followed in the footsteps of scholars as diverse as George I. Sanchez, Carlos Castañeda, and Ernesto Galarza. For example, in an early Peñalosa piece, while noting the criticism of sociological research on the Mexican American, he accepted the assumption that the Mexican American was going through a process of assimilation. The Mexican American "is clearly moving further away from lower-class Mexican traditional culture and toward Anglo-American status."[55] The sociologist Edward Murguía observed that Peñalosa's scholarship was similar to that of Leo Grebler, Joan Moore, and Ralph Guzman in *The Mexican American People*. They shared a belief that Mexican Americans were undergoing a process similar to other European immigrants.[56] Although Peñalosa later mellowed his views, he retained his liberal perspective as evidenced by his views on sociology in a Mexican American studies program.[57]

As Peñalosa's intellectual biography suggests, liberal empirics varied in how they accepted and used their disciplinary tools as well as how they connected their research to community transformation. Essays by psychologists and political scientists Amado Padilla, Edward Casavantes, and Ralph Guzman shared much with Peñalosa's endeavors.[58] More examples of liberal empirics can be found in the early readers, like those by scholars Manuel P. Servín and John H. Burma.[59] Some of the essays that appeared in the special issue of *Social Science Quarterly* in 1973 demonstrated how quantitative research could be part of the liberal empiric camp. One of the better examples was Rodolfo Alvarez's "The Psycho-Historical and Socioeconomic Development of the Chicano Community in the United States."[60] Although these scholars felt more secure with their discipline's tools, their research highlighted the oppression faced by Mexican Americans and the need to challenge these conditions. Their essays were imbued with oppositional spirit.[61]

The radical empirics, however, while accepting the possibility of "good" academic work, began from the acknowledgment that the United States was a fundamentally unfair economic, social, and political system. Liberals might accept the temporary nature of this inequality, but radicals emphasized that this was a deep-seated attribute of the United States. Moreover, radicals wanted to use their research to transform this unequal system. In some cases, radicals incorporated a socialist analysis in their explanation of the Mexican American condition.

Macías, Gómez-Quiñones, and Castro proposed intellectual vision, as articulated in their Concilio piece, and found development in the journal *Aztlán*. Throughout this period, they appeared as editors, coeditors, as well as assistant or contributing editors of *Aztlán*. Together with the rest of the editorial board and various contributors, Macías, Gómez-Quiñones, and Castro developed a loose community of mostly California-based Chicano(a) intellectuals who shared a common vision of Chicano studies. This cohort shared many socioeconomic and political characteristics that supported their mutual assumptions of U.S. society and the placement of Mexican Americans. UCLA Chicanos(as) provided the leadership of the community. The construction of the UCLA Mexican American Cultural Center, with its emphasis on program development and research, paralleled the interest in *Aztlán*.[62] Eventually Macías, Gómez-Quiñones, and Castro would also assert leadership in the Center when Gómez-Quiñones became director. The *Aztlán* editors wanted to present a "critical discussion and analysis on Chicano matters as they related to the group and to the total U.S. society."[63] In seeking to achieve this goal, the editors began to mold the incipient field. Even though it was unclear what direction Chicano studies would evolve, the editors pushed for publications that manifested this new empirical philosophy.

The historian Jesús Chavarría's short introduction to his bibliographic essay exemplified this initially ambiguous vision. He claimed that at the heart of Chicano studies is the discipline of history: "[I]t can . . . offer a basic analytical structure for the totality of the Chicano experience."[64] To be successful with this endeavor, Chicanos(as) needed to rigorously reconceptualize the field. Chavarría felt they ought to begin with a "prudent revisionist attempt at explaining the emergence of the Chicano in the Southwest."[65] In another piece, Chavarría remarked that the educational experience presupposes certain assumptions that arise from a particular historical and cultural setting. "Thus it follows that any curriculum which purports to serve Chicanos," he espoused, "must be rooted in some fundamental way in his culture, his history, in his language."[66] He asserted "that history is the key discipline" necessary to build a curriculum toward self-identity and community service.[67] At the same time, this curriculum has to serve the community. "Pursuing Chicano Studies . . . is not only a matter of sure academic training," wrote Chavarría, "it is also a matter of receiving an education that is going to be relevant to our community."[68]

Although not everyone accepted Chavarría's endeavor to present historical analysis as the mode of comprehending the Mexican American experience, most approved of how *Aztlán* attempted to establish a rigorous analytical and structural analysis for this experience. The push for a structural explication of the Chicano(a) condition, using tools from the social sciences or humanities, became the calling card of the empiric. While articles by Gómez-Quiñones and Carlos Cortes demarcated research on Chicano history,[69] it was Muñoz's piece that amended Chavarría's intellectual vision of Chicano Studies as a discipline.[70] Muñoz used cultural nationalism as a tool to build Empirical Chicano Studies as an academic program. He pointed out how social science, and in particular political science, has ignored Mexican Americans.[71] "That social science has failed to focus on the reality of the Chicano experience cannot be easily disputed," Muñoz said. "However, through both ignorance and misinterpretation, it has succeeded in de-emphasizing the very real problems that have confronted Chicanos in our racist society."[72]

Recalling the work of Romano, Hernández, and Raymond Rocco, Muñoz concluded that this misunderstanding of the Mexican American resulted from "a dominant Anglo perspective which has been predicated on the cultural values and norms of the dominant society."[73] Therefore, the Chicano scholar needs to confront this discourse with a counter-perspective; if not, he will reproduce the dominant view. Muñoz continued: "The Chicano scholar must realize that it is not enough to write critiques pointing out the stereotypes and myths that social science has perpetuated about Chicanos. The crisis that confronts his people is too great and profound and it compels him to develop new paradigms of research and analysis. . . . The challenge before the Chicano scholar is to develop a Chicano perspective of political analysis. A perspective that will assure that his research will be oriented toward the needs of his community."[74] This Chicano perspective should be rooted in the Mexican American condition and the endeavor to resolve this situation by and for Chicanos(as).

Although Muñoz did not complete the task of establishing the framework of this new discipline in this essay, he left it clear that this intellectual paradigm must flow from a particular political agenda. For Muñoz, cultural nationalism guided the construction of an analytical model that would explicate the Mexican American condition and provide a political solution.[75] Unfortunately cultural nationalism—as a concept, ideology, and political device—was problematic, uncontrollable, and amorphous: "our vague, but dominant, ideological expression."[76] For most, it was the political philosophy of el movimiento: "Nationalism appears to be a strongly unifying feature among the methods of operation of the more activist segments in the Chicano [community]."[77] Another voice noted: "Barrio gente began to define and develop their own institutions. The philosophical basis for those institutions became cultural nationalism because nationalism lends itself directly to defining one's self. . . . Cultural nationalism became a rallying point around which Chicanos began to organize."[78]

Gómez-Quiñones added: "Nationalism provided an operative norm for politicalization and community development and provided the rationale and psychological substance for a collective Mexicano identity through the vehicle of symbols and sub-concepts which had the possibilities for wide acceptability."[79] But this nationalist politics, arising in conjunction with the various struggles for national liberation (in Algeria, Cuba, and Vietnam, to name a few) and the writings of nationalist revolutionaries (by the likes of Fanon, Memmi, Castro, Che, Ho, Mao, Cabral) was not homogeneous. Conflict arose over its ideology and praxis.[80] Furthermore, some Chicano(a) scholars found the growing nationalism as a potential problem for Chicanos(as).[81] In the end, cultural nationalism as an intellectual paradigm could not fully explain the Mexican American condition.

In another issue of *Aztlán,* the sociologist Tomás Almaguer transformed cultural nationalism into a "new orientation and basis for further research" as the internal colonial model.[82] While Almaguer's essay was not the first to use the internal colonial model, his work demonstrated how the model could become "central to the evolution of the 'concept of Chicano Studies' because internal colonialism provided a theoretical, a 'social scientific,' explanation for Chicano Studies' ideological role."[83] The model was further expanded theoretically by Mario Barrera, Muñoz, and Charles Ornelas.[84] It was applied by Rodolfo Acuña in the first edition of *Occupied America.*[85] Even Gómez-Quiñones, who was ambivalent about the internal colonial model,[86] saw a "framework of colonial relations and patterns" as possibly the best way to understand the condition of the Mexican American.[87] In the following years, the internal colonial model, with an increasingly Marxist tinge, became the alternative perspective that many *Aztlán* essayists acknowledged as the way to engage in critical research.[88] By 1973, Empirical Chicano Studies had a paradigm.[89]

While it is true that scholars using a variety of Marxist methodologies challenged the internal colonial model, too much was made about the conflict between internal colonialism and Marxism as an intellectual tool: was it race or class? Most scholars used a combination of these methods. Any reading of the two symposia in 1973 at University of California at Irvine and UCLA pointed to the incorporation of aspects of Marxist analysis into internal colonialism.[90] And just as one encountered internal colonialists adopting Marxist conceptions, we could see Marxists turning toward concerns of race and ethnicity. Much controversy could be read in Fred Cervantes's essay, but the differences were more smoke than fire.[91] Cervantes's frustration with the diverse expressions of internal colonialism was a response to its lack of a revolutionary political program, especially if its nationalism resulted in reformist politics. In the final instance, both camps shared a structural explanation of Chicano oppression.[92] When we look at their emphasis on the causes of oppression, we can draw a continuum of race and class between internal colonialism and Marxism. Their differences often came in their political choices, not their intellectual framework.

The next step in the formation of Empirical Chicano Studies was the 1974 special issue of *Aztlán* (volume 5), edited by Muñoz. In this issue, most of the authors expanded the discussion on internal colonialism, with various additions of Marxism, as the key for Chicano studies. Almaguer combined an analysis of capitalist development with colonialism to elucidate the Mexican American experience. Muñoz, like other scholars, indicated the paucity of good literature on Mexican Americans: "very little has been done in basic research and critical analysis of empirical data useful to the interpretation of the Chicano political experience."[93] To resolve this problem, he called for research using the internal colonial model.[94] Barrera followed up on Muñoz's argument. He remarked how political scientists continued to use myths and stereotypes in their analysis of the Mexican American. Barrera criticized the "objectivity" of political science and its narrow disciplinary approach and called for new theoretical approaches.[95] He wrote: "A pressing need is for the creation of new theoretical models for analyzing the realities of U.S. politics, with particular reference to Chicanos."[96]

Thus political science cannot achieve this goal. In fact, Chicano(a) scholars risked co-optation if they remained close to their field. "There is great temptation to accept the assumptions of the profession and the funding agencies," Barrera continued, "since this makes it much easier to work in that environment."[97] Therefore Chicanos(as) need an interdisciplinary model based on a historical perspective that avoids narrow empiricism of traditional academic disciplines. "[S]ubstituting Chicano political scientists for Anglo political scientists will not in itself provide a meaningful discipline," he explained. Rather, "[a] re-definition of the study of politics, which will challenge existing approaches at their theoretical and methodological base is needed to develop effective strategies for change and alternative conceptions of a just society."[98] Barrera contended that to avoid the failures of social science, scholars needed to turn to internal colonialism as the way to understand the Mexican American situation. What Barrera left unclear, however, was the relationship between internal colonialism and his criticism of academic knowledge. What exactly about the internal colonial model offered an escape from disciplinary control and allowed an explication of the contradictions of American society? Moreover, what did interdisciplinary research mean, and how did it fit with internal colonialism? Were a historical perspective and an interdisciplinary model sufficient to avoid the epistemological constraints of academic practices?

While Almaguer, Barrera, and Muñoz utilized the internal colonial model, any close reading of these scholars revealed significant theoretical differences that resulted from their particular understanding of capitalism, colonialism, internal colonialism, and race. Whatever their slant might have been, two issues linked their views together. First was the belief that the internal colonial model could escape the confines of academic knowledge and its stereotype of Mexican Americans. Practitioners of the model often claimed that by using an interdisciplinary or multidisciplinary approach, they could avoid disciplinary blind spots and narrowly defined intellectual practices. The second assumption was that any valid evaluation of the Mexican American had to begin with an examination of structures of oppression and domination. Only then could they develop a politics of transformation. Excavation of these structures necessarily had to draw from several disciplinary methodologies.

Empiricists believed that their analysis could exist outside the academic structures of knowledge. In a revealing footnote, Almaguer asserted in his essay that social science has always been an ideological tool meant to distort history, mystify reality, and justify oppression.[99] Thus there was no good social science; all social science was ideological. He reasoned that the internal colonial model could exist outside of academic knowledge and therefore avoid ideological confusion. For most of these writers, the model avoided the racist contamination present in all the disciplines and provided the only correct theory that could explain the Mexican American condition, offering a real basis for change. For instance, Muñoz contended that the scholar must provide a critical analysis "aimed at the construction . . . of a responsible ideology that can become a foundation for the development of viable strategies for social change in the urban barrios and the creation of alternative institutions conducive to the decolonization of Chicano America."[100] The only way to reach this conclusion was to escape disciplinary bonds. Only an interdisciplinary approach could help Chicanos(as) understand the Mexican American condition. "For it is my belief that Chicano Studies," Muñoz wrote, "due to its interdisciplinary scope as opposed to any traditional discipline, has the potential to more adequately deal with the questions that are underscored in this study."[101] The escape from academic disciplinary controls was to turn to versions of interdisciplinary or multidisciplinary scholarship.

These thinkers further agreed that the only way to understand the Mexican American condition and devise a political response was to comprehend the structures that created domination. The key was to analyze the institutional mechanisms by which dominant groups maintain their power and privilege.[102] As the critical theorist Raymond Rocco has stressed: "These frameworks are essentially interpretive schemes which attempt to account for the *institutional* basis of the subordinate status of Chicanos. This concern to explain the patterns of domination in structural terms, to conceive of them as a result of the characteristics of an interrelated social and political totality, is a common and unifying trait of these efforts."[103]

This structural methodology became the proposed mechanism for Empirical Chicano Studies research. A fusion of internal colonialism and Marxism became the preferred methodological tool to describe the America system of domination. They assumed that this methodology necessarily resulted in an activist program: "This broader approach [study of domination] defines the field of social and political research in terms of the problem or relating theory to practice, thought to action, or as it is now referred to, the problem of praxis."[104] By this methodology, Chicano scholarship brought together theory and praxis. The answer to Barrera's unstated question concerning the epistemological constraints of academic practices was simple. The internal colonial model, with its structural methodology, was not an academic (or bourgeois) enterprise and did not seek academic answers; it was a revolutionary program. The explication of structural reality of a capitalist United States disentangled the Chicano(a) from the academy's structure and rules of operation and prepared him/her for practical political action.

Interdisciplinarity became the conceptual link between the non-academic revolutionary potential of the internal colonial model and a structural methodology. Chicano(a) empirics found themselves defining the interdisciplinary character of their research as the central core to their epistemological revolution within academic research. Interdisciplinary work provided a method and methodology to Chicano Studies scholarship that avoided the limits of traditional social sciences and humanities. At times, some empirics used "interdisciplinary" as a code word for Chicano Studies research in toto, or when they were unsure of their own views on internal colonialism or a structural methodology. In an early essay on history, Gómez-Quiñones proclaimed that Chicano history "will call for rigorous interdisciplinary research and innovative methodology."[105] While he acknowledged the tentative nature of his postulations, he asserted that Chicano history needed a conceptual framework that juggled the relationship among culture, economics, psychology, sociology, and history of the Mexican American—as expressed by various disciplines. Earlier, Chavarría believed that Chicano studies had to take in all the diversity of the Mexican American experience.[106] Thus he maintained a balance in his historical practice between his modified colonial perspective with interdisciplinarity.

As the structural methodology and the internal colonial model dominated *Aztlán,* the journal conveyed the new discipline. The journal had moved from providing a voice for empirics to becoming the journal of Empirical Chicano Studies. Thus *Aztlán* became the lead intellectual organ in Chicano Studies, just at the time *El Grito* ended its first period (1975), and asserted its responsibility as disciplinarian of the incipient field. The change of *Aztlán's* subtitle exemplified this transformation. Initially the subtitle for *Aztlán* was the *Chicano Journal of the Social Sciences and the Arts.* While the title acknowledged its ties to social science and the humanities, the journal positioned itself not as a disciplinary component but as a *Chicano* journal challenging traditional social science research—one among others. By 1975, *Aztlán,* now the *International Journal of Chicano Studies Research,* presented itself as *the* journal whose disciplinary theme was Chicano Studies; a Chicano Studies that the journal itself had helped to create.[107] As the journal was incorporated into academic practices, Chicano Studies research became part of the "universal" search for knowledge. As the journal coeditors noted in the resubtitled journal: "Through the pages of published research, critiques and essays, our scholarship was and is having an impact in our communities and around the world. Our contribution, not only to 'academic literature' but to 'knowledge' is incipient."[108]

Furthermore, to strengthen its participation in knowledge gathering, the editorial committee called for greater involvement in the academic infrastructure, more publications, programs, courses, organizations, libraries, research institutes, archives, and the rest of academic paraphernalia. Rhetorically, the advocates of the new Chicano Studies argued that research could not be done through traditional or established disciplines. The editors called for "transdisciplinary" as well as traditional interdisciplinary work.[109] Increasingly, the paradigmatic break that Muñoz had demanded was translated into using different methods. Thus interdisciplinary, transdisciplinary, and multidisciplinary work becomes the "radical break" in Chicano Studies.

Just like in the first issue, interestingly, Peñalosa wrote the lead piece for the rebaptized *Aztlán*. While presenting a more developed argument than his earlier piece, his position toward social science and academic knowledge remained unequivocal: "Chicano sociolinguistics will have to develop their own theory, which can then be fed into the mainstream of sociolinguistics to challenge and enrich it."[110] From this view, Chicano Studies would provide the intellectual energy to revitalize moribund fields.[111] The earlier rejection of social science was silenced. Instead, Chicano Studies could save traditional academic disciplines.

Empirics never fully balanced internal colonialism, structural methodology, and interdisciplinarity. How these three fitted remained uneven. This balance was made more difficult by the attempt of some empirics to salvage aspects of traditional disciplinary tools. Moreover, given differences over interpretation about how to mix internal colonialism, Marxism, and a structural class analysis, interdisciplinarity became the lowest common denominator that empirics could accept. Given the incertitude of Chicano studies, interdisciplinary work remained a common point of reference for all empirics. For example, Carlos Ortega accepted Muñoz's challenge to develop a discipline of Chicano Studies with its particular paradigm. Yet for Ortega, internal colonialism in any of its configurations was "too narrow, deterministic and unsatisfactory." Rather, he saw a different paradigm on the rise that marked the "uniqueness" of Chicano Studies: "its interdisciplinary and comparative focus."[112]

Through its essays, *Aztlán* successfully placed itself at the head of Empirical Chicano Studies. An excellent example of *Aztlán*'s self-image as the flagship of Chicano Studies was Gilbert Cárdenas's guest editorial statement for an issue in 1976. He wrote: "The articles included in this volume were selected by referee judges, chosen on the basis of scholarly merit, and fitting the overall purpose of this special issue."[113] Cárdenas professed an academic creed with its articles of faith, all learned in the long process of academic training: referred judges, merit, objectivity, and finally, knowledge. In the process, he asked his readers to recognize the limitation of earlier articles (even in *Aztlán*) that had not gone through this process and were therefore of dubious quality. Cárdenas proclaimed with this issue that *Aztlán* provided an example of good scholarly practices and a journal that made available the best research on the Mexican American.

Aztlán was not the only journal that negotiated with the academy. What made *Aztlán* different from its contemporaries was its ability to present itself as a "radical" alternative to other Chicano(a) or ethnic-style academic journals. Given that Anglo journals gave little heed to Chicano(a) issues and Chicano(a) scholarship, *Aztlán* could fill this vacuum and in the process determine what Chicano Studies research was. This situation was reinforced by the lack of academic Chicano journals that dealt exclusively with scholarship. Although *El Grito* had published important and thought-provoking pieces, under Romano's growing influence, the journal was more concerned with the Chicano self-image as constructed through the arts, especially literature.[114] This situation continued under *El Grito del Sol,* when it appeared in 1976. Other journals like *Con Safos* (1968), *Journal of Mexican-American Studies* (1970), *Regeneración* (1970), *El Cuaderno* (1971), *Chicano Law Review* (1972), *De Colores: Journal of Emerging Raza Philosophies* (1973), *Encuentro Feminil* (1973), *Revista Chicano-Riqueña* (1973), *Tejidos* (1973), *Caracol* (1974), and *Bilingual Review* (1974) were limited in scope, short-lived, ambiguous in orientation, or more interested in the arts. Furthermore, some of these journals found themselves in sympathy with a different style of Chicano studies that placed them in conflict with the mission articulated in *Aztlán*. In other words, the new field was surrendered to *Aztlán* and the editors' conception of Chicano Studies.[115]

The National Association for Chicano Studies

By 1975, the discipline of Chicano Studies was set. Institutionalization was established in both student and academic services on many California campuses. Chicano Studies scholars, trained in a myriad of fields, participated in the new academic discipline. Although empirics dominated, scholars from different perspectives formed part of the new discipline as it tussled to establish its space in the university. *Aztlán* had become the prow of the new discipline that would "discover" Chicano knowledge.[116] The faculty, who were hired in the late 1960s and early 1970s and were close to tenure or already associate professors, became the spokespersons for Chicano Studies and arbiters of Mexican American knowledge.

Most Chicano(a) scholars, now settled at different academic institutions, agreed that they needed a scholarly organization and an annual convention like other academic disciplines. Initially organizing within traditional associations like the American Association of Sociology or the American Association of Political Science, Chicanos(as) moved to form a parallel organization outside the associations in their fields of training. At the 1972 annual meeting of the Southwestern Social Science Association, Chicanos(as) in existing disciplinary caucuses formed the National Caucus of Chicano Social Scientists with the purpose to establish a national association.[117] Jaime Sena-Rivera chaired this project and organized the first meeting for Chicano(a) social scientists at New Mexico Highlands University.[118] At this initial meeting in 1973, approximately fifty Chicanos(as) established the direction of the association and Chicano social science.[119] Chicano social science research, they argued, would be problem-oriented; it would be committed scholarship. Chicano practice of social science had to break down barriers between research and action. This would satisfy the "activist" character of Chicano studies. Moreover, social science research was to be interdisciplinary in nature as well as critical and rigorous. Lastly, Chicanos(as) must not limit the scope of their research.[120] The form of this new organization was to be in keeping with the philosophy and direction of the new Chicano social science. Muñoz contended that an "[a]greement was reached that traditional social science was to be discouraged within the proposed association in favor of more critical analysis as afforded by the internal colonial and Marxist class analysis."[121]

Thus the association was a place for Chicano(a) scholars to share their views on working in the academy and to establish a process whereby Chicanos(as) could organize Chicano studies. Most were still working out their understanding of what Chicano studies offered intellectually. While scholars belonged to different perspectives of Chicano studies, empirics dominated the early organization. The organization "was founded to provide an alternative forum for the development of a more critical analysis of the Chicano experience."[122] Thus in conjunction with *Aztlán*, the association helped foster the empiric perspective and orient the discipline.[123] At yearly conventions, Chicano studies scholars would judge up-and-coming scholarship. And if it had quality and merited attention, it would appear in the proceedings whenever they could be published. Here the "senior" scholars mentored the next generation of scholars, and the up-and-coming could express their views and perspective among fellow Chicano(a) academics. The organization formed "part of the first real 'generation' of Chicano scholars."[124] Again, we encounter the subordination to academic logic.[125]

By the time of the second annual convention, close to a hundred Chicanos(as) participated. To underscore the role of activism in the organization, half of the workshops dealt with "action research."[126] By this point, the organizational structure had been established and now was known as the National Association of Chicano Social Scientists (later it would be renamed the National Association of Chicano Studies, NACS). The leadership was principally based in the University of California system.[127] By the third convention, held in 1975 at the University of Texas at Austin, the association was firmly grounded. Some of the major themes at the conference were politics, nationalism, social history, sociolinguistics, labor, folklore, and Chicanos in the Midwest. Of particular interest was a session that year on "Chicano Social Science: The Ethics and Politics of Research."[128] Due to pressure from Chicana scholars and activists, the organizers held a session on "La Chicana" at the end of the conference. *El Mirlo Canta de Noticatlan: Carta Sobre Chicano Studies* reported: "Due to the great interest in the Chicana question expressed by the audience, a Chicana panel was arranged for Saturday."[129] About thirty individuals presented at this conference to about two hundred participants. Close to half the presenters were from California and a third from Texas. In both conventions, the spirit of *El Plan* and *Aztlán* was evident.[130]

The conference in 1976 at El Paso and in 1977 at Berkeley saw a rapid rise in the number of panels, themes, and presenters. In El Paso, one encountered panels on the border, communication, oral history, immigration, La Chicana, schooling, labor, and the concept of national minorities.[131] At Berkeley, aside from what could be defined as activist research, there were panels on health, history, leadership, identity, communication, and regional concerns. Again, California and Texas sent most of the presenters with the majority from California. The

University of California was the most heavily represented of California institutions. Of course, at the California conference, presenters were heavily in favor of Californians, with University of California presenters more than double those from the California state college system and private institutions.[132] By this point, NACS had proven its success and had become one of the pillars that sustained Chicano Studies.

By 1977, NACS was a successful association that managed the growth of Chicano Studies as a discipline. The overpowering logic of the empiric tradition directed the organization. Although occasionally dissenting views or traditions appeared, the vision presented at the New Mexico Highlands University conference, echoing the vision of *El Plan*, resonated throughout these early conventions. Throughout the conferences, empirics progressively established a Chicano research program and agenda for academic work. Empirics' desire to explain the causes of the Mexican American condition paralleled their wish to better the condition of Mexican Americans. These meetings underscored the influence of California, in particular UC-based Chicano(a) scholars (faculty and students). While NACS was not a California product, it was difficult to dismiss the influence of scholars that were in California-based institutions. Californians often played a central role in NACS, as they sat on steering committees at the various national conventions.

Muñoz believed that NACS failed to fulfill his hope of using internal colonialism as the paradigm for Chicano Studies research.[133] Instead, as the organization became more diverse, he found a resurgence of "a scholarship rooted in the dominant paradigms of the established disciplines."[134] This occurred because of the nature of academic work in the university. "The answer lies in the structure of the university," he wrote. "We remain victimized by it and are powerless to control our collective intellectual development. Our survival as faculty is dependent upon how well we meet the criteria for excellence in scholarship as defined by the dominant paradigms."[135] Muñoz had the right answer for the wrong question. Chicano Studies was successful in establishing the paradigm he so much desired. It was not, however, a theoretical perspective (like internal colonialism, Marxism, or even liberalism), but a structural analysis—a style of intellectual work that found legitimacy in the academy.

From a different angle, the scholar Hisauro Garza saw the development of this "objective" approach as good for Chicano social science. He has stated that once the "nationalist reactive and defensive postures" faded, more creative forms of social analysis were possible.[136] If scholars identified too closely with any one model or perspective, they would suffer from rigidity. "This appears to have happened to NACS," wrote Garza. "Many of its members formed their intellectual perspectives not on the basis of a socially detached, ethically-neutral scholarly orientation, but on the basis of deep-seated notions about social justice, equality and liberation."[137] For Garza, the objectivism of social science had returned in full force and saved NACS as well as Chicano Studies.

Arturo Madrid, the literary and cultural critic and education policy expert, organized a conference on the status of Chicanos in higher education.[138] Some of the issues discussed were access to higher education, student support, quality of education, as well as the status of Chicano Studies and the direction of research. The conference took place in Santa Monica in 1975. It provided a forum to address issues of the Chicano in higher education by accepting the structure and procedures of the academy. In a letter to the participants, Madrid stated that given the reality of the "antagonistic academy," "[i]t behooves us then to use the experience, knowledge, and expertise we have gained to develop new structures and new strategies."[139] One could read this conference as a "how to" become an academic broker. Madrid remarked that after the symposium, there was agreement on the need for creating a national commission with solid academic standing. The purpose of this organization was to influence public and private institutional policy, raise and administer funds, provide a framework for discussing issues in higher education, and to create a forum to address their concerns to the Chicano community. The organization would play a central role in channeling funds and providing intellectual support to particular programs and individuals—no doubt sharing the same empiric ideals. Again, we encounter an overlap in the individuals that participated in the symposium and other empiric endeavors and the replication of their thought style.

The transformation of Chicano(a) faculty into brokers was prefigured in the establishment of various University of California organizations. In June 1969, the UC president Charles J. Hitch received a critical letter from the special assistant for Mexican American Affairs. In the letter, Paul Sanchez, who would later resign, was critical of the University of California's efforts toward Mexican Americans. Gómez-Quiñones, representing the Mexican American Cultural Center, participated in a task force that called a statewide meeting to discuss the president's inaction.[140] This resulted in the creation of the University of California Chicano Steering Committee, composed of students, faculty, and staff, in August 1969.[141] Soon, President Hitch appointed a President's Task Force to look into the status of Chicanos(as) in the university. In looking over some of the minutes of the UC Chicano Steering Committee from 1971 to 1972, it is interesting to see academics from various perspectives working together. These were some of the issues discussed: national organization building and participation, Chicano studies at other institutions, bilingual programs, funding, Movimiento Estudiantil Chicano de Aztlán (MEChA), the Educational Opportunity Program (EOP), hiring in the system and affirmative action, conferences, directorship of programs, all special services, as well as discussions on "las chicanas," ideology, and community relations.[142]

To support the University of California Chicano Steering Committee and the Task Force, students decided to organize the University of California MEChA Federación.[143] By 1975, the task force was ready to present its report.[144] Aside from looking at the recruitment and retention of Chicanos(as) in the system, the report focused on public service. The report provided an institutionally legitimate way for Chicano Studies to incorporate community service and therefore fulfill its activist aim. The report used organized research units, like those at UCLA, as a way to satisfy Chicano(a) demands to retain the link to the community and provide a space for activist research. In the *Report of the President's Task Force,* the authors proposed that "[i]t is perhaps within the ORU's [organized research units] that the University currently possesses resources that are of immediate usefulness and importance to the Chicano community."[145] The document reiterated that community-related service and research were central to ORUs. Yet "the first of these responsibilities [cannot be] carried out at the expense of the second."[146] Many were not happy with the report or efforts to follow through on its proposals.[147]

The report manifested how faculty and administration had begun to negotiate for a Chicano space within the University of California system. While problems still had to be resolved, most UC campus Chicanos(as) had begun to accept the logic of the university system. In organizing a meeting of University of California faculty, certain issues, community involvement in particular, had to be restrained. As Jorge Terrazas Acevedo reported in *Chicano Studies Newsletter*: "In my estimation the secondary item of power and liberation within the dimension of community involvement does not stand a chance of obtaining a place in the coming announced agenda unless students and community members obtain commitments from their various representatives to, first of all, list the item within the agenda, then secondly support the conceptualization of community power and liberation for the priority which it deserves from the new caucus emerging from the Chicano Faculty at the University of California."[148] In *El Popo,* one reporter saw this as a meeting of a "Chicano elite."[149] In an article on La Raza Council on Higher Education, the author questioned whether Chicano(a) admissions, Chicano studies professors, and administrators were a form of co-optation.[150]

The success of Chicano Studies as an academic project was closely connected to the support empirics received from philanthropic organizations. This relationship furthered the shift of Chicano Studies to accept academic practices and institutional logic. This institutional reallocation presented itself, for instance, when the Ford Foundation funded the Southwest Council of La Raza (later called the National Council of La Raza).[151] The journalist Armando Rendon reported that in the aftermath of the El Paso conference, Ford provided the money to establish the Council whose task was to support other Mexican American groups as well as carry out its own programs. By September 1968, the Southwest Council was fully operational. Rendon continued that the Council geared itself for the economic development of the barrio through internal efforts. But he stressed that Chicanos(as) and the Council did not have the political savvy to avoid dependence on "private gringo bureaucracy" that Ford and other foundations represented.[152]

In an issue of *Ramparts,* journalists Rees Lloyd and Peter Montague pointed out how the Ford Foundation had set out to develop "a 'safe' leadership for La Raza akin to the NAACP or the Urban League."[153] First they supported the Southwest Council of La Raza and later the Mexican-American Legal Defense and Educational Fund.[154] The political and civil rights activist Bert Corona recalled how Galarza was able to sell the idea of the Concilio to the Ford Foundation that led to Southwest Council. Unfortunately, instead of being the result of grassroots organizing, it was grown from the top down. Moreover, the organization was beholden to the foundation. Thus, "[t]his limited the effectiveness and autonomy of the group and steered it toward more of an establishment perspective."[155] José Angel Gutiérrez, cofounder of the Mexican American Youth Organization and later the La Raza Unida

Party, declared that Ford-funded organizations would be "less account-able and accessible to the Chicano militants."[156] Acuña supported this contention.[157] In addition to Ford, other institutions served to moderate Chicano academic politics.[158]

Empirical Chicano Studies as Chicano Studies

The *Aztlán* essays and the establishment of NACS manifested the dominance of empirics and Empirical Chicano Studies as the epistemo-logical and methodological guide to Chicano research. Three reasons lie behind this success: (1) Empirical Chicano Studies presented a work-able political strategy for Chicanos(as) in the academy; (2) it provided an acceptable and legitimate ground for research and policy conclu-sions; (3) it established and sanctioned a Chicano space in the academy. These distinct and potentially contradictory concerns were reinforced by the use of a structural analysis of oppression. This epistemological gaze legitimated the success of the empirics. These empirics assumed that the best, if not the only, way to comprehend U.S. oppression and discrimination was to elucidate the system of racial, ethnic, and/or class domination. This explained the success of internal colonialism, colo-nialism, and Marxism as tools of analysis. Moreover, many Chicano(a) thinkers further concluded that this structural analysis necessarily provided the basis for an activist program—whether reformist or revo-lutionary. Thus, the political desires expressed by *El Plan* and many Concilio papers could be fulfilled.

The instrumentalist character of the empirics' curricular agenda, unfortunately, distorted the hope of building an oppositional intellec-tual endeavor. *El Plan* harnessed Chicano Studies to resolve immediate political goals. In the process, thinking was reduced to the immediacy of political and social action. The wanting philosophy of chicanismo and cultural nationalism fostered a negative and abstract subjective reason that resonated with the apparent scientific clarity of empiricism. Even historical analysis, whether in its idealist or materialist form, became reified—disconnected, whatever the rhetorical posture, from situated reality. History merely became a tool to explain the pragma-tism of the structural analysis. This pragmatism turned to physical science as the model for all analysis, reiterating the technical character of knowledge.[159] In other words, the political concerns of the Chicano student movements—in particular, the endeavor to seek political power through the academy—subverted the intellectual autonomy and critical spirit of early Chicano thought. This tendency was fortified with the adoption of a structural analysis of domination that legitimated their research by building on academic practices.[160] In the end, as the economist Refugio Rochin has commented, the goals of Chicano Studies were "not so different from the goals that most universities strive for, but in a broader context."[161]

The potential radical critique implicit in the Chicano analysis simply faded. U.S. social sciences and humanities had no problem utilizing a variety of empiricist structural models; these models shared an ahistorical understanding of structures. In contrast, Chicano structural analysis initially grew out of a historicist perspective. Sadly, this perspective was lost as Chicano structural analysis came closer and closer to its Anglo counterpart. Internal colonialism, colonialism, and Marxism sanctioned the metamorphosis of early historical analysis into structural explanations. History became mere background or setting. Unintentionally, these engaged thinkers returned to the empiricism of Anglo social science and academic knowledge.[162]

While empirics desired to avoid American exceptionalism and proposed the creation of a more just society, their intellectual approach returned them to academic practices that resulted in the opposite effect. The development of a structural model to explain the Mexican American condition played into the incorporation of Chicano Studies into the academy. Paralleling the construction of Chicano Studies programs and their incorporation into university practices, Empirical Chicano Studies found its academic niche. The assumption that the internal colonial model or academic Marxism could exist beyond the university quickly faded.

As Empirical Chicano Studies came to be Chicano Studies, it further strengthened its position by disciplining the field using academic accouterments. This did not suggest that fellow non-Chicano(a) academics agreed or even acknowledged these methods and tools. But they could accept its measurability—publications, presentations, curricula vita—and agree on the common search for knowledge. Even in the margins of the university, acceptable procedures and practices legitimized some with power and knowledge, while dismissing others. As critical and as community oriented as Empirical Chicano Studies desired to be, it became an expression of academic practices. In Rochin's overview of Chicano Studies, he never once mentioned questions of knowledge or epistemology. He simply assumed that "good research" would answer that question. Rather, his concerns were about institutions and institution building.[163]

At the same time, we must be wary of accepting *Aztlán's* self-presentation as a radical and therefore oppositional voice. Many essays in *Aztlán* remained tied to its nationalist origins even though articulated through internal colonialism or Marxism. The scholar Alfredo Cuéllar's criticism, influenced by Harold Cruse's *The Crisis of the Negro Intellectual,* confirms the accommodationist side of this perspective. The Chicano nationalist, like his African American counterparts, had not come to any understanding of nationalism and its possible conservative nature.[164] Cruse argued against black nationalism: "But a closer examination of every analysis by each Black Power exponent from SNCC and CORE reveals that while the slogan cast a revolutionary *sounding* theme and a threat of more intense revolt across the land, the *substance* was, in fact, a methodological retreat to black social reforms."[165]

If we leave aside the black power rhetoric, Cruse surmises, we return to traditional reformist African American politics. Like black power activists, Chicano activists learned little from the African American intellectual past and the conflicts among the various African American positions. Thus the black power outlook replayed "the old dichotomy between DuBois–NAACPism and West Indian nationalist–Garveyism."[166] Despite black power's vaunted anti-Americanism, "they were more American than they think" and fell prey to bourgeois aspirations.[167] Just as their political vision led them to return to a collaborationist politics, academically they returned to the academic practices that provided them with professional and intellectual legitimacy.

As the empirics subjugated Chicano Studies to their vision, they marginalized other alternative perspectives. Chicanos(as), who were wary of empiricism in the social sciences and humanities, were progressively forced to retreat from positions of contention. Those who may have endeavored to formulate a Chicano studies around their particular interpretation of critical theory, expressions of existentialism, forms of essentialism, and styles of cultural nationalism became peripheral to the academic project in Chicano Studies. Many Chicana writers, frustrated with the patriarchal character of el movimiento and informed by a feminist agenda, found themselves isolated. The empirics had successfully established their formulation as the only version of Chicano Studies.

Perspectivist Chicano Studies, 1967-1982

Although many intellectuals followed the political and intellectual agenda established by *El Plan de Santa Bárbara,* the empiric position was not the only possible option for Chicanos(as) in the academy. The activism that led to the formulation of *El Plan* also brought to life other configurations of Chicano(a) academic work. In the early years of Chicano studies, multiple Chicano studies coexisted with several possible options of bridging Chicano studies and the academy—formulated in a hostile, aggressive, and turbulent environment. This chapter traces one such tradition, Perspectivist Chicano Studies.

It is difficult to define Perspectivist Chicano Studies. This vision lost the struggle to present itself as a legitimate interpretation of Chicano studies. By the late 1970s, Perspectivist Chicano Studies became an increasingly peripheral and fragmented intellectual agenda, surviving in corners of nonresearch teaching institutions, alternative educational institutions, the arts, and certain community organizations. As victorious Empirical Chicano Studies settled in the prestigious institutions and its works were transformed into the canon of Chicano Studies, perspectivist writers were progressively pushed toward peripheral journals or self-publication. As the empirics further disciplined the field, they apprehended Perspectivist Chicano Studies as at best a quaint romantic vision and at worst as irrational and dangerously apolitical. Because of the success of the empirics, Perspectivist Chicano Studies never had the opportunity to mature into a concise intellectual style, its practitioners often being isolated. This lack of maturity allowed enormous variation among perspectivist writings as well as off-key, if not contradictory, expressions of this style. At the same time, many perspectivists shared a variety of views about the Chicano(a) experience.[1]

This historical experience has made it difficult to name this tradition. Initially I called it "Existential Chicano Studies." As an undergraduate, Donato Martinez indicated that existentialism might be used to understand the Chicano(a) protest.[2] More directly, the scholar Jesse Contreras connected Chicano studies to the legacy of the Mexican antipositivist revolt that took the form of an existentialist phenomenological framework.[3] But readers of earlier versions of this project felt that this term unnecessarily introduced the long history of phenomenology and existentialism into the discussion. While some early Chicano(a) thinkers may have accepted this baggage, others would not.[4] I find the term "perspectivist" more acceptable. In this manner, the influence of Samuel Ramos, Patrick Romanell, Octavio Paz, and José Ortega y Gasset on early Chicano(a) thinkers could be more fully appreciated.[5]

To understand the perspectivist position, it is important to recall the influence Mexican thinkers had on the early development of Chicano studies. In looking over early Chicano studies course syllabi (1968–1975), the influence of Romanell's *Making of the Mexican Mind,* Ramos's *Profile of Man and Culture in Mexico,* and Paz's *The Labyrinth of Solitude* on developing Chicano thought is inescapable.[6] The historian David R. Maciel wrote: "Para los Estudios Chicanos, la historia intelectual de México está íntimamente relacionada en doble forma" (For Chicano Studies, the intellectual history of Mexico is doubly intimately intertwined).[7] These texts provided Chicanos(as) with a particular interpretation of the "Mexican character" and, more important, with a theoretical/philosophical vision about their own identity. Perspectivism could fit well with expressions of Chicano cultural nationalism. Romanell's and Ramos's texts introduced Chicanos(as) to Ortega y Gasset's notion of perspectivism: "a theory of knowledge in 'culturalist' dress."[8] He wrote: "Perspectivism, in brief, is the theory which holds that since reality is composed, like a landscape, of an 'infinite number of perspectives,' some of which we come to know through the 'selective' medium of 'vital reason,' therefore, reality does not possess in itself, 'independently of the point of view from which it is observed, a physiognomy of its own.'"[9]

Reality was thus composed of perspectives; truths were points of view, equally authentic and true: "[T]ruth and error, like life and death, are matters of history and history is a matter of perspectives."[10] What made Ortega y Gasset's position different from pre-Socratic philosopher Protagoras's view that each man was the measure of all things was the need to restore to individuals their national perspectives—a philosophy of culture (*Kulturphilosoph*). A perspective is tied to a particular historical, social, and cultural context. Mexican thinkers, Romanell concluded, had abandoned the various manifestations of rationalism and sought an existential intellectual perspective bound to the Mexican experience. They found a "norm" applicable to Mexico in Ortega y Gasset's pivotal idea: "Yo soy yo y mi circunstancia" (I am myself and my circumstance).[11] Contreras suggested that Ortega y Gasset echoed Nietzsche's perspectivism by adding that one "cannot transcend this totality of self and circumstance to achieve an absolute and impartial knowledge of an objective world; each individual is limited to the perspective of a given self-with-things."[12] Perspectivism found company with Chicano cultural nationalism and chicanismo.

The journal Con Safos did a good job introducing the writing of Ortega y Gasset to Chicanos(as) in 1969.[13] One could argue that the journal shared Ortega y Gasset's position, at least as developed by Mexican existential thinkers. One editorial in the journal explained: "It is rather an attempt at expressing the entire spectrum of feelings that are the soul of the barrio . . . Con Safos is faith."[14] In an interesting student essay, the young philosopher Francisco Vázquez worked Ortega y Gasset, in particular El tema de nuestros tiempos, together with indigenous Mexican philosophy, José Vasconcelos's La Raza Cósmica, and Chicano(a) thought.[15] Vázquez pointed out that El Plan Espiritual de Aztlán came about from the new spiritual sensibility that Chicanos(as) had brought to the intellectual table to challenge materialism and "blind rationalism."[16]

Chicano(a) readings of these texts reinforced the supposed continuity between the "Chicano mind" and the "Mexican mind," while providing an intellectual vision to Chicano politics.[17] Perspectivism's reference to one's circumstances fitted well with the Chicano(a) call for a link between community and university. This allowed them to initiate their research from their position as Chicanos(as) in American society. Moreover, their search for identity could be tied to an anticolonial perspective.[18] For perspectivists, identity and knowledge were linked together. For most, knowledge did not exist outside, framed by some objective and neutral setting. Rather, knowledge was the active result of the researcher and his or her world. Therefore, perspectivists began their intellectual operation with a rejection of the practices of social science research. These scholars sought to establish an oppositional epistemology rooted in the process of Chicano(a) identity formation. Readings of these texts further endowed Chicanos(as) with a theory of being and knowledge that could function as the ground for Chicano studies—"understanding of the Chicano frame of reference."[19]

Perspectivism called into question traditional academic constructions of the Mexican American. Nick Vaca's work provided an example of perspectivist writing. In "Message to the People," Vaca argued that social science literature on the Mexican American flowed from the position of Anglo researchers in relationship to the Mexican American. Thus social scientists created a myth of the Mexican American as a docile people, portrayed as an emerging or changing people. Traditional scholars could not visualize the activism of Mexican Americans because of their belief that Mexican Americans were passive, fatalistic, and unchanging beings.[20] Vaca expanded his argument in a two-part essay that provided a critical overview of social science writing from 1912 to 1970. In his first essay, Vaca noted how early work in psychology and sociology portrayed Mexican inferiority and used a variety of explanations to justify this condition. In the second essay, Vaca observed the success of cultural determinism to explain the Mexican American condition. Unlike Romano's early pieces in El Grito, Vaca highlighted the politics behind this intellectual view.[21] He wrote: "It seems certain that the major reason for the triumph of cultural determinism in the 1950s was ideological. For only by viewing the causality of the social ills of the Mexican-American as stemming from within him—his cultural baggage—all complicity was removed from American society."[22]

Perspectivists formulated a Chicano standpoint that unfolded from the many Mexican American experiences in the United States. "This is what Chicano Studies is all about," Richard Vásquez wrote, "getting the Mexican American . . . to understand himself and his people, his history and his culture, his heritage and his destiny."[23] Critical of social science research and skeptical of academic work, these scholars sought to establish an oppositional epistemology rooted in the process of Chicano identity formation. At the same time, they had to struggle with the practices of the academy.[24] Although their intellectual work created another expression of Chicano studies, their inability to resolve the contradiction of a Chicano academic gave their vision a short life.[25]

Chicanismo and Perspectivist Chicano Studies

As more campuses established Chicano studies programs, activists grew increasingly concerned about the character and direction of these programs—this was especially the case with academic work. What made a Chicano studies course any different from any other course? What should the goals of the curriculum be? To respond that these courses dealt with the "Chicano experience," some felt, was insufficient. For perspectivists, Chicano studies had to provide a vision of life; organization building and institutionalization alone was insufficient. Chicano studies had to deal with existence. An example was Thomas Martinez's essay, presented at the Chicano Studies Summer Institute in 1970.

Chicano studies programs, Martinez observed, needed to foster "a philosophy of living—an alternative set of values to those now persisting in Anglo-American society."[26] Fortunately, he highlighted, Chicanos(as) possessed such an alternative philosophy—chicanismo. While chicanismo is not simply a reaction to Anglo society, it does manifest dissatisfaction with "Anglo-white values."[27] These so-called Anglo values emphasize material achievement to prove self-worth, while chicanismo is about spirituality, honest self-examination, a complete love of life, and consciousness of the here and now. Chicanismo rejects Anglo materialism.[28] Martinez explained that Chicanismo is a variant of the larger humanist tradition missing from mainstream America.[29]

Chicano studies, he maintained, therefore cannot be about social science (or the humanities) alone, but about existence. "It is the 'inner' life that is most important in defining worth of self and others."[30] The problem with the university is not simply academic; it is the qualification of human behavior, responsibility, values, and ethics; its denial of humanism. Martinez warned his readers: "Do not allow the administrative responsibilities for programs to dictate the development of a 'bureaucratic personality' to the exclusion of Chicanismo values."[31] Rather, Chicano studies must continually preserve and promote humanism at the same time to resist the bureaucratic mentality of the academy. "There is a humanistic tradition inherent in the Chicano culture," Martinez wrote. "It embodies an identification with all that is living."[32] The scholar Jorge Terrazas Acevedo appended this idea: "I interpret life in terms of emotion and drama rather than rationality or logic."[33] The scholar Celia Medina continued this line of thinking, writing that the "existential perception of life is that it could be human being-centered."[34]

A variety of political and intellectual communities utilized chicanismo throughout the early period of el movimiento.[35] For most, this spirit embodied the core value of all those struggles with dominant

Anglo society: "Chicanismo [was] the ideology of El Movimiento and of Mexican American politics."[36] Chicanismo drew inspiration from the black power movement and anti-imperialist struggles, such as the Cuban Revolution.[37] For others, chicanismo was also about cultural resistance, cultural nationalism, humanism, and revolutionary praxis. As the activist and scholar Theresa Aragón de Shepro wrote: "Chicanismo is at once an ideology and a cultural expression . . . the main tenets of Chicanismo are humanism and self-determination. It calls for the humanity of man through revolution."[38] For this reason, chicanismo connected to carnalismo; both are rooted in respect.[39] The community and mental health activist Roberto Vargas wrote: "Carnalismo is a brotherhood, it is an understanding and an awareness of the concepts—love, nature, peace, culture, and destiny, that allows this brotherhood to evolve. . . . Carnalismo is the philosophy of the Mexican as he transcends political and social philosophies into humanistic terms."[40]

In an article in *Bronze,* the writer Esmeralda Bernal examined the notion of carnalismo. Some of the people struggling for their rights had detached themselves from materialism. They sought the elements necessary for self-respect and nourishment, enriching their mind through carnalismo. "Carnalismo is that love that we possess for each other," she wrote, "the same love taught by Christianity that somehow got mangled through war, materialism, and computerization."[41] Through carnalismo, Chicanos(as) could unify and avoid being reduced in the materialist melting pot. While Chicanos(as) might demand their piece of the pie, Chicanos(as) could not allow themselves to become inhuman automatons. For some Chicano activists, chicanismo's expression of humanism was a spiritual force;[42] "a way of life, a spiritual calling, a love, a respect, and a duty."[43] Perspectivism was an alternative way of life, different from Anglo society. In this way, the Chicano(a) challenged the dominant belief system and attempted to reconstruct the Mexican American. This reconstruction began with an appeal to pride in a common history, culture, and "race." The scholar Alfredo Cuéllar wrote: "*Chicanismo* attempts to redefine the Mexicans' identity on the basis not of class, generation, or area of residence but on a unique and shared experience in the United States."[44] Chicanismo, like carnalismo, was about *familia.* Acevedo affirmed this idea when he wrote: "I love humanity for everyone is a member of the same family. In Spanish we speak of *la familia, la raza, la sangre,* carnalismo. This is the kind of thing that makes us humanists."[45] He saw *la raza* and *familia* as the totality of interactions and experiences from the ancestors to present-day families.[46]

Alurista articulated this vision of chicanismo and Chicano studies in a position paper for the first California-wide state college Chicano(a) faculty conference. He defined Chicano studies as an instrument to recognize the Chicano(a): "To take cognizance of the Way of Life, the culture which must be cultivated if our Nation is going to rise."[47] Often he utilized indigenous imagery to express his vision. It is only by acknowledging the native spirit, he wrote, that we can resist the engulfing specter of the American way of life. Thus Chicano studies must reflect different practices than other academic endeavors. Chicano studies is about practice, about advocacy for change, a different way of life. Alurista continued: "Practice is the only possible measure of stability in Chicano Studies since the constant influx of Chicano Students will bring more and more theoretical possibilities we must offer a concrete example of what we have nationalized so that as Chicano Students leave our instruction they have learned an alternative way of life which is practicable under any working conditions according to the Seven Principles of Calpulli."[48] The future of Chicano studies, then, rested on the acceptance or rejection of the indigenous way of life.[49]

I do not want to reduce chicanismo to Perspectivist Chicano Studies or vice versa. Chicanismo permeated all Chicano politics and early endeavors to construct Chicano studies in the late 1960s and 1970s.[50] Therefore the language of chicanismo can be found in most, if not all, expressions of early Chicano studies. However, the vision of a living Chicano culture (Ramos's *cultura viviente*) as the central core of Chicano studies, I believe, is what made Perspectivist Chicano Studies distinct from Empirical Chicano Studies. While chicanismo may appear to simply restate the assumptions of cultural nationalism, some have tried to turn the call to culture into a practice that avoids what they perceived as U.S. materialism, hypocrisy, and inhumanity. As the anonymous La Coronela reminded Chicanos(as), cultural nationalism replaced the emptiness created by Anglo brainwashing. It was the instrument by which we could begin to organize the community and by which we took the first step on the road to freedom: "[C]hicanos are creating their own life style under the banner of cultural nationalism."[51] From this vision, the movements of people of color were also part of the larger anti-imperialist struggle. Contreras explained this point further: "What 'Third World' communities have in common is *not* a culture but an experience of discrimination, disadvantage and a failure, on the part of the larger society, to recognize the worth and dignity of the specific culture which each of the different 'Third World' communities experienced in different ways."[52]

Chicanismo as Philosophy

The philosopher Eliu Carranza formulated a possible philosophic framework for Chicano perspectivism. Like Romano, he began with a return to Mexican Americans' heritage and values: "The Mexican American has had to return to his own, his parents', his grandparents' values. This is what has made el movimiento a reality."[53] But a simple return was not sufficient. Carranza demanded that the Chicano honestly confront this past. Not all this heritage was good; some must be cast aside. Once the Chicano accomplished his self-evaluation, he could boldly move into new directions, holding fast to the privilege of self-determination.[54] In this way, he became a human being. He wrote: "Our point of departure is self-determination; our strategy is confrontation and refutation; our enemy is racism; our goal is *Carnalismo*— flesh of my flesh, bone of my bone, and blood of my blood. This is the essence of Chicano humanism."[55] Carranza believed that the Chicano(a) was reborn with the spirit of freedom, truth, and life. This idea marked the start of a "cultural revolution" by which the Chicano came into being, significantly changing his worldview.[56] Carranza emphasized that Chicanos are agents, creators of their own destiny. The cultural revolution was about Chicano self-determination. Thus chicanismo held the key for the new humanism that could save the United States.[57]

This cultural revolution paralleled an analogous transformation of education. Through this new education, the Chicano would decolonize and liberate his mind, permitting him to see himself in the face of his fellows.[58] The Mexican American mind would liberate itself by establishing free universities, Chicano institutes, or autonomous schools of Mexican American studies that would research, articulate, publish, and disseminate knowledge of the Mexican American.[59] Liberating knowledge, Carranza implied, was not legitimated by social science or the humanities; this could only come about by chicanismo.

In a later edition of *Pensamientos on Los Chicanos: A Cultural Revolution,* Carranza reacted to the increasing instrumentalization of Chicano studies; he rejected the rise of Empirical Chicano Studies. While he accepted traditionally defined functions of Chicano studies, such as opposing prejudice and stereotyping as well as serving the community, he added that Chicano studies must help the Chicano(a) to "know himself in his world."[60] The Chicano(a) must dare to be a human being; he/she must be the agent of his/her existence and its meaning. Unless the Chicano(a) is centered in the world as subject, he/she would be engulfed. "[U]nless Mexican American Studies commits itself to new approaches it, like other departments, will find itself readily assimilated into the existing structure as one more department among departments."[61] To play with social science, without Chicano(a) self-determination established, is to ask for co-optation. Carranza explained further: "Another reason that may account for the term's [chicanismo] passing may be a predilection of Chicanos toward the social sciences route to knowledge, in effect, to the neglect of the humanities and philosophy. Thus, Chicanismo was taken to refer not to the world view which it constituted, but to a group 'life style,' deemed suitable for the statistical approach to truth via the social sciences."[62] It is only humanism that can resist this instrumentalization.

Chicano Studies, dominated by empiricism, thus effectively erased the Chicano(a). Carranza reported that "[t]he search for the *essence* of the Chicano and the super-Chicano . . . had become a search for what was not there."[63] Empirically driven Chicano Studies reduced the Chicano(a) and his/her problem to two basic perspectives: the colonial or Marxist model, and this was not sufficient.[64] Rather, we need to understand the Chicano(a) through multiple perspectives. Carranza explained: "For the Chicano Movement is in many respects a coming together of many often diverse points of view. The language of each point of view generates a different perspective concerning our situation, our problems, and the kind of solutions called for. Each perspective is important as one among others."[65]

The "priests of the movement," Carranza lamented, reject this call for perspectivism; they only accept one model of understanding the world when multiple perspectives are needed.[66] Only from an individual's particular perspective can one truly become "active creative participants."[67] "These considerations led me to the proposition that many Mexican-Americans were in possession of the truth of their condition, but had either suppressed it or had learned to ignore it."[68] To create an understanding of the world, Carranza felt, Chicanos(as) must start with their experience, with their being in the world. In this way, they could break the "grinding alienation of prejudice and hatred," and everyone could then develop his or her aspirations.[69] Then Chicanos(as) could explore enchantment, life, death, meaning, and love.[70] And this would result in Chicano(a) liberation.[71]

To challenge Empirical Chicano Studies, Carranza proposed chicanismo as a worldview.[72] He wrote: "The need for a conceptualization of reality from the Chicano perspective has never been a more necessary undertaking than at this time. The fact that it has never been accomplished heretofore is perhaps sufficient reason for burdening the literary world with yet another philosophical work [*Chicanismo as a World View*]."[73] The scholar Mauro Chavez, in a review of Carranza's work on chicanismo, clarified the dichotomy between Chicano studies as social science and as a worldview. By the mid-1970s, Chicano Studies paralleled established disciplines in its academic behavior: "[O]bjectification of knowledge was dependent on assimilating and meticulously applying conceptual models and scientific techniques formalized and legitimized by established disciplines."[74] Although this has been useful, Chavez presented Carranza's counterargument: "The urgent need for theoretical inquiry into the Chicano's conceptualization of reality, i.e. his world view (*weltanschauung*) has continued to inspire intellectual interest in Chicano Studies."[75] Carnalismo opened the door to understanding this ethical imperative. Choosing to adhere to principle was the first step in embracing this Chicano *weltanschauung*.[76]

The poet, essayist, fiction writer, and historian E. A. Mares, in his evaluation of Paulo Freire, provided an addition to Carranza's philosophy by introducing the concept of play. Since beginnings and absolutes are not the issue, then fiesta and *homo ludens* become fundamental, as they allow a playful and nonoppressive manner of experiencing the world.[77] Unfortunately, contemporary society has separated life from fiesta, resulting in alienation. Mares believed that only the Chicano(a) and Native American, among the citizens of the United States, remain in contact with the spirit of play: "The idea of mirth, humor, playfulness as an integral part of life, as an on-going *fiesta*, as a graceful and joyful acceptance of human folly, is as old as the Totonac Period, even older, according to Octavio Paz, and as recent as the insights of a Yaqui man of knowledge."[78] Without fiesta, alienation resulted in dehumanizing structures resting on the mystique of science. Freire's *conscientización*, Mares believed, breaks through this fog by raising questions and then posing an alternative course of action, a true praxis, toward self-determination and self-liberation.[79] This praxis was tied to fiesta. Mares continued: "The celebration of *fiesta* under adverse circumstances, may have a great opportunity . . . for initiating a process of humanization, of restoration of the unity of man and the world, and for the creation of life styles more suitable to a post-technological society."[80] As the feminist philosopher María Lugones suggested in a later piece, knowledge and *juguetear* needed to work as one.[81]

The community scholar José Armas's quest to save Chicano cultural identity was another example of chicanismo as philosophy. He asserted that Chicanos(as) were lost because "there is nothing to distinguish themselves as culturally different Chicanos."[82] To maintain this identity and therefore establish a humanistic society, the Chicano(a) must develop social responsibility, a *doctrina de la raza,* and a process to incorporate all Chicanos(as). With this doctrina, Chicanos(as) can promote their values, maintain their cultural identity, and use "them as ready-made alternatives to what the dominant society has."[83] Armas explained further: "*La Doctrina de La Raza* would be the abc's of Chicanismo. The different themes and concepts selected are those that are needed to maintain the essence of La Raza culture. It is important to understand that the culture is learned. No one is born with culture. They learn their cultural attributes. The doctrina program would teach and reinforce those elements of La Raza culture."[84]

Other essays in *De Colores: Journal of Emerging Raza Philosophies,* edited by Armas, paralleled these ideas.[85] *De Colores,* an outgrowth of grassroots organizing efforts, saw a need for a philosophical direction given their perceived limitations of cultural nationalism: "[W]ithout a redirection, without a formulation of clear ideologies and philosophies, the future of the culturally different Raza in this country is soon going to be all but eliminated."[86] The journal hoped to blend potential intellectual frameworks with practical applications to maintain cultural identity and build a Chicano nation. This could only result from dialectical exchange, critical analysis, self-evaluation, and reflection. But the journal had difficulty in articulating a consistent position, as the title changes of the journal reflected: *De Colores: Journal of Emerging Raza*

Philosophies (1975–1978), *De Colores: Journal of Chicano Expression and Thought* (1978–1982), with *A Bilingual Quarterly* as a sort of subtitle for a limited time.

Perspectivist Chicano Studies as Academic Project

In the early 1970s, a handful of Chicano(a) academics avoided the emerging empiricism in Chicano Studies. Influenced by Mexican and Chicano(a) thought, as well as by debates in Western Marxism and developments in European philosophy, these scholars presented an alternative vision. Although most of these writers did not necessarily recognize such a project, it is clear, with hindsight, that their work presented a rejection of developing Empirical Chicano Studies and instead called for a different academic project.[87] The writings of several early Chicano literary critics allowed their readers to explore a manifestation of Perspectivist Chicano Studies. Juan Rodríguez and Carlos Zamora, for example, argued that the "uniqueness" of the Chicano(a) experience and identity together with humanism and praxis were the engine behind Chicano(a) literature.[88] Zamora pointed out that the praxis of humanism had to be understood as a political act and therefore as the only salvation from "las fuerzas de la dehumanización" (the forces of dehumanization), "[la] cosificación" (reification), and "la enajenación del hombre" (human alienation).[89] Therefore, the artists' humanist praxis was a necessary aspect of the liberation of humanity. Translator and poet Gustavo Segade inserted that this praxis constructed the Chicano(a): "Chicano is a synthesized reality that had to be recognized and affirmed by those who were aware of living it."[90] Chicano literary criticism, rooted in a Chicano(a) perspective born from their living experience, was an essential part of the political battle for self-determination and liberation. Poet and critic Michael Sedano maintained that Chicano movement poets focused on introspection and self-definition rather than on mass action or external scenes.[91] Chicanismo was affirmative, about promise and self-definition.

Some of Rodríguez's early essays probed this vision. The growing consciousness of the Chicano(a), he asserted, demanded self-determination. The Anglo separated the Chicano(a) from his/her history, culture, and raison d'être, leaving him/her "en el mundo vertiginoso del enajenamiento" (in an inconstant alienated world).[92] Through literature, the Chicano(a) encountered and constructed his/her "awareness." He wrote:

"Consecuentemente, un *awareness,* un estar consciente de sí mismo, de su circunstancia respecto a la de los otros, un reconocimiento de su otredad, son el *sine que non* de la búsqueda de identidad del chicano en la literatura" (Consequently, an awareness, an understanding of self, in regard to one's cirsumstances in relation to others, a recognition of otherness, are the sine que non of the search for Chicano identity in literature).[93]

Thus Chicano literature wrote about daily life and thereby showed that the Chicano was part of humanity. Rodríguez explained: "He aquí el postulado básico de toda la literatura chicana: testimoniar la vida particular y, por consiguiente, universal del chicano para asegurarle su sitio correspondiente en la familia de la raza humana, sitio que le pertenece por derecho propio, no divino, ni diabólico" (Here is the reason for all Chicano literature: to give testimony to their unique and universal lived experience and, consequently, to secure its place in the human family, a place it deserves in its own right, neither granted by divine nor diabolic power).[94] The artist was thus able to give the particularities of the Chicano(a) being, especially in relationship with the long struggle against Anglo society, and in the process, breaking alienation that had denied their Chicano(a) being.

To support his point, Rodríguez turned to Tomás Rivera's *Y no se lo tragó la tierra.* Rivera's novel presented "momentos reveladores en la vida de un pueblo en lucha con su circunstancia y consigo mismo" (revealing moments in a people's struggle with their own circumstance and their own self).[95] Rodríquez's exploration of Rivera's novel recalls Ortega y Gasset's famous dictum and the philosophy of perspectivism. In this manner, he restored the Chicano(a) to his/her spot in the continuum of humanity. Yet there could be more. In the essay "La Raza Nueva" that appeared in *Bronze Magazine,* the author wrote: "It represents the need and the ability of man to break the chain of history; a history filled with oppression, chauvinism, aggression, and symbolizes the need of creating a New World by creating a new man who will build his culture on the humanism which history has neglected."[96]

Some who read earlier versions of this book felt that my description of emergent Chicano(a) scholarship in the humanities—in particular, literary criticism—gave the impression that literary critics (and art critics in general) could more easily avoid the pitfalls that faced Chicanos(as) in social science. Furthermore, the introspection of much early Chicano(a) writing necessarily embodied the notion of "yo y mi

circunstancia" (I am myself and my circumstance) and thereby seemed
by necessity to reject empiricism and articulated perspectivism. This
is not the point I wish to make. Rather, I turn to scholarship in the
humanities to demonstrate that no distinction existed between projects
in the humanities or social science. Both could and did suffer from
empiricism. Academic Chicano(a) literary criticism eventually consented
to empiricism. The critic and librarian Ernestina Eger made a similar
point in her examination of a set of short stories by Juan Rodríguez
and Juan Bruce-Novoa.[97] Having said this, it is important that we also
acknowledge that scholarship in the arts could, at times, prove more
resilient to academic pressures, though academic success could often
be more difficult.

Another example of perspectivism in academic work can be found
in the work of José B. Cuéllar and Raymond Padilla. Cuéllar developed
a model of Chicano culture as a way to deal with the bilingual experience of the Mexican American community by building on the various
worldviews of Mexican American culture with special attention to the
ethnoperspective model.[98] Padilla directed his work to the field of bilingual education. In a short essay for *Bilingual Resources,* he made a case
for a Chicano pedagogy that avoided the failures of "affirmational and
reformational education."[99] He turned to his reading of Freire to argue
for a transformational approach. Padilla asserted that the "Chicano
has to undertake an analysis of the *yo y mis circunstancias* . . . [for] . . .
conscientization."[100]

The critical theorists Raymond Rocco's essays provided an example
of academic Chicano perspectivism within social science. He formulated a critical position for Chicano(a) researchers. Scholars uncritically
accept, Rocco began, given concepts or theories as universal. Using
Romano's and Deluvina Hernández's critique of social scientists, Rocco
turned to see what alternatives might exist to traditional social science:
"The point is that there are many dimensions of 'reality' that we never
become conscious of. Our use of concepts, our designation of certain
phenomena as 'facts,' really depends on those aspects of the culture
which are emphasized as significant, which is ultimately determined
by normative criteria."[101] For Rocco, knowledge is not singular nor
homogeneous: "If we are to take the role of scientist seriously, then we
should be dedicated to the search for as many forms of knowledge as
possible."[102] Perspective can provide alternative orientations that generate different research programs. Rocco intimated in his *Aztlán* essay

that "[o]ne of the perspectives we must establish is one based on the experience of people who live in Mexican American community."[103]

But Rocco was unsatisfied with the conclusion that we base a perspective on a group's experience. In a later piece for the *Western Political Quarterly,* he began with a critique, not only of social scientists' research but of social science in general, now grounding his discussion in critical theory: "They [critical theorists] argue that the majority of theorists and researchers have not recognized that the practice of social science rests on a substructure which is essentially philosophical or theoretical in nature and that any analysis of specific frameworks and methodologies must be firmly rooted in a knowledge of the more basic commitments made at the ontological, epistemological, and logical levels."[104] Traditional social science reifies data by abstracting it from relations that provide meaning and significance; it distorts reality. For this reason, Rocco indicated, one must be clear what one is doing and why; otherwise, one accepts the assumptions of social science—objectivity, facts, and truth.[105] It is through praxis in the world that we come to understand knowledge claims.

Chicano scholarship, Rocco observed—attuned to the Marxist, cultural nationalist, and internal colonialist models—sought to explain the patterns of domination through structural terms.[106] This emphasis on one realm of activity exhibits a possible reductionist tendency. One could overcome these limitations by translating issues into a theoretical complex defined by critical theory and praxis. Arguing through the writings of the Mexican philosopher Leopoldo Zea, Rocco specified that the role of the intellectual is to mediate between philosophy and history.[107] This mediation aims at the liberation of *la persona,* resulting in emancipation from domination.[108] It is by interrogating the "concreteness of historical experience" that one comes to self-consciousness.[109] "For philosophy to be philosophy," Rocco stated, "it must achieve consciousness; thought which does not recognize its own circumstances does not reach self-consciousness."[110] These conditions oblige one to practice responsibility. One can infer from Rocco's reading of Zea that just like the "authenticity of Latin American philosophy develops when it begins to assess its circumstances from the perspective of the colonized," so the Chicano(a) would become subject when he/she acts in the world as self-consciousness.[111]

From other social sciences, a few Chicanos(as) took advantage of phenomenologically based research to redirect how their particular disciplines analyzed and structured Mexican Americans. This style of research, influenced by phenomenology and existentialism, provided an alternative vision for sociological and anthropological work. For those who turned to these approaches, the hope was to get at Chicanos(as) as living entities, as subjects in the world. These methodologies limited logo-deductive theory and endeavored either to center on actors' knowledge of their circumstances or allow relevant social and social psychological organization of actors to emerge, using for instance grounded theory or ethnomethodology.[112] Reyes Ramos's use of ethnomethodology was one such example. Ramos highlighted how Mexican Americans made decisions.[113] This phenomenological approach was quite different from the approaches encountered in the work of Peñalosa and Alvarez.[114]

El Alma Chicana Symposium, organized in 1973 at San Jose State by the Graduate Studies Department, provided another example of academic perspectivist writing. Sister Teresita Basso wrote about the existential conflict of identity and commitment that many religious Chicanas faced. In the process, she examined Chicanos(as)' human-ity and values in light of the negative position of women in Mexican American society.[115] Her essay balanced the social call of the Church with the Chicano(a) concern with the community. In a similar vein, Germana Carmen Rodriguez, using the work of Antonio Caso and Erich Fromm, called attention to personhood.[116] From a very different direction, Arturo Amaro examined the impact of capitalist culture on the Chicano(a). After a brief examination of capitalism, he turned to the psychological disorganization of the personality that capitalist culture causes to the individual.[117]

Alfredo Cuéllar's criticism of cultural nationalism fits in the chal-lenge and endeavor to develop a Chicano scholarship that remained outside traditional disciplines. He began his dissertation with a discus-sion of the crisis in Chicano scholarship. Unlike Muñoz, who felt that Chicano Studies' problems appeared because the discipline lacked a paradigm, Cuéllar believed that the crisis was the result of an already existing paradigm. This paradigm, which he called "Chicano revision-ism," exaggerated racial factors, cultural conflict, racism, racialism, and therefore presented a limited theory of social and political change. "Chicano revisionism," Cuéllar wrote, "embodies a very conservative ideology which seeks to bring about change in ideas, sentiments and values. It is completely devoid of any historical vision for the restructur-ing of social institutions."[118] The attempt to conceptualize history as conflict between cultural entities resulted in ethnocentrism and racialism that "ipso facto precludes historical interpretation on the basis of social forces."[119] This is not to say that scholars are not personally committed to radical change. The problem is that cultural nationalism is a vapid concept. For Cuéllar, this sad situation was the result of an academic methodology (fixed on culture and race) that embraced a limited theory of change.[120] The Chicano movement is only radical in style and integrationist in spirit. Cuéllar suggested that Chicanos needed to revisit traditional concepts, like the immigrant model, to continue the battle for equality.

Perspectivist Chicano Studies, however, as an academic field, found it difficult to survive in higher education. Institutions found it difficult to measure and therefore assimilate this approach. Perspectivist research could not be easily broken down into analytical parts; empirics, like other academic fields, saw perspectivist work as subjective and individualistic. Perspectivism simply could not find space in an institution that was centered on an empirical framework. As the anthropologist Octavio Romano explained further: "If there is a cohesive configuration of cultural themes and overriding values which characterize the historical development of American society and its West European . . . heritage, then that configuration can best be summarized as an analytical orientation toward the empirical, physical, and cultural world accompanied by a pervasive belief in the separability of reality into its constituent parts and elements."[121] Moreover, the university, especially the research institutions, set conditions that made this controversial style of intellectual endeavors ineffectual and unworthy. Some sought a solution to this incompatibility by articulating qualitative research into a "positivistic methodology."[122] Contreras, for instance, declared that if Chicano studies was to survive in the academy, it had to "formulate a more coherent standard and methodology that involves both quantitative and qualitative approaches to research."[123]

At the same time, Chicano Studies devoured its opposition. As the student protests died down, the limited space allotted to nontraditional approaches was further restricted.[124] Empirical Chicano Studies could not permit alternative variants to exist because the academic institution would use their "intellectual weakness" as a cause to assault the newly founded programs. Chicano Studies had to dominate its space within the academy if it was to have a political role. In doing so, Chicano Studies acted no differently than any other discipline in higher education.

The administrator Paul Sánchez noted that "Chicano Studies have been absorbed. A traditional strategy of the majority system is to get hit, draw back and then devour whatever is hitting it."[125] In this situation, Empiricist Chicano Studies was simply more malleable to the institution. In this atmosphere, Perspectivist Chicano Studies broke up into different directions, losing its already limited cohesion and unity.

I would not want to leave the impression that perspectivist scholars did not participate in institution building. All scholars active in Chicano studies were fighting for the creation of Chicano studies programs or working to set up and defend these new programs. Thus perspectivists could be found in endeavors to establish the National Association of Chicano Studies, El Concilio Nacional de Estudios Chicanos, and many local Chicano studies programs. An example of the participation of perspectivists in institution building was the six-week summer institute that was developed for Chicano(a) college personnel at Stanford University. The goal of this program was to better prepare instructors in Mexican American Studies. Carranza, Romano, and Vaca played an important role in this institute.[126] Nonetheless, there was a difference between perspectivists' and empirics' understanding of institution building. While both were uncritical, as well as unaware of the limitations of institutions, perspectivists were critical of the political hope that empirics had for organization building.

A Search for Alternative Pathways

For some Chicanos(as), their experience in institutions of higher learning left little hope for developing a radical and critical intellectual perspective within the academy. Education sustained "the constant erosion of the values each [Chicano(a) and native] hold absolute to their unique heritage and culture."[127] At best, Chicano studies might help students survive the institution, but one could not expect permanent change. Eliezer Risco has written about his experience at Fresno State College.[128] "[Y]ou cannot change the system using the system's tools," he reflected. "All you can do is patch up holes. There's is no such thing as a neutral education. It's all political. . . . No amount of Chicano Studies or La Raza Studies is going to change the system's master plan. But maybe Chicano Studies helps Chicanos while they are on those campuses."[129]

The answer, Risco concluded, was to develop alternative counter institutions.[130] Bilingual-bicultural education provided an alternative that was not rooted in the language of Anglos but "in terms of their own [Chicano(a)] cultural identity and linguistic heritage."[131] Acevedo added that "Chicanismo itself is still being defined and molded in the heart and crucible of everyday life. Chicanismo involves Indianismo, Carnalismo, Guerrillismo, and the process of becoming and being."[132] Yet even the alternative schools that appeared in this time period did not fundamentally break with the basic notions of schooling.[133] A possible exception might have been the long-standing D-Q University, located in Yolo County, California. Most of these alternative institutions saw themselves in the mode of the college without walls—examples would be the Colegio Cesar Chavez in Oregon, University of Aztlán in Fresno, or Colegio Jacinto Treviño in Texas.[134] In a more traditional vein was the proposed College of Chicano Studies, which never got off the ground. In the school's curriculum, similar to other colleges, the main objective was "to sensitize the student to the needs of the Chicano community in addition to providing preparation for professional training."[135] A Chicano perspective would permeate the curriculum. Later the Mexican American Studies Center at Claremont tried to secure a grant for founding a Mexican American College.[136]

Of the many alternative institutions that appeared, the most interesting was La Academia de la Nueva Raza, directed by Tomás Atencio. La Academia began from the premise that "education has bypassed La Raza; that the value system underpinning the body of knowledge available to some of us in the course of our education is a foreign one."[137] The "educational systems aggregate events and experiences into a body of knowledge that is then transmitted to others," imposing the system's values.[138] Chicanos needed to seriously question dominant society's values. In a later essay cowritten with Estevan Arellano, Atencio sketched out how institutions, like the university, stifled creativity and limited Chicano freedom.[139] So where are Chicanos(as) to go from here? For Atencio, they turn to what had been hidden in the Mexican American community: "Most of our barrios, farm workers, and rural villages have hidden and locked in their people a profound wisdom and insight into life, cutting through the abstract systems of thought that separate the human species from the natural environment."[140] From the "oro del barrio," the accumulated popular knowledge of the Chicano communities (both past and present), "La Academia proposes to compile a philosophy."[141]

The idea was to use "life experience to build the body of knowledge from which people learn."[142] Atencio further explained: "[T]he preceding argument is sufficient for us to demand a body of knowledge that embodies the Chicano experience. This dictates our tasks: we must dig into our past literature, our folklore, our history which is mostly oral; we must venture into areas related to the social and behavioral sciences and identify individuals and social behavior patterns that may reflect the Chicano experience as we struggle for survival."[143] Therefore, Atencio criticized alternative schools that merely mirrored the traditional system. Rather, he felt, Chicanos(as) must build a body of knowledge from La Raza's experiences and create a learning experience through dialogue—his famous *resolana*.[144] "If there is hope for institutional change," he wrote, "the transition must begin with the reflection of different values and different world views that heretofore have been ignored."[145]

The concept of *la resolana* played a major role in the vision of Atencio and La Academia. In a later piece he cowrote with Consuelo Pacheco, Atencio argued that la resolana had been the communication center of community life before there were radios and televisions. Today, it is still the place were the community shares issues and passes on information. La Academia took "the historic and actual reality of *la resolana* and gives it a new dimension. La Academia has the insight that popular modes of communication, the art and craft of the *resolaneros,* provide an accessible approach to the latent complex of ideas and memories of the *mestizo* experience."[146] Atencio and Pacheco argued that *La Academia* would take an informal social institution and transform it into a communication mechanism that serves to open up discussion and reflection.

Atencio and Arellano recalled how in 1969 a group of Chicanos(as) came together to develop a process Chicanos(as) could use to reflect on the Mexican American experience. The nucleus of mining this wisdom was the framework of personal history, oral history, folklore, and the arts.[147] Out of the community's lore, oral history, community spirit and wisdom, Chicanos(as) would mine "el oro del barrio," uncovering classic Chicano thought—then publishing it in a journal. In this way, one could develop a body of knowledge consistent with Chicano values. Together with La Academia, the goal was to create an atmosphere where individuals could encounter their self-identity through their own culture and history.

Another direction that Perspectivist Chicano Studies developed was certain styles of community service.[148] These perspectivist writers formulated an interactive approach in which the community was not transformed into object or problem. Their response was to push the academy to open their intellectual space to a different logic. This logic started with the living experience of people who became the subject as well as object of their research. By grounding research on lived experience, Chicano(a) scholars confronted social science. This was more than a conflict between macro and micro or quantitative and qualitative styles of research.

The staff at Hijos del Sol, for instance, developed a program for children, youth, and their families based on their experience: "a person's own life experiences comprise a knowledge base."[149] In this way, Samuel C. Martinez and Roberto Vargas wrote, Chicanos(as) could escape the chronic pattern of "El No," referring to the dynamic by which society negates personal and group power manifesting itself in the words "no puedo" (I can't).[150] Martinez and Vargas had earlier developed the concept of "razalogía": "Razalogía has evolved out of the attempt to conceptually describe our approach for developing knowledge that heals, liberates and transforms."[151] This "transformative learning" was the process of creating knowledge "partial to the needs and well-being of the community."[152] What these individuals, who entered community services, learned from the academy had to be completely reconceptualized. "Having critiqued the field of psychology as inapplicable to an understanding of the Chicano reality," Martinez and Vargas recalled, "we eventually agreed that understanding the 'Chicano experience' required sharing from our personal lives."[153]

Thus activity in community services, like La Clínica de la Raza, was guided by razalogía—knowledge *for* Raza *by* Raza. In this process of learning from Mexican American experiences, the activist could move away from "no puedo"—an internal devaluation of self—to a reconceptualization of Chicano power. At this stage, the Mexican American community would assert its self-organization. Martinez and Vargas highlighted: "[We] recognized that our communities require, not merely more professionals or services, but an ideology and activism that seek radical change in our social systems."[154] As razalogía unfolded, it led to the formation of a "progente/provida" network. Clearly the application of razalogía "must be extended beyond the work arena to one's family and community life."[155] By this point, razalogía shifted from its Chicano perspective and became more appropriately "an approach of transformative learning guiding a conscious community knowing toward advancing human/social transformation."[156]

One could even suggest that some Brown Berets, a Chicano(a) nationalist youth group that was initiated in Los Angeles in the late 1960s but soon became national, may have participated in this perspectivist world. In a *La Causa* article by a "Sacramento Beret," the author began by noting that the "proper upbringing" of Chicanos(as) led them to question Anglo expressions of human truth and values. Anglo values are the product of the capitalist system—a system that removes humanity. Therefore, for the Anglo, everything is reduced to a contest, while for Chicanos, it is family, memory, and ultimately humanity.[157]

Perspectivist Chicano Studies on the Essentialist Edge

Perspectivist Chicano Studies suffered from many limitations and distortions that reflected its uneven development and its peripheral intellectual presence. Among those constraints was an ambivalent relationship with essentialism. How Chicanos(as) dealt with who they were could lead to attempts to essentialize concepts like "race" or "nation." Chicano(a) intellectuals highlighted how Anglo scholars reduced Mexicans and Mexican Americans to an essential idea defined by particular attributes. In response, some Chicano(a) cultural nationalists often reduced the "colonizer" to an essence, simultaneously writing about themselves in terms of an authentic given that challenged prior asserted characteristics with an alternate set of qualities. This inversion typically served to suppress other identities and experiences; difference was erased. Given the intensity of political and social battle, this may have been unavoidable.[158] Moreover, essentialist arguments were present in most styles of Chicano studies. Perspectivist writers tried to balance themselves on this edge—at times successfully, but often they created a homogeneous, male, universal, and transhistorical image of the Chicano.

Dan Porath contends that the philosophy of perspectivism was attractive to the "latin mind," given the Mexican/Chicano tragic sense of life. Drawing on his readings of Unamuno, Ortega y Gasset, Romanell, and pre-Columbian Indian mysticism, he believes that the Mexican was born an existentialist. He writes that "[c]ertain 'feelings' are suggested in the deep mysticism of the pre-Conquest world as well as the particular history which Latin America has experienced."[159] Although Porath indicates the role of experience in forming a philosophy of life, he nonetheless roots this vision in the "nature" of the Mexican: "What had been tried then, in attempting to impose the empirical, scientific approach on the Mexican [that is, positivism], was not to allow a system to develop from the Mexican's own experience, but as an attempt to assimilate the Mexican to an outside source. And the Mexican was too Mexican to buy it." [160] The true Mexican, Porath insists, is an existential man.

When he turns to Chicanos(as), he encounters the same spirit. Porath traces this existential spirit from the *pachuco* through César Chávez, "Corky" González, and Romano, to chicanismo. Chicano(a) academics, however, possess a limited understanding of chicanismo. "Very little of what was presented to the Chicano had its origins in the barrio," Porath writes, "primarily because most of these chicano scholars were not barrio oriented—they had escaped long ago and had become successful in the 'mainstream' culture." [161] Chicanismo is about the barrio, about a cultural revolution, about creating a new social being. And most important, Porath continues, chicanismo is about existing in the here and now. As *Con Safos* stated: "It is rather an attempt at expressing the entire spectrum of feelings that are the soul of the barrio." [162] At the same time, some Chicano(a) poets used Indian genesis to create a sense of identity, a romantic, mythic, possibly fantastic history. [163]

Porath's essay provided an example of the unresolved tension between essentialism and the desire to ground this perspective in a Mexican American or Mexican experience/essence. Initially, he writes about a particular Mexican/Chicano mind-set that was tied to some native past. There was an unstated assumption about a genetic existential spirit inhabiting Mexicans and Mexican Americans. At the same time, he argues that this mind-set found expression in particular historical and social settings—for instance, the North American barrio. This tension attempted to sustain the challenge to American culture—whether he was successful is up to the reader.

Another theme that suggested ambivalence with essentialism was Chicanos(as)' use of the native past. At the same time razalogía moved toward transformative praxis, Vargas returned to a romanticized notion of Chicanos(as)' native past. [164] Arnaldo Solis, who influenced razalogía formation, provided an example of this return to native roots—not solely in a racial or cultural sense, but also in its spiritual significance: "Chicano cultural values are recognized to be within the realm of the Chicano or Native American Spirit." [165] In another essay, he added: "It is a shared psychological-spiritual force. At that point we begin to see '*in*

Tloque, in Nahuaque.' The spirit of Unity-Togetherness, as we practice it, begins to emerge."[166] Where did this come from? Solis pointed to our native past, to our "tatas."[167] "We are first of all and at the very core or root of our psyche and spirit, native-americans of any one or some Mexican Indian tribe(s)."[168] From here, Solis believed, we draw our Mexicano-Chicano values, especially harmony, community, and the quest for land.[169]

Following on his understanding of the indigenous past, Mares proclaimed that the Chicano coyote-nature, his "half-breed-ness," is the source of the Chicano movement's strength. The coyote inherits the worldviews of Anglo-America and of Indo-Hispano America and chooses what it wants. Mares maintained that the Chicano(a) "coyote-ness" is key to the search for identity, origins, and meaning: "As the half-breed, the perpetual outsider, he may warn of the danger of fac-tionalism, of authoritarianism drift, of a mirror image of white rac-ism."[170] Therefore, the Chicano(a) is both Indian and Hispanic—"no se trata de estupideces raciales sino de herencias culturales" (this is not about stupid racial thinking but about cultural inheritances).[171] For Mares, many who use the "myth of Aztlán" played into a chauvinistic nationalism that historically has divided humankind.[172] Chicanos(as) need to be wary of this virulent nationalism. Rather, they need to see this myth as a "[c]atalyst for the release of the creative energy of the Chicano people, as a vital image for the transformation of the world in which Chicanos live, and as a unifying construct to provide a dynamic coherency, shape, or form to the rising aspirations of the Chicano."[173] For in the end, these values can also move the Anglo world and create a society that is more introspective as well as concerned with values and the past. The problem, then, is that we know little of our native past.[174]

For some Chicanos(as), the native past and present governed their vision of the world. These authors believed that their Chicano(a) being was tied to that indigenous past/present and sought to revive cultural and spiritual values that had been "lost" after 1848. The Chicano—argued, for example, Justo Alarcón—must return to Mother Earth.[175] Spirituality was at the heart of chicanismo and the barrio was its home. "The main awareness of the movimiento," Alarcón wrote, "has its base in the philosophical attitude that the total unity of the Chicano is the principal spiritual force and that the barrio is the center of the 'living culture.'"[176] Chicanos must rescue these essential values from Anglo materialist hands.

In examining a few of the writings of Alurista and Luis Valdez, the reader can appreciate the different uses of native imagery. Alurista used these images to reveal the limits of Anglo culture.[177] In an essay in *De Colores,* Alurista drew a sharp contrast between the Indian world of harmony and balance and the Anglo world.[178] Valdez, in *Pensamiento serpentino* and other essays, built a worldview around this native imagery and moved toward a belief in its essential meaning.[179] Jesús Treviño recalled that Valdez and El Teatro Campesino accepted a peculiar "neo-Mayan beliefs linked to Christianity."[180] Treviño asserted that Valdez had "taken the *Plan de Aztlán* to its logical conclusion and had devised a Chicano religion based on Christianity and ancient indigenous mythology."[181] Interestingly enough, this led, Treviño continued, to neo-Mayan capitalism! While Alurista and Valdez might have agreed that the Chicano(a)'s native cultural and spiritual past may have (and should have) some impact on the present, they had an equivocal reading of this heritage and its function in the present.[182]

Chicanos(as)' indigenous heritage led to an enormous outpouring of literary and intellectual work. Chicanos(as) often did not separate early Chicano studies from the quest of the Chicanos(as)' real and mythic historical and cultural identity. The use of Indian motifs paralleled preoccupation with the search for identity, an appeal to the great indigenous civilizations of the past as a source of pride, and a quest for a symbolic nexus that could link all Chicanos(as) despite their heterogeneity. Much of the early poetry and art of the Chicano Movement used these motifs and symbols, although its meanings and importance varied. All readings of this native heritage were equivocal. Although the majority balanced themselves between metaphoric and essentialist conceptions of the native past/present, some could not retain this ambivalence.[183]

Some Chicano(a) writers recalled the native past to challenge Western epistemology, avoiding essentialist claims. Faced with the social science leviathan, how did Chicanos(as) challenge and offer a counter epistemology? Francisco Vazquez asserted the need to use epistemological alternatives, such as the Aztec search for truth.[184] In an earlier project, Vazquez suggested that Chicano thought could also serve "to indicate the path to the future of Latin America in the philosophical field."[185] One needs to recognize that Vazquez's "chicanology" project flowed from his understanding of Foucault.[186] Furthermore, he contended that any challenge to the institutions of knowledge was to risk harm: "To speak against the rules of discourse, to speak the words of an emergent knowledge against an established paradigm, is to risk being declared mad, if not physical injury."[187] Padilla expanded on this notion by acknowledging Chicanos(as)' Western heritage (Socratic, Christian, Hegelian, Marxist, Buberian), but regards it as only part of their intellectual tradition. Therefore, Padilla expressed, Chicanos(as) needed to look toward their indigenous heritage and legacy. Not to live in or reestablish this past, but to retake their legitimate heritage.[188] With these resources, Chicanos(as) could engage in "chicanizaje"[189] or Vazquez's "chicanology."[190] To other Chicanos(as), this awareness of the past opened the possibility of "la vida nueva."[191] These readings represent perspectivist visions of their past. The goal is not to resurrect some real or usually mythic past[192] but to begin an epistemological transformation from their situation in the world, their becoming, by taking possession of their past and identity.[193]

At the center of this perspectivist project was self-consciousness. A danger, however, existed on trying to ground this self-consciousness. It was easy to step from a perspectivist analysis over to essentialism and nativism.[194] Perspectivist thinkers often drew links to the Chicano native past to emphasize the existence of alternative worldviews. Some could interpret this as creating a Chicano-centric worldview. But by this point, Perspectivist Chicano Studies as a coherent episteme was fading. David Hayes-Bautista's dissertation on "dis-assimilation" avoided the dance on the essentialist edge by arguing that Chicanos(as) are made and not born. Using grounded theory, participation observation, interviews, and symbolic interaction, he traces how a Chicano(a) gains a sense of ethnic identity. He argues that ethnic identity is a process and therefore there are no particular properties to an identity. Moreover, people can have multiple identities. "Ethnic identification, then, is a changing mode in a shifting matrix."[195] This identity may change over time and place, and "[a] response by one person at one stage of development of ethnic identity will not be the same response made later in the development."[196] Therefore to argue a particular identification of a Chicano(a) is to misunderstand the process of identity formation. Hayes-Bautista's work ends with the vision that a Chicano(a) is about variety as well as an unfinished self. In this way, he escapes any need to establish some essential collection of attributes that constitutes the Chicano(a).

The Evaporation of Perspectivist Chicano Studies

By the early 1980s, Perspectivist Chicano Studies as an alternative style of academic knowing had evaporated. The lack of an established base in the academy undercut the development of a core of perspectivist scholars. Furthermore the rise of structuralism, poststructuralism, feminism, postmodernism, neo-Marxism, and queer theory contested the philosophical ground of the perspectivist camp.[197] But the most damaging impact was the exclusionary politics of empirics.[198] The end result was to vanquish Perspectivist Chicano Studies as a viable alternative. Nevertheless, in challenging Empirical Chicano Studies, perspectivists demonstrated the limitations of this dominant view. They demonstrated that the empirics could not escape the patriarchal, logo-deductive, and instrumentalist reasoning that was at the core of the U.S. academy. Just as Perspectivist Chicano Studies faded, new contestants materialize to critique Empirical Chicano Studies. These fresh provocations took a variety of shapes, from the radical epistemological attacks by queer theorists and postmodernists to the criticism of the exclusionary politics of empirics by multiculturalists, feminists, and those interested in Latino(a) and/or American Studies.

Chicano Studies as an Academic Discipline, 1975-1982

By 1975, empirics had consolidated their control of Chicano Studies. Its competitors were banished. Empirics subjugated the discipline, using their presence in research institutions, especially in California, to manage the field.[1] In these research institutions, empirics had secured the new discipline by resolving the early crises in Chicano studies programs, often by dismissing the "founders" and political activists who had established these programs and renegotiating the relationship between Chicanos(as) and the academy. Academic success, even survival, meant acceptance of the American academic order. Although intellectually the empirics may have differed over perspectives, methods, and political views, these individuals accepted institution building as the first step to academic autonomy, followed by an analysis of the structures of oppression. Chicano(a) empirics brokered with institutions to fortify Chicano Studies spaces within the academy and built institutional links outside of the academy. This paralleled the endeavor to mesh institutional construction with academic production. Even though students and some scholars were unhappy with the new direction of Chicano(a) scholarship and Chicano Studies, the discipline was set and had to be sustained. It was imperative to defend the new homogeneity of the discipline against the "disciples of anarchy."[2]

Ironically, just as empirics began to consolidate Chicano Studies as an academic discipline, many Chicano and Chicana students accelerated their critique of their home campuses' Chicano Studies departments and programs.[3] For some, Chicano Studies on their particular campus had not satisfied their expectations. They felt that these programs had not fulfilled *El Plan de Santa Bárbara*. In contrast, most faculty and administrators in Chicano Studies programs deemed they had been successfully institutionalizing Chicano Studies and *El Plan*. They could point to the increasing number of Chicano(a) students, the expanded curriculum, institutional structures, grant development, and so on. Given these contradictory views, conflict blossomed among Chicanos(as) on many campuses. The historian Mario García contends, for example, that the problems at San Diego State College arose when Chicanos(as) became part of the academic institution; one encountered a "deradicalization of the radicals."

García explained: "[O]ne conclusion concerns the fact that the radicalization that initiated Chicano Studies has become deflated; Chicano Studies, in turn, now represents a bureaucratic organization laden with incompetent and opportunistic faculty members whose sense of commitment to the students and the Chicano Movement leaves much to be desired."[4] The problem, García continued, was that *El Plan*'s answer to governance (the formation of juntas *directivas*) had not worked. The juntas had failed because they could fall prey to faculty control or because faculty avoided their political responsibilities. Moreover, as political scholar Theresa Aragón de Shepro observed at the University of Washington, faculty's ability to co-opt oppositional forces within Chicano Studies was often assisted by administration.[5] The solution to the crisis, García concluded, was to foment radicalism among all sectors of the university, especially the faculty. "Chicano Studies can and will be a viable structure," he wrote, "but first it requires a competent, politically conscious, and, yes radicalized faculty."[6] How could this occur? The answer: Organized students must be active participants in decision-making.[7]

Historian Juan Gómez-Quiñones provided a different take to the problems in Chicano Studies. He began by acknowledging that the future of Chicano Studies was still an open question. As proposed by *El Plan,* the maturation of Chicano Studies necessitated self-determination and self-definition on college campuses. Because Chicano Studies aimed at self-knowledge, community knowledge, and social change, all depended on Chicano self-determination since Chicano Studies situated itself in opposition to the university. This placed Chicano Studies in a certain dilemma; it had to run counter to the university's purpose of serving dominant society, yet remain part of the university. Given this challenge, the academy endeavored to change the objective and purpose of Chicano Studies. Administrators would encourage tendencies within Chicano Studies that would lead to the loss of autonomy of Chicano Studies programs.

At the same time, the presence of a domesticated Chicano Studies provided the university with the façade of being tolerant, liberal, and progressive. Thus Chicano Studies found itself in constant tension between its advocacy role and the institutions' demands for acquiescence that was further accentuated by the capricious behavior of administrators.[8] The apparent conflict in Chicano Studies, Gómez-Quiñones maintained, resulted from the "failure to perceive and make operational the perception of the class and race contradictions between Chicanos/Chicano Studies and the universities" and the "belated recognition of the pervasive, assimilative thrust."[9] Chicanos(as), however, could not conclude that Chicano Studies had failed: "The future of Chicano Studies is yet to be built."[10] The institutional building process thus remained vital to the creation of an active and progressive Chicano Studies in higher education.

At the same time that Chicano Studies faced this "crisis," academic institutions began to clamp down on certain manifestations of ethnic and gender studies. The historian Albert Camarillo wrote that "[a]fter a period of relative calm, 1971–1974, we are now witnessing a pattern of retrenchment by university administrators from their concern for Chicanos and other ethnic groups."[11] The decline of student activism paralleled, possibly permitted, the rise of administrative control. The culturally and politically conservative turn in the United States intensified the pressure on affirmative action, gender and ethnic studies, and intellectuals who took critical positions or engaged as public intellectuals. The Bakke decision regarding the question of affirmative action underscored this conservative reaction.[12]

Nonetheless, Gómez-Quiñones's optimism was well placed; Empiricist Chicano Studies was being constructed and institutionalized even in the environment of retrenchment and internal difficulties in Chicano Studies. Empirics argued that the solution to all these problems was the erection of more extensive academic constructions under Chicano control. Without these institutional structures, Chicanos(as) would have to accept their subordinate and colonial position in the university. Scholars Charles Ornelas, Charles Brazil Ramirez, and Fernando V. Padilla developed this point. They initiated their essay by noting that Anglos controlled knowledge production by regulating publishing outlets and training institutions: "Academic colonialism consists of the dominant members of a society severely excluding the members from the universe of intellectual discourse by sharply restricting their access to the status conferring institutions, relatively limiting their use of the publishing and media outlets, and facilitating the mobilization of bias against the excluded population."[13]

So what could be done? Following the spirit of the earlier piece by Reynaldo Macias, Juan Gómez-Quiñones, and Raymond Castro, Ornelas and his coauthors picked up their argument concerning the need to strengthen Chicano Studies institutionally: "It seems that the only way for a subordinate group to avoid becoming the object of exploitation in the literature is to be properly represented in the professions."[14] Specifically, they suggested that Chicanos(as) needed to crack the bottleneck at doctoral-granting institutions and at the same time to develop alternative paradigms and interpretations.[15] They demanded the creation of publishing outlets that would challenge Anglo control of academic print culture with its rules on peer review and thereby publish alternative research. Journals like *El Grito: A Journal of Contemporary Mexican-American Thought*, *Aztlán: Chicano Journal of the Social Sciences and Arts*, and *Campo Libre: Journal of Chicano Studies* are examples of the institutional success of Chicano Studies. If we leave the journals' intellectual and political differences to the side, Ornelas and his coauthors suggested, "[b]oth journals [*El Grito* and *Aztlán*] are serving to institutionalize the Chicano perspective."[16] Although not stated specifically, the development of a paradigm that could fit emergent Chicano Studies was left to *Aztlán*. *Aztlán* would become "the vehicle of dissemination of these evolving new perspectives."[17]

Chicano Studies Consolidated, 1975–1982: Institution Building

The central step in the consolidation of Chicano Studies was the continuation of institution building, both within and outside the academy. These institutions, empirics emphasized, should be under Chicano control. Only by creating this Chicano space in the university could Chicanos(as) avoid colonization in higher education. Some empirics suggested that only within Chicano-controlled academic spaces could a critique of academic work on Mexican Americans and a rethinking of their experiences occur.

Researcher Carlos Arce's essay on academic colonialism exemplified this point. Following Colombian sociologist and activist Orlando Fals Borda's notion of "colonialismo intellectual," Arce contended that dominant society's intellectuals imposed their "intellectual premises, concepts, methods, institutions, and related organizations on a subordinate group" as well as monopolized "the resources for academic enterprise."[18] Chicanos are academically colonized, he explained. Arce posed that to avoid academic colonization, Chicanos must engage in institution building; Chicanos must establish one of these scenarios: an independent and autonomous Chicano institution or an independent, well-staffed, and endowed Chicano program or center within a conventional university.[19] Given the difficulty of creating independent institutions, however, the only solution is to engage in the building of institutions under Chicano(a) control *within* the academy. Arce rejected Raymond Padilla's transformational model as a model for creating an independent Chicano institution because of his unrealistic insistence on separation. Arce recognized that Chicanos(as) existed on Anglo dominant campuses. He suggested that the only way Chicanos(as) could deal with their colonial status was to create tactical alliances with radicals to usurp control of the academy, to create a radical alternative space—an institutional coup d'état, if you will. He believed that this strategy might have been possible in three or four institutions in Texas and California; he noted in particular UCLA. For Arce, like most empirics, institutionalization was the first step in finding a solution to the colonization of Mexican Americans. From this angle, the survival of the Chicano(a) was not epistemological, but technical.

Like Arce, most Chicano(a) empirics felt that they could remain faithful to their academic programs and *El Plan* if they could construct institutions under Chicano control in higher education. While they often referred to university institutions like Educational Opportunity Program or Chicano Studies, they also sought to construct institutions that would exist outside of the university setting; institutions that hopefully would provide national leadership to Chicanos(a) academics. Many empirics believed that it was necessary to build a national organization to deal with issues of higher education to sustain Chicano Studies at the local level. The aim of developing a national structure that could channel Chicano(a) interventions in higher education has a long history.[20] One endeavor was the proposed National Chicano Commission of Higher Education. In the paper "National Chicano Commission on Higher Education," the authors stated: "In a very real sense the Commission should be an institution in and of itself that is independent of existing institutions."[21] The commission had to provide leadership by articulating Chicano(a) concerns, facilitating and coordinating the definition of issues, creating a forum to discuss concerns, and constructing a mechanism for policies, fund-raising, and fund management. It also had to sponsor and initiate research, disseminate information, and advocate for Chicanos(as).[22]

The commission hoped to achieve these goals by working through academic procedures guided by the political vision provided by *El Plan*.[23] Again, in the paper on the commission, the authors noted that "[i]t will function as a framework for convening meetings to define and discuss issues. It will be a forum for articulating new concerns, for debating priorities, and for discussing strategies for addressing issues and concerns. It will provide a framework for formulation of policy and for responding to agencies and/or institutions, public and private, and seek to become better informed about Chicanos in higher education."[24] Among the issues the commission could deal with were access to higher education (more students, faculty, and administrative personnel), more financial and counseling support, and "additional funds for research and publication."[25] Moreover, the commission also dealt with curricular concerns, ranging from the quality of instruction to the limits imposed by traditional disciplines. Even though the authors of the paper disavowed traditional methods, they wished to establish "acceptable standards."[26]

To build the commission or similar type of organization, Chicanos(as) turned to the Ford Foundation to help organize a conference on the status of Chicanos(as) in higher education.[27] In a letter to participants, policy expert Arturo Madrid stressed that Chicanos(as) stood at an institutional crossroads that would define the future of Chicanos(as) in the academy and their intellectual project. He wrote: "It behooves us then to use the experience, knowledge, and expertise we have gained to develop new structures and new strategies. Let us meet . . . to organize a Chicano Commission on Higher Education which will provide us with a framework for our discussions, a form for our concerns, and a foundation for our efforts. The need, the vision, and the will are there. Ha llegado la hora."[28] In preparation for the conference, the scholar Ronald Lopez was given the responsibility to write up a report on Chicano(a) participation in institutions of higher education.[29] By 1975, the National Chicano Council on Higher Education was established.[30] One task of the council, possibly in response to Ford concerns, was faculty retention by funding midcareer doctoral fellowships.

The role of the Ford Foundation, as mentioned in an earlier chapter, was an issue of concern. Abel Amaya, at the time of the planned establishment of the commission, was a program officer in the division of higher education at the foundation. In looking at Chicano(a) educators, he noted that Chicano(a) education activists had finally "transcended the narrow rhetorical focus of the movement."[31] In particular, he observed that Chicanos(as) had moved away from slogans, utopias, and cult of leadership. The foundation could help sustain this more legitimate effort. Some Chicanos(as) felt that Ford, like other foundations, was trying to moderate forces within ethnic studies. For this reason, the historian and activist Rodolfo Acuña contended that organizations like Ford searched for Chicano(a) institutional gatekeepers. The foundation's policy was to work through selected Chicanos(as) and their organizations to serve their mission, then replace them with other Chicanos(as) and organizations when another mission materialized.

Acuña identified the case of the National Chicano Council on Higher Education. For a while the council received Ford monies to distribute for postdoctoral research; then Ford distanced itself from the organization, "using another set of brokers, who aspired to become the new gatekeepers."[32] At the same time, the Institute for Social Research at the University of Michigan funded the National Chicano Research Network. Eventually, the council and network merged, relocating to the Claremont Graduate School under the leadership of Madrid, who had extensive ties to Ford and other foundations. These organizations, Acuña underscored, presented a paradox. While they may have initially formed part of the Chicano(a) challenge to higher education and the transformation of the community, they quickly became content to only acquire funding for research and thereby determine the success or failure of faculty.

Possibly the most successful empiric endeavor at institution building was the National Association of Chicano Social Scientists. In 1975, *El Mirlo Canta de Noticatlan: Carta Sobre Chicano Studies* reported that the association was "the only national gathering of faculty, students and researchers specifically focusing on Chicano Studies and research."[33] By 1977, the association opened its door to scholarship from the humanities. This concurred with the name change to the National Association for Chicano Studies.[34] Although empirics dominated the vision of the association and its annual conferences, other perspectives of Chicano studies were present. This provided the association with the legitimacy to build and expand. (Earlier chapters examined the beginning years of the association and the successful development of an empiric paradigm with the predominance of California-based teaching and research institutes.) The NACS conferences that followed in the late 1970s and early 1980s served the process of canon formation and the expansion of Chicano Studies research.

Another less-structured institution-building effort was regional conferences and organizations.[35] For example, *La Red/The Net* in 1979 reported conferences on women at Indiana University in Bloomington, bilingual education and public policy at Eastern Michigan University, Chicano mental health at the University of Nebraska at Lincoln, ethnic studies at the University of Wisconsin at La Crosse, Mexican American history at Our Lady of the Lake University, and health planning at California State Polytechnic University in Pomona. Institutions like the Chicano Studies Research Center at UCLA and the Stanford Chicano Studies programs organized symposiums, conferences, and the like to continue the building of the discipline. Often these presentations were then published and could form part of the debate over canon formation in the discipline. In California, the Mexican American Legal Defense and Educational Fund (MALDEF) and Chicanos(as) at UCLA organized the Higher Education Task Force that challenged the Bakke decision. The Bakke decision demanded a renewed stress on Chicano institution building in higher education.[36] In 1977, the task force organized a statewide conference at USC to respond to the Bakke decision.[37] At the same time, at least in Los Angeles, coalitions were built around the Bakke decision, linking up with local political organizations like the Centro de Acción Social Autónoma (CASA).[38]

To underscore the success of institutionalization, Chicano Studies experts internationalized the field. Paralleling the redefinition of *Aztlán* as an international journal, the Chicano Studies Research Center at UCLA, together with the University of Guadalajara, organized the first international symposium on the problems of migrant workers in Mexico and the United States in 1978.[39] The Chicano(a) scholars at the conference represented the intellectual elite who were now guiding the direction of Chicano Studies. Interestingly, as Chicano Studies firmed up its position within U.S. academic institutions, it sought further legitimacy by developing ties with Mexican academic and political structures. While many of the Mexican presenters were connected to Universidad National Autónoma de México, Universidad Autónoma

Metropolitana, El Colegio de Mexico, Universidad de Guadalajara, and other institutions, the symposium also provided space to the Partido Revolucionario Institucional (PRI) state.

At the symposium, Manuel Aguilera Gómez of the Secretaría de Programación y Presupuesto (the cabinet office that dealt with planning and development) and Romeo Flores Caballero of the Presidencia (the office of the president) were present.[40] This desire to establish links with the Mexican state was problematic. It served to highlight the bizarre relationship that existed between a few Chicano activists (such as Reies López Tijerina and José Angel Gutiérrez) and some Chicano(a) academics with the Mexican PRI state. Both Gutiérrez and Tijerina noted with pride their association with President Luis Echeverría Alvarez and President José López Portillo.[41] The historian Ignacio García went so far as to call Echeverría "Mexico's left-leaning president"![42] Many Chicano(a) academics benefited from their ties to the PRI state. At the same time, a few Chicano(a) academics, with ties to CASA, fostered a close relationship with the Mexican Communist Party.[43] This should not seem contradictory, given the Mexican Communist Party's ambiguous (some might say subordinate) relationship to the PRI state.[44]

Continuing the consolidation of Chicano Studies were the publications that followed these conferences. An example was Chicano(a) Studies scholar Isidro Ortiz's edited work that sought to cover all fields of Chicano Studies. Ortiz remarked in his foreword that "the lack of knowledge and critical review of the scholarship was a major deficiency," resulting in a symposium "whose primary objective was to be a critical assessment and discussion of the social science scholarship produced by Chicanos during the 1970s."[45] The symposium and publication sought to bring together experts of "Chicano scholarship in their discipline."[46] What was clear from the essays is that Chicano Studies was much closer to the mainstream than its practitioners wanted to acknowledge.[47] As Ortiz stated: "Chicano social science scholarship will continue to flourish and contribute to the improvement of people of Mexican descent in the United States."[48]

Canon Formation and Chicano Action Research

Institutionalization was closely linked to canon formation, research, publication, and a shared vision of activism, thereby establishing legitimacy and responsibility.[49] To secure this academic legitimacy, Chicanos(as) accepted the institution's definition and criteria for publication. While teaching and service were important, publications were the only element that the institution would accept as measuring academic successes. In a letter by David R. Howton, the chair of the Faculty Welfare Committee at UCLA, this was clearly stated: "Finally—and most seriously—I agree with the conclusion that Chicanos fare poorly (and unfairly) in advancement proceedings because of factors tending to affect adversely their record of tangible scholarly achievement—this point is well taken. My impression is that while some weight is afforded to teaching talent (difficult at best to evaluate), and even less to University and other public service, publication (or other evidence of creativity) is the *sine qua non* that elicits recommendations for promotion."[50] Although others may have been supportive of different forms of measuring academic success, especially if we keep in mind that "equality of opportunity" was not the same as "equality of success," there was no future for any argument that tried to lessen the role and importance of publication for success in the elite institutions like UCLA.[51] Moreover, service in the community, as a major criterion for promotion and tenure, was a nonstarter. The Chicano Studies Center at UCLA, under different administrators, was aware of this reality. Thus the Center shifted away from its earlier community interests. In the Chicano Studies Center report of 1975, the smallest section was devoted to the issue of community service.[52]

While few journals would question the premier position held by *Aztlán*, other journals appeared that helped the institutionalization of Chicano Studies as an academic discipline by providing venues for publication.[53] Since *Aztlán* shied away from literature and *El Grito* had entered a period of decline, the field of Chicano literary expression and criticism needed journals for its developing academics.[54] A few arrived on the scene before the reappearance of *El Grito* as *El Grito del Sol* in 1976. *Revista Chicano-Riqueña* was the most important in this period, appearing in 1973. From a different angle, equally tied to the academic project was *The Bilingual Review/La Revista Bilingue*, appearing in 1974. This journal combined social science research with literary projects. *Caracol* (starting up in 1974), *El Fuego de Aztlán* (from 1975), and *Maize: Cuadernos de Arte y Literatura Xicana* (from 1977) also presented essays and literary projects. But unlike other contemporary journals, they did not try to define themselves solely within an academic niche. They saw their role to express Chicano(a) cultural experiences. Other examples were the short-lived *Tejidos: A Bilingual Journal for the Stimulation of Chicano Creativity and Criticism* and *Metamorfosis.* These were examples of journals that played a key role in the development of the arts and criticism. A potential competitor to *Aztlán* was *Campo Libre,* which appeared in 1981 out of California State University at Los Angeles. Taking a different angle was *Carta Abierta,* which started in 1975. For close to five years, Juan Rodríguez as editor of *Carta Abierta* peeped through the curtain to see what was really cooking in the Chicano(a) academic kitchen. Juan enjoyed bringing out the dirty laundry in Chicano Studies.[55]

The *Hispanic Journal of Behavioral Sciences* provided opportunity for Chicano(a) scholars to publish social science research. As journal editor Amado Padilla suggested, the journal followed in the footsteps of such established scholars as Alfredo Castañeda, Manuel Ramirez III, Edward Casavantes, and others.[56] Readers could find essays examining the Mexican American experience using various epistemologies and methodologies offered by anthropology, economics, linguistics, political science, psychology, psychiatry, public health, and sociology.[57] This journal represented the best in Chicano social science scholarship and offered a consistent flow of publications.

From these publications, Chicano Studies scholars began to draw out guidelines to direct Chicano Studies research. Some of these writings became part of the process of canon formation. These key texts were granted respect and defined as meritorious; they became essential to the education of Chicano Studies acolytes. Establishing this canon, however, was an equivocal task. Given the incomplete status of Chicano Studies in the 1970s, canon formation was replete with political divisions and hesitation. Nonetheless, empiricists dominated the process of canon building by their positions in elite institutions and journal editorships favoring structural analysis. As the canon came into play, the empiricist view of Chicano Studies research was increasingly defined as "action research."

This canon, of course, was not simply composed of a set of texts but also referred to a particular reading of these texts. These texts had to corral the openness of Chicano studies and sustain the agreement that structural concerns were at the heart of Chicano Studies research. Thus the canon enforced the empirics' position that scholarship depended on an undefined Marxist-liberal-colonialist and/or hybrid model that began from the premise that Mexicans and Mexican Americans as a community were under siege by the dominant Anglo-capitalist society. Therefore, together with the institutionalization of Chicano Studies programs was the need for research to be activist and transformative. Chicano Studies research thus started from an excavation of the economic, social, political, and at times ideological structures dominating the Mexican American.

Gómez-Quiñones's "On Culture" was one such pivotal essay in the consolidation of Chicano Studies scholarship and canon formation. This essay furnished an imperative for all those who wished to engage in legitimate Chicano Studies scholarship. For Gómez-Quiñones, Chicano scholarship provided an understanding of the structures of oppression that would result in action research. At the same time, he discarded other Chicano studies alternatives, like cultural nationalism or perspectivism, condemning them for their political analysis and/or lack of praxis. Published in 1977, the article reflected the continuing crisis in Marxism (especially its Leninist-Stalinist variant) because of its inability to deal with culture, subjectivity, and politics. The mid-1970s also witnessed the growing impact of French thought, through the writings of structuralism, poststructuralism, postmodernism, and the rediscovery of Western Marxism (from the writings of Luckas to Gramsci). Although Gómez-Quiñones did not engage this literature, he understood the need to rethink the artificiality of some Marxists' separation of base and superstructure.[58]

In his essay, Gómez-Quiñones searched for cultural space that is political: "[Amilcar] Cabral overstresses culture to the point of implying it is part of the economic-social substructure, rather than what it is: part of the superstructure, a result of contradiction and needs stemming from the base of society. . . . Culture acquires political significance as part of the economic class conflict when it is politicized consciously; of itself it is not the cause of conflict or an expression of resistance."[59] Gómez-Quiñones claimed that culture is both "subjective and objective, both ideal and material," that it "stems" from the base yet "can act" upon the base.[60] To further his argument, he constructed a straw figure of culture. He jumbled high culture, tradition, with social practices, and then separated cultural practices from politics. He claimed that culture on its own has no politics. Thus he concluded that culture "must be joined to politics of liberation for it to be an act of resistance."[61]

Only under specific economic-social crises and national/ethnic/racial conditions can cultural/ideological practices come together as class and cultural resistance.[62] Gómez-Quiñones stressed that cultural production "[w]ithout class identification and political participation . . . is at best neutral. At worst, it becomes deceptive, diversionary, and conservative, thus, supportive of the status quo. Cultural activity quo culture, even in groups ostensibly allied to the political movement, retains this conservative character."[63] Even though he appears to follow Roberto Fernández Retamar and the spirit of Gramsci, Gómez-Quiñones reduced "culture" to a narrow anthropological use of the term and returned the reader to the Leninist-Stalinist vision of cultural producers as distinct from political activists. "The intellectual's role in regard to culture," Gómez-Quiñones wrote, "is one of clarifying values and introducing ideas in order to bring about progress by establishing meaningful patterns of historical judgment or relationships."[64] His resolution reduced the complexity and contradictions of cultural production to a bad reflection of class contradictions. "On Culture," in the final instance, ratified the empiricist agenda and dismissed all other versions of Chicano studies and returned to a Leninist-Stalinist form of Marxism.[65]

The activist and scholar Aragón de Shepro provided an interesting corollary to Gómez-Quiñones's essay. Her essay stressed the failures of chicanismo to examine the contradictions of el movimiento. She argued that some Chicanos have been unable to transform their values, goals, and historical experience into a political ideology. She linked this failure to what I have called Perspectivist Chicano Studies. She noted how the work of Eliu Carranza could not take his rhetoric about values and devised a political strategy to transform the Mexican American condition: "For all intents and purposes, the pursuit of self-determination had not meant effecting fundamental change in the country's political and economic system but attempting to effect procedural change (reforms) which would provide access to fuller participation in the existing system."[66] In the end, chicanismo remains motivated by the logic of the dominant political order. Those who follow chicanismo and cultural nationalism do not question the existing economic order. Only in the mid-1970s, she concluded, do we see the articulation of a political ideology to challenge Chicano(a) powerlessness.[67]

Gómez-Quiñones's essay became a classic in the empiric canon. The emphasis on a structural examination, in his case a class analysis, served to finalize the dismissal of studies that looked at the individual or asserted the heterogeneity of the Mexican American. Moreover, Gómez-Quiñones narrowed the space for scholars who wished to engage in a structural analysis from the perspective of culture (cultural nationalism) and race (internal colonialism). He left little doubt that a Leninist-Stalinist form of materialist analysis was the only acceptable research epistemology and the only effective expression of action research. Gómez-Quiñones's essay also was a call to rethink the origins of Chicano Studies. Early empirics had been haphazard in their grounding of this perspective. He did not make this call explicitly, but his "On Culture" essay demanded a theoretical rethinking of the origins to Chicano Studies. Empirics could not remain tied to discussions on *mexicanidad,* identity, and nationality as proposed by such Mexican intellectuals as Ramos, Paz, Vasconcelos, and others. Their discussion favored the turn to culture and away from class structure and politics. Whether early Chicano(a) thinkers accepted or rejected these Mexican authors, most still agreed that these thinkers were important for understanding Chicano thought and Chicano studies.[68] Some early Chicano(a) writers turned to Vasconcelos's concept of *la raza cósmica* and compared it with La Raza.[69] Others criticized Paz's vision of the pachuco but did not reject his interpretation of *lo mexicano* and *mexicanidad.*

The same concerns led Chicanos(as) to analyze Ramos's vision of the Mexican people. The assumed relationship of lo mexicano and the Mexican American led to a deeper reading of Mexican thought, taking us to other Mexican writers like Alfonso Caso, Gabino Barreda, the Flores Magón brothers, and Leopoldo Zea.[70] But as empirics progressively disciplined the field, the impact of these Mexican authors had to be pushed aside or turned on its head. Where initially students in Chicano studies courses read Paz or Ramos, this was no longer the case. For empirics, it was time to disconnect the Chicano(a) from this predominantly Mexican existential dialogue. Neither internal colonialism nor Marxism could swallow the existential flavor of Paz nor the philosophical/psychological analysis in Vasconcelos, Ramos, and Zea.[71] For these reasons, the empirics sought to resituate the origins of Chicano Studies.[72]

A series of essays by Jorge Klor de Alva highlighted the philosophical shift demanded by "On Culture" and necessary for Empirical Chicano Studies. In an early piece on Chicana poetry, Klor de Alva lashed out against the Chicana quest for authenticity and self-identity. He rejected these desires because they swayed toward existentialism and subjectivism. He maintained that Sylvia Gonzales's effort to ground the universal in the personal was meaningless, leading him to conclude that Gonzales's work reflected the confusion of Chicanas in general.[73] In another essay, he stated that most essays on chicanismo and carnalismo are of doubtful quality because of their subjectivism: "Countless tracts, from the subtle to the muddled, have attempted to depict the essence of such notions as *carnalismo* and Chicanismo."[74] Klor de Alva therefore sought to delegitimate the perspectivist tradition in Chicano studies. Some Chicanos feel, he observed, that what influenced Mexican thought (that is, existentialism) must have influenced Chicano thought as well. "For instance, since existentialism played an important role among academic philosophers in Mexico," he wrote, "we find Chicano intellectuals exaggerating the part existentialism has had in Chicano thought in general."[75] This is not the case.

Klor de Alva disparaged the existential turn as simply too subjective and therefore groundless. He rejected the works of Federico Sánchez, Dan Porath, and Celia Medina.[76] Although they did not necessarily draw on Mexican thinkers or European existential writers, their desire to resolve issues of identity, critical thinking, research, and the academy, given their particular experiences, was unacceptable to Klor de Alva. Possibly favoring the U.S. philosophical tradition, he willingly subjugated philosophy to social science.[77] "Philosophy, after all, cannot be used to replace the social sciences," he explained. "The role of philosophers, therefore, is limited to establishing the logical sense of the valid connections between the conclusions given to me so that the systematic world-views suggested by the data can be reconstructed."[78] Klor de Alva articulated a very U.S. understanding of philosophy as merely a check on the validity and soundness of arguments.[79]

An example of the philosophic shift Klor de Alva suggested was the *Aztlán* issue edited by Oscar Martí in 1983. Martí devoted the issue to the Mexican thinker Gabino Barreda. While the personal intellectual concerns of the editor and the various writers explain the interest in this thinker, what did a study of Barreda's thought mean to Chicanos(as) and Chicano Studies? Klor de Alva presented an interesting illumination. He indicated how Barreda's privileging of systematization, generalization, and empiricism are the same biases shared by Chicano(a) social scientists.[80] Their "various ideologies coincide in presupposing the reality of the empirical world as described by modern science."[81] Few Chicano(a) scholars, Klor de Alva continued, adhere to phenomenology, symbolic interactionism, or ethnomethodology, apparently suggesting that these methodologies do not explain reality. Klor de Alva intimated that the only differences between Barreda and Chicano(a) social scientists are ideological and class differences.[82] What they share, which is more important, is their belief in the laws that guide human behavior and core truths; in other words, a scientific approach.[83] Thus it did not matter whether a scholar used the tools of a traditional discipline or turned to a materialist analysis; the key is an acceptance of a measurable empirical world with given universal laws that can be stated, examined, and applied.

Klor de Alva's removal of ideological position and class differences among intellectuals might not have found support with Chicano Studies Marxists. Yet he was closer to what Chicano Studies demanded. While many Marxists retained their rhetoric of class revolution based on a materialist analysis, as part of the academic institution their Marxism was diluted to an expression of the type of empiricism articulated by Klor de Alva.[84] Whatever the political intention of Gómez-Quiñones, the canonization of "On Culture" necessarily meant a reduction, if not erasure, of the political demands of a class analysis. In the end, the building of the empirical canon of Chicano Studies meant the assumption of a depoliticized structural examination of Mexican American oppression and a call for action research that was articulated within academic and empirical practices—soon to be rearticulated as policy research.

We should not assume, however, that Empiricist Chicano Studies was completely triumphant in erasing the link to existential Mexican intellectuals. Voices still were heard, though typically ignored.[85] For instance, while Chicano social science moved away from problematic Mexican thinkers, certain authors remained close to the perspectivist vision. Federico Sánchez in "Raices Mexicanas" salvaged certain writers from the empiric assault. Sánchez interpreted Romano's attack on social science as following up on Ortega y Gasset's perspectivist conception of philosophy: "search for a point of view on human life."[86] Sánchez asserted that this vision was at the core of Chicano studies: "This Ortegan concept (yo soy yo y mi circunstancia) has served as the basic philosophical foundation of most current Chicano criticisms of Anglo studies about Chicano culture."[87] Moreover, Sánchez read

Chicano(a) acceptance of such authors as Vasconcelos, Ramos, and Paz through this lens. The Chicano(a) attraction for Vasconcelos and Paz arose from her/his existential bond. "[Paz's] existentialism, particularly his thoughts about the relationship between solitude, redemption and communion," Sánchez wrote, "have had a tremendous impact on Chicano intellectuals."[88] Acevedo added that Mexican philosophy from scholasticism to perspectivism is the way for Chicano(a) philosophical orientation: "Some of our steps are leading towards Existentialism, Mysticism, and lastly Intuitionism. This is the pattern in which Chicano philosophy will emerge and develop."[89] This was, however, a lost intellectual cause.

Given the difficulty of coming to an agreement over the different political motivations of their research and theoretical approaches, empiric scholars, using a structural analysis, could agree that the end goal was to better the Mexican American condition. One expression of this type of resolution was to speak of Chicano scholarship as action research. This intellectual project was articulated in an *Aztlán* publication in 1974.[90] The aim of the book was to examine how three scholars, engaged with different Chicano(a) communities, tried to integrate their research with political action. The scholars Mario Barrera and Geralda Vialpando pointed out: "It is research at the service of the community, intended to provide the essential knowledge base from which more effective social and political action can be mounted."[91] Of course, this call for action research was not new. For example, in 1971, the scholars Julian Samora, Ernesto Galarza, and Sergio Elizondo had written about the need to link research and community action.[92] Although one could counterpose the different political positions of Galarza, Guillermo Flores, and Rosalio Muñoz with Samora and Elizondo, they did agree on bettering the Mexican American condition. Action research did not specify any particular research method or methodology aside from placing the burden on structural concerns. This further implied that the research could suggest a variety of policies to better the Mexican American condition.

Yet any expression of action research had to first negotiate its legitimacy with the academy. Scholars who engaged in action research had to use the language of the academy to express their research vision and political hope. They had to use the tools of the academy to assert their aims. In doing so, the possibilities of transforming the Mexican American community had to be grounded in the accepted patterns of academic research. In the end, instrumentalist rationality and technique became the prize medium for research and policy became the new language of action research. This is how the UCLA Chicano Studies Center argued the point: "With the increasing reliance of policy-makers upon the findings of socio-scientific investigations, it has become even more important to *initiate* and *support research* conducted by Chicano scholars so as to issue a realistic component of the Chicano experience."[93]

With the increasing success of Empirical Chicano Studies and the concomitant institutionalization of Chicano Studies in the academy, the language of action research and community service was often translated as policy research. Chicano(a) scholars renegotiated their ties to the community through the production of policy papers, policy research, and policy making. Whether one looked at Chicanos(as) who worked from a traditional discipline or those who tried to challenge academic borders by using Marxism, policy became the new language of activist Chicano Studies.[94] This of course fit with the academy's vision of community service. An example of the dialogue among policy researchers, who sought to remain grounded in Chicano Studies, was an essay by the demographer Leobardo Estrada. He resolved the contradiction between the academy and community by discussing "the significance of bringing Hispanic researchers and policy-makers together."[95] In his essay, Estrada claimed to demystify policy and develop research to support this policy. He began with an empirical method where knowledge stood as a fact awaiting its disinterment followed by policies as an outcome of this investigation. "When the knowledge base is solid," he wrote, "policy-making can be grounded in the analysis of the existing data. In this case, the conclusions drawn are more reliable because they depend less on assumptions."[96] It is time then for "Hispanic" researchers to meet with policy makers and share their facts, so proper policies can be developed and enacted and reject "inadequate policies which overlook or oversimplify ethnic issues and Hispanic subgroup differences."[97]

As the canon formed around the empiric guidelines, action research and policy making increasingly became the language of Chicano Studies research. Most Chicano Studies scholars felt that their intellectual work was potentially leading to a better situation for Mexican Americans. Simultaneously, some scholars who came out of the Chicano movement were receiving tenure as well as preparing the next generation of Chicanos(as) graduate students, a few too young to have been part of the 1960s. All were thinking and writing about their understanding of the Mexican American condition with the goal of improving the lives of Mexican Americans. Moreover, these Chicano Studies scholars shared an epistemological vision of how to explain the world and the situation faced by Mexican Americans. Although the internal colonial models, as Muñoz had hoped, did not become the paradigm of Chicano Studies, the structural approach did become dominant. Whether the structural approach favored a traditional disciplinary methodology and practice or some expression of Marxism, scholars sought to understand the condition of the Mexican American as the result of either the structural weakness of the American system or the oppression of a racist and/or capitalist structure.

From this understanding, empiric scholars could then devise solutions for this condition—whether a set of reformist policies to ameliorate the American system or revolutionary action to overthrow an unjust and unequal system. Furthermore, this structural analysis was combined with institution-building efforts; in fact, intellectual inquiry was facilitated by successful institutionalization. Canon formation, action research, and policy making served to support what Jose Cuéllar has called the growth of the new Chicano social science (and one should add the humanities): "[A] study of the problems and needs of a community, by a member of that community, from the perspective of the Insider, under the direction of that community's representatives, and primarily designed to meet the needs and purposes of the community."[98]

Chicano Studies Research

By the early 1980s, the self-doubt and equivocation about the Chicano empirical project was gone.[99] Scholars had published hundreds of pieces and had established a, albeit fluid, canon. Most scholars agreed on what Chicano Studies research was and how it was part of an activist research program. A score of Chicano(a) faculty sat at the pinnacle of the discipline and exercised their academic power; many were even successful in traditional disciplines. The continuation of work in Chicano Studies underscored the empirics' success. As the educator Norma G. Hernandez wrote: "Knowledge in any field of reasoned inquiry increases incrementally in a process that has been extensively used and continuously examined and refined."[100] The empirics had achieved their goal of founding an academic discipline, marking its terrain, and setting up its particular research methods, methodologies, and epistemology. This section provides a selected overview of Chicano Studies research between 1975 and 1982, focusing on texts that served to demonstrate the consolidation of Chicano Studies as a discipline.

Simultaneously, the discipline began a search to ascertain its intellectual origin. As seen earlier, Chicano Studies' intellectual history had to move away from discussions around *mexicanidad* and identity. Although a few empirics still turned to Mexican thinkers to ground Chicano Studies, various scholars recovered the works of George I. Sánchez and Carlos E. Castañeda, as well as more contemporary scholars such as Américo Paredes, Julian Samora, Ernesto Galarza, and others.[101] Some of their writing would be used to establish an origin for Chicano Studies. Muñoz wrote that "[t]he work done by these four scholars [Sánchez, Paredes, Samora, and Galarza] has been important to the development of Chicano Studies as a new field of study and research and, most importantly, to the establishment of a Mexican academic intellectual tradition in the United States."[102] While Chicano(a) activists had initially been critical of these scholars' works for being traditional and assimilationist, by the time Chicano Studies was consolidated, their works had become more acceptable—albeit with a recognition that it did not fully break with the past.[103] As Ignacio García wrote: "While their works focused on Mexican Americans and were often critical of Anglo academic racism, these scholars stayed within the mainstream of their departments and their field."[104] These scholars, nonetheless, were beatified as early patriarchs of Chicano Studies.[105]

Early scholars had looked at these Chicanos' work, in particular at Samora's, as part of the stereotypical research on the Mexican American. For instance, Theresa Aragón de Sherpo was critical of what she saw as Samora's assimilationist argument.[106] Irene Blea referred to Samora's work as "repressive scholarship," since it was based on the structure of social science that "was inherently demeaning and discriminatory."[107] Samora's essay on Mexican Americans in the Midwest resonated with traditional assimilationist theories of the 1960s as well as with stereotypical pictures of Mexican Americans.[108] Yet by the early 1980s, scholars regarded Samora's work as more complicated than Aragón de Sherpo and Blea had suggested. Clearly, in *Los Mojados,* his discussion about undocumented lives echoed with contemporary experiences. While one might quibble about the setting he provided, his description of undocumented people brought them to the attention of a generation who had not included them in their political discourse.[109] Chicano Studies scholars accepted that Samora, like most of these transitional scholars who had begun their intellectual career before el movimiento, suffered from the limitation of their social science training, yet it was important to acknowledge that these transitional intellectuals wanted to make their research meaningful to a new generation of Chicanos(as). As Chicano Studies was consolidated, Samora and other transitional scholars were rehabilitated.

The work of Manuel Ramírez III and Alfredo Castañeda (like Samora, Paredes, and Campa) provided other examples of Chicano(a) scholars whose intellectual production had begun before el movimiento and developed as they dealt with the new questions that the protests brought to the fore.[110] In *Cultural Democracy, Bicognitive Development, and Education,* for instance, Ramírez and Castañeda presented an explanation of how educational pluralism could promote an environment of learning for the Mexican American child. They explained the positive values of bicultural identity and bicognitive development through the practice of an effective cultural democracy: "A culturally democratic learning environment is a setting in which a Mexican American child can acquire knowledge about his own culture and the dominant culture."[111] They rejected assimilation that sought conformity and dismissal of Mexican American culture and cognitive styles.[112] While their work shed light on the condition of the Mexican American child and education, some Chicanos(as) considered that these authors did not fully consider the social, economic, and political limits of U.S. democracy.[113] At the same time, they drew attention to Chicano(a) scholarship in the field of language acquisition and bilingual/bicultural education.[114] These educational professionals highlighted the failure of the U.S. educational system and established policies to ameliorate this situation.[115]

Because of the differences of opinion about these transitional scholars, in the end there was no consistent origin story for Chicano Studies. Although the turn to older thinkers might have provided some balance against Mexican intellectuals, no particular reading existed. Thus, while some scholars could remain critical of Samora, others could find space for Castañeda. It was clear that Chicano(a) empirics could differ over their views of the origin of the discipline without any major damage to the field. What was more important was how these origin writings reinforced the structural analysis and the formation of action research that was at the heart of Chicano Studies.

The period witnessed a flurry of sociological works that sought a critical social science research—a challenge to the work of earlier liberal empirics who practiced sociology. For instance, Alfredo Mirandé stated in his introduction to a special issue of *De Colores* on "La Familia": "The idea of compiling a special issue on *la familia* emerged from the realization that Chicano scholarship has now moved from the reactive stance which was so prevalent in the 1960s and 1970s to a proactive one in the 1980s. A new generation of scholars has emerged which is both sensitive to the nuance of Chicano culture and sympathetic to it, yet one with the maturity and sophistication to discard naïve and idealized conceptions that are not grounded in the real world."[116] In this issue, Mirandé brought together the recent research on the Mexican American family and introduced a new cohort of Chicano(a) scholars doing Chicano social science. These essays provided examples of quality Chicano Studies research and furnished an example of the debate among Chicano(a) sociologists about the relationship of Chicano Studies and sociology.[117]

One way to examine how some Chicano(a) sociologists looked at their discipline of training and Chicano Studies is to examine the debate between Mirandé and Maxime Baca Zinn, another sociologist. Mirandé challenged sociology's examination of the Mexican American and renewed the call for internal colonialism as a model for Chicano Studies analysis. This paradigm, he continued, rejects the scientism of sociology that presupposes apolitical and neutral research. Chicano sociology, in contrast, approaches "all of sociology, not just the study of Chicanos, from a minority perspective—that is, as members of an oppressed group."[118] With this model, Mirandé believed he brought a Copernican revolution to the field. Baca Zinn questioned Mirandé's vision of Chicano sociology as a revolutionary breakthrough in the field. She did not see Mirandé's position as a rupture in the field; rather, she deemed that Mirandé was simply privileging one theoretical/methodological perspective. She intimated that Mirandé's model had more to do with normal sociology than he was willing to admit. Instead, Chicano sociology must adopt multiple theoretical/methodological positions.[119] Mirandé responded that Baca Zinn had ignored the reality of the colonization of the Mexican American.[120] Mirandé expanded that due to this error, she had lost the difference between the sociology of Chicanos and Chicano sociology. He underscored that Baca Zinn was interested only in sociology and its theories, while he wanted a Chicano perspective to be used to shed light on sociology.

In this debate, Mirandé appeared to have shifted his position. Where he initially argued for a paradigmatic revolution in sociology based on the internal colonial model, his dialogue with Baca Zinn forced him to another, less clear, position. He acknowledged that internal colonialism was a structural theory that was part of sociology and yet could advance our knowledge of Mexican Americans.[121] He was forced to recognize that his desire to challenge sociology could not simply come from using a structural model to explain the Mexican American. So where was the break with sociology? He commented that "[t]heories organic to Chicano culture and world views have yet to be developed"; the revolution against sociology was to develop a theory that came from the Mexican American cultural condition.[122] Instead of advancing internal colonialism, his argument returned to Muñoz's earlier discussion of cultural nationalism. To confuse the situation further, he argued that Chicano methodology was less developed than Chicano theory; a methodology "that permits one to be both researcher and Chicano."[123] Mirandé therefore ended up accepting sociology as a tool for Chicano Studies.

Sociologist and policy writer Estevan Flores's review of Chicano(a) sociological works sought a different resolution to the discussion between Mirandé and Baca Zinn over a Chicano Studies research model. Rejecting the internal colonial and liberal models, Flores brought a Marxist analysis to the Chicano(a) experience and asked for a political strategy to attack discrimination.[124] The pursuit of knowledge could be a dead-end pursuit in itself; "we need to begin to develop political strategy from social scientific data."[125] While one could sympathize with Flores's political aims, he basically accepted the operation of social science research in a Marxist guise. In his endeavor to defend advocacy research, he rested on the sophistication and rigor of social science.[126] Thus Flores concluded that he had no intention to either propose a new paradigm or simply use traditional sociological tools. Research, by showing the contradictions in society, would demonstrate the beneficial effects of change.

"What is necessary," wrote Flores, "is to give more time and energy to using our expertise and data in ways that challenge the exploitative system and ultimately benefit our community and class."[127] Marxist social science was the tool to analyze the Mexican American condition and became the place to construct a Chicano politics. Fellow sociologist Gilbert Cadena and others added: "[W]hat is most critical is not so much how research is conducted but for what purpose it is used. Research findings should result in the betterment of the Chicano community."[128] Even though Flores struggled to formulate an activist Chicano Studies, he surrendered to the discipline. His own interpretation of Marxist scholarship in an academic institution resulted in accepting academic structures and procedures. It became difficult to see where a liberal tradition (or a cultural nationalist tradition like that of Mirandé) ends and a Marxist one begins.

Though theoretically different, the research by Mirandé, Baca Zinn, and Flores attempted to resolve the tension between their training and their work as Chicanos(as) by using sociological or Marxist tools to explore the Mexican American condition and to seek a resolution to this condition. Although they differed in how they negotiated this dilemma, they shared a belief in investigating the structure of oppression to establish a practice to ameliorate this condition. Unfortunately, the academic and institutional practices served to domesticate radical intellectual perspectives as well as channel political challenges to acceptable political action.[129]

Like sociologists, Chicanos(as) trained in anthropology also negotiated their space within their home discipline and Chicano Studies. Without doubt, the most successful early Chicano academic anthropologist was the folklorist Américo Paredes. Paredes's work, part of the transitional scholarship before el movimiento, endeavored to bring the Mexican and Mexican American back into the realm of anthropology with recognition of their condition of oppression.[130] His text *"With His Pistol in His Hand": A Border Ballad and Its Hero* used "El Corrido de Gregorio Cortez" to examine issues of the border, racism and discrimination, the *corrido,* and border folklore with an implied critique of Anglo research on Mexican Americans in Texas.[131] Literary and cultural critic José David Saldívar optimistically referred to Paredes's work as an "antidisciplinary Texas-Mexico border project." In his work on folk songs, Paredes brought the border into the Mexican American intellectual imagination as both a place of intercultural conflict and a space for cultural play and identity construction through cultural resistance.[132] In later works, his writing was more critical of anthropologists who continued to use stereotypical language of Mexicans and Mexican Americans. In his work on jokes and humor, he noted how anthropologists, when they directly addressed their subjects, often missed Mexican verbal art.[133] For the anthropologist Renato Rosaldo, Paredes's ethnography moved beyond stereotype and allowed for cultural change and development. His use of culture provided a space to advance Chicano(a) understanding of the Mexican American.[134]

Yet the work of Paredes, like that of Samora, was often distant to early Chicano(a) activists. It did not resonate with their militancy and their form of cultural nationalism—and I would add vice versa. For instance, in his work on *cancioneros,* Paredes signaled a possible continuity between border heroes and modern-day Chicanos: "For thousands of young Chicanos today, so intent on maintaining their cultural identity and demanding their rights, the Border *corrido* hero will strike a responsive chord when he risks life, liberty, and material goods *defendiendo su derecho.*"[135] But Paredes did not accept the form of nationalism used by Chicano(a) activists. Paredes defended a nationalism that blurred the differences between Mexican and Mexican Americans in South Texas as they produced older expressions of cultural production. But the Chicano(a) presented him with a nationalism that went beyond his notion of *lo mexicano.*

He wrote: "For the Chicano activist has become a victim of the Melting Pot in subtle ways. He comes on like an 'urban ghetto' type rather than like a *mexicano.* His urban-militant style—picked up from other militant minority groups—turns off the traditional Mexican-American, who is one with the Chicano in reverence for *lo mexicano* but who is basically old-fashioned in his values, whether he lives in the *barrio* or on the farm."[136] Paredes saw these Chicano(a) militants as *agringado* hippies who did not "act" Mexican. He did not question his own essentialist vision of the Mexican.[137] His work echoed the patriarchal and nationalist voice of early Chicano scholarship.[138] Yet as Chicano Studies matured, Paredes and his work were reconsidered by many of the same activists, though now older, and a newer generation of scholars. Thus the eighth NACS conference in 1980 was dedicated to Parades for his work "as a pioneer Chicano scholar."[139] In 1977, he wrote the lead article for a collection of essays in the *New Scholar* that was republished in *New Directions in Chicano Scholarship.*[140]

Given the differences between Paredes and early Chicano(a) activists, why did Chicano Studies scholars in the 1980s want to resurrect his work? There were two currents at play. The first was to uncover a more academically acceptable illustration of Chicano anthropology than had been articulated in the early essays of *El Grito*. For this reason, Rosaldo insisted on the superiority of Parades's work over that of Romano. He contended that the early work of Romano and Vaca had been burdened by ideology and therefore they were not able to see beyond the dated anthropology they criticized.[141] Whether this was true or not is unimportant; Rosaldo was giving us another genesis myth to Chicano Studies scholarship and Chicanos(as) in anthropology. In this tale, the good academic researcher vanquished the ideologue and provided a univocal fable for Chicanos(as) in higher education and anthropology.[142]

The second aim was the need to lift the burden that Romano's and Vaca's critique had placed on anthropology—the accusation that anthropology served to stereotype and control the Mexican American. The work of anthropologist José Limón makes this point.[143] In his dissertation, he adopted participation-observation together with open-ended informal interviews to examine the expressive culture of a group of students at the University of Texas at Austin. He acknowledged, like Parades, that Chicanos(as) had neglected anthropological studies—in particular, the field of cultural anthropology. This resulted from Chicanos(as)' distrust of how earlier Anglo scholars had used participant-observation. However, Limón suggested that participant-observation can still be used to understand the Chicano(a) community, especially if we link it to the field of symbolic anthropology. He argued that the work of Romano and Vaca had failed ethnographically. Although they had been the first to raise the warning flags, "a thorough reply to these ethnographies would require new fieldwork among the natives who are supposed to be the carriers of these values," which they did not do.[144] Limón's aim was to engage in the ethnographic work that Romano and Vaca had avoided and thereby provide an alternative use of the discipline's method without reproducing the stereotypical results of earlier Anglo anthropologists.[145] While he acknowledged that the work of early anthropologists was biased,[146] the methods were not to be faulted.[147] Limón, following in the footsteps of Parades, remained satisfied with his discipline's instruments.[148]

Another example of this attempt to massage the criticism of Romano, Vaca, and other writers of the Quinto Sol collective into a softer critique—less forceful, less angry, less critical—ironically appeared in Romano's *El Grito del Sol*. Whether through the lens of liberalism or Marxism,

Chicano(a) anthropologists searched for alternatives either from within the discipline or outside without challenging the premises of the field. In an interesting collection in *El Grito del Sol,* one encountered these various tendencies. As Steven Arvizu, the guest editor of the journal, noted, these essays, initially presented at the annual meetings of the American Anthropology Association and the National Association of Chicano Social Science, allow the reader to appreciate the condition of the Chicano(a) academic in anthropology as well as to see their challenge to the discipline's theory and methodology. Arvizu presented the essays as an endeavor to reflect "on the colonizing aspect of anthropology" to decolonialize the discipline.[149] Arvizu wrote: "Chicanos participating challenge one another to conceptualize and operationalize an alternative to traditional anthropology."[150] In the process, he hoped to "view the world of Anthropology from a Chicano perspective," to deal with issues of the Chicano(a) community.[151] Yet the barbed criticism of the discipline does not end in its delegitimization.[152]

Chicano(a) political scientists faced similar methodological questions as their peers trained in sociology and anthropology. While some scholars saw little hope for their field, others hoped to use tools from the discipline to investigate the Mexican American. Muñoz presented a pessimistic view about the possible impact of political science in Chicano Studies. "Given the limited access Chicanos have had to the discipline of political science and the current state of the discipline," he wrote, "it will be a long time before a substantial body of knowledge of Chicano politics is developed."[153] Yet he recognized that political science had provided Chicano Studies with its first model—internal colonialism. Unfortunately, he continued, a myriad of approaches rent any self-identified Chicano perspective.[154] The inability to formulate a model that could lead Chicano Studies beyond disciplinary practices allowed the resurgence of social science.[155]

For this reason, many Chicano(a) political scientists accepted disciplinary assumptions and methodologies that were grounded in a traditional and structural explication of the United States. An example was F. Chris Garcia and O. de la Garza's *The Chicano Political Experience,* published in 1977.[156] In his dissertation, F. Chris Garcia attempted "to explain why Chicanos remain politically weak by analyzing the Chicano experience according to competing theories of the distribution of power in contemporary America."[157] In his examination he stressed that he had done his "utmost to be objective" by relying on empirical studies asserting the logic of social science scholarship.[158] He traced the pluralist, elitist, and internal colonial models to explain the political process that limited political access to Mexican Americans and the possibilities of change. Thus he concluded that the internal colonial model might be the best description of the historical experience of the Mexican American.[159] However, while this model might explain aspects of the problems Mexican Americans face, it could not explain why they had begun to enjoy political victories.[160] The author believed that the pluralist model best explained the then recent political success in the Southwest.[161] We should not assume that those who remained close to their discipline could not be critical of the Mexican American condition and develop a politics to challenge this reality.[162]

The acceptance of the discipline's tools (whether it be sociology, anthropology, or political science) created a situation that allowed Chicano(a) scholars to build an acceptable model that explained the Mexican American condition and then provided policies to better their situation. One direction of this methodological compromise was the uneasy acceptance of statistics, surveys, and other forms of quantitative research. Often Chicanos(as) would combine a variety of these methods.[163] In 1977, the University of Michigan's Institute for Social Research, under the direction of Leobardo Estrada of UCLA, established a pilot two-week summer program to train Chicano(a) researchers in "selected survey research and demographic methodologies most applicable to research on minority populations."[164] At the same time, the National Chicano Research Network with Stanford University scheduled an intensive training in social research methods at Stanford. By 1979, the University of Michigan had a full-scale summer training institute for researchers in the social and behavioral sciences. Examples of quantitative scholarship in this period were present in the work of Carlos H. Arce, Leobardo Estrada, Amado Padilla, Marta Tienda, and Robert Santos.

Not all Chicanos(as) were happy with this development, however. Rodolfo Acuña, for instance, wrote that Chicano(a) advocacy research was critical of the "abuse of quantitative methodology by Anglo scholars." Implied in this criticism was the idea that Chicano(a) scholars should avoid quantitative research because of its perceived epistemological determinism. Furthermore, as Chicano(a) scholars who used quantitative methods stepped away from their community, "it became popular to regard qualitative methods as soft."[165] Nonetheless, many scholars saw quantitative research, like other social science tools, as neutral.

Chicano(a) empirics in sociology, anthropology, and political science had successfully established a criterion for "good" Chicano Studies research and therefore helped the consolidation of Chicano Studies.[166] The majority of Chicano(a) scholars retained an unhealthy association with their area of training and rationalized their work as an example of multi- or transdisciplinary work. Chicano Studies came to house Chicanos(as) that shared the empiric assumptions of a structural approach and action research, whatever their methodologies or epistemologies. Thus the historian Mario García was right when he observed that Chicano Studies in the mid-1980s was ready to integrate into the mainstream, even if traditional disciplines still had not resolved their own doubts about Chicano research. Chicano Studies as a discipline had matured to the point that it sought equal participation in the academic world.[167] The critic Herminio Rios-C. added to this idea: "During the decade of the 1970s, Spanish surnamed individuals started to invade the previously almost exclusively Anglo American domain in the social sciences. However, with a few notable exceptions (Vaca, Romano, Hernández) the philosophical postures they espoused were not different from those proposed by Anglo American social scientists."[168]

Chicano literary criticism also entered a period of consolidation.[169] In most cases, Chicano criticism remained more eclectic and open than the social sciences—often retaining a contact to their communities. Most early critics followed literary scholar Juan Bruce Novoa's call for a criticism that would allow the "dynamic interplay of many readings, none of which can presume to be absolute."[170] Essays in the journal *Revista Chicano-Riqueña* demonstrated this plasticity.[171] The work of critic José R. Reyna drew on cultural nationalism to understand different types of Chicano cultural expressions; Latin American literary scholar Rosaura Sánchez applied a Marxist approach in her criticism.[172] Scholars Justo S. Alarcón and Sylvia S. Lizárraga employed a traditional academic approach.[173] Cultural critic Tomás Ybarra-Frausto's essay on emergent Chicano poetry tried to weave poetic production with the various aspects of the Chicano struggle.[174]

Although these various readings started from an understanding of the oppression of the Mexican American, they differed over the direction of the criticism. In her dissertation, Evangelina Enriquez asserted the centrality of culture and nationalism through a reading of Franz Fanon, Freire, and Peter Nazareth. She employed Américo Paredes's claim of the "non-passivity of Chicanos in the face of oppression."[175] Influenced by her acceptance of the internal colonial model, she stressed that literary criticism had to center itself on the realities of usurpation, colonization, and discrimination. From this perspective, she placed Bernice Zamora, Juan Rodríguez, and Rolando Hinojosa in the social-cultural camp versus those who sought the universal dimension of Chicano literature, like Max Martinez, Sylvia Gonzales, and Philip Ortego.[176] Trying to bridge these differences were synthesizers like Ricardo Sanchez, Tomás Rivera, Justo A. Alarcón, Bruce Novoa, and Ramón Saldívar.

Yet with the consolidation of Chicano Studies, criticism also had to be corralled; it was necessary for the survival of criticism as an academic project to manage its early wildness that still inhered in cultural nationalism.[177] Thus the many critics and writers who wanted to retain a nationalist orientation had to be disciplined. This tension between art and its "establishment" could be witnessed in the Flor y Canto festivals or Bruce Novoa's examination of Chicano(a) poetry and chicanismo.[178] The best example of this need to create a coherent approach to criticism was Ramón Saldívar's "A Dialectic of Difference: Towards a Theory of the Chicano Novel." Responding to Joseph Sommers's call for a rethinking of literary scholars' theoretical suppositions, Saldívar utilized a poststructuralist criticism to draw out the ideology of difference in three novels. He explored the novels' "paradoxical impulse toward revolutionary and toward the production of meaning."[179] In this fashion, he molded a theory that remained associated with social and historical forces and free from the myth of absolute and universal truths. In the end, this could lead to "the development of a truly 'new' American 'criticism.'"[180] Saldívar provided Chicano Studies criticism with terminology that found parallels in the social sciences.

For many Chicano Studies scholars the answer to the limits of academic research and the praxis demanded by action research was to turn to Marxism. There was no agreement on what they saw as a Marxist methodology or even as a political praxis. The Marxist continuum spread from a liberal academic (often clumsy) expression of social analysis to a Soviet version of dialectical materialism.[181] A good number of Chicano(a) scholars felt that Marxism alone could provide an analytical framework that would allow a proper evaluation of the

Mexican American condition, avoiding the containment imposed by disciplines, and the construction of a radical political practice.

While the work of Gómez-Quiñones, Acuña, and García was part of Chicano(a) Marxists' historiography, there is little doubt that Gómez-Quiñones's work was central to the convergence of Chicano Studies, Mexican American history, and Chicano Marxist history. Although García and Acuña's historical research opened many historical sites, their work remained ambiguous to the disciplining of history in Chicano Studies. The open-ended history that Jesus Chavarría proposed was short-lived. Gómez-Quiñones's role as the senior Chicano Studies historian in the University of California system allowed him to cultivate a generation of scholars that shared aspects of his historical theory and practice. His interest in social history through a materialist framework was adopted by his students and a few peers.[182]

For some, this historical work signaled "the maturation of a young, but growing field of study," eventually making major contributions in the field of social history—in particular, labor history.[183] Chicano historical research benefited from the earlier shift toward social history in U.S. historiography. Many historians accepted Gómez-Quiñones's position that "[t]he most important determining aspect for the Chicano community is its economic role and position."[184] A good example was Luis Arroyo's piece on the direction of Chicano labor studies, which appeared in a special issue of *Aztlán* on labor edited by him and his fellow UCLA student Victor Cisneros. Influenced by the growth of social history and Marxism, Arroyo provided a detailed exploration of this "new" Chicano labor history, highlighting most of the current Chicano historians.[185]

What they shared was a shift from "cultural conflict to materialist explanations of social change."[186] For many Chicano(a) historians, *Aztlán* became the journal that supported Gómez-Quiñones's version of Chicano Marxist historiography. Eight years later, Arroyo reasserted his position.[187] In his earlier bibliographical essay, he observed that *El Grito*, the *Journal of Mexican American History*, and *Aztlán* produced fifty-eight out of eighty articles that appeared between 1970 and 1974 on Chicano(a) history.[188] Yet it was *Aztlán* that specifically cultivated social history with a materialist tinge. The central text was Gómez-Quiñones's *Development of the Mexican Working Class North of the Rio Bravo*.[189] The historian Alex Saragoza does a disservice to his argument when he narrows this early Chicano social history to an "us versus them" nationalist model. Although there were many problems with this social-Marxist research, Saragoza's rhetorical accusation only served to politicize the discussion over the capitalist transformation of the West.[190]

One place to examine Chicano Marxist historiography was the move away from internal colonialism toward a materialist history. Arroyo and Victor Cisneros's essay provided a good example of this turn. Their work, Estevan Flores pointed out, shifted away from the internal colonial model and offered a Marxist integration of race with class. "While the internal colonial model focused on oppression and liberation," he wrote, "those who used the Marxist model dealt more with 'exploitation' and the political economy of the Southwest's growth."[191] By the 1980s, Chicano(a) Marxists had decided to jettison the internal colonial approach in any of its variations. An example of the endeavor to push aside internal colonialism can be found in a symposium dedicated to the second edition of Acuña's *Occupied America*.[192] The sociologist Anastacio "Tatcho" Mindiola Jr. suggested in the introduction that the internal colonial model had overemphasized race relations that in turn had weakened early Chicano research. Now, as evidenced in Acuña's second edition, Chicanos(as) have turned to a class analysis.[193]

Others in the symposium,[194] many who worked at UCLA with Gomez-Quiñones, agreed with this interpretation.[195] Interestingly, Acuña's own interpretation was different from his reviewers. He was critical of Marxists scholars who have "adopted Marxism as a religion" and were intolerant. He suggested that many do not practice what they preach; they adopt lifestyles far removed from the communities they write about.[196] Yet he saw his own intellectual project as a reflection of his time and temperament. Therefore, his use of internal colonialism reflected the time period; *Occupied America* was a necessary project as Chicano Studies was being constructed. If there were flaws, Acuña suggested, they may reflect "the current of the times."[197] He added that he now sees the internal colonial model as primarily relevant to the nineteenth century. However, for the twentieth century, Acuña found other paradigms wanting and turned to historical materialism. Most of the writers found his shift key to the demise of internal colonialism, marking the victory of dialectical materialism.[198]

A different use of Marxism, outside of history, was present in Jose Limón's "Western Marxism and Folklore: A Critical Introduction." Limón explored how Western Marxist commitment to culture, especially art, as a field of lived political relationship—in particular, the work of Gramsci and the Frankfurt school—helped his exploration of folklore. This essay provided an alternative view of culture than is found in Gómez-Quiñones's "On Culture." Unfortunately, while he engaged with a tradition within Marxism that few Chicano(a) scholars utilized, his analysis was wanting. His interpretation was swayed by Perry Anderson's work, that the Frankfurt school, and possibly Western Marxism as a whole, provided a pessimistic outlook and were apolitical. Limón wrote: "They shunned an active engagement in the arena of labor and politics, embarking instead on a program of research, theory building, and critical analysis."[199] Nonetheless, whatever the article's limitations, it provided a different style of Marxism that could avoid many of the Leninist constraints.

Just like earlier success of cultural nationalism and internal colonialism, for a moment Marxism appeared to dominate the field of Chicano Studies. Even academics who felt little sympathy with a Marxist political agenda flirted with Marxism as an academic practice. For many Chicano Studies scholars Marxism was the only authentic method for activist research and a revolutionary praxis—and it avoided academic constraints. Many practitioners of Chicano Studies saw themselves using a materialist analysis together with a coquettish relationship with a variety of Marxist-Leninist political organizations. Of course, whether as a tool of analysis or a political program, Chicano(a) Marxists expressed many variations and differences.

Flores maintained that this Marxist turn was the result of activism in the Mexican American communities. "Chicano Studies and Mexican American Studies were forged out of student and community struggles for access to institutions of higher education," he wrote.[200] Marxism, he asserted, can resolve many issues not dealt with by internal colonialism and expressions of nationalism as well as provide a concrete and transformative political agenda. Internal colonialism and cultural nationalism only provide "critiques of racism, without class perspective, [and therefore] were ultimately reformist."[201] The use of dialectical materialism entailed participation in a Marxist politics. Flores drew attention to scholar activists—in particular, those working on immigration and with CASA.[202] "The scope of Chicano Studies," explained Flores, "was augmented through the social activism of CASA and other groups, while scholarly production on the topic made significant advances for both Marxist thought and Chicano Studies."[203]

In making his argument, Flores privileged a particular expression of Marxist scholarship and politics. First, he asserted a Leninist-Stalinist version of a materialist analysis that left little room for culture and subjectivity. He returned to the model that Gómez-Quiñones's had articulated in "On Culture." Thus alternative Marxist currents were dismissed since they promoted a "reformist" or "infantile" political project. The best Flores could offer in response to the question of the epistemological alternative Marxism offered Chicano Studies was to turn to "grounded theory." Second, he advanced a particular expression of Marxist-Leninist political action. By promoting the cause of CASA, Flores opened himself to the accusation of sectarianism by other Marxist-Leninist organizations that found themselves in conflict with CASA's ideological and political agenda. Simultaneously, his link of academic scholarship to Marxist-Leninist practices limited political practices to an acceptable spectrum.

Flores's case exemplified the potential problem with a particular Marxist scholarship that linked its research to a particular political Marxist praxis. He limited action research scholarship to a Leninist-Stalinist structural analysis and constrained political action in the community to the CASA program. His belief that Chicano(a) scholars in CASA personified the scholar-activist reduced the political options of scholars and left scholarship with a mediocre and inflexible expression of Marxism as an intellectual tool. This may explain why the particular Chicano history that came from UCLA was stillborn. More important, Flores ignored the institutionalization of Marxism into an academic project. While individual scholars fought against oppressive structures, academic practices eroded Marxism as it was molded into particular disciplines. Thus the success of Marxism in Chicano Studies (and Chicano Marxist history) was defined by academic and not political practices.[204] Marxism's political edge was removed in its academic venture. Increasingly, the logic of the academic project became the reasoning of Marxism in Chicano Studies. For this reason, Flores concluded that from "vague criticism to emphasis on internal colonialism to various Marxist interpretations," Chicano Studies had developed as an academic field.[205]

Institutional Support and Academic Consolidation

Whatever the intellectual gyration in Chicano thought, Chicano Studies' success in the academy depended on the existence of a coherent administrative structure. The ability to follow administrative policies made Chicano Studies a vibrant program. This also meant that the institutionalization of Chicano Studies defined the terms of intellectual incorporation. The academic institution was clearly aware of this process of subordination. University of California president Charles Hitch, for instance, understood the centrality of using established procedures to control new and possibly challenging departments and/or programs. In a 1969 letter, he wrote: "I want to remind you that proposals for new departments must be reviewed with the appropriate Academic Senate agencies, must demonstrate academic merit, and must show good reason for establishing a departmental organization. If approved, such departments would operate under the same rules, regulations, and budgetary procedures as other departments of the University."[206] This process served to both legitimate and bind Chicano Studies. Even when external organizations entered the arena, the home institution defined institution building. Thus the establishment of Chicano Studies programs paralleled the development of Chicano Studies as an academic discipline. Furthermore, this dual process demonstrated the subordination of both to the logic of the academy. To understand the success of academic production, it would be good to understand how the institution confined and dictated the direction of Chicano Studies, but I leave this discussion for another time.

Chicano Studies was consolidated as Chicanos(as) built the institutional infrastructure that found an uneasy peace with the general administration of the college and developed a curriculum that acknowledged the premises of customary academic tools and practices. Together these made Chicano Studies a success. In particular, structural analysis as the paradigm of Chicano Studies quickly found space within the academy. Whether this epistemological vision took the methodology of cultural nationalism, internal colonialism, Marxism, or traditional disciplinary practices, it encountered a possible though troubled existence in the academy. Yet, like the structural analysis, the proposed methodologies did not challenge intellectual practices or break the disciplinary boundaries created by the training of Chicano(a) scholars. When Chicano Studies spoke of its revolutionary break, it increasingly was reduced to some challenge to disciplinary work (inter-, trans-, multidisciplinary). This did not deny that scholars produced enormous amounts of research and in the process created a better understanding of the Mexican American condition. In less than a decade, Chicano(a) scholars expanded the knowledge about their community by using a wide variety of methods and methodologies. Their research provided the background for community-based policies and activities that transformed parts of the community and tweaked American exceptionalism. Although this work did not overturn the American imaginary and its power structure, these policies did resolve some anomalies faced by Mexican Americans. What it did not do was to break academic practices or challenge knowledge as they knew it. Chicano Studies, like other academic disciplines, took its place in the institutional hierarchy and mirrored the ethical dynamic that all academics learned in their transition from initiate to high priest.

Chicanas, the Chicano Student Movements, and Chicana Thought, 1967-1982

Although some Chicana scholars found an intellectual space in the perspectivist or empiricist camp, a number desired a different intellectual program. Women began the intellectual work of constructing a feminism that first challenged Chicano political practices, then aspects of Chicano studies, before turning to an articulation of Chicana Studies. Often through these stages of criticism, a few Chicana scholars came to question the entire Chicano studies project and even academic work as a whole. Paradoxically, this Chicana venture and its assertion of autonomy occurred at the moment that Empirical Chicano Studies consolidated its control over Chicano(a) academic work. Therefore the disciplinarians of Chicano Studies curtailed the Chicana challenges at all levels. Given the sexism and racism of higher education and the sexism within el movimiento, it should not be surprising that Chicanas had a longer struggle to articulate an independent intellectual project within the academy. This chapter describes Chicana thought as it unfolded from a gendered critique of el movimiento toward the development of the foundation of a feminist construction of Chicana and Chicana(o) studies.

Chicana thought was grounded in the struggles of race, class, gender, and sexuality. Chicanas found themselves involved in tense battles with Chicanos and Anglos as well as with other Chicanas. The Chicano student movements' exclusionary politics, for instance, obligated women to formulate a different political practice within the movements and at times to construct a separate politics altogether. Thus the inception of a Chicana intellectual tradition ran parallel to the various political battles Chicanas had to conduct for their identity and autonomy. This chapter maps out the early Chicana struggles with the wider society and el movimiento as the opening step to understand the various Chicana intellectual endeavors. As the scholar Alma García has argued, Chicana feminist discourse developed through the Chicana struggle with sexism within their communities and the racism of the larger society. In this process, "Chicana feminists constructed a feminist ideology based on their specific experiences as women of color."[1]

To capture the interface of political choices with intellectual production, I briefly explore Chicanas' political practices outside the academy. Given the exclusionary practices of el movimiento and the racism and sexism of Anglo society, and higher education specifically, Chicanas often found themselves outside of the academy and beyond the centers of Chicano power.[2] While they may have sought a place in the university, many Chicanas were unable or unwilling to accept the terms of such a contract. Therefore, they had to express themselves intellectually through nontraditional venues as they contested male- and/or Anglo-dominated sites. Given the various levels of Chicana oppression, they could not contend with only one site (or region) of oppression, but from the start Chicanas had to contest multiple and changing sites of domination.

The need for flexibility also had to do with the limited number of Chicanas in higher education and the mechanism by which they were silenced. This did not mean that women were not active. The historian and feminist Martha Cotera, for instance, noted thirty-four different Chicana workshops, conferences, caucuses, meetings, symposiums, seminars, and committees between 1970 and 1975—the vast majority took place outside the academy.[3] This activism created a firestorm over the "role of the Chicana" in both el movimiento and Chicano studies, often leading to a critique of both. Out of this critique, some Chicana intellectuals endeavored to rethink their relationship with the academy, Chicano studies, and knowledge in general. Many moved toward a feminist perspective, "Chicana feminism," and a "Third World" or "women of color feminism" that was ultimately explored in the landmark work *This Bridge Called My Back*. Chicana scholars took seriously the critical intellectual arguments that most practitioners of Chicano studies had put aside.[4] They in turn reformulated these criticisms through their life experiences.

Chicanas, El Movimiento, and the Chicano Student Movements

The literature on el movimiento has been a male expression; there has not been sufficient effort to present women in their various roles.

Unlike el movimiento's "founding fathers," women like Francesca Flores, Martha Cotera, Elizabeth Martinez, Mirta Vidal, Enriqueta Longauex y Vásquez, and Anna NietoGomez have been, at least until recently, historically edited.[5] Attention is still devoted to male heroes, especially with the recent publications of their histories and autobiographical stories, while female activists are remembered in passing and peripherally. At the National Association of Chicano and Chicana Studies conferences, we still hear the early history through the same lens. I do not excuse myself, since I have also devoted much ink to a masculinist interpretation. Simultaneously, to state that the early politics was patriarchal does not mean that women were not present. More research is needed to excavate the role of women during this period. There is more to learn about Chicana activists who headed up their campus student organizations, like Olga Martinez at Foothill College's MEChA or Lupe Valizan at Ventura Community College's UMAS, or women who edited student periodicals, like Lori Mejia Briscoe of University of California at Riverside's *Adelante* or Alexandrina Esparza of San Jose State's *El Machete*.

Chicanas were active in both el movimiento and the Chicano student movements; their activism unfortunately was typically framed within patriarchal politics. As the scholar Sonia López has reminded us: "[T]hough Chicanas were active from the inception of the Movement, they were generally relegated to traditional roles played by women in society."[6] El movimiento was about men, led by men, defined by men, and masculinist in its rhetorical practices and intellectual perspectives. Women's participation was submerged; their voices silenced.[7] Women had to submit to male fantasies, as García explained it: "While being good wives and mothers in the tradition of our people, Chicanas also want to use their intelligence skillfully to strengthen and benefit all Raza."[8] It was incumbent on Chicanas to break this monopoly by introducing a gendered appraisal of Chicano politics.[9]

Chicanas who struggled for their space and identity within these movements typically faced three choices. First, they could simply acquiesce to given political practices and submerge their identity and gender concerns. Second, they could endeavor to create a space for "women's concerns" within these patriarchal movements, often negotiating their autonomy away. Third, they could reject Chicano patriarchal politics altogether and propose a nonpatriarchal politics. Often this meant to join the general women's movement—albeit with enormous conflict with white women. In the early 1970s, Chicanas had to negotiate among these three options, often moving among the three. No individual ever expressed only one position; rather, women mixed them together and through their political lives continued to blend these options. Often, when using the writings of one Chicana to demonstrate a particular political perspective, it could be possible to use a different writing to show another point of view. This did not result from Chicanas' inability to take a position. Rather, this was the consequence of the difficulty to make their politics concrete—that is, to articulate a particular program, organization, and so on, given male constraints on Chicanas.[10]

The situation faced by Chicanas was made more complex by cultural nationalism and the need to frame their initial political choices through this perspective. The dominance of men in the movements was reinforced by the ideology of cultural nationalism that rested on the centrality of patriarchy within their constructed tradition of Mexican/Chicano culture.[11] The Chicano activist Rodolfo "Corky" Gonzales provided an example of this attitude: "I recognize too much of an influence of white European thinking in the discussion. I hope that our Chicana sisters can understand that they can be front runners in the revolution, they can be in the leadership of any social movement, but I pray to God that they do not lose their *Chicanisma* or their womanhood and become a frigid *gringa*. So I'm for equality, but I still want to see some sex in our women."[12] El movimiento had little interest in ending patriarchy.[13] From the start, Chicanas had to contest cultural nationalism as part of patriarchy; García went so far as to propose that cultural nationalism was irreconcilable to feminism.[14] It was patriarchy that led to the development of women's groups within MEChA and the eventual need to separate from the organization.[15]

At the same time, many of these same Chicanas retained an ambivalent relationship with cultural nationalism. While Chicanas raised their voices "in a collective feminist challenge to the sexism and male domination that they were experiencing with the movimiento," they also sought to retain an ambiguous link with el movimiento's nationalist articulation.[16] "From their nationalist base," García wrote, "these Chicana activists began to evolve also as feminists."[17] Many early Chicana activists used a redefined notion of nationalism and *chicanismo* as a unifying worldview. This did not mean that Chicanas closed their eyes to sexism.[18] Rather, Chicanas acknowledged that their struggle was against both sexism and racism.[19] "As a result, feminism, as articulated by women of color, represented an ideology and political movement to end patriarchal oppression within the structure of a cultural nationalist movement."[20]

For this reason, García believes that the Chicanas' struggle was both nationalist (redefined) and gendered, opening up the possibility for Chicana feminist thought. Activists and scholars Elizabeth Martínez and Ed McCaughan have distinguished Chicanas' use of nationalism and chicanismo. For Chicanas, chicanismo did not simply affirm nationhood but reflected a sense of peoplehood coming together to survive oppression and cultural assimilation as well as to affirm their humanity. "We see the Chicanismo of working-class people as a movement against exploitation and oppression," they wrote, "a reflection of the reality of living in a racist society where the working class is segmented along racial lines."[21] Elena Garcia, from a different angle, has maintained that Chicana consciousness was part of chicanismo. She stresses that Chicanas were working within a cultural context and therefore had little connection with the women's movement: "As Chicanas we respect our men. We respect the home, the family."[22] While Chicanas prize home and family, they recognized that their place would not *only* be in the home with family. As Elena Garcia has exemplified, many Chicanas were willing to continue an ambivalent relationship with cultural nationalism since it was perceived as an emancipatory politics.[23]

The feminist activist Anna NietoGomez's "La Feminista" provided a summary of the different tendencies within the early Chicana movement.[24] After calling attention to the various oppressions that Chicanas face (racism, sexism, and "sexual racism"),[25] she notes that some rejected feminism as irrelevant and Anglo-inspired.[26] Many activists reasoned that if Chicanos did oppress women, this was the system's fault: "It is the economic structure that forces the Chicano to oppress the women because the whole world oppressed him."[27] Racism was seen as the predominant issue facing Chicanos(as) and to deal with sexism was to be drawn away from struggle. NietoGomez calls women who accepted this reasoning "loyalists." These Chicanas "were ready to defend their men against Anglo feminist infiltration in order to survive racial-economic oppression."[28] For the activist and anthropologist Adelaida Del Castillo, these "[n]onfeminists expressed the popular sentiments of the movement by reiterating that men were not the problem and that it was the responsibility of women to be supportive of them and of the movement in general."[29] Women who hold a contrary view, the "feministas," are perceived as antifamily, anti-Chicano/Mexican culture, anti-man, middle class, individualistic, materialistic, and therefore against el movimiento. They are seen as being on an Anglo bourgeois trip and are therefore driven by a non-Chicano set of values: ambition, selfishness, and competition.

The difference between nonfeminists or loyalists and feminists was therefore the weight they gave to race versus gender. An expression of this split was present at the first National Chicano Student Conference in Denver in 1969. The Chicana workshop at the conference has been used to exemplify the split between loyalists and *feministas*. Journalist and activist Enriqueta Longauex y Vásquez provided one of the first insights into the Denver workshop.[30] She recorded that when the women made their report to the full conference, the presenter simply stated: "It was the consensus of the group that the Chicana woman does not want to be liberated."[31] Longauex y Vásquez questioned why the presenter had not expanded on this statement. Maybe the women were "going along with the feelings of the men at the convention" as the best possible political option at the moment.[32] Given that Chicanas at the conference understood the key role women were playing in the movement, how to explain this particular political statement?

For Longauex y Vásquez, when Chicanas step out of the household to find work, their immediate family oppression multiplied. "Not only does she suffer the oppression that the Anglo woman suffers as a woman in the market of humanity," she explained, "but she must also suffer the oppression of being a minority person with a different set of values."[33] Thus the limits placed on the Chicana by the paternalistic rules of Mexican American social practices are reinforced by the general patriarchal and cultural practices she faces on a daily bases. Because of these experiences, Chicanas bring much to el movimiento; they realize that the struggle is not simply waged by the individual, but is a commitment from the family. For this reason, Longauex y Vásquez continued, "[w]hen a family is involved in a human rights movement, as is the Mexican American family, there is little room for a woman's liberation movement alone."[34] The reality of the Chicano(a) struggle is a total struggle by which women "help liberate the man and the man must look upon his liberation with the woman at his side."[35] Longauex y Vásquez interpreted the Denver resolution not so much as a rejection of women's liberation but as a recognition that the Chicano struggle had to be a community and family struggle.

How can we read Longauex y Vásquez's exegesis of the conference?
Did she articulate a loyalist or feminist position?[36] On the one hand,
she highlighted the dual oppression Chicanas faced (racism and sexism)
as well as the patriarchal nature of Chicano/Mexican culture. Without
doubt, this part of her analysis could place her among the feministas.
On the other hand, her political choice to accept the family, and other
expressions of nationalism, as central to the political struggle, suggested
that the "Chicana woman does not want to be liberated" without the
Chicano.[37] With this reading, she could be seen as a loyalist. While
NietoGomez's contends that a clear distinction exists between loyalist
and feminist, it is difficult to place particular activists cleanly in one or
the other camp. As Longauex y Vásquez's explication of the women's
position at the Denver conference demonstrates, most Chicanas fluctu-
ated between the two positions, with shifting valuations of race and
gender.[38] It seems that NietoGomez's delineation was based on what she
perceived to be the best tactical position to take relative to Anglo society, the women's movement, and Chicano sexism. Given a particular
situation, political tactics shifted according to the conflicting demands
of race and gender. Women's political positions varied because of their
articulation (or lack thereof) of a gendered analysis of el movimiento's
cultural nationalism and their determination of the negative impact
of Chicano patriarchy. Because of this continuum of choices, even the
most radical Chicana activists would still identify (at particular points)
with the collective Chicano struggle.[39] For this reason, one person's
loyalist might be someone else's feminist and vice versa.

Simultaneously, the difficulty in distinguishing loyalists and feministas reflected male-imposed limitations on women's political choices.[40]
The historian Cynthia Orozco has highlighted four sexist ideologies
that emerged from Chicana confrontation with el movimiento: "(1) 'El
problema es el gabacho no el macho'; (2) feminism was Anglo, middle-
class, and bourgeois;[41] (3) feminism was a diversion from the 'real' and
'basic' issues, that is, racism and class exploitation; and (4) feminism
sought to destroy 'la familia,' supposedly the base of Mexican culture
and the basis for resistance to domination."[42] Of course, one can add
the perennial complaint that women wanted to be men.[43] Chicanos told
Chicanas that the search for a space for gender was void.[44] Therefore,
some feministas found themselves in battle with both men and women
who refused to recognize the importance of sexism.[45]

These differences among Chicanas exploded at the first National

Chicana Conference held in Houston in 1971: "The contradictions of the role of 'La Mujer' in the Movement, were crystallized at the First National Chicana Conference held in Houston Texas in May 1971, where more than 600 Chicanas from 23 states participated."[46] The activist Mirta Vidal believes that the conference manifested a rising consciousness among Chicanas, marking a break with the statement made by women at the Denver youth conference. This new consciousness was foreshadowed at workshops set up by women at the Mexican American Political Association (MAPA) conference in Wisconsin, the three youth conferences in Denver, the United Farm Workers Organizing Committee (UFWOC) boycott conference in Texas, the Mexican American National Issues conference in Sacramento, the action of women in La Raza Unida Party, and the Los Angeles pre-Houston conference. Furthermore, numerous publications—in particular, *Regeneración, El Grito del Norte,* and *Hijas de Cuauhtémoc*—articulated this consciousness.

At the Houston conference, Chicanas discussed women's control of their bodies (sex, abortion, birth control, marriage), how to break the pattern of patriarchal practices, child care, and education. They rejected the Church's use of religion to control women and their bodies. Chicanas spoke about the changing women's role in the family. Some argued that attempts to preserve *la familia* and other aspects of the Mexican cultural heritage were only another mechanism used to keep women in their place. The issue of reproductive rights became a point of contention. At the same time, the women recognized el movimiento by acknowledging *El Plan de Aztlán* and calling on men to support their multileveled struggle.[47] Women, Vidal claimed, have awakened to the triple form of oppression they face: "as members of an oppressed nationality, as workers, *and* as women."[48]

Issues of women's control over their bodies, however, clashed with the philosophy that marriage and motherhood were central to el movimiento. In response to these discussions, a contingent of women walked out of the conference. For journalist and activist Francisca Flores, "the women who believe that women in the Chicano community must submit to the dominance of the men walked out."[49] She contends that the right of self-determination by Mexican American and Mexican women over their bodies is not simply a white feminist issue.[50] Rather, the problem is a Chicano philosophy that believes a Chicana's place is in the home, fulfilling her role as mother, and that any attempt to challenge this position is an attack on Mexican and Chicano culture and heritage.[51] In response to this viewpoint, Flores avowed: "OUR CULTURE HELL!"[52] For Flores, the criticism launched against Chicanas who sought to reclaim control over their bodies hid problems within the community.[53] Elizabeth Olivarez has elaborated on Flores's critique of the walkouts. She acknowledges "that the discrimination against her within her culture in many instances took the same form as with her Anglo and black counterparts and, in some instances, took a more oppressive form as a consequence of certain contributing factors."[54] Activist and scholar Consuelo Nieto has added that Chicanas must demand their position within the women's movement, "which allows her to practice feminism within the context of her own culture."[55]

UCLA Chicanas, some of whom had participated in the Houston walkouts, saw the conference differently. For these women, the conference did not deal with the central issue of self-determination; rather, the discussions were controlled by "reformists," "feminists," and "self-appointed arbitrators."[56] They believed that the feminists had argued that the family unit was the enemy, while *movimiento* Chicanas" maintained that "ours is a struggle of a people, la Raza, for self-determination and survival and that in our struggle we will fight to keep those values that make us Raza and not lose sight of our philosophical and intellectual heritage."[57] Chicana womanhood had to be understood within the concept of Aztlán. Furthermore, to underscore their point, critics of the conference alleged that the white conference organizers (the YWCA) had excluded barrio Chicanas.[58] Thus a local barrio organization had asked Chicanas to protest the conference. The UCLA contingent asserted that two-thirds of the participants walked out and continued the conference in the barrio and affirmed the statements of *las madres* of San Diego: "[e]s nuestro deber como hermanas, madres, y compañeras luchar por el bien estar de la familia y de nuestra gente" (it is our duty as sisters, mothers, and partners to struggle for the health of the family and our community).[59] Furthermore, they called upon all to protest the war in Vietnam and to affirm *El Plan Espiritual de Aztlán*.

To support these women's critique, *La Gente de Aztlán*, a UCLA Chicano(a) campus paper, republished an essay by Velia Garcia. The editors appeared to want their readers to link Garcia's criticism of the white women's movement with Chicana criticism of the conference. Garcia's piece had originally appeared in Berkeley's *Chicano Studies*

Newsletter. She starts by stating that the women's liberation movement "seems to hold little or no appeal for the majority of Chicanas on the University campus."[60] The women's movement premise was unacceptable to many Chicanas. White women were struggling against the influence of white men; in contrast, Chicanas and Chicanos struggled *together* against the forces of racism and economic exploitation.[61] Yet Garcia acknowledged that there were issues that Chicanas and the women's movement could agree on. Clearly, the two groups agreed in the struggle for equal access to education.

Moreover, the radical faction in the women's movement understood the role of racism in the United States. Unfortunately, they focused on the "maleness of our present social system."[62] This was a problem. "We aren't oppressed by Chicanos," Garcia wrote, "we're oppressed by a system that serves white power and depends upon a white majority for its survival and perpetuation. In our struggle we identify our men, not white women, as our natural allies."[63] This was not to suggest that no difference existed between Chicanas and Chicanos. Certainly, Chicanas resented the romanticized notions men have about Chicanas and the limited roles they perceive women could accomplish. But they got together around *la familia.*[64] Garcia asserted that Chicanos(as) are a communal people who value cooperative, interpersonal relationship. Their notion of *familia* is different from that of the white middle-class nuclear family.[65]

In this spirit, we can also add Longeaux y Vasquez's essay that appeared in José Armas's *El Cuaderno.*[66] She fears that the women's movement is a threat to Chicano culture by its "attack" on the family. She maintains that Chicanas have to be Chicanos(as) first; "we want to walk hand in hand with our Chicano brothers, with our children, our *viejitos*, our *Familia de La Raza.*"[67] At the center of Chicano(a) concerns, Longeaux y Vasquez argues, are our children, who represent our only means of cultural survival.[68] Chicanas and Chicanos need to work together to fight a colonial structure that is trying to destroy the family. She also seems to reject abortion as a Chicana choice.[69] While Chicanos(as) might feel sympathy with the women's movement, Chicanas cannot identify with their struggle. "In the white women's liberation movement," Longeaux y Vasquez explained, "we see issues that are relevant to that materialistic, competitive society of the Gringo."[70] It is in fact this competitive perspective that led white women to conclude that men are the enemy. For this reason, their demands for equality mean different things to the Chicana and the Chicano movement. Longauex y Vásquez restates her premise: the Chicana "chooses to become a Chicana PRIMERO (first), to stand by and for her people, then she has become stronger by joining the struggle and endurance of her people."[71] Chicanas cannot blame Chicanos for their oppression: "Our men are not the power structure that oppresses us as a whole."[72]

I believe that Velia Garcia's and Longeaux y Vasquez's essays, in conjunction with the various critiques of the Houston conference, might represent an expression of a loyalist position. These essays did not deny the existence of sexism in el movimiento; they differed with the feministas on how to deal with sexism. Part of the problem was their inability to balance gender, race, and culture. Loyalists often reduced gender to an epiphenomenal concern that was politically ineffectual—a simple diversion for middle-class white women. They refused to put gender on the same level as race and culture, nor could they perceive how issues of the body could be important to the Mexican American community. At the same time, the women's movement was used as a boogey-woman. They accepted a stereotypical picture that presented the women's movement as only Anglo and upper- and middle-class. There was even a reluctance to engage the black women's movement.

The determining issue for loyalists was the impact of nationalism. Some women who wished to transform their communities felt they had to remain tied to el movimiento and therefore negotiate their autonomy. They accepted nationalism as the only tool for the political transformation of the Mexican American community and by implication acknowledged a romanticized notion of the family. They felt that the Houston Chicanas had jettisoned the only political tool available to challenge Anglo domination in favor of gender. To accuse them of being male-identified would be too strong; nonetheless, their desire to be active politically, especially in those early years, blinded them to the possibility of gender as a political and intellectual tool. This put them into direct confrontation with women who were progressively being pushed aside by el movimiento because of their feminist politics.[73]

In a fascinating poem, Elma Barrera and NietoGomez express their frustration with the events of the Houston conference. While they had organized the conference with good intentions, they start their poem, it ended in a fiasco—the walkout. Its failure, they add, changed the lives of some: "We really had no idea, women, Chicanas could be so misinformed about one another."[74] They were accused of being man-haters, against Chicanos and Chicanas, socialists, communists, middle-class, women's libbers, and so on. These women came with the experience on "[h]ow to criticize, protest, demand, take-over. . . . And more than anything, condemn each other." "Si supieran," Barrera and NietoGomez lament, "esas mujeres la agonía que nos causaron" (If those women only knew what harm they have caused us).[75] Maybe, paraphrasing their words, people will not remember the events of this conference, but we learned about "mujeres in the movement . . . About how some of us operate . . . right or wrong."[76] The problem is the failure of Chicanas to understand themselves and their differences together with a particular style of protest. Barrera and NietoGomez were shocked that Chicanas would resort to the same tactic that Chicanos had used against Anglos. One cannot escape the frustration they felt with Chicanas as a whole.[77]

The women who walked out of the Houston conference laid claim to representing the interest of Chicanas—especially on college campuses.[78] Their notion of how to work with Chicanos and their particular articulation of nationalism and/or eventually Marxism evolved into *the* Chicana position. For example, Bernice Rincon has indicated that Chicanas developed a strategy that would enable them to be "women people, rather [than] chattels or pets," retaining a balance between men and women.[79] As proof of this alliance, women had to reject the women's movement since it was unable to see beyond women's liberation. The statement that "one had to avoid the white feminist movement" became a mantra.[80] An early illustration of this was the MEChA Chicana Caucus at Stanford University in 1970. These women decided that they were not interested in joining the Anglo woman's liberation movement, since they did not want to compete with men. Rather, "[w]e want to be in on the decision making if we are 'leaders' and to work beside our men as equals."[81] Henri Chavez has written that "[t]he woman and the man must collaborate effectively without feeling humiliated."[82] As Sylvia Delgado has suggested, men must understand that liberation cannot be just for some.[83]

How deep was the division among Chicanas? Clearly the events in Houston left many hurt feelings. The nationalist articulations that led to the walkouts increasingly dominated Chicanas(os) on campuses. Some women decided that they could not work with Chicano-dominated organizations. While they were willing to battle by accepting a muted expression of nationalism, they also wanted to harmonize their politics with gender. Often this meant moving away from the mainstream of el movimiento. Thus, many women turned toward Chicana-centered organizations. NietoGomez embodied such a turn. She argued that the tension among Chicanas resulted from not understanding the differences and similarities between the Anglo and Chicana feminists and their movements. While they may be both women, they have different ethnic, cultural, and class positions. Chicanas share with other women issues that affect them as women, such as welfare, birth control, abortion, and employment. However, because of racism, these issues take on another dimension. Chicanas must reject Anglo feminists' beliefs that the problems of women can unite women and overcome racial differences. This is evident in the many attempts to participate with the Anglo women's movement.[84] Thus, although Chicanas share certain problems as women, the issues become distinct because of race.[85] The Chicana needs to contest both racism and sexism to deal with the oppression of poverty. Ironically, just like Chicanos demanded that Chicanas leave behind their concerns with gender, many white women's organizations demanded that Chicanas leave race behind—also in the name of solidarity.[86]

Chicana and Latina feministas constructed many organizations to develop their social and political agendas. Among these groups were the Comisión Feminil Mexicana, Mexican American National Women's Association (MANA), Hispanic Women's Council (HWC), Mujeres Unidas, Mexican American Business and Professional Women, National Chicana Coalition, Mujeres Pro-Raza Unida, Chicana Caucus of the National Women's Political Caucus, and others.[87] To fully understand Chicana/Latina political behavior, it is important to explore the positions taken by these organizations. Often they had conflicting views that appeared in particular settings, like the United Nations conference for the International Women's Year in Mexico City in 1975.[88] Unfortunately, this book cannot do justice to this important topic.

An alternative to the loyalist-feminist dichotomy was a developing expression of Chicana(o) socialism. The activist and scholar Adelaida Del Castillo has argued that Chicana organizing had a limited impact on el movimiento, especially in light of a nationalist resurgence in the 1970s: "It appeared, however, that a resurgent nationalism of the Chicano Movement drove many to confuse stereotypic traditional male/female concepts for actual viable roles. Paradoxically, while Mexican students fought for the democratic rights of Mexican people in general, the manner in which they implemented much of their political and organizational activities particularly limited the democratic participation of women."[89]

Del Castillo blames this situation on the ideological limitations of the Chicano movement: the limits placed on women's leadership role, the nasty campaigns against women, the multiple levels of sexist attitudes, and the structural character of organizations that dichotomized men and women's activity. Her solution was to turn to a class analysis to understand the condition of women.[90] "The personal, sociopolitical, and economic oppression of women contributes directly and indirectly to the power of capitalist oppression."[91] Del Castillo was not the first to articulate a socialist-feminist position. Josefina Lopez, for instance, proclaimed that Chicanas must struggle together with men in order to deal with discrimination, hunger, housing, education, unemployment, and the defense of the Chicano(a) culture.[92]

One could argue that the Chicana movement went in three directions—sometimes parallel, at others times at cross-purposes. In one direction were the women who organized the Houston conference. They turned their attention to creating and working with both Chicana and white organizations at a regional and national level. While a few of these women tried to negotiate with nationalists and/or Marxists, more often they sought to retain a relationship (often acrimonious) with the larger women's movement. These Chicanas many times found themselves excluded from the centers of Chicano studies power. In another direction were Chicanas who remained within el movimiento, albeit with ambivalence. These women understood the problem of sexism in society, the Chicano(a) community, and el movimiento. Yet they were willing to accept limitations if they could struggle for justice with el movimiento (La Raza Unida, the Crusade, or campus organizations like MEChA). The last current was Marxist Chicanas who avoided nationalist and feminist ideologies and organizations. Some pushed for a particular Marxist-Leninist organization. The difference among these currents was the balance activists sought to give race, gender, and class.[93]

Chicana Herstory and Critiques of Chicano Studies

Alma García has noted three approaches Chicanas used to bring their experiences into the frame of Chicano(a) intellectual production and

Chicano studies.[94] The first was to search for Chicanas as great women. This vision was to challenge the stereotype of Chicanas as passive, docile, and submissive. The second approach revised the Chicano(a) experience by focusing on Chicana participation in the labor force. The third method focused on the hierarchical relation that existed between men and women. This "approach explains the social location of Chicanas by emphasizing gender as a major explanatory variable."[95] According to García, some scholars within this camp articulated a theoretical synthesis of race, class, and gender.[96] García concludes that a combination of all three approaches is the only way to redefine the study of women within Chicano studies.

One particular set of Chicana writings sought to explicate the Chicana condition through an uncovering of herstory. These writings established a Chicana scholarly orientation and an initial intervention in Chicana theory and feminism. An early example of a Chicana periodical that bridged political action and intellectual production was the *Hijas de Cuauhtémoc* (1971). The *Hijas* "marked a critical historical moment in the development of Chicana feminist theories and practices and a gendered shift in the print culture of the Chicano movement."[97] Like other publications, the *Hijas* "provided a forum for Chicanas to dialogue across regions and social movement sectors, which was crucial to the formation of Chicana feminism."[98] In the first issue, essays reflected the debate among Chicanas about their political relationship with Chicanos and their organizations. In one essay, Rosita Morales argued that the Chicano movement did not necessarily benefit Chicanas, especially when one considered education. Morales underscored that the problem was culture: "La cultura mexicana no expone a La Chicana a mejores expectaciones otra de llegar a ser ama de casa" (Mexican culture does not provide Chicanas any better expectation than becoming a housewife).[99]

An essay by the Orange Country Brown Berets took a different direction. These women were critical of the disrespectful behavior of the Brown Berets Chicanos and their denial of women's potential role as activists. The authors observed that Brown Beret men were driven by their stereotypes of women: "These stereo-types are the byproducts of deep-macho hang-ups BATOS DEL MOVIMIENTO have."[100] These men assumed that they were leaders, while women were meant to do the chores. Men believed that the family was the central place for the reproduction of Chicano culture as an oppositional force. In contrast, the Orange County Brown Berets stressed that Chicanas have always been involved in social movements and therefore must be allowed to support and, more important, participate in the organization. The essay ended with a typical disclaimer. The position they presented was not about women's liberation ("that's a white thing") but about the liberation of La Raza, which all Chicanos(as) have to achieve together. Just like Chicana activists, the women in the Brown Berets struggled to balance their analysis of gender with race and culture, to avoid accusations of diverting el movimiento. In this way, essays published in *Hijas* moved between political debate and herstory.

From the start, Chicanas elaborated a Chicana version of herstory to contest a Chicano and Anglo narrative that either left Chicanas out or turned women into some form of camp follower. A series of essays drew attention to "heroic" women such as the *soldaderas* of the Mexican Revolution or intellectuals like Sor Juana Inez de la Cruz. The writer Gema Matsuda provided a quick overview of this women-centered history in the first part of her essay.[101] Adelaida Del Castillo's essay on Malinche/Marina/Malintzin Tenépal was the best example of this style of writing.[102] Feminist scholar Maylei Blackwell contended that the study of women's history provided "a sense of historical agency" that had been denied to Chicanas.[103] Ramon Gutierrez pointed out that Chicanas shifted the point of origins for the study of the Mexican American experience. While Chicanos used 1848 as the break, Chicanas began their history with 1519, and in that way placed gender and conquest at the center of Chicano(a) history. Thus, herstory created an epistemological shift away from chicanismo and carnalismo to *mexicanidad* and *mestizaje*.[104] But Chicana-story was only the beginning.

Encuentro Feminil was the first journal to identify itself as feminist. Given birth by women from the student group "Hijas de Cuauhtémoc" and possibly the local Third World Liberation Front, the journal had an independent life from the organization.[105] They shared an understanding that "our struggle is racial as well as sexual."[106] The journal editors recognized that it was necessary to challenge the picture that Chicanas were second-class citizens. This did not mean that Chicanas wanted "to emulate men, instead we'd like to see the efforts of enlightened women bring about the correction of inconsistencies and injustices now present."[107] Chicanas fought for feminism as an effort to struggle for all Chicanos(as). They explained that "feminism is not necessarily incompatible with our people's struggle, nor does it distract from our Movement's effort; instead, it can enhance them."[108] The editors at *Encuentro Feminil* retained gender at the center of their political and intellectual concerns; they saw gender as complementary to race and culture in el movimiento. Many of the articles in the journals of the time reflected this vision.

Anna NietoGomez played a central role in both Hijas de Cuauhtémoc and *Encuentro Feminil*.[109] Her intellectual work provided the building blocks for Chicana feminism. Writers as diverse as Adelaida Del Castillo and Cynthia Orozco have recognized the centrality of NietoGomez's work. Del Castillo, for instance, has documented that while a student at California State College at Long Beach, NietoGomez organized and taught courses on La Chicana. With others, she set up the journal *Hijas de Cuauhtémoc*. Later, NietoGomez was the catalyst for the "first Chicana feminist journal, *Encuentro Feminil*." Her essay "La Feminista," Del Castillo points out, "along with the work of Martha Cotera of Texas represents one of the most important statements of Chicana feminism of the period."[110] Orozco has emphasized that NietoGomez was both an intellectual and an activist.[111] She presented the first written expression of a Chicana feminism that articulated an intellectual agenda *for* Chicanas *by* Chicanas. It was NietoGomez's spirit that permeated Hijas de Cuauhtémoc and *Encuentro Feminil*.[112]

In her piece "Madres por Justicia," NietoGomez highlighted the type of analysis one encountered in *Encuentro Feminil*. She affirmed the need to understand government policy toward welfare recipients— in particular, the Talmadge Amendment to the Social Security Act— and to develop a political strategy to contest how politicians dealt with women and minorities on welfare. Aside from presenting an analysis of the inadequacy of welfare and its impact on Chicanas, NietoGomez directed attention to organizations like Madres de Justicia that were organizing to defend the rights of poor women, especially the work of Alicia Escalante, who organized the Chicana Welfare Rights Organization. This essay bridged the concerns of the Chicana community with the academy and in the process provided a possible action to change existent conditions.[113] NietoGomez worked closely with organizations that sought to improve the conditions for poor Chicanas and to develop courses on the Chicana to challenge the masculinist vision of Chicano studies.

Another essay in *Encuentro Feminil* was Corinne Sanchez's "Higher

Education y La Chicana?" Here the author discussed the situation Chicanas were facing in education—in particular on the college campus. Just as Chicanos had earlier questioned whether educational opportunity programs were working for them, Chicanas were now asking the same question. Sanchez examined the curriculum "choices" women made in college. Chicanas have little input on program activities, no presence in decision-making positions, and need to fight with males who have degrading conceptions of women.[114] What are the possible solutions? She proposed to develop a Chicana ad hoc committee to recommend how to integrate women in these programs, write a position paper to analyze the status and needs of college women, and recruit and hire Chicanas in administrative positions.

In the essay "The Chicana Perspectives for Education," NietoGomez expanded on Sanchez's ideas. She summarized many of her earlier ideas, and more sharply declared her differences with the loyalists. She made it clear that "motherhood" and the family are *not* the definition of women or the Chicana. "As more and more Chicanas begin to realize their aspirations through higher education," NietoGomez wrote, "motherhood no longer becomes the primary goal in the 'typical' Chicana's life."[115] It is not even the place to start the conversation about Chicana options. She followed this with a critique of society's endeavor to construct women and rationalize their discrimination. She ably used Anglo women's critique of patriarchy to explore gender stereotyping with the racial constructions of Chicanas, especially when it came to the family: "The identity of a Chicana is often defined as the girlfriend, wife, or sister of a particular man."[116] She expanded on resolutions from the Houston conference that dealt with sex, birth control, and abortion. In the process, she also threw down the gauntlet to those Chicanas(os) who appeared to suggest that Chicanas should accept their roles as mothers and nurturers because that was part of Chicano/Mexican culture and the struggle. NietoGomez said: "It perpetuates the idea that the only way she can change society is to bring more brown faces into the world."[117] She stressed that "[i]t is important that the Chicano movement recognize the sexual as well as the racial discrimination of this society, and how it manifests itself within the movement."[118] Only when we deal with sexual oppression between Chicanos and Chicanas can there be an effective movement.

NietoGomez concluded the essay with a plan of action for "Estudios de la mujer chicana." Like Chicanos who demanded courses that analyzed and sought solutions for the Mexican American experience, NietoGomez made the same call for Chicanas. Given the paradigms in Chicano studies, the study of the Mexican American experience did not deal with women and the prejudice they face by a patriarchal and racist society and the Mexican American community. Therefore Chicanas needed courses that could help them create a sense of identity and understand their role in society. NietoGomez suggested classes like the "The Chicana in Education," "The History of the Chicana," "The Chicana and the Law," "Religion and La Mujer," "The Cultural-Psycho-Physiological Realities de la Mujer y el Hombre," and a possible class on the human body. The goal was to institute parallel courses on the Chicana with already established courses on the Chicano experience; it is not enough to have simply one universal class on La Chicana. During a Mujer workshop at a MEChA conference at California State University at Northridge in 1972, where NietoGomez had begun teaching, she proposed that all Chicano studies majors take at least one course on the Chicana.[119]

By 1976, NietoGomez made her points more sharply in her discussion of Chicana feminism. This was part of her reaction to the growing presence and success of loyalists and the establishment of Empirical Chicano Studies. She dismissed any discussion that somehow Chicanas and feminism did not go together. In her piece "Chicana Feminism," she took exception to the need to explain that feminism is not an Anglo issue: "I resent the usual remark that if you're a feminist you have somehow become an Anglo or been influenced by Anglos."[120] She proclaimed that feminism is a worldwide issue that has been at the center of women's concerns. Therefore the "differences" between the Chicana feminist movement and the Anglo women's movement are "irrelevant." Furthermore, she explained, the attempt to dismiss the Anglo women's movement as middle class is false. The women's movement is as diverse as the Chicano movement; Chicanas can be liberal feminists, radical feminists, Marxists, and women's liberationists. Chicanas needed to make the Chicano movement responsive to Chicana issues; the movement must "address itself to the double standard about male and female workers, and making it live up to its cry of Carnalismo and community responsibility."[121] The problem, she said, is male denial. NietoGomez recognized that Chicanos may not have power, yet they seem "to try to compensate for that lack of power with the use of 'male privilege'—coming down with the double standard."[122]

But not all women who participated in *Encuentro Feminil* thought alike or agreed on their understanding of the relationship between Chicanas and el movimiento.[123] Adelaida Del Castillo, for instance, sought a closer tie to el movimiento and wanted to retain greater distance from the women's movement. "We're not going to ally ourselves to white feminists who are part of the oppressors," she wrote.[124] A great cultural difference existed between Chicano and Anglo cultures. While Chicanas may share certain issues with white feminists—like welfare, education, child care, birth control, the law, and so on—they mean different things because of cultural and class differences. It is unfortunate, however, that Chicanos do not understand the importance of Chicana feminism. She called for increased communication among Chicanos(as) so that a united movement could exist.

The work of writer and activist Martha Cotera provided another expression of early Chicana herstory. Her *Profile on the Mexican American Woman* (the historical sections were republished in *Diosa y Hembra: The History and Heritage of Chicanas in the U.S.*) provided the first text on the Chicana experience.[125] Cotera's book straddled the aim of developing a political response to Chicanos and Anglos, while providing an introduction to Chicanas' endeavors to explain and narrate their experience. In her historical narrative, Cotera detailed the continuity with earlier Mexican and Mexican American female activists. Reacting to accusations of being "*agringadas*," "anglocized," "feminists," and "anti-traditionalists," she sought to disprove men's (and society's) stereotype of Mexican women.[126] This research, she wrote, "has provided ample evidence about the high status and the strength of the Mexican and Mexican American woman."[127] Cotera's text was a political manifesto against Chicano political dismissal of the Chicanas' role in the past and present as well as a call for participation in community work.[128] Chicana feminism needed to engage both issues of sex and race.[129] Yet Cotera concluded that the main issue for women, like men, was racism and the destruction of Chicano(a) cultural traditions.[130] "What is stronger: racism or sexism?" she asked, "I believe racism."[131]

The critic Sylvia Gonzales provided a different approach to the concerns expressed by NietoGomez and Cotera.[132] Her interest was literature and literary criticism. In her essay she described a conference she designed on Latin American writers, with a central role for Chicanas. She illustrates the tension among women writers at the Inter-

American Women Writers Congress (1976): "the San Jose Congress . . . was a microcosmic venture into the contemporary attitudes and status not only of women, but also cultural values and traditions."[133] Women reflected the same division as men over the role of gender. Nonetheless, the problem remained men's obstructionist role. Gonzales expressed that "[i]t is the Chicano who must move aside and allow the Chicana a place in the creative world of words, canvas and music."[134] Chicanas struggled to make sure that their writing received the attention it deserved.[135] An issue of *De Colores,* also known as *La Cosecha,* was dedicated to Chicana writings. Nevertheless, questions over leadership, Gonzales believed, still undercut Chicana unity as evident at the National Hispanic Feminist conference in 1980.[136]

Sylvia Gonzales used Paulo Freire's *Pedagogy of the Oppressed* as a way to think about the academic Chicana project. She argued that "[t]he works of Freire can serve as significant foundations for a feminist pedagogy."[137] She understands the process of "concientización" to mean self-actualization. When looking at the state in which women found themselves, she recorded that the duality of Chicana oppression is much more fluid than typically conceived. Gonzales added that the emphasis on economic deprivation created a hierarchy of oppression that often can make women's issues irrelevant. By using Freire's notion of power, Chicanas could understand that such a hierarchy of oppressions only helps women's pacification. "Freire has said that in order for the oppressed not to become oppressor," Gonzales wrote, "the violence of the oppressor must be eliminated. Discrimination, racism, sexism are violent acts that kill the spirit and the very essence of the person affected."[138] The path toward a resolution to oppression is education. "Thus, a feminist education would be the tool for linking knowledge of our oppression with a new statement of power."[139] Gonzales then turned to the situation of the Chicana to begin this transformation. She believes that this change must begin within the Chicana first. Self-awareness is the catalyst for action. "Women must not force change on others," she explained, "but instead require change by changing themselves."[140] Then the process of establishing a new order can start. Gonzales pointed out the universality of the Chicana's cause.[141]

The intellectual work of Chicanas like NietoGomez, Cotera, and Gonzales grew out of their political involvement.[142] Their essays and those in the early feminist journals would be difficult to see solely as academic literature; their works were political and polemical. Other contemporaries who followed in their footsteps added to the development of this early Chicana thought, even though they had divergent and often competing views.[143] Differences in class, sexual orientation, political strategies, political goals and objectives, academic status, and relationships with white feminist organizations and Chicanos were central to this variety of intellectual expressions of Chicana herstory and their criticisms of el movimiento. But all these works set the foundation for the next stage of Chicana intellectual work.[144]

Three different intellectual agendas guided Chicanas' recovery and examination of their experiences as well as the development of a theoretical expression for Chicana thought. First was the work of Chicanas who examined the double oppression Chicanas faced: race, ethnicity, nationality, or culture, in addition to gender. Chicanas faced oppression because of their status as women by men of all colors; they faced rejection by white women because of their ethnicity, race, national origins, and/or culture. Chicanas differed on how they saw the equilibrium of these two features, at times paralleling the political split among activists. A second perspective found in some Chicana writings was the impact of Marxist theory in understanding the Chicana condition. Chicanas differed over the relationship they attached to class with race, ethnicity, nationality, culture, as well as gender in understanding the Mexican American women's experience. In the majority of cases, class was the determining factor in explaining the Chicana condition. The last possible option was the least developed. To capture the Mexican American women's experience, one negotiated through the interplay of race, ethnicity, nationality, culture, class, and gender. The difficulty in this approach arose from sustaining the independence of the categories and then tracing their interaction. The Mexican American women's experience could not be reduced to simply an explanation of her race, ethnicity, nationality, culture, class, and gender experience as independent experiences. The "intersection" meant more than just the addition of the three oppressions.

Chicana Intellectual Production
and the Genesis of Chicana Feminisms

The next cohort of Chicanas in the university benefited from the political and intellectual work of these trendsetters. Based on their work, academic Chicanas constructed an intellectual and physical space for themselves and other Chicanas within the academy. Many commenced from their social science or humanities training, like most male scholars, and found themselves in the perspectivist or empiricist camp. Others conflicted with their training and the various Chicano studies perspectives; they ended up looking for some alternative. Yet many of these women came together because of their need to negotiate with gender—especially if they were forced to reduce gender's importance in a hierarchy of oppressions. Their work, often in conflict over how to understand gender, created the terrain for a women-centered perspective within Chicano studies. The institutionalization of Chicano Studies under empiric control did little to ameliorate the sexism within both el movimiento and Chicano Studies. Orozco holds that Chicano intellectuals saw race or class (or a hybrid of both) as the determining factors in understanding the Mexican American experience. Gender, she emphasizes, was irrelevant to their analysis. She uses Rodolfo Acuña's *Occupied America* as an example of this type of analysis. As a result, scholars suppressed feminism and repressed feminists, leaving Chicano Studies underdeveloped. Orozco concludes that scholars had to understand the significance of gender for the field to truly grow.[145]

Flirting with Empirical Chicano Studies yet seeking a space for gender was the work of Margarita Melville. In her introduction to *Twice a Minority: Mexican American Women,* she comments that Chicanas have not been present in social science literature, except in a few discussions about the family. Melville provides empirical data on Mexican American women that was not stereotypical. The essay portrays "a population of women who attempt, with varying degrees of success, to fit into the mainstream of American life without losing their identity as Mexicans or their love of many aspects of Mexican culture."[146] Melville accepts a process of assimilation that leaves Chicano(a) identity intact. She hopes that this empirical data will make Mexican American women more visible and provide Anglo society as well as Mexican American men with information to gain an insight into the Chicana experience. She draws attention to Chicanas who are minorities because of both their race and gender.[147] In the end, Melville calls for "advocative social science" that responds to the needs and values of the population.[148]

Sociologist Maxine Baca Zinn's work should be read in conjunction with Melville. Like Melville, she demonstrated strong control of social science literature. She was critical of the assumptions this literature made of Chicanos, especially Chicanas. In her piece "Gender and Ethnic Identity among Chicanos," she demonstrates the negative depictions of Chicanas produced by social science. She offers the reader a different and more flexible understanding of gender and ethnicity in order to understand Mexican American life conditions. Baca Zinn points out Chicanas' multiple identities that flow from the interaction of these categories. "[I]f we are to comprehend the nature of Chicana identity," she wrote, "we had best attempt to understand the dynamic relationship between gender and ethnicity."[149] By redefining ethnic and gender identities, Chicanas provide a double reading of the concept that reveals their subordination as women of color. Baca Zinn hopes that research will come to a point where Chicanas(os) no longer have to ask whether gender or ethnicity is more important. In a different essay she reexamines this point by exploring Chicano masculinity. She again uses the tools of social science to provide a critique of the cultural stereotype of machismo, without dismissal of patriarchal power relations.[150] As Karen Mary Davalos has characterized it, Baca Zinn's work was an example of scholarship that moved beyond Romano's and Paredes's critiques of Anglo anthropological work. In particular, Davalos draws attention to Baca Zinn's introduction of Chicana subjectivity as it overlapped with the politics of research.[151] In this fashion, Baca Zinn's work problematized the cultural analysis of the Chicana experience— in particular, the family.[152]

Melville's and Baca Zinn's work typified the initial analysis of Mexican American women's experience as both women and as a racial/ethnic group. The educator Cecilia Cota-Robles de Suarez has written of this dual nature: "The Chicana . . . carries a double burden when it comes to stereotypes. For not only is she discriminated against as a woman, but she is also discriminated against as a member of an ethnic group which has a long history of prejudicial treatment by the dominant society."[153] The research of many Chicana scholars toiled to understand the relationship of gender and race/ethnicity/culture in the Chicana experience. This was clear in many articles that appeared in *Regeneración, Encuentro Feminil,* and off and on in *El Grito del Norte.* As more women successfully learned the art of their academic disciplines and wrote articles, they provided a collection of essays that examined the condition of Mexican American women by looking at Chicanas' double oppression. A series of articles in the *Hispanic Journal of Behavioral Sciences* from 1982 provided a nice example.[154] Following in their footsteps was Lea Ybarra's work.[155] Nor should one think that the double-minority perspective faded over time. We encounter this perspective well into the 1980s. For instance, Marcela Lucero has asserted that Chicanas were "fighting not only sexism but also racism, and in some cases marianism."[156]

Coming from a different angle was Adaljiza Sosa Riddell's "Chicanas and El Movimiento." Sosa Riddell calls for research that looks at gender, race, and class. She believes that the most important issue faced by el movimiento is Chicanas. Like other writers, she discloses the defensive attitude of Chicanos toward the Chicana challenge. However, she explains this reaction as the result of "externally-imposed stereotypes" about Chicanas.[157] Sosa Riddell builds on Chicano(a) criticisms of social science to shift the explanation of Chicano behavior away from concepts like machismo and therefore by implication sexism. She writes: "Machismo is a myth propagated by subjugators and colonizers who take pleasure in watching their subjects strike out vainly against them in order to prove themselves still capable of action."[158] This becomes a political problem because Chicanas act upon these false beliefs.[159] "Chicanas may come to believe the external realities as equitable to the internal conditions. This is a dimension of being colonized."[160] Thus Sosa Riddell found little use for the women's movement. Chicanas who fall for that political orientation, with its emphasis on gender, break with the movement and her people. The solution is to integrate the Chicana into the movement so as to diminish the influence of external groups' manipulation of Chicanas.[161] Sosa Riddell did not provide an explanation of sexism within the Chicano(a) community. While her call for an articulation of gender, race, and class sought to go beyond research on the dual nature of Chicana oppression, her work did not accomplish this goal.

Some Chicanas shared issues with Perspectivist Chicano Studies. For instance, Isabelle Navar's *Regeneración* essay, which had initially appeared in *Encuentro Feminil*, drew attention to the different values that existed between Chicanas and the Anglo system. She criticized the U.S. "materialist system of values" that takes away our compassion and excitement and "produces a collective monster nation."[162] Fortunately, Chicanos(as) have been able to retain their emotions—culture and love as well as their strength and endurance that allows them to make their own decisions.[163] This feature has surprised, Navar pointed out, many Chicanos who "imagine us as they would have us, too often a shadow of their unrecognized desires."[164]

Another example was an essay by educator and activist Gracia

Molina de Pick. She stressed how el movimiento and the women's movement have depicted and constructed Chicanas. It is important to understand the Chicana experience.[165] Activist Bernice Rincon's piece tried to
combine the trajectories in Navar's and de Pick's essays.[166] Like Navar,
she drew attention to the different value systems that exist between
Anglos and Mexicans. She then noted how "traditionalist" Chicanos
idealized Chicana womanhood. She ended by drawing attention to
Chicanas' desires for recognition and responsibility.[167] Even Cotera's
piece in *La Luz* provided yet another example of this perspective vision
among Chicana thinkers, bringing us close to an essentialist view of
the Chicano(a). She argued: "This unique cultural history and genetic
blend had made us heirs to an aggregation of cultural values with very
specific moral, philosophical and religious traditions."[168]

One of the first books to deal with Chicanas was written by Evangelina Enríquez and Alfredo Mirandé.[169] Much of the work recapitulated what many women had written earlier; they merely provided a
colonialist framework to explain the "triple oppression" of Chicanas.
Instead of drawing attention to gender, race, and class, the authors
contend that Chicanas are "victims of attempted cultural genocide,"
gender oppression, and "an additional burden of internal oppression
by a cultural heritage that tends to be dominated by males and exag-
gerates male domination over women."[170] The text provided a historical, sociological, and literary overview of the experience of Mexican
American women from these three angles.[171] An example of Enríquez
and Mirandé's position was their discussion of the Chicano family.
They retained an intellectual relationship with nationalism through
their use of colonialism.[172] In their analysis of the family, they discuss
the difference between Anglo and Chicano families through their supposed cultural traits. They state that "Anglos are more individualistic,
so that even the family itself idealizes the development and accomplish-
ments of the individuals, whereas Chicanos are more oriented toward
the group and seek to enhance its welfare."[173] Furthermore, Enríquez
and Mirandé argue that Chicanos(as) place a greater emphasis on
familism and respect, deriving greater emotional gratification. In the
process, like much earlier literature, they are critical of myths created
by social science research on the Mexican American family. Ironically,
the authors reproduced a family that subordinated women by creating
an equally mythical Chicano version of the family.

The last chapter in Enríquez and Mirandé's book deals with Chicana feminism. They spend three-quarters of the chapter regurgitating much of Chicana herstory. They claim that this account forms the base of contemporary Chicana feminism. They then turn to their understanding of Chicana feminism. The authors claim that although "Chicana feminism is not impervious to Anglo feminism," "its roots are in Mexicana-Chicana feminism."[174] Enríquez and Mirandé see the rise of this perspective as the result of frustration when hard work and dedication go without recognition. They recognize that pressure was placed on Chicanas to forgo their concerns. They turn to NietoGomez's work to develop their argument.

Enríquez and Mirandé differ from NietoGomez because, while they acknowledge that both the Chicano movement and women's movement provided little space for Chicanas, they conclude that Chicanas need to work in combination with el movimiento. They write: "Chicana feminists hold that liberation will come neither from the Anglo women's movement nor from the Chicano movement but from a unique Chicana movement that works closely or in conjunction with the *movimiento* but is not subordinate to it."[175] In the end, the authors argue that the Chicana movement cannot be independent and different from the Chicano movement nor can it be tied to the white women's movement. The reason Chicanas will have to struggle with Chicanos, albeit in some nonoppressive setting, is due to the realities of colonization. In the process, the authors resurrect machismo by retaking the concept from Anglo social scientists and using Armando Rendon's vision of men in struggle for nationhood.[176] In the end, Mirandé and Enríquez added little to the understanding or development of Chicana feminism, but rather used the discussion to minimize Chicana criticisms of patriarchy in Chicano and Mexican culture. In fact, their turn to nationalism and the internal colonial model served to discount Chicano sexism.

Just as some Chicanas turned to the social sciences or the humanities to articulate an activist academic program, other Chicanas turned to Marxism with the same hope. Whatever Marxist orientation was used, these early Chicana Marxists articulated a position in which gender as well as race and ethnicity were subsumed by their class analysis.[177] For instance, Rosaura Sánchez in her 1977 piece examined the transformation of Chicana's social role as women entered the labor force and participated in labor struggles. She assumes that as Chicanas became workers "opportunities will develop to achieve independence and create new social roles which will not limit women to subservient positions."[178]

While she is cognizant of the limits imposed by "traditional roles of homemaker and housekeeper," Sánchez shies away from putting these patriarchal practices at the center of understanding Chicana reality or in any theoretical explication. Thus she concluded that Chicana professionals should acknowledge the working-class experience of the majority of Chicanas and "identify with their struggle rather than with middle class feminist aspirations."[179]

Linda Apodaca's essay "The Chicana Woman: An Historical Materialist Perspective" was the first extended endeavor to examine the Chicana experience from a Marxist perspective. Her piece explored the history of the Southwest from a materialist view. She contended that earlier perspectives that began by looking at culture and nationalism blocked any fundamental understanding of Chicanas. Only a class analysis, she explained, would lead to an understanding of the Chicana condition and a political plan of action.[180] She believed that the "particular subjugation of women must be understood in terms of class contradictions." To support her point, she provided a historical overview of the different modes of production and their transitions from the time of the Mexica to the present.[181]

The 1982 UCLA Chicano Studies Research Center international symposium on Mexicana/Chicana history offered an extended conversation over the role of Marxism within Chicana scholarship.[182] Although not all the presenters used a materialist perspective, many of the scholars did, forming a basis for *Between Borders: Essays on Mexican/Chicana History*.[183] While this text claimed to represent the most developed Marxist analysis of the Chicana experience that was possible in this period (early 1980s), much of it repeated Apodaca's earlier analysis. But it also included essays that demonstrated the limits of Chicana Marxism. One example was Juan Gómez-Quiñones's "Questions within Women's Historiography." Gómez-Quiñones recognized the erasure of women's experience in historical research as well as the unequal distribution of goods and power along gender lines and the propagation of practices that sustain this disadvantage. He wrote: "To understand the course of women in history and their situation at any given time requires understanding particular production priorities and organization of society in relation to how production is organized and how the young are cared for and trained."[184]

Gómez-Quiñones made the discussion of gender as dependent on production and economic organization of capitalist society alone, tying the discussion to reproductive labor. In fact, he left no space for any independent role for gender. He criticized recent "idealist" trends that suggested that feminism is "grounded in a distinct theory and episte- mology."[185] As if to mark the impossibility of such an epistemic shift, Gómez-Quiñones wrote: "What must be considered in any case is the possibility of a gendered differentiated epistemology for if demonstrated it would be a paradigmatic revolution of unprecedented proportions." He concluded that all "feminist writing is either an elaboration or cor- rection of this [Simone de Beauvoir's *The Second Sex*] magnificent critique which is the fulcrum of women studies discourse and at its base is undeniably Marxist and Western."[186] For Gómez-Quiñones, then, the "most innovative insights [produced by women's scholarship] are social and cultural rather than conceptual or methodological, i.e., how we know and are taught as opposed to how we organize and gather what we know."[187]

Cultural critic Sonia Saldívar-Hull hit the mark when she referred to Marxist analysis as limited for the Chicana experience. "To com- pletely understand the complexities of the Chicana and Chicano sub- jectivity in the greater borderlands of the United States," she wrote, "discussions of gender and sexuality are central in our oppositional and liberatory projects."[188] Like those scholars who used nationalism or turned to the dual nature of Chicana oppression, Marxists limited the role of gender in their endeavor to examine the Mexican American and Chicana experiences. Although these Marxists called attention to gender and race, they could not integrate these realities in their understanding of class. Their attachment to a Leninist-Stalinist version of Marxism left little space in the split of base and superstructure to assess how ideology and subjectivity are aspects of class and labor or a more complex understating of class.

One position that received little attention was the Third World per- spective. In reading the initial history of "Las Mujeres" at University of California at Santa Cruz, one can see an attempt to understand Chica- nas from a perspective that was open to all women of color. In this way, they sought to understand the Chicana condition from a more varied and concrete approach. In 1982, the women in this group organized a Third World Workshop with women from University of California at Berkeley, Stanford, and other northern California campuses.[189] By placing the Chicana within a world context of women's oppression and struggles for national liberation, they believed that Chicanas could find a space to talk about gender, race, and class—without surrendering one to the other.

While many scholars referred to the "triple oppression" of women, few articulated a theoretical or methodological position that could direct research outside the limits imposed by academic disciplines. For example, while a special issue of *Frontiers* on Chicanas pointed out that they "suffered from triple oppression—that of racial/ethnic discrimination, sexual discrimination, class bias, and often further discrimination because of their bilingualism," the articles did little to examine this condition or provide a methodology to explore these oppressions in interaction. In fact, like many pieces of this time period, the use of the term "triple oppression" was primarily rhetorical. Even by the early 1980s, Chicana scholars had not come to terms with how this triple oppression played itself out. In a review essay, Baca Zinn acknowledged that a "complete understanding of how capitalism, patriarchy, and racism operate together to subordinate women of color awaits conceptual development and empirical study."[190] She suggested that this possible analysis would not approach the three axes as separate and distinguishable. Rather, the three categories would coexist and influence each other to form identity. Thus, she called for a refinement of structural frameworks, though not at the expense of microlevel analyses. The scholar must start with the everyday worlds in order to "locate social experiences in a set of *social* relations."[191]

Unfortunately, the intellectual work of Chicana scholars received little respect and legitimacy in the university and throughout Chicano studies. Chicanas found little acceptance for their analysis of their experiences in the new institutions created by Chicano(a) campus activism.[192] Chicano studies remained both politically and intellectually a male bastion. Chicanos and a Chicano perspective dictated the institutional and intellectual practices of Chicano studies. Women who were able to enter this newly minted academic discipline faced programs that were dominated by men who acted out stereotypical assumptions about women's and men's fantasies about the role of women within a variety of patriarchal ideologies, methodologies, and epistemologies.

Chicanas even had to negotiate with men in their own conferences on "La Chicana." It was not unusual to find men, sometimes *only* men, presenting about the Chicana experience. One example was the symposium "Educación en Luz," organized by Mujeres del Movimiento at the University of California at Berkeley. There were twenty-three guest speakers, only eight were women.[193] At California State College at Los Angeles, women denounced Chicano studies as "an all male chauvinistic clique" driven by "sexist attitudes." When a course was offered on Chicanas' involvement, a man was scheduled to teach the class.[194] Possibly the most telling case of the tension between Chicano studies and Chicana scholars was the tenure case of Anna NietoGomez and California State College at Northridge.[195]

The same problem is evident in publications and organizations. Chicana perspectives did not find a space in the main journals unless they accepted the position of perspectivist or empirical scholarship. An example was the 1973 special issue of El Grito, edited by Estela Portillo.[196] Chicanas had to develop their own journals or publish in peripheral periodicals to express their views of the world around them.[197] Some examples of these journals were La Palabra: Revista de Literatura Chicana, Comadre, Encuentro Feminil, Hijas de Cuauhtémoc, La Cosecha, and Third Women. Chicanas also formed new organizations, like Mujeres en Marcha, who organized the panel discussion at the 1982 National Association of Chicano Studies (NACS), and published a recapitulation of their presentations and discussion in Chicana in the 80's: Unsettled Issues.[198] An organization closely tied to Mujeres en Marcha was Mujeres Activas en Letras y Cambio Social (MALCS). MALCS was organized in 1981 with support from the Chicano Studies Program and Women's Studies at the University of California at Davis. In a 1983 declaration, MALCS spoke of itself as an organization of working-class women whose values were derived from their location: "Our history is the story of working people." They saw their academic work tied to community involvement—in particular, to the condition of women.[199]

The 1982 NACS panel provoked discussion about issues of gender inequality and generated suggestions to remedy the problems women faced in the organization.[200] The women presented a sublimation of the various expressions of Chicana liberal feminism, Chicana Marxism, and Chicana cultural nationalism that dominated the 1970s. These feminists explored three issues: to separate gender exploitation from other forms of oppression, to examine the relationship among Chicanas and Chicanos, and to specify the differences that women of color had from white women and men of color.[201] The presentation recapitulated the situation Chicanas found themselves relative to el movimiento, often repeating arguments developed earlier by NietoGomez and others.[202]

Policy advocate and scholar Teresa Córdova used the image of La

Malinche to trace how Chicanas were constructed into traditional and stereotypical roles. When women rejected these strictures, they were criticized for their divisiveness, their aggression, and their middle-class feminism. "But all we are told serves to diffuse the understanding of the imbalance of power that is the function of male dominance—or patriarchy." The scholar Margarita Decierdo continued the discussion by calling attention to the restrictions placed on Chicanas in the 1960s. She drew attention to the loyalists who willingly ignored the issues of sexism to battle other political, economic, and social concerns. Thus she was critical of movimiento activists that "neglected to embrace socioeconomic, political issues critical to women" and therefore limited its success. Educator Gloria Cuádraz called on women to challenge the structures and practices of patriarchy, while historian Deena González presented on the differences between Chicana and Latina expressions of feminism and white middle-class feminism. In particular, González proclaimed that the struggle of other women of color in the United States and Mexican feminists helped her move toward "self-discovery, of recovery, and of renewed identification" and therefore an "intimate liberation that feminism induces."[203] In closing the panel presentation, Córdova, drawing on Francisco Vazquez's work, called for both a "chicanology" and a "chicanalogy" to disrupt the body of knowledge that oppressed Chicanas and for the construction of a Chicana feminist perspective. It was a plea for an intellectual challenge against both Anglocentric, Chicanocentric, and phallocentric interpretations of the world.[204]

Chicanas retained a tense dialogue with women's studies. The anthropologist Patricia Zavella, in a later essay, has argued that a fundamental difference existed "in ideology and epistemology between Chicana studies and women's studies, and within feminist theory as a whole."[205] Chicanas kept their distance from the feminism articulated by the women's movement that accentuated differences in cultural style and politics. She underscored Baca Zinn's position that Chicana scholars avoided concepts from feminist theory.[206] Yet, Zavella continued, as Chicanas' ambivalence toward Chicano scholarship and el movimiento metastasized, Chicanas had to develop their *own* Chicana feminist institutional and academic supports, at times drawing from women's studies.[207] This move, she averred, demands a reformulation of the articulation of race, class, and gender from a Chicana perspective and experience.

Third World Chicana Feminism

By the early 1980s, Chicana scholars had come to the point that retelling herstory and a continued analysis of the condition of Chicanas was no longer sufficient.[208] Their position echoed a similar position in women's studies: "The story is no longer about the things that have happened to women and men and how they have reacted to them; instead it is about how the subjective and collective meaning of women and men as categories of identity have been constructed."[209] Chicanas recognized that their intellectual quest, just like Chicano studies, had reached a cul-de-sac. Chicanas' use of various models to understand their oppression seemed trapped within a cycle of arguments that had first been articulated by women in the early 1970s. None of the models had been able to deliver an analysis that looked at gender, race, and class as interrelated factors. The Chicana intellectual project seemed on the verge of an epistemic and methodological break. But what did this mean? Would it be a breakdown or a breakthrough? Where would it come from?

Norma Alarcón, together with other women who published in *Revista Mujeres* or *Third Women*, hinted at this rupture when she evoked a different way to theorize about Chicanas and women of color. In the initial issue of *Third Women*, Alarcón elicited self-invention. She contended that women need to invent themselves; to engage in historical reconstructions is not sufficient: "Third Women is one forum, for the self-definition and self-invention which is more than reformism, more than revolt."[210] Moreover, she suggested that this could not be done only by Chicanas; rather, it would involve all women of color. The future of Chicanas in Chicano studies has to be beyond the criteria so far present in any practice of Chicano studies. Unfortunately, Alarcón did not clarify what this meant.

Alarcón's position was not new. Earlier Chicanas had prefigured this notion of writing as a way to explore the multiple aspects of identity.[211] Rita Sanchez's essay, "Chicana Writer Breaking Out," reflected this hope. She began by noting that writing could be a revolutionary act since through writing a woman can come to understand the condition of colonization and the forces of racism and gender that limited her options; yet it allowed her to transcends these bonds and make choices that determined her life. "By becoming a writer," Sanchez wrote, "the Chicana has to have already rebelled against a socialization process that would have her remain merely the silent helpmate."[212] For Sanchez, the reality of her experiences as a Chicana placed her at the heart of the struggle. It is by communicating this experience to other Chicanas that together they express a Chicana view. Thus, it is in the "confrontation" with another like her that a new source of power is born and becomes a real source of change.

Sanchez drew attention to Antonia Castañeda's work on Chicano literature and the "Chicano collective voice." In particular, Castañeda wrote about how "así nos habremos dado en préstamo los unos a los otros" (that we are on loan to one another).[213] Sanchez challenged the empirics by placing the subjective act of writing at the core of praxis: "Writing, breaking the silence, subjective as it may appear, becomes a monumental and collective act because it signifies overcoming, freeing oneself from the confines and conditions of history."[214] By writing, Chicanas could create "spiritual zones," where they might remain safe from the corrupting influence of technocratic society. Women must not remain silent; to remain silent is to be guilty. Women must speak to all women, "Chicana, Black, Asian, White, any woman, any age, child, sister, wife, aunt, or friend."[215] The poet and writer Marcela Trujillo Gaitan has phrased this issue as such: "Literature is a medium and a praxis whereby we can start to question our oppression . . . [and deal] with our everyday problems."[216]

Without doubt, the definitive articulation of Third World feminism came with the publication of *This Bridge Called My Back* in 1981. This collection of essays, poems, and short stories opened up an oppositional feminist discourse.[217] What made *This Bridge* so radical was the epistemic break that lesbians of color formulated in the early 1980s by building on their multiple identities.[218] In its wake, the collection disrupted Chicano Studies, providing an articulation of Chicanas' triple oppression and a way to challenge this imposed limit. *This Bridge* succeeded in spanning and connecting the political and intellectual realms without privileging academic criteria in sustaining this link. By placing itself on the ethical platform of "listening to each other and learning each other's ways of seeing and listening," as well as the personal location of knowledge, the essays in the book subverted endeavors to constrict the interaction of race, class, and gender.[219] By rejecting separatism yet acknowledging difference, these writers sought to present a dynamic interaction among these various identities in their efforts to understand collective experiences through their personal experiences.[220]

In this interchange on "third world feminism in the U.S.," these women created a space for a radical rearticulation of any expression of ethnic studies and a strategy for revolution. The work represented a rethinking of identity—not as pieces (woman, race, color, sexuality, class, and so on) but as dynamic and coupled components. The scholar and activist Gloria Anzaldúa portrayed this image in this way: "Think of me as Shiva, a many-armed and legged body with one foot on brown soil, one on white, one in straight society, one in the gay world, the man's world, the women's, one limb in the literary world, another in the working class, the socialist, and the occult world. A sort of spider woman hanging by one thin strand of web."[221]

One of the central shifts in *This Bridge* was to place the individual and her personal experiences at the center of discussing the collective.[222] To write from a "theory in the flesh" asserted the collective stories of oppression that echoed in the individual's personal body as one struggled in naming oneself through the telling of one's story.[223] Anzaldúa wrote: "The act of writing is the act of making soul, alchemy. It is the quest for the self, for the center of the self, which we women of color have come to think as 'other'—the dark, feminine."[224] Oppression was thus embodied in each writer and took shape as they wrote their experiences. This writing, at the same time, gave visibility to their differences and created the condition for political action by constructing a space "to talk about our own fears and misconceptions about each other."[225]

Culture, often depicted through the relationship of mother and daughter, stood at the center of a theory of the flesh. Yet this was not some return to cultural nationalism. The authors tussled to sustain the tension within culture, as it appeared as simultaneously as oppressor and liberator. Some women called attention to culture as the place to begin the dialogue about liberation; it was not the end. The writer, poet, and playwright Cherríe Moraga expands on this point: "What I know about loving, singing, crying, telling stories, speaking with my heart and hands, even having a sense of my own soul comes from the love of my mother, aunts, cousins."[226] Yet it was also the space that erased differences and tried to subject all to a particular embodiment. "The relationship between mother and daughter," Aurora Levins Morales wrote, "stands at the center of what I fear most in our culture."[227] Moreover, culture sustained an environment that fed racism among Third World people as well as the denial of the existence of lesbians and gay men.[228] Lastly, there was no resolution to this friction. Acknowledging differences was the only way to build coalitions. Feminist scholars Barbara Smith and Beverly Smith explained it this way: "What *I* really feel is radical is trying to make coalitions with people who are different from you. I feel it is radical to be dealing with race and sex and class and sexual identity all at one time."[229]

This Bridge also remained coupled to the earlier themes developed by women of color—the racism of white feminism. The activist, poet, and writer Audre Lorde remarked that white feminism continues to see women as singular: "all women suffer the same oppression simply because we are women."[230] This denial of difference served to strengthen patriarchy. White feminist stereotypes of women of color culture reasserted the racial privilege of white women, where women of color were assumed to be more sensual, less cerebral; more oppressed, less political.[231] Particularly frustrating was Anglo women's demand that women of color were responsible to educate them about race and racism.[232] This was not to suggest that the turn to race was the answer—for difference goes beyond merely adding race, culture, color, class, sexuality, or immigrant status into the mix.[233] There was an implied understanding that separatism (whether national or gender) in any form was politically stagnant. On this point, Barbara Smith stated: "We sometimes think of separatism as the politics without a practice." Beverly Smith developed the idea further: "One of the problems of separatism is that I can't see it as a philosophy that explains and analyzes the roots of all oppression and is going to go toward solving it."[234]

Lorde's seminal essay "The Master's Tools Will Never Dismantle the Master's House" formulated the break that allowed women of color to reformulate an intellectual framework to explain the condition of people of color. It allowed women of color to develop a political program for change without returning to the established academic practices of explaining these conditions. She began by drawing attention to the centrality of difference. She argued that "academic arrogance" dismisses the creative function of difference: "Difference is that raw and powerful connection from which our personal power is forged."[235] It is by taking this difference that women of color can discover their power, since they cannot use the master's tools to dismantle the master's house. This criticism was sharply directed against women who insisted on using the master's tools.[236] "The failure of the academic feminists to recognize difference as a crucial strength," Lorde wrote, "is a failure to reach beyond the first patriarchal lesson."[237] Thus to deny race, sexuality, and class is to return to the master's concerns over universality and the reproduction of patriarchy. It is essential for all to "reach down into that deep place of knowledge inside herself and touch that terror and loathing of any difference that lives there. . . . See whose face it wears."[238] Lorde ended with the notion that "the personal as the political can begin to illuminate all our choices."[239]

From a different perspective, Anzaldúa called attention to the spiritual side of women of color that comes from the voice within women. She called for the struggle that allows women to use their vulnerability to unite others against oppression. Third world feminism thus summons women "to work with those people who would feel at home in *El Mundo Zurdo, the left-handed world*: the colored, the queer, the poor, the female, the physically challenged."[240] It is the two-way path of the Mundo Zurdo—from self and outward to society—that we can think of transforming society. At best, in the left-handed world, those left outside of dominant society can come together to create their space. At the same time, however, Anzaldúa remained aware of the limits to unity. She called attention to "our own racism, our fear of women and sexuality"—a fear of betrayal.[241]

This Bridge provided an insurmountable challenge to earlier Chicana thought and Chicano studies. The various writers afforded Chicanas a way out from the constraints of Chicana herstory, a narrative of the hierarchical relation that exists between men and women, and a rhetorical synthesis of race, class, and gender. I somewhat differ with Maylei Blackwell, who is critical of scholars who "periodize the formation of women of color political identity as originating in the 1980s, marked by the publication of *This Bridge*."[242] Although she is correct that many scholars have dismissed the long historical trajectory to the appearance of this text, the collection marked a quantum leap in Chicana thought and political direction. While *This Bridge* returns us to the early Chicana movement that sought to balance intellectual and political work, by placing greater emphasis on difference and moving away from universality, these writings reasserted identity without a static nationalism or any attempt to privilege any particular factor in identity construction.

In doing so, they complicated Chicano(a) endeavors to describe the Mexican American experience through any particular paradigm or assumptions that methodologies and their methods were a neutral technology. This particular move put the question to the quest of Chi-

cano studies for a perspective that would allow Chicanos(as) to explicate their experience. In particular, *This Bridge* offered a vision that
was incomprehensible to Chicano Studies since it questioned the entire
enterprise. Their articulation of feminism questioned the apparatus of
the Chicano Studies discipline and the academy as a whole.[243] It is a pity
that almost a decade would pass before Chicanos and some Chicanas
would take seriously the promise of *This Bridge*. The historical evolution of Chicano studies would have been quite different had many more
Chicanos(as) read closely *This Bridge Called My Back*—and followed
its ethics.

Conclusion

In 1968, there were many Chicano studies that sought to establish a space in U.S. higher education. Fourteen years later, there remained one dominant expression of Chicano studies at major universities. Many of the earlier versions had been vanquished, often pushed to peripheral areas of the academy (colleges and nonresearch universities). By 1982, Chicano Studies had become a uniform disciplinary practice with a particular set of methods conveyed as "action research" that sought to disclose the structures of Mexican American oppression and develop the politics/policies to transform this situation. Whether formulated by Marxists, nationalists, or liberals, Chicano Studies had its epistemological core, methodologies, and policy goals. Simultaneously, the American academy allowed this disciplinary practice to find a space within its ivory tower—albeit not in the tallest tower or in the building closest to the central quad. For both the institutional gatekeepers and the Chicano Studies practitioners, it became easier to think of the discipline as "interdisciplinary," "multidisciplinary," or "transdisciplinary." In the end, Chicano Studies was established as a discipline that had negotiated its space within the U.S. academy.

Beginning in the mid-1960s, Chicano(a) campus activists struggled with administrators over admissions, student services, and retention of Mexican American students. A few called for the reformation of American academic knowledge and its system of distribution. These campus activists sought to disrupt the pact among professors, their acolytes, and the selective intellectual tradition. Moreover, they set out to manifest the link between U.S. academic knowledge with American exceptionalism and imperialism. These revolutionary challenges, paralleled by other campus communities, were summarized in the students' demand for Chicano studies. Chicano studies was to be a space controlled by Chicanos(as) and driven by Chicano social and political

concerns uniting with the struggle of el movimiento. Chicano(a) campus activists began to design what they felt was the best expression of
Chicano studies, always in negotiation with the administration. These
programs echoed the various local, ideological, and political issues that
motivated campus activists—reflecting nationalist, racial, gender, and
administrative concerns. Although activists often conflated issues, they
sought to bridge their understanding of social and political transformation with academic practices. Thus out of the California Bay Area,
they had the first scholarly endeavor to write Chicano studies. As the
title stated, *El Grito: A Journal of Contemporary Mexican-American
Thought* expressed an oppositional academic Chicano studies that was
not part of the social sciences or humanities.

Through the essays in *El Grito*, this book traced the shift from
a critique of some social science research to a rejection of the social
sciences and the assumptions behind U.S. academic knowledge. The
demand for objectivity was shown to be a cover for biased research and
the denial of the researcher. All academic social sciences and humanities research on the Mexican American was therefore partial. The only
possible Chicano(a) response was to engage in a form of standpoint
research, where the researcher was a participant. So long as research
was separated into object and subject, the Chicano(a) would never be
understood and the Chicano(a) researcher would never be. Chicano
research thus had to start from the standpoint of the Chicano(a) and his
or her position in U.S. society—not from an assumed impartial social
science or humanities based on academic disciplinary methodologies.

Another conceptualization of Chicano studies was present in *El
Plan de Santa Bárbara*. The participants of *El Plan* wrote that the
Chicano(a) struggle for self-determination and liberation would benefit from the strategic use of education. This strategic plan rested on
creating autonomous institutions in the academy that would be under
Chicano(a) control. Chicano research, in turn, would develop the tools
and knowledge necessary for the community's transformation. This
often meant that the social sciences, the humanities, and policy programs might be used to achieve this political goal. By 1969, one could
see a Perspectivist and Empiricist Chicano Studies; *El Grito* and *El
Plan* manifested these divergent ways of thinking of Chicano studies as an academic enterprise. This difference was illustrated in their
readings of the UCLA's Mexican American Study Project. Examples of
these Chicano studies were Raymond Padilla's "A Critique of Pittian

History" and Deluvina Hernández's *Mexican American Challenge to a Sacred Cow*. These essays exemplified the emerging Chicano studies traditions. Although their views overlapped at many points, they manifested two styles of thinking about academic research, intellectuals, and Chicanos(as).

The initial intellectual vision presented in *El Plan* initially was not as well developed as those that appeared in *El Grito*. However, many intellectuals stepped forward to remedy this situation. They began from the premise that the struggle for Mexican American freedom demanded the disruption of the structures of oppression. But what were these structures and how did they operate? Chicano(a) empirics turned to the study of these structures from a variety of political and ideological orientations (liberal, nationalist, and Marxist) and used theoretical perspectives drawn from their disciplinary training. Thus Empirical Chicano Studies developed a research paradigm that studied these oppressive structures, whether as the result of colonialism, internal colonialism, class oppression, or the simple failings of the American system. Once Chicanos(as) figured out the system of oppression, they would devise a political plan to challenge and then change this situation. This vision was articulated in several essays in *Aztlán: Chicano Journal of the Social Sciences and the Arts*. The research by Carlos Muñoz, Tomás Almaguer, and Mario Barrera presented a possible model to explain Mexican American oppression. By 1973, *Aztlán* proclaimed a fusion of internal colonialism and Marxism as the preferred methodological tool and the proposed mechanism for Empirical Chicano Studies research. In the process, *Aztlán* became the lead journal of Empirical Chicano Studies. Tied to empiricist endeavors to explore structural inequality, however, established an ambivalent relationship with social science research and the belief in the possibility of "good" social science.

Building on standpoint epistemology, the critique of the social sciences, with a Chicano reading of Jose Ortega y Gasset, Samuel Ramos, and Octavio Paz, Perspectivist Chicano Studies required an oppositional epistemology rooted in the formation of Chicano(a) identity. Perspectivists set out to transform the oppressive institutions in the United States, not by structural transformation, but by articulating a philosophy of life—rejecting what was seen as Anglo materialism and rationalism. Some referred to this lifestyle as chicanismo and a few connected it to carnalismo. For this expression of Chicano studies the problem with the university was not academic or institutional; rather, it was its denial of responsibility, values, ethics, and humanism. Thus Eliu Carranza believed that the Chicano(a) needed a cultural revolution that could not coexist within the U.S. academy. Essays in *De Colores: Journal of Emerging Raza Philosophies* and *Con Safos* struggled to blend this perspectivist intellectual framework with practical applications to maintain cultural identity and build a Chicano(a) nation.

Perspectivist Chicano Studies could not establish itself in the U.S. academy. Even though select scholars from the humanities, social sciences, and education engaged in perspectivist research, academic institutions could not digest this research as easily as empiricist research. At the same time, Empirical Chicano Studies could not let this alternative survive since the academy would interpret this multiplicity of Chicano studies as a weakness and possibly a demonstration of the unsuitability of Chicano studies in the American academy. Thus the voice of Perspectivist Chicano Studies in major universities was quieted; it survived in alternative teaching institutions and community services. By the late 1970s and early 1980s, Perspectivist Chicano Studies as an alternative style of academic knowing had evaporated, in a few cases replaced by structuralism, poststructuralism, or postmodernism.

As Perspectivist Chicano Studies faded, Empirical Chicano Studies consolidated its hold on the discipline by continuing institution building, both within and outside the academy. Examples of this endeavor were the proposed National Chicano Commission of Higher Education, the National Association for Chicano Studies, and a whole series of regional and local conferences. Together with institutionalization came canon formation, research, publication, and a shared vision of activism. As internal colonialism fell into disfavor, empiric scholars used the language of action research to refer to the link between structural analysis and political action. With the success of Empirical Chicano Studies and the institutionalization of Chicano Studies in the academy, the language of action research and community service was translated as policy research. This reinforced the relationship of Empirical Chicano Studies and the academy. By the early 1980s, Chicano Studies scholars had published hundreds of pieces and had established a canon, many playing the role of policy consultants and policy decision makers.

The initial struggle of Empirical Chicano Studies for institutional space within U.S. higher education, ironically, softened empirical activists' critique of the academy and academic-based knowledge production.

The demand for institutions under Chicano(a) control was not as radical as initially perceived. Furthermore, this same experience facilitated Chicano Studies' ability to accommodate an intellectual space. Because of their acceptance of good social science and humanities research as well as policy research, Chicano Studies found that it could engage in academic research as defined and constructed by American higher education. As Empirical Chicano Studies consolidated its hold, it negotiated an acceptable, if not equal, relationship with the academy. Simultaneously, major U.S. universities could have the new discipline, often as a major and at times as a program or department. The attainment of departmental status became the mark of success for Chicano Studies.

The belief that academic practices were neutral, and therefore could be turned to the use of the Mexican American community, grounded Chicano Studies on a traditional and instrumentalist Enlightenment vision. Chicano Studies equated knowledge to power and reduced it to technology. Chicano Studies programs, even when bolstered by student activism, did not escape the instrumentalist logic and practices of the academy. "Learning about ourselves" was rooted in paradigms, institutional processes, and intellectual formats derived from the academy and society. Critical thinking was transformed into an objective, impersonal, self-activating process whose purpose was the domination of existence and the alienation of the individual and thought.[1] Chicano and Chicana scholars may have been critical of Anglo research and methods of research, yet they remained naïve about the whole operation of academic knowledge, its reproduction, and its dissemination. In the end, Chicano Studies based itself on the same conservative and manipulative Socratic agenda of "know thyself" as the rest of the academy.

The certainty felt by Chicanos(as) concerning the relationship between the academic project and the community blinded them to the authoritarianism in this project. They did not conceptualize how reason was harnessed to the interests of the bourgeois social system, as evident at the university. Chicano Studies approached the issues in their barrios through the same instrumentalist reason (no matter how radical their political rhetoric). As the critical theorist Max Horkheimer wrote: "Today even outstanding scholars confuse thinking with planning. Shocked by social injustice and by hypocrisy in its traditional religious garb, they propose to wed ideology to reality, or, as they prefer to say, to bring reality closer to our heart's desire, by applying the wisdom of engineering to religions."[2]

Somehow the scholar-activists were to take the university back to the community, applying their skills in the barrios. Like the rest of society, the activism of Chicano Studies looked "upon the world as a world of facts and things, and fail[ed] to connect the transformation of the world into facts and things with the social process." Much like the technocrats, the activists forgot that "[t]he task of critical reflection is not merely to understand the various facts in their historical development . . . but also to see through the notion of fact itself, in its development and therefore in its relativity."[3] This instrumentalist vision was further manifested in a "Leninist" line when dealing with the community—not in any ideological or political sense, but in the assumption of a vanguard and leadership role of the university/activist student. Chicanos(as) retained a hidden assumption, reinforced by the university, of a politically unsophisticated Chicano(a)/Latino(a) community. Because the barrio did not "behave" like the political literature (no matter what orientation) said they should, many assumed it needed organization and leadership from without. Should we as Chicanos(as) then be surprised that the "Hispanic policy maker" is the primary product of the university today? Chicano Studies was neither more backward nor had a greater propensity to these tendencies than other initially oppositional academic projects. Marxism, existentialism, structuralism, feminism, postmodernism, poststructuralism, cultural studies, postcolonial studies, and the like, in their own ways, have found their place in the academy and ultimately became incorporated.[4]

Chicana criticism of the movement and its patriarchal practices together with the formation of a Chicana feminism questioned the disciplinary approach of Chicano studies and Empirical Chicano Studies in particular. A fierce debate among Chicanas(os) brought to the surface contradictions in el movimiento. Out of this maelstrom, Chicanas, together with other women of color, articulated a feminism that sought to understand the intersectionality of race, gender, and class in U.S. society. For some it was clear that to only look at a structural analysis of gender, race, and class would make it difficult to get to the intersectionality or allow the understanding of other identities in the U.S. polity, like sexuality. Chicanas' criticism reoriented Chicano(a) scholarship back to the intellectual chaos of earlier days. Thus, as Chicano Studies triumphantly found its place in U.S. higher education, an alternative vision of Chicano(a) studies had appeared that was premised on the demise of Chicano Studies and the coming of something totally different.

In Medias Res

Since Chicano(a) studies is still practiced today, my study of this discipline stops in the middle of this history. Today Chicano(a) studies is a vibrant field of intellectual work and inquiry. Recently, doctoral programs have been instituted in the field. Thousands of essays explore the Mexican American and Latina(o) experiences in the United States. More has been done to understand the transnationalism of Mexican American and Latino(a) communities. In the process, the phallocentrist, heterosexist, and nationalist character of Chicano studies has been questioned, allowing scholars to reconceptualize the field as Chicano(a) studies, Chicana(o) studies, and Chicana(o) and Latino(a) studies—to name a few possibilities. Some scholars have also elaborated a Chicana studies that speaks to the Chicana experience. Other disciplines borrow from the field. Aside from producing more data on the Mexican American and Latino(a) populations, non-Chicano studies scholars have engaged theoretical frameworks that Chicana(o) intellectuals have developed in the process of understanding their experiences. In particular, the works of Chicana lesbian scholars have added to the growth of Chicano(a) studies and other disciplines as well. Although the ideas present in *This Bridge Called My Back* may have been initially ignored, this is no longer the case.

To trace the intellectual history of Chicano(a) studies after 1982, I would have to develop another, longer volume. Instead, I would like to hint at particular articulations of Chicano(a) studies. Clearly, I cannot provide a thorough overview of the changes in the field since 1982. It was an intense period that saw the retreat of Chicano Studies and a return to the multiplicities of Chicano(a) studies. By the early 1990s, there were different currents of Chicano(a) studies scholarship as well as a resistance to Chicano Studies. It is not a coincidence that this period also marked the weakening of the journal *Aztlán*. The rupture of Chicano Studies allowed the interlinking with ideas and positionalities that works like Gloria Anzaldúa's *Borderlands/La Frontera* (1987), Patricia Hill Collins's *Black Feminist Thought: Knowledge, Consciousness, and the Politics of Empowerment* (1990), the essays in Anzaldúa's *Making Face, Making Soul/Haciendo Caras* (1990), and *Cultural Studies* (1990) brought to the fore. One might call this period a Chicano(a) renaissance.

Yet the academy did not relax its role; it reasserted its authority and control. Although many academic disciplines were unhappy with the feminist and postmodern turn, the institution was able to find space for this perspective. While the debates with postmodernism in fields like science studies, literary criticism, and history were severe, postmodern scholars were able to negotiate their space. At the same time, much like Marxism a generation earlier, postmodernism's critical edge was blunted as it found its space in the academy. The same phenomenon unfolded with feminism and postmodernism in Chicana(o) studies as the twentieth century came to an end. While initially the institution had denied Gloria Anzaldúa its imprimatur, years later and in death, this was no longer an issue. At the National Association of Chicano and Chicana Studies (NACCS), the old home of Chicano Studies, it is acceptable if not *de rigueur* to cite the work of Chicana feminists, Chicano(a) postmodernists, and Chicano(a) queer theorists. Some of the founders of Chicano Studies now include some of these works in their own research and musings on the Mexican American.[5]

I follow three lines of thought as a tentative conclusion. First, I would like to see how the call presented in *This Bridge Called My Back* was picked up (and ignored) in the years after its appearance by looking at the direction of scholarship in the 1980s. Then I highlight two articulations of Chicano(a) studies: Chicano(a) Cultural Studies and Transnational Chicano(a)/Latino(a) Studies. Chicana feminism— together with a wide-raging set of poststructural, postmodern, and Marxist writings—provided the new Chicano(a) studies variations and multiple directions to grow. I look at two trends. The last point I address is a discussion of where Chicano(a) studies can go now. I argue for an ethical turn. These concluding themes were influenced by a Chicano Studies survey at the University of California at Berkeley in 1978. I cite three students' surveys:

(1) As a Chicana, I cannot overemphasize the need to have Chicanas on the faculty. I was once told by a former male member of the faculty that Chicanas didn't care who was on the faculty "as long as she had tits." That type of mentality was not unusual.

(2) I wish there was a course about sexuality for Chicanos. Mainly by the fact that I find it quite disenchanting to realize that many Chicanos are intolerant to homosexuality. That is one reason why I shy away from some Mexican organizations because they some-times mock certain aspects of life they don't even understand. I hope

it doesn't sound like I'm trying to deny my culture, because I'm not. It's just factual, some Mexicans are intolerant to homosexuality.

(3) You must go beyond simply Chicano Studies and into the LATINO experience. This could be done by simply adding a few courses on the Latino and would not have to radically change your program. I am Nicaraguan. Your program with the exception of a course on Chile has emphasized the Chicano. I feel that rather than the study of the Chicano it should have been the Latino with less emphasis on the Mexican American. The non-Chicano has been entirely ignored at Berkeley. For example, let us examine a Central American who wants to learn about his culture. Aside from one course on Mayan civilization and a survey of Mexico and Central American anthropology, there is nothing, not even a history class. I am not knocking your program, I feel now more than before a need for such a program. One must know his roots, I had to learn mine by myself without any credit or anything.[6]

For these students, Chicano Studies as practiced at UC Berkeley needed a fundamental rethinking. They felt that there was no space to examine gender, sexual orientation, the transnational character of Chicano studies, or Latino(a)-ness. This concern could be encountered on other campuses. It was their concerns that helped me formulate the themes I wish to address in this conclusion.

The 1980s and Building on *This Bridge Called My Back*

With the successful establishment of Chicano Studies, the 1980s started as the decade of Chicano Studies research. Not only had the next generation of Chicano scholars come on the scene, the third generation was in preparation. Many of the early scholars had become associate or full professors. Major research universities had hired their Chicano Studies experts; at other institutions core programs were expanded. Chicano Studies was a successful academic program ready to challenge the other disciplines for its space in the university. Mario García declared that "Chicano studies in the 1980s is coming of age, and this decade will witness continued growth, together with new and challenging issues and questions posed by Chicano intellectuals."[7] Even though some encountered problems,[8] Carlos Muñoz Jr. could contend: "The state of Chicano Studies research is a healthy one, for in spite of the pessimistic forecasts about the future of our programs that have been made since the 1970s, a small but significant number of us have survived in the university."[9]

Though empirics may have banished their enemies from the field, a few opponents lurked in the shadowy margins. For these scholars, Chicano Studies could not explain the Chicano(a) experience as a whole. As Pedro Cabán has noted for Latino(a) Studies: "Although often informed by Marxist and structuralist analysis, much of the academic production of this period (late-1960s to mid-1980s) failed to interrogate adequately the practice and mechanism of race, gender, and sexual orientation oppression within the national formation."[10] The same can be stated for Chicano Studies. For Cabán, the reliance on historical and political analysis reflected a male-centered and nationalist discourse. Feminists, gay writers, and postmodernists/poststructuralists/neo-Marxists whispered (increasingly louder) questions about Chicano Studies as an academic enterprise. These and other voices called for a critical questioning of the Chicano Studies intellectual project and a rejection of the epistemological gaze of the social sciences and humanities.[11] Other scholars added that self-discovery, self-determination, and self-construction could not proceed from academic disciplines. They demanded a return to subjectivity, identity, lived experience, story, and play. Some Chicana feminists turned to a standpoint epistemology for the construction of knowledge. The point was to commence with who they were, what was their experience, and how they engage the world with that experience.[12]

Most of these concerns about Chicano Studies were drowned out, however. Even in the late 1980s, Chicana feminism remained outside the "mainstream" of Chicano Studies.[13] A southern California National Association for Chicano Studies (NACS) *foco* conference held at Loyola Marymount University in 1987 exemplified the failure of these voices to penetrate the dialogue on Chicano Studies.[14] To many of the participants, something was amiss with Chicano Studies, especially in light of the tensions at the UCLA Chicano Studies Research Center.[15] But in looking back at the responses to this crisis in Chicano Studies, one is struck by the conventional solutions proposed: some posed the need to engage in an activist scholarship;[16] others advanced the demand for a viable research paradigm;[17] and a few called for a return to organization building.[18] As Deena Gonzales, Teresa McKenna, and Emma Perez have noted, few scholars were willing to engage in rethinking Chicano

Studies through an understanding of gender or any other alternative perspective.[19]

A piece by Rodolfo Acuña highlighted this traditionalist solution. Building on Jorge García's call for activist research at the NACCS *foco* meeting, Acuña argued that a Chicano Studies scholar must be both researcher and a politically committed individual.[20] Acuña echoed the NACS "Preamble": reject "integrationist perspective which emphasized consensus, assimilation, and the legitimacy of societal institutions" and challenge "the structures of inequality based on class, racial, and sexist privileges in this society."[21] Since he did not acknowledge epistemological concerns, however, the reader is returned to institutional priorities. Acuña believed that the fight for a core department was the central legitimate vehicle to produce Chicano Studies research. "What can be agreed upon," he wrote, "is that Chicanos should control the direction of their own discipline."[22] Following academic logic, Acuña judged that once Chicano Studies became a department, it would become an equal member of the governing body of the university, and "it participates in its deliberations on what knowledge will be available to students."[23]

More extreme was the position taken by Ignacio García, who felt that the intellectual practices that women, gays, and some Chicano(a) scholars had introduced undercut *El Plan de Santa Bárbara* and were destructive to Chicano Studies.[24] He wrote: "Postmodern sectarianism—lesbian-feminism, neo-Marxism, and a militant form of Latinoism—is another challenge to the field since the 1980s."[25] For García, these new intellectual directions were not rooted in working-class communities but rather in a sterile self-serving professionalism, opportunism, and "Hispanic revisionism."[26] This situation, he continued, was strengthened by the arrival of faculty who were not involved in the struggles for Chicano Studies and the retreat of older tenured faculty, creating a vacuum in the leadership of Chicano Studies and organizations like NACS. He concluded that "[t]he scholarship coming from this particular group of scholars is both academically and socially insignificant and provides little to debate on the Chicano(a) experience."[27] The only solution to this crisis was a return to *El Plan* that would allow the development of a new paradigm, community involvement, and more regional autonomy.

But alternative voices would not bend and continued to reassert another Chicano(a) studies.[28] These initial voices came from Chicanas who called for the use of gender as a method to dislodge Chicano Studies from its dominant position. Others soon followed who brought out new understandings drawn from their readings of *This Bridge Called My Back*. *This Bridge*'s challenge to Chicano Studies and the opening of possibilities for the survival and transformation of the discipline cannot be overestimated. Although I cannot trace the multiple (and often conflicting) impact of *This Bridge*'s epistemological and ontological revolution here, I suggest we trace two traditions that flow from *This Bridge* and that are reinforced in *Borderlands/La Frontera* and *Making Face, Making Soul: Haciendo Caras*.[29] I select these trends because they paralleled some of the concerns those Berkeley students requested in 1978. The two tendencies are Chicano(a) Cultural Studies and Transnational Chicano(a)/Latino(a) Studies. This is only a suggestive reading; I am engaged in a whiggish reading. In other words, in the back of my mind, I am also asking how current trends in Chicano(a) studies are prefigured in these earlier texts.

Although much has been written about Anzaldúa's use of the border, race, or *mestizaje* as both metaphor and material, in *Borderlands/La Frontera* she also straddled the personal and collective as she articulated a space for *los atravesados*. She conveyed a cultural nationalism that echoed, rejected, and overcame culture. This allowed her to explore the notion of *la facultad*, a sense that preceded reason and permitted some (females, homosexuals, dark skinned, outcasts, persecuted, marginalized, and foreigners) to witness "the faces of feelings, that is, behind which feelings reside/hide."[30] Anzaldúa's initial ontological move opened to an epistemology of *travesía*.[31] This knowing was not rooted in academic practices; it turned toward "*la conciencia de la mestiza*" and "*nepantilism*."[32] At the heart of this epistemic call was a dialectical "tolerance for contradictions, a tolerance for ambiguity."[33]

Making Face, Making Soul continued the ontological shift toward an epistemic frame built around identity self-construction.[34] Anzaldúa wrote that "*[M]ujeres-de-color* speak and write not just against traditional white ways and texts but against a prevailing mode of being, against a white frame of reference."[35] She added that we need an epistemology that would "rewrite history using race, class, gender and ethnicity as categories of analysis, theories that cross borders, that blurs boundaries—new kind of theories with new theorizing methods."[36] Yet she warned the reader, following "Audre Lorde, about the danger of using the 'master's tools.'"[37] She explored the role of the creative act as a spiritual or psychic endeavor and its connection to culture and creativity. This spiritual-cultural move may be what Anzaldúa is best remembered for in the generations to come. At the same time, like in *This Bridge*, the various writers reject endeavors to separate folks and instead make a call to resistance. "Making face" is about dignity and self-respect as it appears as play.[38]

These books retain an ambivalent relationship with Chicano(a) academic practices. Although many scholars cite and explore themes from these books, the texts themselves remain peripheral to the academy. This difficulty comes from the authors' dismissal of academic writing and presentation as well as their rejection of academic "objectivity." Today, Chicano(a) studies has come to see these texts as a point of departure for a new intellectual practice. Often the perceived limits of *Making Face*'s arguments were supplemented with other non-Chicano(a) intellectuals: some turned to Foucault, Lacan, or Derrida; others to Hall, Said, and Williams; and yet a few others to Irigaray, Spivak, or Kristeva. Whether the turn to these writers made Chicana feminism more adaptable to the academy, I am not ready to say. But it did spark a resurgence in Chicano(a) theorizing.

From this early theorizing, the shift toward a Chicano(a) Cultural Studies can be traced from Renato Rosaldo's *Culture and Truth: The Remaking of Social Analysis* (1989) through Ramón Saldívar's *Chicano Narrative: The Dialectics of Difference* (1990), the essays in *Criticism in the Borderlands: Studies in Chicano Literature, Culture, Ideology* (1991, edited by Héctor Calderón and José David Saldívar), *Cultural Studies* (1990, edited by Angie C. Chabram and Rosa Linda Fregoso), Genaro Padilla's *My History, Not Yours: The Formation of Mexican American Autobiography* (1993), Carl Gutiérrez-Jones's *Rethinking the Borderlands: Between Chicano Culture and Legal Discourse* (1995), and Rosaura Sánchez's *Telling Identities: The Californio testimonios* (1995).[39] While other works should be added to this list, I selected these to follow the impact of a "cultural turn" in Chicano(a) studies. This turn was made possible by the weakening of Chicano Studies due to the work of Chicana feminist writers, at times interwoven with structuralist, poststructuralist, and postmodern scholarship.

These Chicana(o) scholars, reacting to a myriad of objections to academic knowledge, returned to the early quest to decenter academic production. As the sociologist and feminist Liz Stanley has penned, academic knowledge is centered on the Cartesian ideas about science, knowledge, research procedures, theories, and expertise[40] that in turn is protected by a wide variety of gatekeepers, publishers, organizational and professional structures, and the nature of expertise.[41] As earlier, Chicanos(as) believed that they could contest this Cartesian framework and its process of incorporation by turning learned intellectual accouterments upon themselves—to question core concepts and methods of institutional academic knowledge. Chicanos(as) believed that by asserting the priority of ontology (as identity) as well as calling attention to the existence of multiple knowledges based on their diverse positions and lived experiences, they could shift U.S. academic practice off its center.

Rosaldo, arguing from changes in anthropology, wrote that an epistemological shift occurred in ethnographic research. By acknowledging that the ethnographer and the native are "positioned subjects" with distinctive mixes of insight and blindness, he believes that anthropologists can remake social analysis. With this Copernican shift, traditional conceptions of truth and objectivity, endowed with institutional authority, lose their monopoly status. This epistemic break underscores the limitations of traditional modes of composition with its traditional tools and procedures of analysis. Rosaldo overturned the image of the lone ethnographer as the detached observer driven by neutrality, impartiality, and value-free inquiry, in search of the "grammar" of particular communities, presenting his or her data in an appropriate narrative style. Rosaldo purported to break objectivism's monopoly on truth claims by stressing the interplay of structure and agency. This would allow the researcher to explore his or her subjects from a multitude of positions. One approach to achieve this goal, he noted, is the processual analysis (like thick description) that highlights change over structure. Analysts could thereby become social critics driven by ethical concerns.[42]

Using a different language, the critic Carl Gutiérrez-Jones argued a similar point. Chicano literary theorizing, he observed, lies in its movement beyond all-encompassing categories into an analysis of the processes how Chicano(a) art engaged the world.[43] In this way, Chicano(a) narratives challenge hegemonic modes of thought. Ramón Saldívar added that Chicano(a) narratives, as oppositional ideological forms, signify the imaginary ways in which people live out their lives in a class society and overturn hegemonic American culture that seeks to prevent them from attaining knowledge of society as a whole.[44] These authors argued that we need to read Chicano(a) literary texts as works that intentionally exploit their peripheral status and exclusion from the cannon.[45]

Emma Perez's book on the "decolonial imaginary" provides an example of a particular Chicana feminist perspective.[46] Perez sees history as a series of narratives; therefore, the task of the historian is to deconstruct the systems of thought that frame these stories. By introducing the concept of the decolonial imaginary, she wishes to draw out the transformative nature of Chicana agency.[47] The decolonial imaginary is the "lag" between dominant colonial imaginary and a utopian postcolonial project; it is the space where differential politics and social dilemmas are negotiated and the silent gain their agency. Perez wrote: "The historian's political project, then, is to write a history that decolonizes otherness."[48] She suggests that the "technologies" of desire/sexualities/gender are the point of departure for this new approach. A third-space feminist analysis can bring the decolonial imaginary into play and help us move beyond woman as an essential category.[49] Perez turns to Anzaldúa's work, which she describes as a new postnationalist project in which *la nueva mestiza* is the privileged subject of an interstitial space.[50]

The second tradition is Transnational Chicano(a)/Latino(a) studies. Although few scholars would debate the centrality of the border, some would disagree that Chicano(a) studies necessarily needs to establish a link with Latin American (including Caribbean) scholarship. While one could make an argument that this shift might be a continuation of early Chicano internationalism, I believe that this is an attempt to initiate a conversation among Latin Americans and Latinos(as).[51] Unlike the earlier Chicano Studies–Mexico interchange of the 1970s or the internationalization of Chicano(a) studies through conferences in Europe, the present engagement decenters Chicano(a) studies by acknowledging its trans-Mexican, multi-racial/-ethnic, and migrant identities.[52] The homogeneous Mexican was recognized as a political construct of post–Revolutionary Mexico. At the same time, Chicana feminists and lesbians, together with voices of Central American migrants, disrupted a static notion of the Mexican American and Chicano(a). Implied in this deconstruction was how to proceed with some new expression of collectivity. Transnational Chicano(a)/Latino(a) Studies accepts a volatile Chicano(a) identity that moves away from intellectual articulations to those that are formed though particular lived experiences. Moreover, this exchange is not driven from one direction or the other; rather, it appears as a dialogue.

As Latin Americans reclaim "area studies" and propose a "Latin American Subaltern Studies" or a "Critical Latin American Studies," some crossed the gulf between this new Latin American Studies to Chicano(a) studies.[53] Some Chicano(a) scholars returned the favor by linking Chicano(a) studies to the new critical Latin American Studies. This dialogue, with an echo to earlier Chicano(a) and Puerto Rican conversations, led a few scholars to rethink Chicano(a) studies through the lens of the Latino(a) condition. Such an exchange of ideas was sustained by *Latino Studies* in 2006. Maybe this interaction might elude the resurrection of a Mexican-centered notion of *mestizaje* with its attenuated myth of racial democracy. Transnational Chicano(a)/Latino(a) Studies permits scholars to assert the African, Asian, and Native heritages of Chicanos(as) as Latinos(as) without recourse to ladino frameworks. While politically Chicano(a) studies departments and programs are fighting the use of the term "Latino(a)," intellectually a number of Chicano(a)/Latino(a) scholars have shifted by borrowing from the "schools" that have developed around Enrique Dussel, Walter Mignolo, Maria Lugones, and Ramón Grosfoguel.

As much as these two Chicano(a) studies traditions have to offer intellectually, they have to negotiate with U.S. higher education for their existence. The cultural or transnational turn could not sustain an oppositional stance in higher education. Chicano(a) studies, like earlier Chicano Studies, accommodated itself within the academy and established a safe alternative space. Given the nature of the hidden curriculum, however, academic politics cannot reform U.S. higher education. So what are the possible options for the future of Chicano(a) studies? I propose a third option for those of us who still struggle with the academic limits to improve the world we inhabit.

A Possible Future: An Ethical Turn

Just like students, Chicano(a) and Latino(a) academics often find ourselves caught between our hopes and institutional practices that subordinate and discipline us. The hidden curriculum functions against both students and faculty, while our research can "orientalize" our communities. Possibly more pernicious is how the institution manages our personal interactions. How often do we find ourselves "enforcing" institutional regulations against each other? Procedures for admissions, hiring, evaluations, tenure, full professorship, as well as judgments on research and publications become mechanism where we function as gatekeepers. Is this situation unavoidable? Is there anything we can do?

Frankly, I am not sure. Nonetheless, I would like to follow up on a plea that Anzaldúa articulated in *Making Face*: Chicanas(os) need to be careful on how they deal with each other. Specifically, she wrote: "They have us doing to those within our own ranks what they have done and continue to do to us—*Othering* people."[54] To avoid this "othering," Anzaldúa asks that we begin "identifying emotionally with a cultural alterity, with the *Other*."[55] Her call to ethics suggests a different intervention in the academy and Chicano(a) studies. Anzaldúa asks us to look at how we *engage* each other. This ethical turn questions the centrality we have given to ontological and epistemological issues as well as our battle for institutional spaces.

Current Chicano(a) and Latino(a) research still struggles with understanding the Mexican American and Latino(a) conditions. Some scholars start from ontology and move to epistemology, while others do the reverse. Yet in the end, something seems amiss. These multiple ways of knowing, recognition of the multiplicities of being, and understandings of power do little to transform the world. Chicano(a) studies seems satisfied with epistemological puzzles and encounters with multiple identities, while hope remains trapped within the language and practices of instrumentalism. In the academy, we engage each other with the same unethical procedures we have been taught. While Chicano(a) scholars have won the academic battle, we have lost the war for justice. The ability to transform our neighborhoods and our places of work remains utopian.

In *Sometimes There Is No Other Side*, Rudy Acuña has demonstrated that a bifurcation exists among Chicano(a) scholars. Many are willing participants in the dominant paradigm; then there are some that "epistemologically and politically" challenge "the dominant [positivistic Eurocentric] paradigm."[56] Acuña sharply criticizes the first group: "My [legal] case also taught me a lot about Chicana/o studies scholars. They are part of the culture of the university, and subject to its reward system. They crave acceptance by the academy, to the point that much of their research is tailored to fit what the institution wants." Acuña goes on to explain the reason for this attitude: "The main reason for this, I believe, is that an essential part of positivistic logic is to evade responsibility for one's actions and recognition of one's true motives— in this case, opportunism and a lack of political commitment."[57]

Simultaneously, Acuña argues that Chicano(a) studies is a space where the dominant paradigm does not operate (or at least is recognized and questioned for what it is) due to Chicano(a) studies community interests.[58] Chicano(a) studies' oppositional role, Acuña continues, comes from an "interdisciplinary approach to teaching and research."[59] Chicano(a) studies scholars retain an autonomous and activist position in the academy by building on "experiential" and "qualitative" knowledge. This, he adds, can only come from retaining an association with the community. For Acuña, this is "advocacy research in the tradition of W.E.B. Du Bois, since it has a moral and societal purpose."[60] Because of Chicano(a) studies' potential oppositional role, it has not gained acceptance within academia. Acuña concludes that the problem that exists among Chicano(a) scholars arises from faculty who are not engaged in advocacy research.

While I disagree with Acuña's call for advocacy research since it keeps us in the realm of instrumentalism, I fully support his call to responsibility. To make this ethical turn, we cannot return to the instrumental thinking of advocacy research. The work of the philosopher Emmanuel Levinas might help us meditate about the turn to ethics as a point of departure for our role as academics. Just as Edmund Husserl set out to put ontology at the center by displacing epistemology, Levinas will displace ontology with ethics.[61] The modern era, Levinas comments, witnessed the switch from identification and appropriation of being by knowledge to the identification of being and knowledge. Knowledge, as an activity, appropriates and grasps the otherness of the known. "To know amounts to grasping being out of nothing or reducing it to nothing," he writes. "Removing it its alterity."[62]

In consuming otherness, being is reduced to presence and representation; the cogito appropriates the Other (*autrui*). Levinas explains: "Here the known is understood and so *appropriated* by knowledge, and as it were *freed* of its otherness."[63] By violently reducing the other to my sphere of ideas, the *I* closes off contact with the real person. Knowledge does not put us in communion with the other; rather, it is always about solitude and the ego. For this reason, Western modes of knowledge, derived from totality, must be disrupted in order to break the violence of metaphysics.[64] Ethical obligation, Levinas argues, therefore cannot arise from the logical and ontological universality or reason; rather, moral responsibility takes hold immediately before understanding or discussion on part of the subject.[65] In his essay "Ethics as First Philosophy," Levinas turns to an examination of nonintentional consciousness:[66] "[c]onsciousness of consciousness, indirect, implicit and aimless, without any initiative that might refer back to an ego."[67] This implicit consciousness precedes all intentions and is pure passivity. We turn to a point before thought originates.[68] It is a consciousness that signifies "not so much a knowledge of oneself as something that effaces presence or makes it discreet."[69] Passivity precedes the formulation of any metaphysical ideas by which "the very justice of the position within being is questioned."[70]

Historically, the response of my being-in-the-world has meant "the usurpation of spaces belonging to the other man whom I have already oppressed or starved, or driven out into a third world."[71] My being, however, cannot be justified in the usurpation of somebody else's place but in appeal to responsibility. It is when I face the face of the other (proximity) that I am summoned and called back to responsibility. This responsibility is as if I were devoted to the other person before being devoted to myself. It comes before my freedom and before my being. "It is the responsibility of a hostage which can be carried to the point of being substituted for the other person and demands an infinite subjection of subjectivity."[72] It is in the surrender of the ego of its sovereignty that one finds ethics and the question of the meaning of being. In Levinas's words: "The human is the return to the interiority of non-intentional consciousness, to *mauvaise conscience,* to its capacity to fear injustice more than death, to prefer to suffer than to commit injustice, and to prefer that which justifies being over that which assures it."[73] Subjectivity is subjection to the other. At this point, substitution arises directly from being held hostage by the other. Being a subject means to be in the grips of the Other.

This responsibility for the Other does not begin with my decision. It comes from a "prior to every memory," an "ulterior to every accomplishment, before and beyond essence."[74] For this reason, the response cannot be contained, historically reconstructed, thematized, or comprehended. My responsibility for the Other commands me and ordains me to the Other; I am ordered toward the face of the Other to listen.[75] Again, Levinas: "The response which is responsibility, responsibility for the neighbor that is incumbent, resounds in passivity, this disinterestedness of subjectivity, this sensibility."[76] In *Totality and Infinity,* Levinas uses the concept of infinity to avoid the totalizing and violent language of knowledge and metaphysics and to explore that space in subjectivity where we welcome the Other: "The trace of a past in a face is not the absence of a yet not-revealed, but the anarchy of what has never been present, of an infinite which commands in the face of the other, and which, like an excluded middle, could not be aimed at."[77] But the Other and I do not form a unit. The Other remains outside my grasp—outside totality. The relationship that can exist only proceeds from the I to the Other, as a face-to-face.[78] "It is therefore to *receive* from the Other beyond the capacity of the I, which means exactly: to have the idea of infinity."[79] In this face-to-face, where we recognize the Other as master, we encounter truth and justice.[80] From Levinas's *Ethics and Infinity*: "[T]he saying is the fact that before the face I do not simply remain there contemplating it, I respond to it."[81]

When we encounter the face, it is naked; it is by itself, without reference to system. Thus the face comes to us destitute; it demands our response. To recognize the Other is to recognize a hunger and to give, to speak.[82] In discourse, the Other presents himself or herself as interlocutor, as him or her over whom I cannot have power.[83] The urgency of response engenders me for responsibility. To be attentive is to recognize the mastery of the Other.[84] The notion of saying places us before the questioning. Responsibility is precisely a saying before anything is said.[85] The act of saying is from the start as "the supreme passivity of exposure to another."[86] To engage the face is to speak with the world; the face-to-face commits me to the human fraternity.[87] By thinking of subjectivity in terms of proximity, Levinas makes sure the notion of responsibility is universal. The "an-archy" of proximity, as the scholar Fabio Ciaramelli stresses, between the Other and me renders my responsibility infinite. Everyone is called upon to become a "me" in a relation of responsibility with the other; the claim made on me by another is made to everyone.[88] "Ethics occurs as an an-archy, the compassion of being."[89]

Acuña asked us, as Chicanos(as), to explain why we have not challenged the U.S. paradigm. I suggest that the failure came from our preoccupation with unmediated theorizing. Although this has produced much interesting intellectual production and provided an alternative view of the world, it has not dealt with the issue that was (and is) at the heart of el movimiento: justice. Simultaneously, as academic Chicanos(as), we do not listen; we are unable to look awry. Even in their most radical dress, Chicano(a) intellectuals fall into an "abstract rationalistic inventiveness," that abstract critical activity from the social world.[90]

This has reinforced our Sisyphean search for theoretical closure. This was simply another totalizing effort to absorb (and observe) otherness. Our focus on epistemology and ontology, reinforced by our desire to be part of U.S. higher education, has led us away from responsibility. So we are now at a point to make this ethical turn—both as academics and as individuals. Where this might lead us, I am not certain.

I hope that my playing with Levinas might permit Chicanos(as) to reconsider responsibility from outside the frame of morality. While consciousnesses and epistemological questions still demand our attention as Chicanos(as), we need to acknowledge our ethical practices, especially in the academy. While Levinas's argument about substitution may sound abstract and return us to the deity, and maybe Derrida's criticism that Levinas remains trapped in totalizing thought has merit, the vision I would like to take from him is his call for our engagement with each other *without* our endeavor to control. As Chicanos(as), in various hierarchical relationships with one another, we cannot accept academic practices as neutral. To do so is to turn our back on justice and self-determination. Thus, if there is any role for a Chicano(a) studies in our intellectual lives, we need to return to Anzaldúa's comment about how we treat others; it is to balance our academic quests with our commitment to each other, and then to our communities.

Notes

Introduction

1. I have retained "Chicano studies" and "Chicano" because its usage reflects the gendered politics and epistemology of the Chicano movements. Soldatenko, "Constructing Chicana."

2. I use the term "Chicano studies" to refer to the plurality of Chicano studies. In contrast, "Chicano Studies" refers to the version of Chicano studies that ultimately found academic success in many university research institutions.

3. Martinez, "'*Chingón* Politics.'"

4. Bixler-Márquez, *Chicano Studies*.

5. By "method," I refer to research techniques or practices, such as surveys or interviews. "Methodology" is a perspective or theoretically informed framework that may or may not have its appropriate research techniques. "Epistemology" is defined as "a theory of knowledge which addresses central questions such as: who can be a 'knower,' what can be known, what constitutes and validates knowledge, and what the relationship is or should be between knowing and being" (Stanley and Wise, "Method, Methodology, and Epistemology," 26).

6. Williams, *Marxism and Literature,* 115.

7. Ibid.; Williams, "Future of Cultural Studies"; Said, *World, the Text, and the Critic*; Ross, *Origins of American Social Science*; and Schürmann, "Concerning Philosophy."

8. Margolis, *Hidden Curricula*.

9. "Alternative" seeks to adapt to existing power relations, while "oppositional" questions and hopes to replace existing dominant relations (Williams, "Base and Superstructure," 82).

10. Ross, *Origins of American Social Science,* 59.

11. Rosen, *World Split Open,* xiv.

12. Ross, *Origins of American Social Science,* 60–61.

13. Said, *World, the Text, and the Critic ,* 21.

14. Singh, *Black Is a Country,* 17.

15. Ibid., 19–20.

16. Ibid., 31.

17. DuBois, *Souls of Black Folks*.

18. Olguin, "Politics of Criticism as a Criticism of Politics."

19. Romano-V., "Anthropology and Sociology of the Mexican-American"; Romano-V., "Historical and Intellectual Presence of Mexican-Americans"; and Romano-V., "Social Science, Objectivity, and the Chicanos."

20. Olguin, "Politics of Criticism as a Criticism of Politics," 40.

21. It is important to keep in mind that I am looking at the formation of an academic discipline instead of a political strategy (Contreras, "Ideology of the Political Movement," 3).

22. Williams, "Future of Cultural Studies," 152.

23. Ibid., 156.

24. Ibid., 157.

25. Ibid.

26. Lugones, "Purity, Impurity, and Separation," 459.

Chapter 1. The Genesis of Academic Chicano Studies

1. Because most early protests and Chicano(a) academics were in California, my research tends to have a California focus. I use examples from California that tend to overemphasize the role of the state. In reality, Chicano studies was being developed throughout the Southwest. As more scholars study this period, a more complete picture will surely emerge. I would hypothesize, nonetheless, that the patterns encountered in California were similar to those elsewhere.

2. See, for example, Padilla, "Chicano Studies at the University"; Padilla, *Chicano Studies Revisited*; Muñoz Jr., *Youth, Identity, Power*; and Contreras, "Ideology of the Political Movement."

3. Furet, *Interpreting the French Revolution*.

4. See Gómez-Quiñones, *Mexican Students Por La Raza*; Muñoz Jr., *Youth, Identity, Power*; Navarro, *Mexican American Youth Organization*; and Chávez, *"¡Mi Raza Primero!"*

5. Gilabert, *El Habito de la Utopia*; and Berman, *Tale of Two Utopias*.

6. See Manuel and Manuel, *Utopian Thought in the Western World*, 4.

7. Ibid., 5.

8. Jacoby, *End of Utopia*, 105.

9. Every utopia is bound to reproduce its particular world (Manuel and Manuel, *Utopian Thought in the Western World*, 23).

10. Gilabert, *El Habito de la Utopia*, 9–10. All translations of the original Spanish-language text are mine.

11. McLaren, *Schooling as a Ritual Performance*, 34.

12. On the "institutional imaginary," see Castoriadis, *Imaginary Institution of Society*. McLaren, *Schooling as a Ritual Performance*, 142–143.

13. Bloch, *Spirit of Utopia*.

14. Giroux and McLaren, "Paulo Freire, Postmodernism, and the Utopian Imagination," 146.

15. Levy, "Utopia and Reality in the Philosophy of Ernst Bloch," 176.

16. Levitas, "Educated Hope," 70.

17. Ibid., 66.

18. Giroux and McLaren, "Paulo Freire, Postmodernism, and the Utopian Imagination," 146.

19. Kellner, "Ernst Bloch, Utopia, and Ideology Critique."

20. Bronner, "Utopian Projections," 168.

21. Giroux and McLaren, "Paulo Freire, Postmodernism, and the Utopian Imagination," 149.

22. Marcuse, "Repressive Tolerance," 83.

23. Ibid., 85.

24. Marcuse, *Essay on Liberation*, 13.

25. Horkheimer, "Authoritarian State," 18.

26. Ibid., 11; and Paz, *The Other Mexico*, 68.

27. Horkheimer, "Authoritarian State," 19.

28. Marcuse, "Repressive Tolerance," 87.

29. Bakhtin, *Rabelais and His World*, 6.

30. Ibid., 7, 19, 47, and 95.

31. Castoriadis, *Imaginary Institution of Society*, 71.

32. Bakhtin, *Rabelais and His World*, 273.

33. Ibid., 10.

34. Ibid., 123 and 276 (quotation).

35. Levy, "Utopia and Reality in the Philosophy of Ernst Bloch," 177.

36. Berman, *Tale of Two Utopias*, 47–48.

37. Castoriadis, *Imaginary Institution of Society*, 62.

38. Marcuse, "Repressive Tolerance."

39. Chávez, "¡Mi Raza Primero!," 47.

40. Macias, "The Ultimate Pendejada."

41. "Editorial," *El Grito* 1, no. 1 (1968): 4.

42. Muñoz, "Development of Chicano Studies," 7.

43. Ybarra-Frausto, "Chicano Movement," 97.

44. Vaca, "Message to the People," 1.

45. Ibid., 3 and 7.

46. Davalos, "Chicana/o Studies and Anthropology," 18–19.

47. García, "Creating a Consciousness," 6.

48. Romano-V., "Minorities, History, and the Cultural Mystique," 8; and Romano-V., "Anthropology and Sociology of the Mexican-American," 13–14.

49. Romano-V., "Minorities, History, and the Cultural Mystique," 10; Romano-V., "Anthropology and Sociology of the Mexican-American," 23; and Vaca, "Mexican-American in the Social Sciences," Part I and II; and Montiel, "Social Science Myth."

50. Romano-V., "Anthropology and Sociology of the Mexican-American," 24.

51. Romano-V., "Goodbye Revolution," 81.

52. Romano-V., "Mugre de la cancíon," 52.

53. Rodolfo Salinas reiterated this view in *Con Safos* (Salinas, "Chicano Power"). Oscar Martinez parallels this point in the same issue Martinez, "Manifest Mexicanism," 35.

54. Romano-V., "Anthropology and Sociology of the Mexican-American," 25; and Olguin, "Politics of Criticism as a Criticism of Politics."

55. In Fraire-Aldava, "Octavio Romano," 165.

56. Romano-V., "Historical and Intellectual Presence of Mexican-Americans," 35.

57. Ibid., 37.

58. Ibid., 39.

59. Ibid., 40.

60. Ibid., 34.

61. Ibid., 41.

62. Romano-V., "Minorities, History, and the Cultural Mystique," 11.

63. Romano-V., "Book Review of: *North From Mexico*," 52.

64. Romano-V., "Don Pedrito Jaramillo"; Romano-V., "Donship in a Mexican-American Community"; and Romano-V., *Geriatric Fu*, 63–68.

65. Romano-V., "Book Review of: *North From Mexico*," 55.

66. Ibid.

67. Romano-V., "Social Science, Objectivity, and the Chicanos," 4.

68. Ibid., 5. In a later piece, Romano phrased this point as follows: "If there is a cohesive configuration of cultural themes and overriding values which characterize the historical development of American society and its West European intellectual, philosophical and political heritage, then that configuration can best be summarized as an analytical orientation toward the empirical, physical, and cultural world accompanied by a pervasive belief in the separability of reality into its constituent parts and elements" (Romano-V., "Constitutional Issues," 10).

69. Ibid., 5–6.

70. Contreras, "Ideology of the Political Movement," 179.

71. Romano-V., "Social Science, Objectivity, and the Chicanos," 7.

72. Ibid., 12.

73. Romano-V., "Introductory Comments"; Romano-V., "Un Telefono"; Romano-V., "Yo no perdi nada . . . "; Romano-V., "The Chosen One"; Romano-V., "Plegaria"; and Romano-V., "Notes on the Modern State."

74. Romano-V. and Rios C., "Quinto Sol and Chicano Publications," 3.

75. Ibid., 5.

76. Romano-V., "Introduction," 2.

77. Romano-V., "Tonatiuh International," 1.

78. "Demagogues may come and demagogues will go, but the art of a people is timeless—following its own rules that transcend the limited focus of ambition as well as the biological routine of death and oblivion" (Romano-V., "Introduction," *El Grito* 2, no. 3 (1969): 2). For a different reading of Romano, see García, "Creating a Consciousness."

79. Ortega, "Introduction," vii.

80. Romano-V., "Introductory Comments," 8.

81. Chicano Coordinating Council on Higher Education, *El Plan*; Muñoz Jr., "Quest for Paradigm"; Muñoz, "Development of Chicano Studies"; and Contreras, "Ideology of the Political Movement."

82. Marin, *Spokesman of the Mexican American Movement*, 13.

83. *Inside Eastside* 2, no. 7 (1969): 37

84. Treviño, *Eyewitness*, 104.

85. Chicano Coordinating Council on Higher Education, *El Plan*, 10; Nuñez and Contreras, "Principles and Foundations of Chicano Studies," in *Chicano Discourse*, 32.

86. Chicano Coordinating Council on Higher Education, *El Plan*, 13.

87. Nuñez and Contreras, "Principles and Foundations of Chicano Studies," in *Chicano Discourse,* 35; and Padilla, "Chicano Studies at the University."

88. Nuñez and Contreras, "Principles and Foundations of Chicano Studies," in *Chicano Discourse,* 33.

89. Gómez-Quiñones, *Chicano Politics,* 123.

90. Muñoz Jr., "Quest for Paradigm," 24.

91. Nuñez and Contreras, "Principles and Foundations of Chicano Studies," in *Chicano Discourse,* 33.

92. Chicano Coordinating Council on Higher Education, *El Plan*, 94.

93. Ibid., 70.

94. Ibid., 43 and 95–96.

95. Ibid., 47.

96. Navarro, *Mexican American Youth Organization,* 71.

97. García has argued that current weakness in Chicano(a) studies results from the failure to either fully or truly implement *El Plan* (García, "The Chicano," 353, 354).

98. Padilla, "Chicano Studies at the University," 157.

99. Ibid., 154.

100. Ibid., 48.

101. Chicano Coordinating Council on Higher Education, *El Plan*, 13; Muñoz, "Development of Chicano Studies," 13; and Contreras, "Ideology of the Political Movement," 1.

102. Chicano Coordinating Council on Higher Education, *El Plan*, 74.

103. Fleck, *Genesis and Development of a Scientific Fact,* 38.

104. Ibid., 41.

105. Grebler, Moore, and Guzman, *Mexican American People.*

106. Ibid., 575.

107. Ibid., 592.

108. Chicano Coordinating Council on Higher Education, *El Plan*, 75.

109. Vaca, "Message to the People," 2.

110. Ornelas, "Book Review of the Mexican-American People," 14.

111. Padilla, "Critique of Pittian History," 4.

112. Ibid., 16.

113. Padilla could never overcome his own desire to negotiate with the academy and the possibilities offered by *El Grito* thinkers. In later works, he turned to traditional social science. He accepted the academy and its academic devices. This contradiction was most obvious in his almost ceaseless struggle to square the circle by trying to create a radical (transformative) pedagogy within a traditional school of education. Ironically, his Sisyphean endeavor ended up authenticating traditional academic pedagogic patterns. Moreover, his academic practices reinforced the standards and ethics of higher education.

114. Hernández, *Mexican American Challenge to a Sacred Cow,* 48.

115. Ibid., 45.

116. Ibid., 50.

117. Ibid., 49.

118. In another essay, following Max Weber, Hernández wrote in favor of "subjective understanding" (Hernández, "La Raza Satellite System").

119. Memorandum, "Chicano Studies Program in California," 1970, Ronald Lopez Collection, UCLA Chicano Studies Research Center Library.

120. Memorandum, "Feasibility Study for College of Chicano Studies," 1972, Ronald Lopez Collection, UCLA Chicano Studies Research Center Library.

121. Alurista, "Chicano Studies: A Future," n.d., Deborah Weber Collection, UCLA Chicano Studies Research Center Library.

122. Ibid, 3.

123. Rochin, "Short and Turbulent Life of Chicano Studies," 888.

124. Memorandum by UMAS, n.d., Ronald Lopez Collection, UCLA Chicano Studies Research Center Library, 1.

125. Acuña, "Chicano Studies," 2.

126. California State University at San Diego, Chicano Studies Catalog, 1969 (mimeograph).

127. Acuña et al. *Chicano Studies SDSU*, 1973.

Chapter 2. Empirics and Chicano Studies

1. Most scholars remained ambivalent in their understanding of the Chicano(a) academic's political role. "The university today graduates thousands of students who will 'go out into the world.' These students are trained to perpetuate the 'system' as it exists today. . . . If we really believe that we can change the society by going into the barrios and ghettos, we are truly victims of our fantasies" (Memorandum by Ronald Lopez, n.d. Ronald Lopez Collection, UCLA Chicano Studies Research Center Library, 6).

2. Olguin, "Politics of Criticism as a Criticism of Politics," 80.

3. Rochin, "Short and Turbulent Life of Chicano Studies," 888.

4. Ramos, "A mi me dieron el talento."

5. Lopez and Enos, *Chicanos and Public Higher Education*, H-7.

6. Gómez-Quiñones, *Chicano Politics*, 104.

7. García, *Chicanismo*, 8.

8. Nogales, "Chicanismo and Education."

9. At the same time, chicanismo conveyed the sins of patriarchy (La Coronela, "Cultural Nationalism," 3).

10. Lopez and Enos, *Chicanos and Public Higher Education*, H-7.

11. Muñoz, "Development of Chicano Studies," 13.

12. Ortega, "Introduction," ix.

13. Muñoz Jr., *Youth, Identity, Power*, 141.

14. Padilla, "Chicano Studies at the University," 268; Contreras, "Ideology of the Political Movement," 1; "Proposal for Mexican American College," n.d., Ronald Lopez Collection, UCLA Chicano Studies Research Center Library; García, "Juncture in the Road"; and Memorandum, "Feasibility Study for College of Chicano Studies," 1972, Ronald Lopez Collection, UCLA Chicano Studies Research Center Library.

15. Ross, *Origins of American Social Science*; and Said, *World, the Text, and the Critic*.

16. Gómez-Quiñones, *Chicano Politics*, 140.

17. Chicano Coordinating Council on Higher Education, *El Plan*, 16–18.

18. Alejandro, "Chicano and Higher Education," 44.

19. García, "Creating a Consciousness," 14.

20. Memorandum by Ronald Lopez, n.d. Ronald Lopez Collection, UCLA Chicano Studies Research Center Library.

21. Contreras, "Existential Phenomenology," 195.

22. Ronald Lopez, Reflections, n.d., Ronald Lopez Collection, UCLA Chicano Studies Research Center Library, 5.

23. Memorandum by Rene Nuñez, n.d., Ronald Lopez Collection, UCLA Chicano Studies Research Center Library, 3.

24. Ibid.; Minutes of the Mexican American Cultural Center, Steering Committee Meeting, December 5, 1969, Library Collection, UCLA Chicano Studies Research Center Library.

25. Agenda Chicano Studies Institute, June 13, 1970, UCLA Chicano Studies Research Center Library Collection.

26. Alejandro, "Chicano and Higher Education"; and Armas, "National Concilio for Chicano Studies"; and Amaya, "On Chicanas in Higher Education."

27. Gómez-Quiñones, *Mexican Students Por La Raza*, 31–35; and Muñoz Jr., *Youth, Identity, Power*, 134–136.

28. "El Concilio Nacional de Estudios Chicanos," v.

29. Guerra, "What Are the Objectives of Chicano Studies?," 8.

30. Rivera, *On Chicano Studies*.

31. Elizondo, "Critical Areas of Need," 4.

32. Guerra, "What Are the Objectives of Chicano Studies?," 9.

33. Elizondo, "Critical Areas of Need," 3.

34. López, "Role of the Chicano Student," 14.

35. Sánchez, *La Raza Community*, 1.

36. Guerra, "What Are the Objectives of Chicano Studies?," 11.

37. Elizondo, "Critical Areas of Need," 4.

38. Samora and Galarza, "Research and Scholarly Activity."

39. Macías, Gómez-Quiñones, and Castro, "Objectives of Chicano Studies." In a committee meeting of the UCLA Mexican American Cultural Center, Castro recognized that their summer institute presentation could provide the curricular vision for the new Chicano studies major at UCLA (Minutes of the Mexican American Cultural Center, Steering Committee Meeting, Library Collection, UCLA Chicano Studies Research Center Library).

40. Macías, Gómez-Quiñones, and Castro, "Objectives of Chicano Studies," 31–32.

41. Ibid.,32.

42. Ibid., 31.

43. Ibid.

44. Ibid., 32–33.

45. Ibid., 32.

46. An example of the acceptance of the academy's notion of "objectivity" was a proposed NBC television series on Mexican Americans (Memorandum by Ramon L.

Ponce, April 27, 1971, Ronald Lopez Collection, UCLA Chicano Studies Research Center Library, 2).

47. This was not the only endeavor to define Chicano studies. During the same time period, a six-week summer institute was set up at Stanford University to improve "the general quality of the instruction in the Mexican-American field" (see John J. Johnson, National Endowment for the Humanities Project Grant Application, November 12, 1969, Ronald Lopez Collection, UCLA Chicano Studies Research Center Library; Memorandum, "Summer Institute in Chicano Studies June 22–July 31, 1970," Ronald Lopez Collection, UCLA Chicano Studies Research Center Library).

48. Muñoz Jr., "Quest for Paradigm," 24–25; and Navarro, *Mexican American Youth Organization*, 73.

49. Muñoz Jr., "Quest for Paradigm," 24–25.

50. Mexican American Cultural Center, Chicano Journal Proposal—Draft, August 16, 1969, UCLA University Archives, Record Series 401 Box 127.

51. Peñalosa, "Recent Changes Among the Chicanos," 1; and Peñalosa, "Toward an Operational Definition."

52. Hernández, "La Raza Satellite System," 32.

53. Rivera, *On Chicano Studies*, 40.

54. The reader should not confuse the liberal position with the attempt by some Anglo scholars to write about the Chicano or to publish Chicano works without any reference point, such as Wagner and Haug, *Chicanos*.

55. Peñalosa, "Changing Mexican-American in Southern California," 257.

56. Murguía, *Assimilation, Colonization, and the Mexican American People*.

57. Peñalosa, "Recent Changes Among the Chicanos"; Peñalosa, "Sociology in a Mexican American Studies Program: Some Tentative Recommendations," n.d., Ronald Lopez Collection, UCLA Chicano Studies Research Center Library.

58. Padilla, "Psychological Research and the Mexican American"; Casavantes, *New Look at the Attributes*; and Guzman, "Politics and Policies of the Mexican-American Community."

59. Servín, *Awakened Minority*; and Burma, *Mexican-Americans in the United States*.

60. Alvarez, "Psycho-Historical and Socioeconomic Development."

61. Hernández, Estrada, and Alvírez, "Census Data"; Garcia, "Orientations of Mexican American and Anglo Children"; Gutiérrez and Hirsch, "Militant Challenge to the American Ethos"; Rochin, "Short and Turbulent Life of Chicano Studies"; Ramirez III, "Cognitive Styles and Cultural Democracy"; Ramos, "Case in Point"; and Alvarez, "Psycho-Historical and Socioeconomic Development."

62. See the entire issue of *Mexican American Cultural Center: Carta Universitaria* 1, no. 1 (1969).

63. "Mexican American Cultural Center and Aztlán," vi.

64. Chavarría, "Précis and a Tentative Bibliography," 133.

65. Ibid., 134.

66. Jesús Chavarría, "Chicano Studies," *Social Science Quarterly* 52, no. 1 (1971): 175.

67. Ibid., 177.

68. Ibid., 178.

69. Gómez-Quiñones, "Toward a Perspective on Chicano History," 1; Cortes, "CHICOP"; and Muñoz Jr., "Quest for Paradigm," 26.

70. Muñoz's intellectual work has consistently endeavored to come to terms with the intellectual project of Chicano(a) thought. He has worked to critically understand what we do as Chicano(a) intellectuals.

71. Muñoz, "Toward a Chicano Perspective," 18–10.

72. Ibid., 18.

73. Ibid., 21.

74. Ibid., 24.

75. Ibid., 17; Muñoz, "On the Nature," 99–100; Muñoz Jr., "Quest for Paradigm," 21; Gómez-Quiñones, Chicano Politics, 104.

76. Blanco, "Unidad," 5.

77. Hernández, "La Raza Satellite System," 14.

78. Ortiz, "On Ideological," 17.

79. Gómez-Quiñones, Mexican Students Por La Raza, 28.

80. Muñoz Jr., Youth, Identity, Power, 146; Gómez-Quiñones, Mexican Students Por La Raza, 12; and Gómez-Quiñones, Chicano Politics, 19.

81. Vaca, "Black Phase"; and Vaca, "Negro Movement."

82. Almaguer, "Toward the Study of Chicano Colonialism," 7.

83. Contreras, "Ideology of the Political Movement," 283.

84. Barrera, Muñoz, and Ornelas, "Barrio as an Internal Colony."

85. Acuña, Occupied America, 1st ed.

86. Gómez-Quiñones, "Toward a Perspective on Chicano History," 39; and Gómez-Quiñones, Chicano Politics, 19.

87. Gómez-Quiñones, "Toward a Perspective on Chicano History," 5; Gómez-Quiñones, "On Culture"; and Muñoz Jr., Youth, Identity, Power, 148.

88. Ortega, "Introduction," x.

89. García, "Internal Colonialism and the Chicano," 27; Muñoz Jr., "Quest for Paradigm," 30; Muñoz Jr., Youth, Identity, Power, 148; Gutiérrez, "Spanish-Language Radio"; and Alvarez, "Psycho-Historical and Socioeconomic Development."

90. García, "Internal Colonialism and the Chicano"; and "Symposium at Irvine."

91. Cervantes, "Chicanos as a Post Colonial Minority"; Segade, "Identity and Power"; Vigil, "Marx and Chicano Anthropology"; Gonzalez, "Critique of the Internal Colony Model"; and Mindiola, "Marxism and the Chicano Movement."

92. Minjares, "Chicanos for Political Unity"; "Una ideología," Nuestra Cosa 2, no. 2 (1973); and Prensa Popular 1, no. 6 (1974).

93. Muñoz, "Politics and the Chicano," 1.

94. Ibid., 4.

95. Barrera, "Study of Politics and the Chicano," 16.

96. Ibid., 16.

97. Ibid., 23.

98. Ibid., 24.

99. Almaguer, "Historical Notes on Chicano Oppression," 52–53.

100. Muñoz, "Politics of Chicano Urban Protest," 11.

101. Ibid., 16.

102. Rocco, "Critical Perspective on the Study of Chicano Politics," 561.

103. Ibid., 566.

104. Ibid., 560.

105. Gómez-Quiñones, "Toward a Perspective on Chicano History," 1.

106. Chavarría, "Précis and a Tentative Bibliography," 175.

107. The Chicano Studies Center at UCLA manifested this victorious spirit.

108. "Co-Editors Note," iv.

109. Ibid., iv–v.

110. Later Peñalosa would turn to world system as an approach to explain Chicano sociolinguistics.

111. Peñalosa, "Sociolinguistic Theory," 9. Amaya noted how Chicanos(as) in higher education were becoming stronger scholars as they moved away from the narrow pursuit of activism (Amaya, "On Chicanos in Higher Education," 40).

112. Ortega, "Introduction," xi.

113. Cárdenas, "Introduction," 141–142.

114. One should note the tension between the *Aztlán* editorial board and Octavio Romano (Minutes of Mexican American Cultural Center, Editorial Board Meeting, December 5, 1969, UCLA University Archives, Record Series 401 Box 127, 2).

115. In Mexican American history, one journal tried to challenge the direction *Aztlán* had established by returning to the traditional practices in the discipline with a traditional outlook. The *Journal of Mexican American History* (*JMAH*) saw itself as a response to "the opportunism, crass politics and misleading publicity" of Chicano(a) academics ("Editorial," *JMAH*; and Navarro, "Condition of Mexican-American History," 44). Unfortunately the journal would not last.

116. Soldatenko "Quincentenary of an Erasure"; and McClintock, *Imperial Leather*.

117. Letter by Jaime Sena Rivera, February 14, 1973, National Association of Chicano Studies Association, Library Collection, UCLA Chicano Studies Research Center Library; *National Caucuses,* 1, no. 1. One could point to La Junta de Sociológicos Chicanos, the Chicano caucus in the American Sociological Association, as a precursor to National Caucus of Chicano Social Scientists (Letter by Jaime Sena Rivera, September 13, 1971, National Association of Chicano Studies Association, Library Collection, UCLA Chicano Studies Research Center Library; Letter by Reynaldo Flores Macías, September 16, 1971, National Association of Chicano Studies Association, Library Collection, UCLA Chicano Studies Research Center Library; Letter by Jaime Sena Rivera, September 23, 1971, National Association of Chicano Studies Association, Library Collection, UCLA Chicano Studies Research Center Library).

118. *National Caucus,* 1, no. 1. In a letter Rivera noted that an Association of Chicano Historians was established and could be contacted through the UCLA Chicano Studies Center (Letter by Jaime Sena Rivera, February 14, 1973, National Association of Chicano Studies Association, Library Collection, UCLA Chicano Studies Research Center Library).

119. Aside from members of the site committee, no tenured or senior faculty were present (*National Caucus,* 1, no. 1).

120. Macías, *Perspectivas en Chicano Studies,* 214–216.

121. Muñoz Jr., "Quest for Paradigm," 30–31.

122. Garza, "Origins and Evolution of an Alternative Scholarship," 41.

123. Ibid., 43.

124. Barrera, Camarillo, and Hernandez, "Introduction," 3.

125. Garza, "Origins and Evolution of an Alternative Scholarship," 45.

126. *National Association* 1, no. 2; 1, no. 3.

127. *National Association* 1, no. 3: 1.

128. *El Mirlo* 2, no. 9.

129. *El Mirlo* 2, no. 8: 250. One can also see a continuation with an earlier Symposium on "La Mujer Chicana" held at Notre Dame (*El Mirlo* 2 , no. 7).

130. *El Mirlo* 2, no. 7; 2, no. 8; and 2, no. 9.

131. *El Mirlo* 3, no. 10.

132. *National Caucuses*; and Macias, *Perspectivas en Chicano Studies.*

133. Muñoz Jr., "Quest for Paradigm," 31.

134. Ibid., 34.

135. Ibid., 35.

136. Garza, "Origins and Evolution of an Alternative Scholarship," 40.

137. Ibid., 45.

138. Included in the initial planning committee for the conference were Eugene Cota-Robles, Juan Gómez-Quiñones, Ricardo Griego, and Carlos Blanco-Aguinaga.

139. Letter by Arturo Madrid, 1974, Ronald Lopez Collection, UCLA Chicano Studies Research Center Library.

140. Minutes of the Mexican American Cultural Center, Steering Committee Meeting, December 5, 1969, UCLA University Archives, Record Series 401, Box 127.

141. University of California Chicano Steering Committee, "Proposal for a University of California Student Lobby Intern for Chicano Affairs," 1974, Larry Trujillo Collection, University of California at Berkeley, Ethnic Studies Library Archives, Box 32, 1.

142. Minutes from Meeting of University of California Chicano Steering Committee at Irvine, October 9, 1971, UCB Ethnic Studies Library Archives, Juan Gonzales Collection Box 2; Minutes of University of California Steering Committee Meeting, January 22, 1972, Juan Gonzales Collection, UCB Ethnic Studies Library Archives; Minutes of University of California Steering Committee, February 19, 1972, Juan Gonzales Collection, UCB Ethnic Studies Library Archives, 2; John Gonzales, Report of University of California Steering Committee of 8-19-72, August 30, 1972, Juan Gonzales Collection, UCB Ethnic Studies Library Archives Box 2; Memorandum, "Notes Taken from a Workshop Report Delivered at the University of California MEChA Conference Held in Upland, Califas," 1972, Library Collection, UCLA Chicano Studies Research Center Library.

143. Ibid.

144. By 1975, the University of California Chicano Task Force finally came out with its report on the status of Chicanos(as) and its recommendations (*El Mirlo* 2, no. 10; 3, no. 1; 3, no. 7; 3, no. 8; 3, no. 9; 3, no. 10).

145. *Report of the President's Task Force,* 115.

146. Ibid.

147. Memorandum, "Unase Raza!!," 1975, UCB Ethnic Studies Library Archives, Juan Gonzales Collection, Box 2; Memorandum, "Huelga General," 1976, Juan Gonzales Collection, UCB Ethnic Studies Library Archives, Box 2.

148. Acevedo, "U.C. Chicano Faculty Meeting."

149. "Chicano 'Elite' in the Universities."

150. "La Raza Council on Higher Education."

151. Sierra, "Political Transformation of a Minority Organization"; Vigil, *Crusade for Justice,* 52–53; issues from *Agenda.*

152. Rendon, *Chicano Manifesto,* 125.

153. Lloyd and Montague, "Ford and La Raza," 10.

154. Olveira, *MALDEF*; and Romano-V., listserv e-mail message in chicle@unm .edu, March 15, 2000.

155. Garcia, *Memories of Chicano History,* 229.

156. Gutiérrez, *Making of a Chicano Militant,* 118.

157. Acuña, *Occupied America,* 3rd ed., 380–381.

158. I do not want to follow current conservatives who argued that Ford manipulated Mexican Americans (Funk, "Foundation Aiding Militants"; and Skerry, *Mexican Americans*).

159. Horkheimer, *Eclipse of Reason,* chapter 1.

160. Ross, *Origins of American Social Science.*

161. Rochin, "Short and Turbulent Life of Chicano Studies," 888.

162. Ibid., 889–893.

163. Ibid.

164. Cuéllar Jr., "Theory of Politics"; and Cruse, *Crisis of the Negro Intellectual,* 409.

165. Ibid., 546.

166. Ibid., 552.

167. Ibid., 560.

Chapter 3. Perspectivist Chicano Studies

1. Rios-C., "Historical and Comparative Content and Linguistic Analysis," 278.

2. Donato Martinez, "Existentialism and the Chicano Movement: Revolt of the Chicano/a Community," n.d., Library Collection, UCLA Chicano Studies Research Center Library.

3. Contreras, "Existential Phenomenology," 1.

4. Villarreal argued that Rivera's protagonists existed in an existential (Sartrean) universe (Villarreal, "Existentialism and . . .").

5. Carranza, *Pensamientos on Los Chicanos,* 2nd ed.; Porath, "Chicanos and Existentialism," 13; and Duran and Bernard, *Introduction to Chicano Studies.*

6. Romanell, *Making of the Mexican Mind*; Ramos, *Profile of Man and Culture*; and Paz, *The Labyrinth of Solitude.*

7. Maciel, "Introducción," 85.

8. Romanell, *Making of the Mexican Mind,* 152.

9. Ibid., 161.

10. Ibid., 161.

11. Ibid., 164.

12. Contreras, "Existential Phenomenology," 94.

13. Ortega y Gasset, "La superioridad Anglo-Sajona vista."

14. "Editorial," *Con Safos,* 1, no. 1, 1.

15. Francisco Vázquez, "Chicano Thought," January 10, 1971, Ronald Lopez Collection, UCLA Chicano Studies Research Center Library.

16. Ibid., 31–33.

17. "Interview with Octavio Paz"; and Blanco-Aguinaga, "El laberinto fabricado por Octavio Paz."

18. Contreras, "Existential Phenomenology," 3.

19. "Chicano Intellectual Thought, ca. 1968–1969," Library Collection, UCLA Chicano Studies Research Center Library.

20. Vaca, "Message to the People"; Rios-C. added that Vaca's 1967 piece analyzed many of the same themes, used a similar approach, and arrived at conclusions similar to those Romano used later (Rios-C., "Historical and Comparative Content and Linguistic Analysis," 24).

21. Vaca, "Mexican-American in the Social Sciences," Part I and Part II; Vaca, "Comparative Study of Values."

22. Vaca, "Mexican-American in the Social Sciences," Part II, 46. Padilla's bibliographical work continued in Vaca's line as he examined publications on Chicanos(as) between 1848 and 1970 (Padilla, "Apuntes para la documentación").

23. Vásquez, "Chicano Studies," 207.

24. Alurista, "Chicano Studies: A Future."

25. Vázquez, *Chicano Thought,* 36.

26. Martinez, "Chicanismo," 35.

27. Martinez, *Chicanismo,* 36.

28. Ibid., 4–6.

29. Martinez, "Chicanismo," 37.

30. Martinez, *Chicanismo,* 3.

31. Martinez, "Chicanismo," 39.

32. Martinez, *Chicanismo,* 7.

33. Acevedo, "Chicano Thought and Value," 114.

34. Medina, *Chicanos, Existentialism and the Human Condition,* 34.

35. Gómez-Quiñones, *Chicano Politics,* 104–105.

36. Aragón de Shepro, *Chicanismo and Mexican American Politics,* 1; and Cuéllar, "Perspective on Politics," 149.

37. Cuéllar, ""Perspective on Politics," 151; and Acevedo, "Two-Headed Jaguar," 4–5.

38. Aragón de Shepro, *Chicanismo and Mexican American Politics,* 12.

39. Marrufo, "What Is Carnalismo?," 1–2; Vargas, "Carnalismo"; and "La Causa" (in *La Raza*).

40. Vargas, "Carnalismo," 17.

41. Bernal, "Chicano en pensamiento."

42. "Concerning the Conceptualization of Chicanismo."

43. De Leon, *Chicanos*, 4.

44. Cuéllar, "Perspective on Politics," 153.

45. Acevedo, "Chicano Thought and Value," 114.

46. Ysidro Macías added the notion of *compadrazgo* (Macías, "Chicano Movement," 138).

47. Alurista, "Chicano Studies: A Future," 2.

48. Ibid., 4.

49. Ortego, *Montezuma's Children*.

50. García, *Chicanismo*, 8.

51. La Coronela, "Cultural Nationalism," 3.

52. Contreras, "Existential Phenomenology," 161; 233–237.

53. Carranza, *Pensamientos on Los Chicanos*, 1st ed., 4.

54. Carranza, *Chicanismo*, 10; and Castillo, "An Essay," 3.

55. Carranza, *Pensamientos on Los Chicanos*, 1st ed., 16.

56. Ibid., 8; and Carey-Herrera, *Chicanismo*, 32.

57. For a different read of Paz, see Carranza, "Cultural Erosion."

58. Carranza, *Pensamientos on Los Chicanos*, 1st ed., 18.

59. Ibid., 16.

60. Carranza, *Pensamientos on Los Chicanos*, 2nd ed., 19.

61. Ibid., 21.

62. Carranza, *Chicanismo*, 129.

63. Carranza, *Pensamientos on Los Chicanos*, 2nd ed., 17.

64. Carey-Herrera, *Chicanismo*, 134.

65. Carranza, *Pensamientos on Los Chicanos*, 2nd ed., 18.

66. Ibid., 52.

67. Ibid., 18.

68. Carranza, *Chicanismo*, 131.

69. Carranza, *Pensamientos on Los Chicanos*, 2nd ed., 19.

70. Ibid., 26.

71. Ibid., 25; and Acevedo, "Chicano Thought and Value," 98.

72. Carranza, *Chicanismo*, 130.

73. Carranza, *Chicanismo*, 132.

74. Chavez, "Review Essay," 95.

75. Ibid.

76. Carey-Herrera, *Chicanismo*, 150–157; and Vázquez, *Chicano Thought*, 36.

77. Mares, "Fiesta of Life," 6.

78. Ibid., 10.

79. Ibid., 9.

80. Ibid., 14.

81. Lugones, "Playfulness 'World'-Travelling, and Loving Perception," 390–402.

82. Armas, "Doctrina de La Raza," 43.

83. Ibid., 44. In "The White Problem," Cantu and Peralez observed Chicanos(as) love their children more than Anglos because of their humanistic values (Cantu and Peralez, "The White Problem," *Chicanismo* 1, no. 3 [1970]: 7).

84. Armas, "Doctrina de La Raza," 44.

85. For a discussion of problems between Armas and other journals like *Rayas* and *Caracol*, see the last issue of *Rayas* 4 (1979).

86. Armas, "Editorial," 7.

87. Poblano, "Introduction," 10.

88. Rodríguez, "Donde esta la onda," 3–5; Rodríguez, "La búsqueda de identidad," 170–178; Zamora, "Humanismo y Praxis Artistica," 3; and Armas, "Introduction to La Cosecha," 10.

89. Zamora, "Humanismo y Praxis Artistica," 3.

90. Segade, "Toward a Dialectic of Chicano Literature," 4; and Segade, "Introduction to Floricanto," 3.

91. Sedano, "Chicanismo in Selected Poetry," 44.

92. Rodríguez, "La búsqueda de identidad," 7.

93. Rodríguez, "Donde esta la onda," 162.

94. Rodríguez, "La búsqueda de identidad," 8.

95. Rodríguez, "Acercamiento a cuatro relatos de," 16.

96. "La Raza Nueva" (in *Bronce Magazine*).

97. Eger, "Conflicto en Academia," 183–189.

98. Cuéllar, "Model of Chicano Culture for Bilingual Education."

99. Padilla, "Transformational Education," 2. A literary expression of this argument appeared in *NABE* (Padilla, "Transformación Chicana; Chicano Transformation").

100. Padilla, "Transformational Education," 3. Unfortunately Padilla sought to institutionalize perspectivism as a method—at least in the field of education (Padilla, "Transformational Education," 5–6). Here he shared the same assumptions as those within the empiricist camp.

101. Rocco, "Chicano in the Social Sciences," 92.

102. Ibid.

103. Ibid., 93.

104. Rocco, "Critical Critical Perspective on the Study of Chicano Politics," 562.

105. Ibid., 557. Rocco, "Chicano Studies and Critical Political Theory," 255.

106. Rocco, "Critical Perspective on the Study of Chicano Politics," 561.

107. For Romanell, Zea is another "neo-Orteguian 'circumstantialist'" (see Romanell, *Making of the Mexican Mind*, 176).

108. Rocco, "Marginality and the Recovery of History," 42.

109. Ibid., 43.

110. Ibid.

111. Ibid., 45.

112. Vaca took his criticism of social science seriously, as demonstrated by his dissertation (see Vaca, "Sociology through Literature.")

113. Ramos, "Case in Point," 905–919.

114. Jaime Calvillo's project on Teatro Campesino reflected a perspectivist analysis (see Calvillo, "Between Heaven and Earth," 38–39).

115. Basso, "Emerging Chicana Woman Religious."

116. Rodríguez, "Antonio Caso, Erich Fromm y el Chicano."

117. Amaro, "Chicano in a Capitalist Society."

118. Cuéllar Jr., "Theory of Politics," 25.

119. Ibid., 21.

120. Ibid., 37.

121. Romano-V., "Constitutional Issues," 10.

122. Contreras, "Existential Phenomenology," 173–174.

123. Ibid., 175.

124. *De Colores*, 1, no. 1 (1973): 10.

125. Sánchez, "Memoirs of a Chicano Administrator," 53.

126. Letter by John J. Johnson, 1970, Ronald Lopez Collection, UCLA Chicano Studies Research Center Library; Memo by John J. Johnson, 1970, Ronald Lopez Collection, UCLA Chicano Studies Research Center Library; Nogales, "Letter," 1970; and Memorandum, "List of Participants," 1970, Ronald Lopez Collection, UCLA Chicano Studies Research Center Library.

127. "Editorial," *Deganawidah*. Exemplifying the difference between schooling versus education see "Education."

128. See the entire issues of *Raices* 1, no. 2-2, no. 2 (1970–1971).

129. Risco, "Before Universidad de Aztlán," 46.

130. Arturo Flores, editor of *Con Safos,* agreed with this point ("Interview: Art Flores," *El Mestizo* 2, no. 1 [1972]: 10–11, 14). From a different angle, Machado saw these programs as unacceptable (see Machado, *Listen Chicano!,* 144).

131. Ortego, "Chicano Education," 29.

132. Acevedo, "Two-Headed Jaguar." In another piece, he suggests that Chicanos(as) "use the system to beat the system" by taking over certain campuses and programs (Acevedo, "Some Solutions in Chicano Higher Education," 155).

133. Galicia, "Chicanos and Schools"; Macías, Webb de Macías, and De La Torre, *Educación Alternativa*; Garcia, "Political Socialization of Mexican Americans"; Acevedo, "Some Solutions in Chicano Higher Education," 155–159; and Hernandez, "Schools for Mexicans."

134. "D-Q University" stands for Deganawidah-Quetzalcoatl University. Some tribal members feel that the spelled-out name of the university can be offensive. It was founded in 1971, accredited in 1977. Unfortunately the university lost its accreditation in 2005. There is a campaign to reestablish the institution. "Colegio Cesar Chavez" *Agenda* (1976); Carlos Maldonado, *Colegio Cesar Chavez, 1973–1983: A Chicano Struggle for Educational Self-Determination* (New York: Garland Press, 2000); "Chicano Movement in Action." The Colegio Cesar Chavez in Mount Angel, Oregon, was established in 1973 and remained open until 1983. It was the first accredited independent four-year Chicano college. Universidad de Aztlán was established as a four-year instituion in 1971, together with the Colegio de la Tierra (community college). They were to serve the farm-working community by providing alternatives to traditional postsecondary education. It closed in the early 1970s. The Colegio Jacinto Treviño was established in Mercedes, Texas, in 1969. Because of internal conflict in 1971, some of the faculty and staff moved to the new Juarez-Lincoln University (1971–1979). Eventually the Colegio closed in the mid-1970s.

135. "Edward T. Quevedo, College of Chicano Studies Feasibility Study, 1972," Ronald Lopez Collection, UCLA Chicano Studies Research Center Library, 82.

136. Memorandum, "Conceptual Basis for the Establishment of a Chicano College," n.d., Ronald Lopez Collection, UCLA Chicano Studies Research Center Library; Memorandum, "Proposal for Securing a Planning Grant to Study the Feasibility of Founding a Mexican American College," n.d., Ronald Lopez Collection, UCLA Chicano Studies Research Center Library.

137. Atencio, "La Academia de la Nueva Raza: Su Historia," 6.

138. Ibid., 97.

139. Atencio and Arellano, "Mining and Processing el Oro del Barrio," 16–17.

140. Ibid., 18.

141. Atencio, "La Academia de la Nueva Raza: El Oro del Barrio," 6.

142. Atencio, "La Academia de la Nueva Raza: Su Historia," 7.

143. Atencio, "La Academia de la Nueva Raza: Sus Obras," 7.

144. Atencio, "La Academia de la Nueva Raza: El Oro," 4.

145. Atencio, "La Academia de la Nueva Raza: Su Historia," 101.

146. Atencio and Pacheco, "Concept of la Resolana," 14.

147. Atencio and Arellano, "Mining and Processing el Oro del Barrio," 18.

148. Atencio also drew attention to transforming social services (Atencio, "Survival of La Raza"). For people sharing similar perspectives on social services, see Social Casework; Medina, Chicanos, Existentialism and the Human Condition, v.

149. Martinez and Hijos de Sol staff, Hijos del Sol, 19.

150. Martinez and Vargas, Razalogía, 78. They continued the earlier criticism by Armand Sanchez; see Armand J. Sanchez, "The Definers and the Defined: A Mental Health Issue," El Grito 4, no. 4 (1971): 4–11.

151. Martinez and Vargas, Razalogía, 2.

152. Ibid., 3.

153. Ibid., 8.

154. Ibid., 16.

155. Ibid., 22.

156. Ibid., 26.

157. Sacramento Beret, "Why a Brown Beret Formed or Emerged in the Southwest?"

158. An example is Javier H. Salazar, Chicano—A Process Toward a Concept of Unity, available online at http://www.aztlanacademy.org/xicanoPhilosophy.html (unfortunately, this document is no longer accessible at this URL).

159. Porath, "Chicanos and Existentialism," 13.

160. Ibid., 11.

161. Ibid., 18.

162. Con Safos, 1, no. 1 (1968): 1. "If El Grito was international and academic, the urban barrios of Los Angeles spawned Con Safos, a feisty compendium of literature, art and documentary reporting" (see Ybarra-Frausto, "Chicano Movement," 98). Ybarra-Frausto added that El Pocho Che from northern California went further than Con Safos's cultural nationalism. As part of the ferment that came with the Third World strikes, the journal brought together artists in an ongoing political praxis that linked raza struggles with international revolutionary movements (ibid., 100–103).

163. Sedano, "Chicanismo in Selected Poetry," 55.

164. Vargas, *Provida Leadership,* 6.

165. Solis, "Chicano Mental Health," 52.

166. Solis, "Traditional Chicano Centering," 18.

167. Bustamante, "La Ciencia en la Tradición," 11–17.

168. Solis, "Chicano Values: Living," 30.

169. Solis, "Chicano Values—Part III," 16–20; Bustamante, "Spiral of Cultural Identity Development"; Bañas, "Donde Estas," 15–77; Bañas, "Donde Estoy"; and Castorena, "La Raza Nueva," 1–2.

170. Mares, "El Coyote," 22.

171. Mares, "Introduction," 17.

172. A possible example of this type of argument is Castorena's piece in *Regeneración* (see Castorena, "La Raza Nueva," 1). A similar view appears in the editorial statements of *De Colores.*

173. Mares, "Introduction," 47.

174. The *danzante* Andés Segura has argued that to achieve unity with these values and past, Chicanos(as) needed a new mentality that can come to the Chicano(a) through dance (Segura, "Continuidad de la tradición filosófica Nahuatl," 20–26).

175. Justo S. Alarcón, "Historical and Cultural Concepts of Chicanismo," 1973, Chicano Collection, Arizona State University Library, 23.

176. Ibid., 24.

177. Alurista, "The Nightmare of the 'Amerikkkan' Dream," n.d., Library Collection, UCLA Chicano Studies Research Center Library, 9–10.

178. Alurista, "Chicano Cultural Revolution," 23–33. See also the letter in *UCLA MEChA Newsletter* 3 (1973): n.p.

179. Valdez, *Pensamiento serpentino*; Valdez, "Tale of La Raza"; and Valdez, "Notes on Chicano Theatre."

180. Treviño, *Eyewitness,* 325.

181. Ibid., 329.

182. Klor de Alva believes that this indigenous interest began to fade by the mid-1980s (Klor de Alva, "California Chicano Literature," 19).

183. Empirics were uncomfortable with Valdez's use of "idealized elements" (*Pensamiento serpentino*).

184. Vázquez, "Aztec Epistemology," 74–79; and Vázquez, "Chicano Studies and a Liberal Arts Education," 37.

185. Vázquez, "Chicano Studies and a Liberal Arts Education," 34.

186. Francisco Vázquez, "Foucault's Disagreement with Husserl's Phenomenology," 1974, Ronald Lopez Collection, UCLA Chicano Studies Research Center Library.

187. Vázquez, "Philosophy in Mexico," 28.

188. Padilla, "Freireismo and Chicanizaje," 79.

189. Ibid.

190. Vázquez, "Chicanology," 116–147.

191. Sánchez, "Looking Back on Chicano Thought," 39–42; and Sánchez, "Raices Mexicanas," 75–87.

192. Carey-Herrera has argued "[t]he choice of identifying with the mythology of an ancient Chichimecan culture was more important as a social statement than as a historical fact" (Carey-Herrera, *Chicanismo*, xi).

193. I believe the editorial direction in *El Grito del Sol* reflected this vision. Less clear was the presence of this perspective in the journal *Campo Libre: Journal of Chicano Studies,* in particular essay by Roberto Cantú (Cantú, "Nota preliminary").

194. Romano-V., listserv e-mail message in chicle@unm.edu, September 30, 1999.

195. Hayes-Bautista, "Becoming Chicano," 34.

196. Ibid., 50.

197. An example of work that avoided the constraints of the empirics and yet went beyond the limits of perspectivist scholars is Mary Romero's work. Her dissertation ably combined a dialectical perspective with a colonial model. "Writings by Fanon, Freire, and others provided alternative explanations of social relationships in a capitalist society in contrast to former social science paradigms that ignored oppression and defined its consequences as a stage toward modernism and part of the development of capitalism" (see Romero, "Transformation of Culture through Appropriation," 284).

198. One must draw attention to the politics among perspectivists and with empirics (*Carta Abierta* 1 [1975]: n.p.); and "Letter by Octavio Ignacio Romano-V.," January 24, 1980, Library Collection, UCLA Chicano Studies Research Center Library).

Chapter 4. Chicano Studies as an Academic Discipline

1. California remained central to Chicano Studies development in these early years (*Guide to Chicano Studies Departments, Programs, and Centers*).

2. García, *Chicanismo*, 61.

3. Muñoz, "Development of Chicano Studies," 14.

4. García, "Chicano University," 352.

5. Aragón de Shepro, "Nature of Chicano Political Powerlessness," 259–260.

6. García, "Chicano University," 353.

7. Nuñez and Contreras, "Principles and Foundations of Chicano Studies," in *Chicano Discourse.*

8. Gómez-Quiñones, "To Leave to Hope or Chance," 156–157.

9. Ibid., 159.

10. Ibid., 166.

11. Camarillo, "Chicanos and the New University Crisis," 1.

12. In 1975, Allan Bakke sued the University of California for denying him admission to University of California Davis Medical School because of the affirmative action policy. In 1976, the California Supreme Court ruled in Bakke's favor. Two years later, the U.S. Supreme Court ruled that special admission quotas were unconstitutional, although race could be used among the criteria when considering admission.

13. Ornelas, Ramirez, and Padilla, *Decolonizing the Interpretation,* 1.

14. Ibid., 27.

15. Ibid., 5–6, 25.

16. Ibid., 38.

17. Arce, "Chicano Participation in Academe," 100.

18. Ibid., 77.

19. Ibid.

20. One could also note the Chicano California workshop and conference on higher education (Memorandum, "Chicano Statewide Workshop-Conference on Higher Education, Agenda," 1969, and Memorandum, "Chicano Statewide Workshop-Conference on Higher Education, Schedule," 1969, Ronald Lopez Collection, UCLA Chicano Studies Research Center Library).

21. "National Chicano Commission on Higher Education," 12.

22. Ibid., 21–23.

23. Ibid., 9.

24. Ibid., 3.

25. Ibid., 7.

26. Ibid., 8.

27. Arturo Madrid, "Proposal for Funding a Conference of the Status of Chicanos in Higher Education," July 23, 1974, Ronald Lopez Collection, UCLA Chicano Studies Research Center Library, 2; Memorandum, "Symposium on the Status of Chicanos in Higher Education," 1975, Ronald Lopez Collection, UCLA Chicano Studies Research Center Library; Ronald W. Lopez, "Chicano Participation in Institutions of Higher Education in the United States: Issues and Responses," n.d., Ronald Lopez Collection, UCLA Chicano Studies Research Center Library; and Lopez, Madrid-Barela, and Macías, *Chicanos in Higher Education.*

28. Letter by Arturo Madrid, n.d., Ronald Lopez Collection, UCLA Chicano Studies Research Center Library.

29. Memorandum by Arturo Madrid, n.d., Ronald Lopez Collection, UCLA Chicano Studies Research Center Library; and Lopez, "Chicano Participation in Institutions of Higher Education."

30. The initial members were drawn from participants of the Symposium on the Status of Chicanos in U.S. higher education held in 1975 (Arturo Madrid, "The Mid-Career Post-Doctoral Fellowship Program of the National Chicano Commission on Higher Education: A Proposal," n.d., Library Collection, UCLA Chicano Studies Research Center Library, 7).

31. Amaya, "On Chicanas in Higher Education."

32. Acuña, *Occupied America,* 3rd ed., 381.

33. *El Mirlo* 2, no. 7.

34. Beginning in 1978 *La Red/The Net* began a section on "Noticias de NACS at times with report from regional focos."

35. "Flyer for Agenda Political Economy Symposium on Political Economy, Power, and Chicano Politics," 1977, Library Collection, UCLA Chicano Studies Research Center.

36. Higher Education Task Force, "Position Statement," 1976, Ronald Lopez Collection, UCLA Chicano Studies Research Center Library, 2; Juan Gómez-Quiñones, "Bakke and the Mexican Community," 1976, Ronald Lopez Collection, UCLA Chicano Studies Research Center Library, 7; Carlos Haro and Rosa Mar-

tinez Cruz, "Coalition Formed to Oppose Bakke," *El Mirlo* 4, no. 1 and 2; Haro, *Bakke Decision*; and Haro, *Criticisms of Traditional Postsecondary School*.

37. Juan Gómez-Quiñones, Memo, 1977, Ronald Lopez Collection, UCLA Chicano Studies Research Center Library; Memorandum, "Higher Education Task Force—MALDEF," n.d., Ronald Lopez Collection, UCLA Chicano Studies Research Center Library.

38. Chávez, *"¡Mi Raza Primero!,"* 112.

39. Given the close relationship between the UCLA Chicano Studies Center and CASA, it made sense to have a conference on the situation of migrant labor.

40. Chicano Studies Center, Press Release, June 28, 1978, Library Collection, UCLA Chicano Studies Research Center Library; Memorandum, "Primer Simposio Internacional," June 21, 1978, Library Collection, UCLA Chicano Studies Research Center Library.

41. Tijerina, *They Called Me "King Tiger,"* 176, 214–215; and Gutiérrez, *Making of a Chicano Militant*, 110, 224, 234–239.

42. García, *United We Win*, 211.

43. Chávez, *"¡Mi Raza Primero!,"* 113.

44. For a different discussion on the links between Chicanos(as) and the Mexican state, see García-Acevedo, "Return to Aztlán."

45. Ortiz, "Foreword," v–vi.

46. Ibid., vi.

47. Valdez, Camarrillo, and Almaguer, *State of Chicano Research*.

48. Ortiz, "Foreword," vii.

49. Nobleza C. Asuncion-Lande, "Chicano Studies: Current Status and Future Directions," 1976, Chicano Collection, Arizona State University Library, 11.

50. Letter by David R. Howton, July 8, 1975, UCLA University Archives, Record Series 85, Box 6, 1.

51. Draft letter by Alexei Maradudin, n.d., UCLA University Archives, Record Series 85, Box 6.

52. Ethnic Study Center Review Committee for Vice Chancellor David Saxon, "Report on Five Year Review," April 17, 1975, UCLA University Archives, Record Series 85, Box 26, 45.

53. Muñoz, "State of the Art," 51.

54. Sedano, "Chicanismo in Selected Poetry," 120.

55. I find it difficult to place *La Luz* (founded in 1972) because it did more than just address academic issues.

56. Padilla, "Notes on the History of Hispanic Psychology."

57. Padilla, "Editorial."

58. He did not find the arguments of Western Marxist of value (see Gómez-Quiñones, "Critique on the National Question").

59. Gómez-Quiñones, "On Culture," 5.

60. Ibid., 6.

61. Ibid., 8.

62. In the process, Gómez-Quiñones argued the "genetic inheritance" of Chicanos(as)' Indian past, their commonality as workers, and the unity of all Mexicans on either side of the Rio Bravo (ibid., 9–10).

63. Ibid., 18–19.

64. Ibid., 22.

65. I am puzzled when contemporary writers have praised this essay's argument. Given the level of discussion opened up by the first English translations of Foucault's *The Order of Things* (1970) and *The Archeology of Knowledge* (1972) and the debate in British journals over Althusser's position, I am surprised by the attention given to this essay and its rather weak attempt to link class, culture, and history (Pérez, *Decolonial Imaginary*, 16; and Darder and Torres, "Latinos and Society," 3).

66. Aragón de Shepro, "Nature of Chicano Political Powerlessness," 185.

67. Ibid., 179–186; and Buzon and Phillips, "Institutional Completeness and Chicano Militancy."

68. Jorge Klor de Alva, "Philosophy/Psychology," 1975, Library Collection, UCLA Chicano Studies Research Center Library, 169; and Klor de Alva, *Introduction to Mexican Philosophy*.

69. García, "José Vasconcelos and La Raza"; and Juárez, "José Vasconcelos and La Raza Cósmica."

70. Simultaneously one cannot ignore the influence of the work of Patrick Romanell and R. A. Caponigri.

71. Klor de Alva, "Gabino Barreda and Chicano Thought," 344; and Weinstein and Weinstein, "Problematic of Marginality in Mexican Philosophy."

72. One might suggest that Gómez-Quiñones was involved in this development of an origins myth with his work on Ricardo Flores Magon (Gómez-Quiñones, *Sembradores, Ricardo Flores Magon*).

73. Klor de Alva, "Critique of National Character." Sylvia Gonzales has suggested that his attitude was reflective of his elitist, macho, and Mexican attitude toward Chicanos and Chicanas (Gonzales, "Congress of InterAmerican Women Writers," 14).

74. Klor de Alva, "Chicano Philosophy," 157.

75. Ibid., 151.

76. In an essay on Mexican thought, Klor de Alva appreciated the complexity of Mexicans' struggle with *mexicanidad* (see his "Being, Solitude, and Susceptibility"). When he dealt with Chicano thought, he did not extend the same evenhandedness. Contrast this with Vázquez's work—in particular, "Philosophy in Mexico."

77. Schürmann, "Concerning Philosophy."

78. Klor de Alva, "Chicano Philosophy," 150.

79. Klor de Alva, "Philosophy/Psychology."

80. Klor de Alva, "Gabino Barreda and Chicano Thought," 347.

81. Ibid., 348.

82. Ibid.

83. Ibid., 352.

84. Vaillancourt, *When Marxists Do Research*.

85. Segade, "Identity and Power," 85.

86. Sánchez, "Raices Mexicanas," 77.

87. Ibid.

88. Ibid., 83.

89. Acevedo, "Chicano Thought and Value," 117; Vázquez, "Philosophy in Mexico"; Rocco, "Marginality and the Recovery of History"; and Padilla "Transformational Education."

90. Barrera and Vialpando, *Action Research*.

91. Ibid., 3.

92. Samora and Galarza, "Research and Scholarly Activity"; and Elizondo, "Critical Areas of Need."

93. "Annual Report Fiscal Year 1972–1973," n.d., UCLA Chicano Studies Research Center Library, Library Collection, 12.

94. Garcia, "Chicano Unemployment in the Seventies."

95. Estrada, "Responsibility to Know and the Ability to Understand," 25.

96. Ibid., 26.

97. Ibid., 30.

98. Cuellar, "El Oro de Maravilla," 1.

99. Barrera, Camarillo, and Hernandez, *Work, Family, Sex Roles, Language*.

100. Hernandez, *Reality and Goal Orientation*, 62.

101. Muñoz, "Development of Chicano Studies," 16; and Paredes, *Humanidad*.

102. Muñoz Jr., "Quest for Paradigm," 22.

103. Ibid., 20–22; and Bixler-Márquez, *Chicano Studies*, vi.

104. García, "Juncture in the Road," 182.

105. Rodríguez, "Chicano Studies Pioneer Praised."

106. Aragón de Shepro, "Nature of Chicano Political Powerlessness."

107. Blea, *Toward a Chicano Social Science*, 8.

108. Samora and Lamanna, "Mexican-Americans in a Midwest Metropolis"; Samora and Simon, *History of the Mexican-American People*. Arthur Campa's and De Hoyos's early works echoed Samora's stereotypical assumptions of the Mexican American community (Campa, "Culture Patterns of the Spanish Speaking Community"; and De Hoyos, "Occupational and Educational Levels of Aspiration").

109. Samora, *Los Mojados*.

110. Other writers that shared much with Ramírez III and Castañeda can be read in Johnson and Hernández-M., *Educating the Mexican American*.

111. Ramírez III and Castañeda, *Cultural Democracy*. 24.

112. Another example would be Cabrera, "Study of American and Mexican-American Culture Values"; and Cabrera, *Strategies for Education of Chicanos*.

113. Poblano, *Ghosts in the Barrio*.

114. For a summary of the issues in bilingual bicultural education at the time, see Trueba, "Issues and Problems"; Gonzalez, "The Status of Bilingual Education Today"; and essays in *NABE*.

115. From a more radical perspective, Macías, Webb de Macías, and De La Torre drew attention to the reality that alternative education in and of itself could not transform the condition of the Chicano(a) (see Macías, Webb de Macías, and De la Torre, *Educación Alternativa*; and Macías, "Schooling"). Other essays by educators that developed Chicano thought can be found in Bernal, Garcia, and Zamora, "Bilingual Education at the Crossroads"; Hernández-Chávez, "Meaningful Bilingual Bicultural Education"; Hernández-Chávez, Cohen, and Beltramo, *El*

leguaje de los Chicanos; Carranza, "Language Attitudes and Other Cultural Attitudes"; Trueba and Wright, "On Ethnographic Studies and Multicultural Education"; Trueba "The Meaning and Use of Context"; and Cotera, "Sexism in Bilingual Bicultural Education."

116. Mirandé, "Introduction," 2–3. Here he was building on his earlier essay (see Mirandé, "Chicano Family").

117. Burrola and Rivera, *Chicano Studies Programs at the Crossroads,* 10.

118. Mirandé, "Chicano Sociology: A New Paradigm for Social Science," 304.

119. Baca Zinn, "Sociological Theory in Emergent Chicano Perspectives," 267–268.

120. Mirandé, "Sociology of Chicanos or Chicano Sociology?," 499.

121. Ibid., 505.

122. Ibid.

123. Ibid., 506.

124. Flores, "Chicanos and Sociological Research," 27. For an earlier use of Marxism, see López y Rivas, *Chicanos.*

125. Flores, "Chicanos and Sociological Research," 31.

126. Ibid., 33.

127. Ibid., 34.

128. Cadena et al., "Chicano Sociology," 20.

129. Chicanos(as) of course continued to work through liberal empirical models (see Sena-Rivera, "Extended Kinship in the United States"; and Sabagh and Lopez, "Religiosity and Fertility").

130. Saldívar, *Border Matters.*

131. Paredes, *"With His Pistol in His Hand."*

132. Paredes, *Texas-Mexican Cancionero.*

133. Paredes, "Folk Medicine and the Intercultural Jest"; and Paredes, "On Ethnographic Work Among Minority Groups."

134. Rosaldo, *Chicano Studies.*

135. Paredes, *Texas-Mexican Cancionero,* xviii.

136. Ibid., 171–172.

137. Davalos, "Chicana/o Studies and Anthropology," 39.

138. Cotera, "Deconstructing the Corrido Hero." 153.

139. *La Red/The Net* 28 (1980).

140. Romo and Paredes, *New Directions in Chicano Scholarship.*

141. Rosaldo, "Anthropological Perspectives on Chicanos," 62–66.

142. Davalos provided a more nuanced approach to understanding the differences and similarities between Romano and Paredes (see Davalos, "Chicana/o Studies and Anthropology," 22–25; 38–39).

143. Paredes had made this argument in his essay "On Ethnographic Work Among Minority Groups," where he asserted the possibility of avoiding the errors of Anglo anthropologists.

144. Limón, "Expressive Culture of a Chicano Student Group," 15.

145. A small part of the dissertation appeared in Limón, "Agringado Joking in Texas Mexican Society."

146. William Madsen, *The Mexican-Americans of South Texas* (New York: Holt, Rinehart and Winston, 1964).

147. Rosaldo, *Chicano Studies*, 13.

148. For this reason, Rubalcava argued that Limón's conception of culture was static, undialectical, and conservative (see Rubalcava, "Assimilation Among Urban Chicanos")

149. Arvizu, "Introductory Comments," 12.

150. Ibid., 13.

151. Ibid., 16. Their word appears to prefigure modern anthropology (Davalos, "Chicana/o Studies and Anthropology," 32.)

152. At the same time, some of the essays tried to bridge the gap between understanding the community with bringing change to the community (see Rios, "An Approach to Action Anthropology"; Valadez, "In Search of a Perspective"; and Fernandez Kelly, "Third World Women in Multinational Corporations").

153. Muñoz, "State of the Art," 51.

154. Ibid., 53–54.

155. Rocco, "Critical Perspective on the Study of Chicano Politics," 566.

156. F. Chris Garcia and Rudolph O. de la Garza, *The Chicano Political Experience: Three Perspectives* (North Scituate, Mass.: Duxbury Press, 1977); De la Garza, "Mexican-American"; and Bareno, "Mexican-American Political Experience."

157. Garcia, "Political Socialization of Mexican Americans," xi.

158. Ibid., xii.

159. Ibid., 38–39.

160. Ibid., 60–61.

161. Ibid., 119; Berrios, "Socialization in a Mexican American Community"; and Tirado, "Mexican American Minority's Participation."

162. De la Garza, "Politics of Mexican Americans."

163. Garcia, "Political Socialization of Mexican Americans"; Garcia, *La Causa Politica*; and Ambrecht and Pachon, "Ethnic Political Mobilization."

164. *La Red/The Net* 2 (1977): 3.

165. Acuña, *Occupied America,* 3rd ed., 381. Chicano(a) scholars used a variety of grounded research. An example was Castañon García's use of symbolic analysis to explain the Mexican American (García, "Teatro Chicano and the Analysis of Sacred Symbols").

166. I find this to be the case for psychology as well. Unfortunately, I am unable to trace the work of Chicanos(as) in the field. Nonetheless, much of the work I read remained firmly tied to the field, such as the essays in Carrol A. Hernández, ed., *Chicanos: Social and Psychological Perspectives*, 2nd ed. (St. Louis, Mo.: C.V. Mosley Comp., 1976). An exception would be Rubalcava's dissertation.

167. García, "Introduction."

168. Rios-C., "Historical and Comparative Content and Linguistic Analysis," 318.

169. Much of what I have to say about criticism can be applied to cultural production as expressed, for instance, in later Floricanto festivals (see Kanellos, "Meditaciones: De Flores"; and Reyes Cárdenas, "Floricanto II: Afterimages," *Caracol* 1, no. 11 [1975]: 4–7). While *Caracol* retained an ambivalent relation-

ship with the new Chicano Studies agenda, some of the essays that appeared in the periodical served to coalesce a Chicano Studies version of literary criticism and cultural studies. For some, *Caracol,* under the leadership of Celio Garcia-C. offered an alternative to Chicano literature—"todo lo que prometió y no cumplió *El Grito*" (*Carta Abierta* 1 [1975]: n.p.).

170. Novoa, *Chicano Poetry,* viii.

171. The editors saw the journal as building on the cultural encounter among Latinos and *latinófilas* ("Nota preliminary," i).

172. She provided a historical reading of Chicano bilingualism in Sánchez, "Chicano Bilingualism."

173. Reyna, "Tejano Music as an Expression"; Reyna, "Raza Humor in Texas"; Reyna, "Mexican American Prose Narrative in Texas"; Sánchez, "La crítica marxista"; Alarcón, "La meta crítica chicana"; and Lizárraga, "Observaciones acerca."

174. Ybarra-Frausto, "Chicano Movement."

175. Enriquez, "Towards a Definition of," 38.

176. Ortego, "Backgrounds of Mexican American Literature."

177. Alurista, *Anthology of Chicano Literature*; and Martinez, "Necessity for Chicano Literary Critics."

178. Vento, *Festival Flor y Canto II*; Armas, "Introduction," in *Flor*; and Novoa, *Chicano Poetry.*

179. Saldívar, "Dialectic of Difference," 88.

180. Ibid., 89.

181. An inept example of Marxism can be found in Vigil, "Marx and Chicano Anthropology."

182. Gómez-Quiñones, "First Steps."

183. Camarillo, "'New' Chicano History," 10.

184. Gómez-Quiñones, "First Steps," 13.

185. Camarillo, "'New' Chicano History," 9.

186. Arroyo, "Notes on Past, Present and Future Directions," 138.

187. Arroyo, "State of Chicano Labor History."

188. Arroyo, *Bibliography of Recent Chicano History Writings.*

189. Gómez-Quiñones, *Development of the Mexican Working Class.*

190. Saragoza, "Significance of Recent Chicano-related Historical Writings."

191. Flores, "Mexican-Origin People in the United States," 114.

192. Acuña, *Occupied America,* 2nd ed.

193. Mindiola, "Introduction."

194. De Leon, "*Occupied America*"; Romo, "Reconstruction of Chicano History"; and Zamora, "Critical Comments on *Occupied America.*"

195. Mario Garcia had made this point earlier (García, "Internal Colonialism and the Chicano"). I find it difficult to place Mario Garcia's first major work on El Paso with this Chicano Marxist camp. Given his earlier interest with historical materialism and Marxism, his first book avoided a Marxist analysis of the condition of Mexicans and Mexican Americans in the United States. Rather, his work was closer to a traditional social history (see García, *Desert Immigrants*).

196. Later he charged that the lack of change within the barrios was due to the appearance of a new class of Chicano(a) intellectuals "who have assumed the role of critics rather than leaders who participate in the struggle to politicize the community" (Acuña, "La Generación," 6). These brokers manipulated the symbols of nationalism, which had been so effective to bring unity to the community, for their self-interest.

197. Acuña, *Occupied America,* 1st ed., vii; Acuña, "Making."

198. One could add that a similar shift could be found in Barrera's work. He had also moved away from earlier expressions of internal colonialism by grafting liberal and Marxist models in his theory of racial inequality in "Class Segmentation" or the more developed *Race and Class.*

199. Limón, "Western Marxism and Folklore," 37.

200. Flores, "Mexican-Origin People in the United States," 108. Interestingly, this view supported the genesis myth of Chicano Studies.

201. Ibid., 110.

202. Ibid., 115.

203. Ibid., 117.

204. Some Chicano(a) scholars turned to "world system" (Ojeda, "International Class Politics of Capital and Labor Flows"; and Montejano, "Frustrated Apartheid"). A critique can be found in Montejano, "Is Texas Bigger Than the World-System?."

205. Flores, "Mexican-Origin People in the United States," 121. For an attempt to write a history of the Mexican Americans from a Marxist perspective, see Borrego, "Capitalist Accumulation and Revolutionary Accumulation."

206. Letter by Charles J. Hitch, January 27, 1969, UCLA University Archives, Record Series 401, Box 127, 1.

Chapter 5. Chicanas, the Chicano Student Movements, and Chicana Thought

1. García, "Introduction," 7.

2. Fernandez, "Abriendo Caminos on the Borderland."

3. Cotera, "Feminism."

4. Davalos, "Chicana/o Studies and Anthropology," 25.

5. For a general overview, see Barry, "Women's Participation in the Chicano Movement."

6. López, "Role of the Chicana," 16.

7. Vigil, *Crusade for Justice,* 114.

8. García, "The Chicana."

9. Unfortunately, Chicano paternalism often remains in current research (see Gutiérrez, *Making of a Chicano Militant,* 106; Navarro, *Mexican American Youth Organization,* 111; and García, *Chicanismo,* 64).

10. Orozco, "Sexism in Chicano Studies."

11. Hobsbawm and Ranger, *Invention of Tradition.*

12. "Corky" Gonzales as quoted in "Why a Chicano Party?," 9.

13. Orozco, "Sexism in Chicano Studies," 11.

14. García, "Development of Chicana Feminist Discourse," 221.

15. Blackwell, "Contested Histories," 63.

16. García, "Introduction"; García, "El feminismo chicano," 3; and Una Chicana, "Abajo con los machos," 30–31.

17. García, "Introduction," 3.

18. García, "Development Chicana Feminist Discourse," 222; and Medina, "Chicanas Live in Aztlán Also."

19. Lopez Saenz, "Machismo, No!"; and Oeste, "Mujeres Arriba y Adelante."

20. García, "Introduction," 4.

21. Martínez and McCaughan, "Chicanas and Mexicanas," 55.

22. Garcia, "Chicana Consciousness: A New Perspective, a New Hope."

23. Fernandez, "Abriendo Caminos on the Borderland." The attempt to find an acceptable expression of nationalism continues into the present. The writer Ana Castillo has called attention to the "philosophy of the male-dominated Chicano Movement." However, Castillo is attracted to certain cultural and nationalist attributes of Chicanismo. She argues that women can "assert a pride in their ethnicity," accepting a form of cultural nationalism without falling into patriarchy (see Castillo, *Massacre of the Dreamers*, 33 and 59).

24. It is important to see NietoGomez's work as part of an intellectual collective.

25. NietoGomez, "La Feminista."

26. Rosen, *World Split Open,* 46.

27. NietoGomez, "La Feminista," 35.

28. Ibid.

29. Del Castillo, "Mexican Women in Organization," 12.

30. A similar presentation was made by Chavez, "Women of the Mexican-American Movement."

31. Longauex y Vásquez, "Woman of La Raza," 20.

32. Ibid., 21.

33. Ibid., 22.

34. Ibid., 23.

35. Ibid., 24.

36. Vigil, *Crusade for Justice,* 97; 401–402.

37. For a discussion of her cultural nationalism, see Oropeza, "Introduction."

38. This split among Chicanas manifested itself at other conferences: the UCLA conference "Corazon de Aztlán" held in 1969, the two caucuses at Raza Unida Conference in 1970, and the Chicana Regional Conference held in Los Angeles in 1971.

39. Segura and Pesquera, "Beyond Indifference and Antipathy," 79.

40. For example, in many MEChAs, Chicanas were accused of being disruptive to the political aims of the organization when they pointed out the machismo and sexism within the organization (Rodarte, "Machismo vs Revolution," 37).

41. Ironically, in the same process, some Chicanas created a straw figure of the white women's movement, paralleling Chicano stereotypes of Chicanas. The women's movement was presented as separatist and antimale, often reducing it to National Organization for Women, ignoring the younger women's liberation movements and African American women's articulation of sexism (Rosen, *World Split*

NOTES TO PAGES 136-139   217

Open, 74–91); and Segura and Pesquera, "Beyond Indifference and Antipathy," 70–72).

42. Orozco, "Sexism in Chicano Studies," 12. For the nationalists, the family was a major battlefield with the Anglo world (Tijerina, *They Called Me "King Tiger,"* 12–13).

43. Moreno, "Quieren ser hombres?," 24–25.

44. Saragoza, "La Mujer in the Chicano Movement." Left unexplored was the impact that the sexual revolution and the libertine counterculture had on Chicanas(os). How much did the changing sexual mores alter gender relationships and foster tensions among them? On the one hand, men increasingly treated movement women with disrespect; on the other hand, as women gained sexual emancipation, they demanded the right to redefine sex. In the process, women asserted the difference between the sexual revolution and women's liberation, while men insisted on confusing the two. Ironically, Chicanos(as) could agree with Betty Freidan's fear of the "lavender menace" to their movement.

45. NietoGomez, "La Feminista," 37.

46. López, "Role of the Chicana," 24.

47. Mirta Vidal, "Women: New Voice of La Raza," available online at http://clnet.ucla.edu/research/docs/chicanas/women.htm.

48. Ibid., 3.

49. Flores, "Conference of Mexican Women Un Remolino," 1.

50. NietoGomez, "Chicana Identify," 9.

51. Rincon, "La Chicana" (1971).

52. Flores, "Conference of Mexican Women Un Remolino," 1–2; Memorandum, "OUR CULTURE HELL! Feminism in Aztlán," 1972 Library Collection, UCLA Chicano Studies Research Center Library.

53. Delgado, "Young Chicana Speaks Up," 5–7; Flores, "Chicano Attitudes Toward Birth Control"; and Orendain, "Sexual Taboo y La Cultura?."

54. Olivarez, "Women's Rights and the Mexican American Woman," 40.

55. Nieto, "The Chicana," 42.

56. Racho, "Houston."

57. Ibid.

58. "National Chicanas Conference," 17.

59. Racho, "Houston Chicana Conference." Blackwell claimed that the walkout at Houston was staged by women who "were sent by a certain fraction of Chicano nationalists based in Los Angeles" (Blackwell, "Contested Histories," 76). It would be interesting to trace the links between the UCLA women, UCLA MEChA, and the earlier protest in May 1970 on the UCLA campus, and the participation of some of these women in the UCLA Chicano Studies Center.

60. Garcia, "La Chicana and Women's Liberation," 7.

61. Ibid.

62. Ibid.

63. Ibid.

64. For a different read, see Flores "The New" and Encuentro Femeníl, "La Vision Chicana," 48.

65. Thus, it is important that Chicanas and Chicanos marry each other. This is not due to any "mingling of the bloods," but due to the fact that interracial marriage leads to the weakening of the ties of La Raza.

66. Longauex y Vásquez, "Soy Chicana Primero"; and Longauex y Vásquez, "Third World Women Meet."

67. Longauex y Vásquez, "Soy Chicana Primero," 17.

68. She finds support for her position from García-Camarillo and de la Torre, "Mujeres en el movimiento"; and García-Camarillo, "Equal Rights Amendment."

69. Longauex y Vásquez, "Soy Chicana Primero," 19–22.

70. Ibid., 18.

71. Ibid., 22.

72. Ibid., 19.

73. Evelyn Jasso and Alberta Snid, "La conferencia de mujeres por la raza," Library Collection, UCLA Chicano Studies Research Center Library; "La Conferencia de Mujeres por La Raza," 224; and NietoGomez, "La Feminista," 39

74. Barrera and NietoGomez, "Chicana Encounter," 49

75. Ibid., 50.

76. Ibid., 51.

77. Elma Barrera felt that the women who walked out of the Houston conference had failed to understand the fundamental issues that women faced (Barrera, "Statement," available online at http://clnet.ucla.edu/research/docs/chicanas/vidal .htm).

78. Sonia López provides a third way to construe the Houston split in 1971. She agreed with most interpreters that there were two trends among Chicana activists. One group did not see the "importance of dealing with several contradictions as they existed between Chicanas and Chicanos in the Movement" (see López, "Role of the Chicana," 26). Rather, they concerned themselves primarily with issues of el movimiento. Another group wanted to organize Chicanas around the contradictions between el movimiento rhetoric and its practices. López suggested that in the end neither position dealt with the social and political contradictions. For López, if Chicanas want to bring about social change, they must engage all people and understand the objective conditions that give rise to inequality. As Apodaca stated: "To do this they need to see class society as the basic contradiction" (see Apodaca, "Chicana Woman," 73).

79. Rincon, "La Chicana" (1971), 15.

80. Gonzales, "The Latina Feminist," 45.

81. Rincon, "La Chicana" (1971), 18.

82. Chavez, "The Chicanas," 14.

83. Delgado, "Chicana," 3. Another example we could look at was the participation of Chicanas in La Raza Unida Party ("Raza Unida Party," 232–333; Chapa, "Mujeres Por La Raza Unidad," 3–5; Cotera, Chicana Feminist, 8; "National Chicano Political Conference"; and Flores, "Equality").

84. At the same time, we should not assume that Chicanas who associated with organizations dominated by Anglo women remained silent.

85. Cruz, "A Mis Hermanas."

86. Cota-Robles de Suarez, "Sexual Stereotypes."

87. Matsuda, "La Chicana Organizes"; Flores, "Conference of Mexican Women Un Remolino"; Flores, "Comisión Femenil Mexicana"; Nava, "Chicana and Employment"; Gonzales, "Sex Role Stereotypes"; Aragón de Valdez, "Organizing as a Political Tool for the Chicana"; Saavedra-Vela, "Hispanic Women in Double Jeopardy"; Espinosa, "Hispanas"; "The 1977 National"; Ortiz, "Rearguarders Thesis and Latina Elites"; Rosen, *World Split Open*, 290; Diehl and Saavedra, "Hispanas in the Year of the Woman," 16–19; Votaw, "Cultural Influences on Hispanic Feminism"; Maymi, "Fighting to Open the Doors"; Burciaga "1977 National Women's Conference," 8; and Robinson, "Are We Racist," 23.

88. Sotomayor, "La Década de la Mujer," 2; Saavedra-Vela, "Hispanic in Double Jeopardy"; Burciaga, "1977 National Women's Conference," 9; and "Chicanas," *Somos* (1978).

89. Del Castillo, "Mexican Women in Organization," 7.

90. Del Castillo, "Introducción; and Mora, "Tolteca Strike."

91. Del Castillo, "Mexican Women in Organization," 13–16. In the same book, Carlos Vásquez presented an ideological attack against "petty bourgeois feminism" and its "lack of ideological clarity." As most Marxist Chicanos, he could not conceive of a class analysis that gave equal space to gender. It is significant that Del Castillo shied away from Vásquez's language; Vásquez stated that "[i]t is necessary to differentiate between those who saw the enemy as men, and those who came to understand that sexism emanates from exploitative class relations and the resolution can only be found in class struggle." Del Castillo presented a more nuanced argument (Vásquez, "Women in the Chicano Movement," 28).

92. Josefina Lopez, "Chicana Women's Statement," n.d., Library Collection, UCLA Chicano Studies Research Center Library, 49; and Christian Smith, "Interviews with Four Chicanas in the Student Movement," UCLA Chicano Studies Research Center Library Collection, 1985, p. 9.

93. I do not want to suggest a one-to-one relationship between Chicana activism and Chicana intellectual thought. Rather, Chicanas' political behavior formed the setting for Chicana thought.

94. García, "Studying Chicanas," 19.

95. Ibid., 24.

96. Ibid., 19–24.

97. Blackwell, "Contested Histories," 59.

98. Ibid., 71.

99. Morales, "La mujer todavia impotente," 2.

100. Orange County Brown Berets, "Adelitas Role."

101. Matsuda, "La Chicana Organizes."

102. Del Castillo, "Malintzin Tenépal." Candelaria's essay on the same topic was extremely underdeveloped and confused (Candelaria, "La Malinche, Feminist Prototype").

103. Blackwell, "Contested Histories," 69.

104. Gutierrez, "Community, Patriarchy, and Individualism," 51–53.

105. Blackwell, "Contested Histories," 80.

106. "Preface," *Encuentro Femenil*, 1.

107. "To Think . . . To Act," 36.

108. Ibid.

109. Castillo, *Massacre of the Dreamers*, 33–35.

110. Castillo, "Introduction," xiv.

111. Orozco, "Sexism in Chicano Studies," 16.

112. In the second issue of *Encuentro Femenil*, the editors provided an overview of the development of Chicana intellectual thought up to that point. They noted the special issues in *El Grito del Norte*, edited by Betita Martinez, and *Regeneración*, edited by Francisca Flores, the two newsletters, *Comisión Femenil Mexicana* and *Chicana Service Action Center Newsletter*, as well as the articles collected by Dorinda Moreno Gladden and the Chicanas at California State University at San Francisco in *La Mujer En Pie de La Lucha*.

113. NietoGomez, "Madres por Justicia"; NietoGomez, "Chicanas in the Labor Force"; and NietoGomez, "Employment Discrimination."

114. Sanchez, "Higher Education y La Chicana?," 31.

115. NietoGomez, "Chicana Perspectives for Education," 39.

116. Ibid., 50.

117. Ibid., 42.

118. Ibid.

119. NietoGomez, "Chicana Perspectives for Education," 58–59; NietoGomez, "Un Proposito Para Estudios Femeniles."

120. NietoGomez, "Chicana Feminism," 3.

121. Ibid., 4; and Sánchez, "Imágenes de la Chicana."

122. NietoGomez, "Chicana Feminism," 5.

123. Of course we still encounter articles in other journals that sought to see women joined in struggle with men (Cruz, "La Mujer Latina").

124. Encuentro Femeníl, "La Vision Chicana," 46.

125. Cotera, *Profile in the Mexican American Woman*; and Cotera, *Diosa y Hembra*.

126. Cotera, *Profile in the Mexican American Woman*, 9, 152.

127. Ibid., 10.

128. Mireles, "La mujer en la communidad."

129. Cotera, *Chicana Feminist*, 17.

130. Ibid., 18, 23; and Cotera, "Chicana Identity."

131. Cotera, "Chicana Caucus," 25.

132. Gonzales "Congress of InterAmerican Women Writers," 10.

133. Gonzales, "Chicana in Literature," 51.

134. Building on Gonzales's suggested criticism, Bernice Zamora notes how the profession of criticism left little space for the existence of Chicana critics (see Zamora, "Chicana as a Literary Critic," 18; Zamora, "Our Truth Our Voice"; and Zamora, "Editorial").

135. Gonzales, "Organizations"; *El Mirlo* 6, no. 5 (1980); and Gonzales, "The Latina," 46.

136. Gonzales, "Toward a Feminist Pedagogy," 50.

137. Ibid.

138. Ibid.

139. Ibid., 51.

140. Much of the research for the National Chicana Foundation can be read within this tradition (see Cota-Robles Suárez and Anguiano, *Every Woman's Right*).

141. Lucero notes the importance of the work of Sylvia Gonzales, Dorinda Moreno, Flo Saiz, and Martha Cotera in preparation for *Estudios Femeniles*, edited by Anna NietoGomez and Corrine Sanchez in 1973 (see Lucero, "Resources for the Chicana Feminist Scholar").

142. García, "Introduction," 9.

143. Although these women writings were at the heart of Chicana herstory and the critique of gender relations, Chicanos and some Chicanas questioned their interpretations, often calling attention to what they perceived as their lack of academic credentials. These women's writings were often placed outside of Chicano studies except when the course on "La Chicana" was taught.

144. At the same time, we should keep in mind Chicana scholars who remained discipline-bound, like Maria Herrera-Sobek, Reyes Rachel Madrigal, Irene Isabel Blea, or Josefina Estrada Veloz. Their research on Chicanos and Chicanas fit traditional disciplinary research, and their conception of gender, at best, was filtered through their training (see Herrera-Sobek, "Metodos útiles para la enseñanza"; Madrigal, "La Chicana and the Movement"; Blea, "Brujeria"; and Veloz, "Chicana Identity").

145. Orozco, "Sexism in Chicano Studies."

146. Melville, "Introduction," 1. At the end of her introduction, she calls attention to "class status." Unfortunately, her use of "class status" was tied to traditional social-science jargon in which employment, education, and class aspirations were thrown about to explain attitudes and behavior (Melville, "Introduction," 7). In another essay, she also drew attention to the impact of migration on women's identity (Melville, "Mexican Women Adapt").

147. Melville, "Introduction," 2. Melville's introduction did not do justice to her work as a social scientist. I find her essay in *American Ethnologist* among the better academic essays in this period (Melville, "Ethnicity").

148. Ibid.

149. Baca Zinn, "Gender and Ethnic Identity among Chicanos," 21.

150. Baca Zinn, "Chicano Men and Masculinity."

151. Davalos, "Chicana/o Studies and Anthropology," 28.

152. Baca Zinn, "Chicano Family Research"; and Baca Zinn, "Ongoing Questions in the Study of Chicano Families."

153. Cota-Robles de Suarez, "Sexual Stereotypes," 17.

154. Vasquez, "Confronting Barriers to the Participation"; Gándara, "Passing Through the Eye of the Needle"; Ortiz, "The Distribution of Mexican American Women"; and Andrade, "Social Science Stereotypes of the Mexican American Women."

155. Ybarra, "When Wives Work"; and Ybarra, "Empirical and Theoretical Developments."

156. Lucero, "Resources for the Chicana Feminist Scholar," 393. "Marianismo" is used in reference to the Virgin Mary and her place in Roman Catholic theology. Some also use the term to refer to an ideal conception of femininity that women are supposed to live up to—modest, virtuous, and sexually abstinent.

157. Sosa Riddell, "Chicanas and El Movimiento," 156.

158. Ibid. For a different contemporary reading of machismo, see Trujillo, "Terminology of Machismo"; for a supporting position see Gallegos y Chávez, "Northern New Mexican Woman."

159. In particular, she was upset with arguments like those made by Linda Peralta Aguilar. Aguilar argues that while much had been written about employment discrimination directed against Chicanos, little had been noted about "employment discrimination directed at Chicanas, not only from Anglo male employers, but potential Chicano employers as well" (Peralta Aguilar, "Unequal Opportunity and the Chicana," 45). She notes that often Chicanas' main opposition in job opportunities was from Chicanos.

160. Sosa Riddell, "Chicanas and El Movimiento," 162.

161. Building on this vision was her coauthored essay on Parlier, California (see Sosa Riddell and Aguallo, "Case of Chicano Politics").

162. Navar, "La Mexicana," 4. Another version appeared in *Agenda* (1974).

163. In a proposal to the Social Science Research Council, Navar states she would like to develop a "theoretical humanistic understanding of the Chicano American culture" (Isabelle Navar, "Towards a Transformation of Culture and Consciousness: A Chicana Perspective," 1973, Library Collection, UCLA Chicano Studies Research Center Library, 1). See also Isabelle Navar, "Como Chicana Mi Madre," 1973 Library Collection, UCLA Chicano Studies Research Center Library.

164. Navar, "La Mexicana," 5.

165. Molina de Pick, "Reflexiones Sobre El Feminismo" (*Regeneración*).

166. Rincon, "Chicanas on the Move."

167. Rincon, "La Chicana: Her Role in the Past and Her Search for a New Role in the Future."

168. Cotera, "La Nueva Hispana y Hispanidad," 8.

169. An earlier version of parts of the text appeared in *De Colores* (see Enríquez and Mirandé, "Liberation, Chicana Style").

170. Mirandé and Enríquez, *La Chicana*, 12–13.

171. Some of the literary discussion reappeared in Enriquez's dissertation (Enriquez, "Towards a Definition of").

172. In her review of *La Chicana*, Baca Zinn highlights that Mirandé and Enríquez reduced Chicana feminism to a distinctive aspect of Mexican cultural heritage. In the end, they failed to distinguish structural and cultural dimensions of social organization (Baca Zinn, "Mexican-American Women in the Social Sciences," 263–264).

173. Mirandé and Enríquez, *La Chicana*, 107.

174. Ibid., 234.

175. Ibid., 241.

176. Mirandé struggles to salvage the term "machismo" by trying to construct a mythical Chicano family (Mirandé, "Reinterpretation of Male Dominance," 474). He concludes "the Chicano family is not male-dominated and authoritarian . . . but egalitarian" (ibid., 477). He further adds that the macho in the family was not about power, but responsibility and providing for the family.

177. Macías, *Perspectivas en Chicano Studies,* 240; and Clarisa Torres, Sonia Lopez, and Enriqueta V. Chavez, "It Is a Class Struggle!," ca. 1974, Library Collection, UCLA Chicano Studies Research Center Library.

178. Sánchez, "Chicana Labor Force," 6.

179. Ibid., 14. To be fair, Sanchez's early use of Marxism was much more subtle than I have argued here. Note her discussion of Chomsky's work (Sánchez, "La gramática transformacional"). Thirteen years later, Sánchez took a different approach to this question. She rearticulated her quest for a materialist perspective by rethinking how to retain a "subject status" (Sánchez, "History of Chicanas," 5). There was another side of her work that was traditional and fit discussions on language assessment and bilingualism (Sánchez, "Critique of Oral Language Assessment Instruments"; and Sánchez, "Chicano Bilingualism").

180. Apodaca, "Chicana Woman," 72. A potential early project was proposed by Rosalinda Gonzalez, a study of working-class women in the United States (in particular Chicanas), through the lens of dialectical and historical materialism (Macías, *Perspectivas en Chicano Studies,* 234).

181. She extended some of her points in a later essay, where she was critical of Chicana feminist thought as a variant of liberal feminism that supported the middle-class aspirations of women (Apodaca, "Double Edge Sword").

182. *El Mirlo* 9, no. 3–4 (1982).

183. Del Castillo, *Between Borders.*

184. Gómez-Quiñones, "Questions Within Women's Historiography," 93.

185. Ibid.

186. Ibid., 94.

187. Ibid., 95. Given this view, he could not share Orozco's definition of feminism as "all-encompassing" since it is a theory, a method, and a practice which seeks to transform human relations (Orozco, "Sexism in Chicano Studies," 14).

188. Saldívar-Hull, *Feminism on the Border,* 33.

189. Carrillo, "History of Las Mujeres." In a later issue of *Revista Mujeres,* Elisa Dávila writes: "En este número, como en los anteriores de *Revista Mujeres,* ni encontramos, ni queremos presentar imagines abstractas o discusiones teóricas sobre la mujer latina, de color, o del tercer mundo. Por el contrario, lo que leemos es el testimonio y/o la poetización de sus vivencias concretas, y la reflexión personalizada de todo aquello que como seres humanos nos caracteriza y como grupo nos unifica" (In this issue of *Revista Mujeres,* as in earlier ones, we do not find nor do we want to present abstract images or theoretical discussions about Latinas either of color or from the third world. On the contrary, what we read is the testimony and/or the poetic expressions of their life experience, and the personal reflection of all that makes us part of humanity and brings us together)." (Dávila, "A manera de introducción," 2.)

190. Baca Zinn, "Mexican-American Women in the Social Sciences," 268.

191. Ibid., 269.

192. NietoGomez, "Un Proposito Para Estudios Femeniles."

193. "Mujeres del Movimiento, Symposium: Educación en Luz," 1975 Library Collection, UCLA Chicano Studies Research Center Library.

194. MEChA, "Chicano Studies Accused of Fostering Male Chauvinism"; and "History of the Chicana," n.d., UCLA Chicano Studies Research Center Library Collection, 2.

195. Barry, "Women's Participation in the Chicano Movement," 69.

196. As Fernandez has pointed out, many of the voices in the collection spoke with a gender-defined voice even though they retained an ambiguous relationship with Chicano nationalism and accommodated to the male vision of women as passive (Fernandez, "Abriendo Caminos on the Borderland").

197. Armas, "Introduction to La Cosecha," 3.

198. Mujeres en Marcha, *Chicanas in the 80's*. Gilberto García observes that by the 1975 conference, Chicanas had raised the issue of greater participation of women on panels (García, "Beyond the Adelita Image").

199. "MALCS Declaration."

200. The women who participated on this panel were Teresa Córdova, Margarita Decierdo, Gloria Cuádraz, Deena González, Sylvia Lizárraga, Linda Facio, and Lita de la Torre; other women in this organization were Murilia Flores, Guadalupe Frías, and Beatríz Pesquera. Mujeres en Marcha, *Chicanas in the 80's*, 2.

201. Ibid., 1–2.

202. Ibid., 7.

203. Ibid., 10; Decierdo in ibid., 23–24; and González in ibid., 26.

204. Little followed the panel presentation; Chicanos were not concerned about bringing Chicanas and a Chicana perspective into Chicano Studies. To place pressure on the organization, some of the panel presenters helped organize the Chicana Caucus. The caucus presented a resolution that the 1984 conference theme be "Voces de la Mujer." Thus the twelfth annual conference (1984) held in Austin, Texas, had women as the focus of the conference (Córdova et al., "Preface"; Irene Campos Carr et al., Letter, 1983 Library Collection, UCLA Chicano Studies Research Center Library; and García, "El feminismo chicano"). Even though Irene Blea had been elected NACS's first female national chair in 1978, this had little impact on the intellectual direction of the organization.

205. Zavella, "The Problematic Relationship of Feminism and Chicana Studies," 28.

206. Ibid., 28; and Baca Zinn, "Mexican-American Women in the Social Sciences."

207. Trujillo Gaitan, "Dilemma of the Modern Chicana Artist and Critic."

208. Baca Zinn, "Mexican-American Women in the Social Sciences," 260.

209. Scott, *Gender and the Politics of History,* 6.

210. Alarcón, "Hay que inventranos," 4.

211. Among African American women, it is important to draw attention to the Combahee River Collective statement in 1974 as an early step in this direction further developed in "A Black Feminist Statement," by Barbara Smith, Beverly Smith, and Demila Frazier that appeared in 1977 (Kelley, *Freedom Dreams,* 148–149).

212. Sanchez, "Chicana Writer Breaking Out," 31.

213. Ibid., 34.

214. Ibid.

215. Ibid., 37.

216. Trujillo Gaitan, "Dilemma of the Modern Chicana Artist and Critic," 9; and Rebolledo, "Maturing of Chicana Poetry," 145.

217. Fernandez, "Abriendo Caminos on the Borderland."

218. García, "Development of Chicana Feminist Discourse," 226–227.

219. Bambara, "Foreword," vii; and Moraga, "Preface," xvi.

220. Anderson, "Separatism, Feminism, and the Betrayal of Reform," 437; Clarke, "Lesbianism," 128; and Molina, "Fragmentations."

221. Anzaldúa, "La Prieta," 205.

222. I find Alarcón's reading of *This Bridge Called My Back* as whiggish. While I might be willing to discuss postmodern notions of the subject, I am not sure that Alarcón's critique of standpoint epistemology and the subject are helpful in engaging the text. Alarcón is right to draw attention to difference and its challenge to white women's theorizing on gender, but I am not certain that the various authors in *This Bridge* are arguing from the position of a decentered subject in the process of shifting through their various identities. For this reason I am not sure that *This Bridge* leads to this: "To grasp or reclaim an identity in this culture means always already to have become a subject of consciousness. The theory of the subject of consciousness as a unitary and synthesizing agent of knowledge is always already a posture of domination" (Alarcón, "Theoretical Theoretical Subject(s) of *This Bridge*"). To argue difference and multiple voicing does not necessarily lead to a fractured subjectivity or none at all (disidentity). For a more thorough critique, see Moya, "Chicana."

223. Moraga, "Entering the Lives of Others," 23.

224. Anzaldúa, "Speaking in Tongues," 169.

225. Cameron, "'Gee, You Don't Seem Like an Indian from the Reservation,'" 49.

226. Moraga, "La Güera," 30.

227. Morales, "'. . . And Even Fidel Can't Change That,'" 56.

228. Cameron, "'Gee, You Don't Seem Like an Indian from the Reservation,'" 49; Valerio, "It's in My Blood," 44; Yamada, "Invisibility Is an Unnatural Disaster," 37; and Smith and Smith, "Across the Kitchen Table," 124–126.

229. Smith and Smith, "Across the Kitchen Table," 126.

230. Moraga, "La Güera," 30.

231. Moschkovich, "'—But I Know You," 82; Chrystos, "I Don't Understand Those Who Have Turned Away," 69; and Davenport, "Pathology of Racism," 86.

232. Moschkovich, "'—But I Know You," 79; and Yamada, "Asian Pacific American Women," 71.

233. Moraga, "Between the Lines," 105–106; and Smith and Smith, "Across the Kitchen Table."

234. Smith and Smith, "Across the Kitchen Table," 121.

235. Lorde, "Master's Tools Will Never Dismantle" (1981), 99.

236. In another rewrite of this essay, Lorde wrote: "*For the master's tools will never dismantle the master's house. They may allow us temporarily to beat him at his own game, but they will never enable us to bring about genuine change*" (Lorde, "Master's Tools Will Never Dismantle," 1984, 112).

237. Lorde, "Master's Tools Will Never Dismantle" (1981), 100.

238. Lorde, "Master's Tools Will Never Dismantle" (1984), 111.

239. Lorde, "Master's Tools Will Never Dismantle" (1981), 101; Lorde, "Master's Tools Will Never Dismantle" (1984), 113. This also overturned the tokenism of women of color (Alarcón, "Chicana's Feminist Literature," 189).

240. Anzaldúa, "El Mundo Zurdo," 196.

241. Anzaldúa "La Prieta," 198.

242. Blackwell, "Contested Histories," 60. The year 1981 played a central role in the development of Chicana thought. As a reaction to the National Women's Studies Association Conference, women of color articulated a "U.S. Third World Feminism" (Sandoval, "Feminism and Racism," 55–71).

243. In the wake of *This Bridge* came Cherríe Moraga's *Loving in the War Years: Lo que nunca pasó por sus labios* (1983), which continued with the ideas expressed in the earlier text. Saldívar-Hull argued that Moraga generated a theoretical space for Chicana lesbian feminism and development of "feminism on the border" (Saldívar-Hull, *Feminism on the Border,* 34). She added that Moraga's work links to the work of other women of color (in particular, the Combahee River Collective) and presented a further development of Third World feminism (Saldívar-Hull, *Feminism on the Border,* 50).

Conclusion

1. Horkheimer and Adorno, *Dialectic of Enlightenment,* 25.

2. Horkheimer, *Eclipse of Reason,* 184.

3. Ibid., 81–82.

4. Liz Stanley and Sue Wise astutely noted in 1983 that feminism was becoming closed, fixed, and developing its own rigid orthodoxies. For this reason, feminism could no longer rest on providing a radical feminist critique because "it accepts existing social science assumptions, beliefs, ways of working and ways of viewing the world, and is concerned with removing sexism from these rather than producing any more radical alternative" (Stanley and Wise, *Breaking Out,* 16).

5. I want to underscore that the various articulations of Chicano(a) studies in no way suggests a weakening of U.S. academic practices.

6. Memorandum, "Chicano/Latino Student Survey," 1978, Larry Trujillo Collection, UCB Ethnic Studies Library Archives.

7. García, "Introduction," 10.

8. Burrola and Rivera, *Chicano Studies Programs at the Crossroads,* 8; Corona, "Chicano Scholars and Public Issues"; and Mirandé, "Research/Curriculum in Chicano Studies," 2.

9. Munoz Jr., "Quest for Paradigm,," 35.

10. Cabán, "Moving from the Margins to Where?," 14.

11. Vázquez, "Chicanology"; and Rocco, "Chicano Studies and Critical Political Theory."

12. Moraga and Anzaldúa, *This Bridge Called My Back.*

13. Gonzalez, McKenna, and Perez, "Background Paper on Chicana and Chicano Studies."

14. The association is divided into regional groups that are called *focos.*

15. Muñoz Jr., *Youth, Identity, Power,* 159; "Chicano Studies"; Editorial, "A Question"; Cruz, "Chicano Studies"; and Haro, "Chicano Studies."

16. García, "Background Paper."

17. Mirandé, "Research/Curriculum in Chicano Studies."

18. Nuñez and Contreras, "Principles and Foundations of Chicano Studies," in *Symposium on Chicano Studies.*

19. Gonzalez, McKenna, and Perez, "Background Paper on Chicana and Chicano Studies."

20. Acuña, "Chicano Studies," 7–8.

21. National Association for Chicano Studies, "Preamble," i.

22. Acuña, "Chicano Studies," 5.

23. Ibid., 6.

24. García, "Juncture in the Road," in 187.

25. Ibid., 189.

26. Ibid., 191–193.

27. Ibid., 193.

28. In *Sometimes There Is No Other Side,* Acuña seems more open to the epistemological questions raised by many non–Chicano Studies practitioners (ibid., 37, 59, and 99).

29. Anzaldúa, *Borderlands/La Frontera*; and Anzaldúa, *Making Face, Making Soul.*

30. Anzaldúa, *Borderlands/La Frontera,* 38.

31. Ibid., 87.

32. Ibid., 77–78.

33. Ibid., 79.

34. Anzaldúa, *Making Face, Making Soul,* xxv.

35. Ibid., xvii.

36. Ibid., xxv.

37. Ibid., xxiii.

38. As María Lugones has reminded us: "To play in this way is then an act of resistance as well as an act of self-affirmation" (Lugones, "Hablando cara a cara/ Speaking Face to Face," 46).

39. Rosaldo, *Culture and Truth*; Saldívar, *Chicano Narrative*; Calderón and Saldívar, *Criticism in the Borderlands*; Padilla, *My History, Not Yours*; Gutiérrez-Jones, *Rethinking the Borderlands*; and Sánchez, *Telling Identities.*

40. Stanley, "Introduction," 4–5.

41. Addelson, "Knowers/Doers and Their Moral Problems," 266.

42. Rosaldo, *Culture and Truth,* 181. Sánchez used Californio "testimonials" as a way to construct a collective identity by their endeavor to recenter themselves textually (Sánchez, *Telling Identities,* x–xiii). However, she hesitated to allow these narratives to dictate our understanding of marginality. Using a composite Marxist model, she criticized the reduction of all theoretical foci to textuality, which she claimed is "the research dominant" of the postmodern era. Reality is not reducible to our knowledge or experience of it. For this reason, discursive formations must be analyzed as ideological frameworks (ibid., 39).

43. Gutiérrez-Jones, *Rethinking the Borderlands,* 29.

44. Saldívar, *Chicano Narrative,* 6.

45. Ibid., 205. Gutiérrez-Jones, however, pointed out that these Chicano(a) narratives might be assimilated into an academic framework that is ideologically structured around notions of pluralism, humanistic universalism, and liberal-legal consensus at the expense of historically situated cultural conflict (Gutiérrez-Jones, *Rethinking the Borderlands*, 31). He called attention to how institutions accommodate and control the process of cultural translation of Chicano(a) public discourse (ibid., 55). Saldívar, at times critical of integrative reform of U.S. literary history, suggested that this reform might turn out to be a counter hegemonic move to renew, defend, and modify, but not to undo earlier forms of dominance (Saldívar, *Chicano Narrative*, 216). Yet in the end, Saldívar's notion of "dialectics of difference" manifested a hope in a truly radical reconstruction of U.S. literary history that seeks Chicano(a) narrative to form a dialogical system to help integrate canonical works as well as resistance literatures (ibid., 217–218).

46. Pérez, *Decolonial Imaginary*.

47. The search for women and agency can also be found in Gonzalez, *Refusing the Favor*.

48. Pérez, *Decolonial Imaginary*, 6.

49. Ibid., 23.

50. Ibid., 25. At the same time, the challenge to Chicano Studies began to dissolve the fetish that had developed in Chicano(a) understanding of the relationship between social science research and community. Instead, we see a reconceptionalization of social science that tried to avoid the disciplinary models and reconciled that the relationship between research and community service was equivocal and complex (Zavella, *Women's Work and Chicano Families*; Romero, *Maid in the U.S.A.*; and Pardo, *Mexican American Women Activists*).

51. Mariscal, *Brown-Eyed Children of the Sun*, 8; and Oropeza, *Raza Si!*, 92–102.

52. This is also different from the comparative approach adopted by Barrera (see his *Beyond Aztlán*).

53. Rodríguez, *Latin American Subaltern Studies Reader*; and Poblete, *Critical Latin American and Latino Studies*.

54. Anzaldúa, "En rapport, In Opposition," 143

55. Ibid., 145.

56. Acuña, *Sometimes There Is No Other Side*, 37, 59, 99.

57. Ibid., 215–216.

58. Ibid., 107.

59. Ibid.

60. Ibid., 221.

61. Levinas, "Martin Heidegger and Ontology"; and Levinas, *Ethics and Infinity*; Greisch, "Face and Reading." Malonado-Torres in *Against War* provides another use of Levinas that merits our attention.

62. Levinas, *Totality and Infinity*, 44.

63. Levinas, "Ethics as First Philosophy," 76.

64. Levinas, *Totality and Infinity*, 21.

65. Ciaramelli, "Levinas's Ethical Discourse," 85–86.

66. While Husserl was successful in isolating the "idea of an originary non-theoretical intentionality," he still bases his theory on representation, the objectifying act. Levinas responds that "[t]he labour of thought wins out over the otherness of things and men" (Levinas, "Ethics as First Philosophy, 78).

67. Levinas, "Ethics as First Philosophy," 79.

68. In *Otherwise Than Being or Beyond Essence,* Levinas argues that the original "saying" (*le dire*) sets an order more grave than being and antecedent to being. Unfortunately, it can be betrayed in the "said" (*le dit*); "whether one can at the same time know and free the known of marks which thematization leaves on it by subordinating it to ontology" (Levinas, *Otherwise Than Being,* 7). The "otherwise than being" is stated in a saying that must be unsaid. "Spoken words are meant to be fragments of intersubjective chains of exchange and conversation" (see Adriaan Peperzak, "Presentation," in *Re-Reading Levinas,* edited by Robert Bernasconi and Simon Critchley [Bloomington: Indiana University Press, 1991], 60). In saying so, I expose myself to the other, and this involves pain and suffering. The order of the said, however, takes us back to logos and its synoptic structures.

69. Levinas, "Ethics as First Philosophy," 80.

70. Ibid., 82.

71. Ibid.

72. Ibid., 84.

73. Ibid., 85.

74. Levinas, *Otherwise Than Being,* 10.

75. Levinas, *Ethics and Infinity,* 86–95.

76. Levinas, *Otherwise Than Being,* 14–15; and Ciaramelli, "Levinas's Ethical Discourse," 88.

77. Levinas, *Otherwise Than Being,* 97.

78. Levinas, *Totality and Infinity,* 39.

79. Ibid., 51.

80. Ibid., 72.

81. Levinas, *Ethics and Infinity,* 88.

82. Levinas, *Totality and Infinity,* 75.

83. Ibid., 84.

84. Ibid., 178.

85. Levinas, *Otherwise Than Being,* 43.

86. Ibid., 47; Ciaramelli, "Levinas's Ethical Discourse," 87.

87. Levinas, *Totality and Infinity,* 215.

88. Ciaramelli, "Levinas's Ethical Discourse," 90–95. Philippe Nemo asks Levinas about the other's responsibility to me. "Perhaps, but that is *his* affair" (Levinas, *Ethics and Infinity,* 98). The relationship, Levinas adds, is a nonsymmetrical one. I am responsible for the other without waiting for reciprocity. "Responsibility is what is incumbent on me exclusively, and what, *humanly,* I cannot refuse" (Levinas, *Ethics and Infinity,* 101).

89. Cohen, "Translator's Introduction," 10.

90. Merod, *Political Responsibility of the Critic.*

Bibliography

Journals

Agenda: National Council of La Raza
Atisbos
Aztlán: Chicano Journal of the Social Sciences and Arts
Bronze
Calmecac
Campo Libre: Journal of Chicano Studies
Caracol
Carta Abierta
CFM Report
Chicana Service Action Center Newsletter
Chicanismo
Chicano Student Movement
Chicano Studies Newsletter
Chilam Balam
Con Safos
Confluencia
Corazon de Aztlán
Critica: A Journal of Critical Essays
Cry of Color
Cultural Studies
De Colores: Journal of Emerging Raza Philosophies
El Cuaderno
El Grito: A Journal of Contemporary Mexican-American Though
El Grito del Norte
El Grito del Sol
El Mestizo
El Mirlo Canta de Noticatlan: Carta Sobre Chicano Studies
El Popo
Encuentro Femenil
Epoca
Hijas de Cuauhtémoc

Hispanic Journal of Behavioral Sciences
Imágenes de la Chicana
Journal of Mexican American History
La Causa
La Luz
La Onda
La Red/The Net
Metas
Mexican American Cultural Center: Carta Universitaria
NABE: Journal of the National Association for Bilingual Education
National Association of Chicano Social Scientists Newsletter
National Caucuses of Chicano Social Science
Nuestra Cosa
Perspectives in Mexican American Studies
Prensa Popular
Que Pasa
Raíces
Rayas
Regeneración
Revista Chicano-Riqueña
Si Se Puede
Somos
Third Women
UCLA MEChA Newsletter

Published Sources

Acevedo, Jorge Terrazas. "Chicano Thought and Value." In *Third World Philosophy,* edited by Heydar Reghaby, 102–128. Berkeley, Calif.: Lewis Publishing, 1974.

———. "Some Solutions in Chicano Higher Education." In *Ghosts in the Barrio: Issues in Bilingual-Bicultural Education,* edited by Ralph Poblano, 153–159. San Rafael, Calif.: Leswing Press, 1973.

———. "Two-Headed Jaguar Threatens Emerging Chicanismo Through Conservative Ideas." *Cry of Color* 1, no. 1 (1970): 4–5.

———. "U.C. Chicano Faculty Meeting." *Chicano Studies Newsletter* 1, no. 2 (1970): 4.

Acuña, Celia, et al. *Chicano Studies SDSU.* San Diego: N.p, n.d.

Acuña, Rodolfo. "Chicano Studies: A Public Trust." In *Chicano Studies: Critical Connection Between Research and Community,* edited by Teresa Córdova, 2–13. Albuquerque, N.Mex.: National Association for Chicano Studies, 1992.

———. "La Generación de '68: Unfulfilled Dreams." *Corazon de Aztlán* 1, no. 1 (1983): 6–7.

———. "The Making of *Occupied America*." In *Occupied America: A Chicano History Symposium*, edited by Rodolfo Acuña, 14–27. Houston: Mexican American Studies Program, University of Houston, 1982.

———. *Occupied America*. San Francisco: Canfield Press, 1972.

———. *Occupied America: A History of Chicanos*. 2nd ed. New York: Harper and Row Publishers, 1981.

———. *Occupied America: A History of Chicanos*. 3rd ed. New York: Harper and Row Publishers, 1988.

Acuña, Rodolfo F. *Sometimes There Is No Other Side: Chicanos and the Myth of Equality*. Notre Dame, Ill.: University of Notre Dame Press, 1998.

Addelson, Kathryn Pyne. "Knowers/Doers and Their Moral Problems." In *Feminist Epistemologies*, edited by Linda Alcoff and Elizabeth Potter, 265–293. New York: Routledge, 1993.

Aguilar, Amparo. "International Women's Conference in Mexico City: June 19–July 3, 1975." *Caracol* 2, no. 1 (1975): 11, 16.

Alarcón, Justo S. "La meta crítica chicana." *Revista Chicano-Riquena* 10, no. 3 (1982): 47–52.

Alarcón, Norma. "Chicana's Feminist Literature: A Re-Vision Through Malintzin/ or Malintzin: Putting Flesh Back on the Object." In *This Bridge Called My Back: Writings by Radical Women of Color*, edited by Cherríe Moraga and Gloria Anzaldúa, 182–190. New York: Kitchen Table, 1981.

———. "Hay que inventranos/We Must Invent Ourselves." *Third Women* 1, no. 1 (1981): 4–6.

———. "The Theoretical Subject(s) of *This Bridge Called My Back* and Anglo American Feminism." In *Criticism in the Borderlands: Studies in Chicano Literature, Culture, and Ideology*, edited by Héctor Calderón and José David Saldívar, 28–39. Durham, N.C.: Duke University Press, 1991.

Alejandro, Franco. "The Chicano and Higher Education"—The 'National Concilio for Chicano Studies." *Hojas: A Chicano Journal of Education*, 40–46. Austin, Tex.: Juarez-Lincoln Press, 1976.

Almaguer, Tomás. "Historical Notes on Chicano Oppression: The Dialectics of Racial and Class Domination in North America." *Aztlán* 5, no. 1 and 2 (1974): 27–56.

———. "Toward the Study of Chicano Colonialism." *Aztlán* 2, no. 1 (1971): 7–21.

Alurista [Alberto Baltazar Urista Heredia]. "The Chicano Cultural Revolution." *De Colores* 1, no. 1 (1973): 23–33.

———, et al. *An Anthology of Chicano Literature*. Los Angeles: University of Southern California Press, 1976.

Alvarez, Rodolfo. "The Psycho-Historical and Socioeconomic Development of the Chicano Community in the United States." *Social Science Quarterly* 53, no. 4 (1973): 920–942.

Amaro, Arturo. "The Chicano in a Capitalist Society." In *The Third Annual El Alma Chicana Symposium*, edited by Randall Jimenez, unpaginated.

San Jose: California State University Associated Students and Mexican-American Graduate Studies Department, 1973.

Amaya, Abel. "On Chicanas in Higher Education." *La Luz* 3, no. 3 (1974): 4.

Ambrecht, Biliana C. S., and Harry P. Pachon. "Ethnic Political Mobilization in a Mexican American Community an Exploratory Study of East Los Angeles, 1965–1972." *Western Political Quarterly* 27, no. 3 (1974): 500–519.

Anderson, Jackie. "Separatism, Feminism, and the Betrayal of Reform." *Signs: Journal of Women in Culture and Society* 19, no. 2 (1994): 437–449.

Andrade, Sally J. "Social Science Stereotypes of the Mexican American Women: Policy Implications for Research." *Hispanic Journal of Behavioral Sciences* 4, no. 2 (1982): 223–244.

Anzaldúa, Gloria. *Borderlands/La Frontera.* San Francisco: Spinsters/Aunt Lute Books, 1987.

———. "El Mundo Zurdo: The Vision." In *This Bridge Called My Back: Writings by Radical Women of Color,* edited by Cherríe Moraga and Gloria Anzaldúa, 195–196. New York: Kitchen Table, 1981.

———. "En rapport, In Opposition: Cobrando cuentas a las nuestras." In *Making Face, Making Soul/Haciendo Caras: Creative and Critical Perspectives by Women of Color,* edited by Gloria Anzaldúa, 142–148. San Francisco: Aunt Lute Foundation Books, 1990.

———. "La Prieta." In *This Bridge Called My Back: Writings by Radical Women of Color,* edited by Cherríe Moraga and Gloria Anzaldúa, 198–209. New York: Kitchen Table, 1981.

———. "Speaking in Tongues: A Letter to Third World Women Writers." In *This Bridge Called My Back: Writings by Radical Women of Color,* edited by Cherríe Moraga and Gloria Anzaldúa, 165–174. New York: Kitchen Table, 1981.

Anzaldúa, Gloria, ed. *Making Face, Making Soul/Haciendo Caras: Creative and Critical Perspectives by Women of Color.* San Francisco: Aunt Lute Foundation Books, 1990.

Apodaca, Maria Linda. "The Chicana Woman: An Historical Materialist Perspective." *Latin American Perspectives* 4, no. 12–13 (1977): 70–89.

———. "A Double Edge Sword: Hispanas and Liberal Feminism." *Critica: A Journal of Critical Essays* 1, no. 3 (1986): 96–114.

Aragón de Shepro, Theresa. *Chicanismo and Mexican American Politics.* Seattle, Wash.: Centro de Estudios Chicanos, 1971.

———. "The Nature of Chicano Political Powerlessness." Ph.D. dissertation, University of Washington, 1978.

Aragón de Valdez, Theresa. "Organizing as a Political Tool for the Chicana." *Frontiers* 5, no. 2 (1980): 7–13.

Arce, Carlos H. "Chicano Participation in Academe: A Case of Academic Colonialism." *El Grito del Sol* 3, no. 1 (1978): 75–104.

Armas, José. "Doctrina de La Raza." *De Colores* 1, no. 2 (1974): 38–47.

————. "Editorial." *De Colores* 1, no. 1 (1973): 4–9.

————. "La Familia de la Raza." *De Colores* 3, no. 2 (1976): 1–55.

————. "The National Concilio for Chicano Studies." *La Luz* 3, no. 3 (1974): 41–42.

Armas, José, and Bernice Zamora. "Introduction." In *Flor y Canto IV and V,* edited by José Armas et al., 10–11. Albuquerque, N.Mex.: Pajarito Publications, 1980.

Armas, Linda Morales. "Introduction to La Cosecha." *De Colores* 3, no. 3 (1977): 3–5.

Arroyo, Luis Leobardo. *A Bibliography of Recent Chicano History Writings, 1970–1975.* Los Angeles: UCLA Chicano Studies Center Publications, 1975.

————. "Notes on Past, Present and Future Directions of Chicano Labor Studies." *Aztlán* 6, no. 2 (1975): 137–149.

————. "The State of Chicano Labor History, 1970–1980." In *Chicanos and the Social Sciences: A Decade of Research and Development (1970–1980),* edited by Isidro D. Ortiz, 1–8. Santa Barbara, Calif.: Center for Chicano Studies, 1983.

Arvizu, Steven F. "Introductory Comments." *El Grito del Sol* 3, no. 1 (1978): 11–16.

Atencio, Tomás. "La Academia de la Nueva Raza: El Oro del Barrio." *El Cuaderno* 3, no. 1 (1973): 4–15.

————. "La Academia de la Nueva Raza: Su Historia." *El Cuaderno* 1, no. 1 (1971): 4–9.

————. "La Academic de la Nueva Raza: Sus Obras." *El Cuaderno* 2, no. 1 (1972): 6–13.

————. "La Resolana." *El Cuaderno* 4, no. 1 (1976): 2–4.

————. "The Survival of La Raza Despite Social Services." *Social Casework: Journal of Contemporary Social Work* 52, no. 5 (1971): 262–268.

Atencio, Tomás, and Consuelo Pacheco. "The Concept of la Resolana." *Agenda* 10, no. 1 (1980): 14–15.

Atencio, Tomás, and Estevan Arellano. "Mining and Processing el Oro del Barrio." *Agenda* 8 (1975): 16–21.

Baca Zinn, Maxine. "Chicano Family Research: Conceptual Distortions and Alternative Directions." *Journal of Ethnic Studies* 7, no. 3 (1979): 59–71.

————. "Chicano Men and Masculinity." *Journal of Ethnic Studies* 10, no. 2 (1982): 29–44.

————. "Gender and Ethnic Identity among Chicanos." *Frontiers* 5, no. 2 (1980): 18–24.

————. "Mexican-American Women in the Social Sciences: Review Essay." *Signs: Journal of Women in Culture and Society* 8, no. 2 (1982): 259–272.

————. "Ongoing Questions in the Study of Chicano Families." In *The State of Chicano Research on Family, Labor, and Migration,* edited by Armando Valdez, Albert Camarrillo, and Tomás Almaguer, 139–146. Stanford, Calif.: Stanford Center for Chicano Research, 1983.

———. "Sociological Theory in Emergent Chicano Perspectives." *Pacific Sociological Review* 24, no. 2 (1981): 255–272.

Bakhtin, Mikhail. *Rabelais and His World.* Cambridge: MIT Press, 1968.

Bambara, Toni Cade. "Foreward." In *This Bridge Called My Back: Writings by Radical Women of Color,* edited by Cherríe Moraga and Gloria Anzaldúa, vi–viii. New York: Kitchen Table, 1981.

Bañas, L. K. "Donde Estas? Conflicts in the Chicano Movement." *Caracol* 3, no. 11 (1977): 15–17.

———. "Donde Estoy?" *Calmecac* (1981): 28–33.

Bareno, John Meza. "The Mexican-American Political Experience in Colton, California." Ph.D. dissertation, U.S. International University, 1978.

Barrera, Elma, and Anna NietoGomez de Lazarin. "Chicana Encounter." *Regeneración* 2, no. 4 (1975): 49–51.

Barrera, Mario. *Beyond Aztlán: Ethnic Autonomy in Comparative Perspective.* Notre Dame, Ill.: University of Notre Dame Press, 1988.

———. *Race and Class in the Southwest: A Theory of Racial Inequality.* Notre Dame, Ill.: University of Notre Dame Press, 1979.

———. "The Study of Politics and the Chicano." *Aztlán* 5, no. 1–2 (1974): 9–26.

Barrera, Mario, Albert Camarillo, and Francisco Hernandez. "Introduction." In *Work, Family, Sex Roles, Language,* edited by Mario Barrera, Albert Camarillo, and Francisco Hernandez, 1–8. Berkeley, Calif.: Tonatiuh-Quinto Sol International, 1980.

Barrera, Mario, Alberto Camarillo, and Francisco Hernandez, eds. *Work, Family, Sex Roles, Language.* Berkeley, Calif.: Tonatiuh-Quinto Sol International, 1980.

Barrera, Mario, and Geralda Vialpando, eds. *Action Research: In Defense of the Barrio. Interviews with Ernesto Galarza, Guillermo Flores, and Rosalio Muñoz.* Los Angeles: Aztlán Publications, 1974.

Barrera, Mario, Carlos Muñoz, and Charles Ornelas. "The Barrio as an Internal Colony." In *Politics and Peoples in Urban Society,* edited by Harlan Hahn, 281–301. Beverly Hills, Calif.: Sage Publications, 1972.

Barry, Naomi M. "Women's Participation in the Chicano Movement." *Latino Studies Journal* 8, no. 1 (1997): 47–81.

Basso, Teresita. "The Emerging Chicana Woman Religious." In *The Third Annual El Alma Chicana Symposium,* edited by Randall Jimenez, unpaginated. San Jose: California State University Associated Students and Mexican-American Graduate Studies Department, 1973.

Berman, Paul. *A Tale of Two Utopias: The Political Journey of the Generation of 1968.* New York: W.W. Norton and Company, 1996.

Bernal, Esmeralda. "Chicano en pensamiento: Regreso a la humanidad." *Bronze* 1, no. 2 (1968): 6.

Bernal, Jose J., Neftali Garcia, and Gloria Zamora. "Bilingual Education at the Crossroads: A Rationale for Political Action." *NABE* 3, no.2 (1979): 61–71.

Berrios, Lizardo. "Socialization in a Mexican American Community: A Study in Civilizational Perspective." Ph.D. dissertation, New School for Social Research, 1979.

Bixler-Márquez, Dennis J., et al., eds. *Chicano Studies: Survey and Analysis.* Dubuque, Iowa: Kendall/Hunt Publishing Co., 1997.

Blackwell, Maylei. "Contested Histories: *Las Hijas de Cuachtémoc,* Chicana Feminisms, and Print Culture in the Chicano Movement, 1968–1973." In *Chicana Feminism: A Critical Reader,* edited by Gabriela F. Arredondo et al., 59–89. Durham, N.C.: Duke University Press, 2003.

Blanco-Aguinaga, Carlos. "El laberinto fabricado por Octavio Paz." *Aztlán: Chicano Journal of the Social Sciences and Arts* 3, no. 1 (1972): 1–12.

———. "Unidad del trabajo y la vida." *Aztlán: Chicano Journal of the Social Sciences and Arts* 2, no. 1 (1971): 1–5.

Blea, Irene Isabel. "Brujeria: A Sociological Analysis of Mexican American Witches." In *Work, Family, Sex Roles, Language,* edited by Mario Barrera, Alberto Camarillo, and Francisco Hernandez, 177–193. Berkeley, Calif.: Tonituh-Quinto Sol International, 1980.

Blea, Irene I. *La Chicana and the Intersection of Race, Class, and Gender.* New York: Praeger Publishers, 1992.

———. *Toward a Chicano Social Science.* New York: Praeger, 1988.

Bloch, Ernst. *The Spirit of Utopia.* Translated by Anthony A. Nassar. Stanford, Calif.: Stanford University Press, 2000.

Borrego, John Gerald. "Capitalist Accumulation and Revolutionary Accumulation: The Context for Chicano Struggle." Ph.D. dissertation, University of California at Berkeley, 1978.

Bronner, Stephen Eric. "Utopian Projections: In Memory of Ernst Bloch." In *Not Yet: Reconsidering Ernst Bloch,* edited by Jamie Owen Daniel and Tom Moylan, 165–174. London: Verso, 1997.

Burciaga, Cecilia Preciado. "The 1977 National Women's Conference in Houston." *La Luz* 7, no. 11 (1978): 8–9.

Burma, John H., ed. *Mexican-Americans in the United States: A Reader.* Cambridge, Mass.: Schenkman Publishing Co., 1970.

Burrola, Luis Ramón, and Hose A. Rivera. *Chicano Studies Programs at the Crossroads: Alternative Futures for the 1980s.* Albuquerque, N.Mex.: Southwest Hispanic Research Institute, 1983.

Bustamante, Ana Luisa. "La Ciencia en la Tradición." *Calmecac* (Spring 1982): 11–17.

———. "Spiral of Cultural Identity Development." *Calmecac* (Winter 1984): 46–52.

Buzon, Bert C., and Diana Buder Phillips. "Institutional Completeness and Chicano Militancy," *Aztlán* 11, no. 1 (1980): 33–64.

Cabán, Pedro A. "Moving from the Margins to Where? Three Decades of Latino/a Studies." *Latino Studies* 1, no. 1 (2003): 5–35.

Cabrera, Ysidro Arturo. "A Study of American and Mexican-American Culture Values and Their Significance in Education." Ed.D., University of Colorado, 1963.

———, ed. *Strategies for Education of Chicanos*. Niwot, Colo.: Sierra Publications, 1978.

Cadena, Gilbert, Alfonso Chavez, Deborah Chavez, and Alfredo Mirandé. "Chicano Sociology: A Critical Evaluation and Synthesis of Chicano Paradigms." In *The Chicano Struggle: Analyses of Past and Present Efforts*, edited by John A. García, Theresa Córdova, John R. García, 12–25. Binghamton, N.Y.: Bilingual Press, 1984.

Calderón, Héctor, and José David Saldívar, eds. *Criticism in the Borderlands: Studies in Chicano Literature, Culture, Ideology*. Durham, N.C.: Duke University Press, 1991.

Calhoun, Cheshire. "Justice, Care, Gender Bias." *Journal of Philosophy* 85, no. 9 (1988): 451–463.

Calvillo, Jaime Dario. "Between Heaven and Earth: *Actos* of El Teatro Campesino." Ph.D. dissertation, University of Minnesota, 1981.

Camarillo, Alberto. "Chicanos and the New University Crisis." *La Onda* 1, no. 11 (1975).

Camarillo, Albert M. "The 'New' Chicano History: Historiography of Chicanos of the 1970s." In *Chicanos and the Social Sciences: A Decade of Research and Development (1970–1980)*, edited by Isidro D. Ortiz, 9–17. Santa Barbara, Calif.: Center for Chicano Studies, 1983.

Cameron, Barbara. "'Gee, You Don't Seem Like an Indian from the Reservation.'" In *This Bridge Called My Back: Writings by Radical Women of Color*, edited by Cherríe Moraga and Gloria Anzaldúa, 46–52. New York: Kitchen Table, 1981.

Campa, Arthur L. "Culture Patterns of the Spanish Speaking Community." In *Selected Readings Materials on the Mexican and Spanish American*, edited by George Garcia, 29–36. Denver, Colo.: Commission on Community Relations City and County of Denver, 1969.

Candelaria, Cordelia. "La Malinche, Feminist Prototype." *Frontiers* 5, no. 2 (1980): 1–6.

Cantú, Roberto. "Nota preliminary: De Samuel Ramos a Emilio Uranga." *Campo Libre: Journal of Chicano Studies* 1, no. 2 (1981): 239–272.

Cárdenas, Gilbert. "Introduction." *Aztlán* 7, no. 2 (1976): 141–152.

Carey-Herrera, Patrick. *Chicanismo: Hypothesis, Thesis and Argument*. Torrance, Calif.: Martin Press, 1983.

Carranza, Elihu. *Chicanismo: Philosophical Fragments*. Dubuque, Iowa: Kendall/Hunt Publishing Co., 1978.

Carranza, Eliu. "Cultural Erosion." In *Ghosts in the Barrio: Issues in Bilingual-Bicultural Education*, edited by Ralph Poblano, 61–69. San Rafael, Calif.: Leswing Press, 1973.

———. *Pensamientos on Los Chicanos: A Cultural Revolution.* 1st ed. Berkeley: California Book Co., 1969.

———. *Pensamientos on Los Chicanos.* 2nd ed. Berkeley: California Book Co., 1971.

Carranza, Michael Anthony. "Language Attitudes and Other Cultural Attitudes of Mexican American Adults." Ph.D. dissertation, University of Notre Dame, 1977.

Carrillo, Ana, et al. "History of Las Mujeres." *Revista Mujeres* 1, no. 1 (1984): 4–5.

Casavantes, Edward J. *A New Look at the Attributes of the Mexican American.* Albuquerque, N.Mex.: Southwestern Cooperative Educational Laboratory, 1969.

Castillo, Ana. *Massacre of the Dreamers: Essays on Xicanisma.* Albuquerque: University of New Mexico Press, 1994.

Castillo, Ralph Cruz. "An Essay Concerning Chicano Philosophy." *Caracol* 1, no. 11 (1975): 3.

Castorena, Jose. "La Raza Nueva: The Fire That Does Not Consume Itself." *Regeneración* 1, no. 3 (1970): 1–2.

Castoriadis, Cornelius. *The Imaginary Institution of Society.* Cambridge: Polity Press, 1987.

———. *Philosophy, Politics, Autonomy: Essays in Political Philosophy.* Oxford: Oxford University Press, 1991.

Cervantes, Fred A. "Chicanos as a Post Colonial Minority: Some Questions Concerning the Adequacy of the Paradigm of Internal Colonialism." In *Perspectivas en Chicano Studies,* edited by Reynaldo Flores Macías, 123–136. Los Angeles: UCLA Chicano Studies Center, 1977.

Chapa, Olivia Evey. "Mujeres Por La Raza Unidad." *Caracol* 1, no. 2 (1974): 3–5.

Chavarría, Jesús. "A Précis and a Tentative Bibliography on Chicano History." *Aztlán* 1, no. 1 (1970): 133–141.

———. "Review Symposium: Professor Grebler's Book: The Magnum Opus of a Dying Era of Scholarship." *Social Science Quarterly* 52, no. 1 (1971): 11–14.

Chávez, Ernesto. *"¡Mi Raza Primero!" (My People First!): Nationalism, Identity, and Insurgency in the Chicano Movement in Los Angeles, 1966–1978.* Berkeley: University California Press, 2002.

Chavez, Henri. "The Chicanas." *Regeneración* 1, no. 10 (1971): 14.

Chavez, Jennie V. "Women of the Mexican-American Movement." *Mademoiselle* 82 (April 1972): 150–153.

Chavez, Mauro. "Review Essay: Carranza's Chicanismo." *Journal of Ethnic Studies* 7, no. 3 (1979): 95–100.

"Chicana Regional Conference." *La Raza Magazine* 1, no. 6 (1971): 43–45.

"Chicana Symposium." *La Raza* 2, no. 10 (1969).

"Chicanas." *Somos* 1, no. 1 (1978): 9–10.

"Chicanas." *Somos* 1, no. 3 (1978): 46.

Chicano Coordinating Council on Higher Education. *El Plan de Santa Bárbara: A Chicano Plan for Higher Education.* Santa Barbara, Calif.: La Causa Publications, 1970.

"Chicano 'Elite' in the Universities," *El Popo* 1, no. 1 (1970). "Chicano Movement in Action: Colegio Jacinto Treviño." *Magazín* 1, no. 1 (1971): 3–7.

Chrystos. "I Don't Understand Those Who Have Turned Away from Me." In *This Bridge Called My Back: Writings by Radical Women of Color,* edited by Cherríe Moraga and Gloria Anzaldúa, 68–70. New York: Kitchen Table, 1981.

Ciaramelli, Fabio. "Levinas's Ethical Discourse between Individuation and Universality." In *Re-Reading Levinas,* edited by Robert Bernasconi and Simon Critchley, 83–108. Bloomington: Indiana University Press, 1991.

Clarke, Cheryl. "Lesbianism: An Act of Resistance." In *This Bridge Called My Back: Writings by Radical Women of Color,* edited by Cherríe Moraga and Gloria Anzaldúa, 128–137. New York: Kitchen Table, 1981.

"Co-Editors Note." *Aztlán* 6, no. 1 (1975): i–v.

Cohen, Richard A. "Translator's Introduction." In *Ethics and Infinity,* by Emmanuel Levinas, 1–15. Pittsburgh, Pa.: Duquesne University Press, 1985.

"Colegio Cesar Chavez." *Agenda* (1976).

Collins, Patricia Hill. *Black Feminist Thought: Knowledge, Consciousness, and the Politics of Empowerment.* Cambridge, Mass.: Unwin Hyman, 1990.

"Concerning the Conceptualization of Chicanismo." In *The Third Annual El Alma Chicana Symposium,* edited by Randall Jimenez, unpaginated. San Jose: California State University, Associated Students and Mexican-American Graduate Studies Department, 1973.

Contreras, Jesse A. G. "Existential Phenomenology and Its Influence on Mexican and Chicano Philosophy of Education." Ph.D. dissertation, University of California at Berkeley, 1984.

Contreras, Raoul. "The Ideology of the Political Movement for Chicano Studies." Ph.D. dissertation, UCLA, 1993.

Córdova, Teresa, et al. "Preface." In *Chicana Voices: Intersections of Class, Race, and Gender,* edited by Teresa Córdova et al., ix–xi. Colorado Springs: National Association for Chicano Studies Publication, 1986.

Corona, Bert N. "Chicano Scholars and Public Issues in the United States in the Eighties." In *History, Culture, and Society: Chicano Studies in the 1980s,* edited by Mario T. García et al., 11–18. Ypsilanti, Mich.: Bilingual Press/Editorial Bilingue, 1983.

Cortes, Carlos E. "CHICOP: A Response to the Challenge of Local Chicano History." *Aztlán* 1, no. 2 (1970): 1–14.

Cota-Robles de Suarez, Cecilia. "Sexual Stereotypes—Psychological and Cultural Survival." *Regeneración* 2, no. 3 (1973): 20–21.

———, and Lupe Anguiano. *Every Woman's Right: The Right to Quality Education and Economic Independence.* Newton, Mass.: Women's Educational Equity Act Publishing Center, 1981.

Cotera, María. "Deconstructing the Corrido Hero: *Caballero* and Its Gendered Critique of Nationalist Discourse." *Perspectives in Mexican American Studies* 5 (1995): 151–170.

Cotera, Martha. "Chicana Caucus." *Magazín* 1, no. 6 (1972): 25–26.

———. *The Chicana Feminist.* Austin, Tex.: Information Systems Development, 1977.

———. "Chicana Identity." *Caracol* 2, no. 6 (1976): 14–15, 17.

———. *Diosa y Hembra: The History and Heritage of Chicanas in the U.S.* Austin, Tex.: Information Systems Development, 1976.

———. "Feminism: The Chicana and Anglo Visions: A Historical Analysis." In *Twice a Minority: Mexican American Women,* edited by Margarita B. Melville, 217–234. St. Louis, Mo.: C.V. Mosby Co., 1980.

———. "La Nueva Hispana y Hispanidad." *La Luz* 8, no. 4 (1979): 8–9.

———. *Profile in the Mexican American Woman.* Austin, Tex.: National Educational Laboratory Publishers, Inc., 1976.

———. "Sexism in Bilingual Bicultural Education." In *Bridging Two Cultures,* edited by Martha Cotera and Larry Hufford, 181–190. Austin, Tex.: National Educational Laboratory Publishers, 1980.

Cruse, Harold. *The Crisis of the Negro Intellectual.* New York: Quill, 1984.

Cruz, Miriam. "La Mujer Latina." *Revista Chicano-Riqueña* 2, no. 2 (1974): 19–21.

Cruz, Patricia. "A Mis Hermanas." *Imágenes de la Chicana* 1 (n.d.).

Cuéllar, Alfredo, Jr. "A Theory of Politics: The Idea of Chicano Revisionism." Ph.D. dissertation, Claremont University, 1976.

———. "Perspective on Politics." In *Mexican Americans,* edited by Joan W. Moore. Englewood Cliffs, N.J.: Prentice-Hall, 1970.

Cuéllar, José B. "A Model of Chicano Culture for Bilingual Education." In *Ethnoperspectives in Bilingual Education Research: Theory in Bilingual Education,* edited by Raymond Padilla, 179–204. Ypsilanti, Mich.: Bilingual Press, 1980.

———. "Social Science Research in the U.S. Mexican Community: A Case Study." *Aztlán* 12, no. 1 (1981): 1–21.

Cuellar, José Bernardo. "El Oro de Maravilla: An Ethnographic Study of Aging and Age Stratification in an Urban Chicano Community." Ph.D. dissertation, UCLA, 1977.

Darder, Antonia, and Rodolfo D. Torres. "Latinos and Society: Culture, Politics, and Class." In *The Latino Studies Reader: Culture, Economy and Society,* edited by Antonia Darder and Rodolfo D. Torres, 3–26. Malden, Mass.: Blackwell Publishers Ltd., 1998.

Davalos, Karen Mary. "Chicana/o Studies and Anthropology: The Dialogue That Never Was." *Aztlán* 23, no. 2 (1998): 11–45.

davenport, doris. "The Pathology of Racism: A Conversation with Third World Wimmin." In *This Bridge Called My Back: Writings by Radical Women of Color,* edited by Cherríe Moraga and Gloria Anzaldúa, 85–90. New York: Kitchen Table, 1981.

Dávila, Elisa. "A manera de introducción." *Revista Mujeres* 1, no. 2 (1985): 2–5.

De Hoyos, Arturo. "Occupational and Educational Levels of Aspiration of Mexican-American Youth." M.A. thesis, Michigan State University, 1961.

De la Garza, Rudolph. "Mexican-American Voters: A Responsible Electorate and Resources." *Graduate Studies Texas Tech University* 14 (1977): 63–76.

———. "The Politics of Mexican Americans." In *The Chicanos: As We See,* edited by Arnulfo D. Trejo. Tucson: University of Arizona Press, 1979.

De Leon, Arnoldo. "*Occupied America* I and *Occupied America* II: A Comparison of the Nineteenth Century." In *Occupied America: A Chicano History Symposium,* edited by Rodolfo Acuña et al., 28–34. Mexican American Studies Monograph Series No. 3. Houston, Tex.: Mexican American Studies Program, University of Houston, 1982.

De Leon, Nephtali. *Chicanos: Our Background and Our Pride.* Lubbock, Tex.: Trucha Publications, 1972.

Del Castillo, Adelaida R., ed. *Between Borders: Essays on Mexican/Chicana History.* Encino, Calif.: Floricanto Press, 1990.

———. "Introduction." In *Between Borders: Essays on Mexican/Chicana History,* edited by Adelaida R. Del Castillo, v–xv. Encino, Calif.: Floricanto Press, 1990.

———. "Introducción." *Fem* 10, no. 4 (1986): 1–2.

———. "Malintzin Tenépal: A Preliminary Look into a New Perspective." *Encuentro Femenil* 1, no. 2 (1974): 58–77.

———. "Mexican Women in Organization." In *Mexican Women in the United States: Struggles Past and Present,* edited by Magdalena Mora and Adelaida R. Del Castillo, 7–16. Los Angeles: Chicano Studies Research Center Publications, 1980.

Delgado, Sylvia. "Chicana: The Forgotten Woman." *Regeneración* 2, no. 1 (1971): 2–4.

———. "Young Chicana Speaks Up on Problems Faced by Young Girls." *Regeneración* 1, no. 10 (1971): 5–7.

Diehl, Paula, and Guadalupe Saavedra. "Hispanas in the Year of the Woman: Many Voices." *Agenda* (1976): 14–21.

Donna. "Chicanas Meet Indo-Chinese." *El Grito del Norte* 4, no. 4–5 (1971): n.p.

Dubois, W.E.B. *The Souls of Black Folks.* 1903; reprint, New York: Dover Publications, 1994.

Duran, Livie Isauro, and H. Russell Bernard, eds. *Introduction to Chicano Studies: A Reader.* New York: Macmillan Comp., 1973.

"Editorial." *Con Safos* 1, no. 1 (1968): 1.

"Editorial." *Deganawidah Quetzalcoatl University Report* 1, no. 21 (1971).

"Editorial." *El Grito* 1, no. 1 (1968): 4.

"Editorial." *Journal of Mexican American History* 1, no. 1 (1970): iii–v.

"Editorial." *Journal of Mexican American History* (1971): iii–iv.

"Education as a Process of Liberation." *Inside the Beast* 1, no. 13 (1973): 7–12.

Eger, Ernestina N. "Conflicto en Academia: Tres Cuentos Chicanos." In *Flor y Canto IV and V*, edited by José Armas and Justo Alarcón, 183–189. Austin, Tex.: Pajarito Press, 1980.

"El Concilio Nacional de Estudios Chicanos." *Epoca* 1, no. 2 (1971): i–iii.

Elizondo, Sergio D. "Critical Areas of Need for Research and Scholastic Study." *Epoca* 1, no. 2 (1971): 1–7.

Encuentro Femenil. "La Vision Chicana." *Regeneración* 2, no. 4 (1974): 46–48.

Enríquez, Evangelina Mirande. "Towards a Definition of and Critical Approaches to Chicano(a) Literature." Ph.D. dissertation, University of California at Riverside, 1982.

Enríquez, Evangelina, and Alfredo Mirandé. "Liberation, Chicana Style: Colonial Roots of Feminist Chicanas." *De Colores: A Bilingual Quarterly Journal of Chicano Expression and Thought* 4, no. 3 (1978): 7–21.

Espinosa, Anita L. "Hispanas—Our Resources for the Eighties." *La Luz* 8, no. 4 (1979): 10–13.

Espinosa-Larsen, Anita. "Machismo: Another View." *La Luz* 1, no. 4 (1972): 59.

Estrada, Leobardo F. "The Responsibility to Know and the Ability to Understand: Policy-making with Hispanic Perspectives." *Metas* 1, no. 3 (1980): 25–30.

Fernandez Kelly, Maria Patricia. "Third World Women in Multinational Corporations—The Mexican-American Border." *La Red/The Net* 25 (1979): 2.

Fernandez, Roberta. "Abriendo Caminos on the Borderland: Chicana Writers Respond to the Ideology of Literary Nationalism." *Frontiers* 14, no. 2 (1994): 23–50.

Fleck, Ludwik. *Genesis and Development of a Scientific Fact.* Translated by Fred Bradley and Thaddeus J. Trenn. Chicago: University of Chicago Press, 1979.

Flores, Estevan T. "Chicanos and Sociological Research: 1970–1980." In *Chicanos and the Social Sciences: A Decade of Research and Development (1970–1980),* edited by Isidro D. Ortiz, 19–45. Santa Barbara, Calif.: UCSB Center for Chicano Studies, 1983.

———. "The Mexican-Origin People in the United States and Marxist Thought in Chicano Studies." In *The Left Academy: Marxist Scholarship on American Campuses, Vol. 3,* edited by Bertell Ollman and Edward Vernoff, 103–137. New York: Praeger, 1986.

Flores, Francisca. "Comision Femenil Mexicana." *Regeneración* 2, no. 1 (1971): 6.

———. "Conference of Mexican Women Un Remolino." *Regeneración* 1, no. 10 (1971): 1–5.

———. "Equality." *Regeneración* 2, no. 3 (1973): 4–5.

Flores, Kathy. "Chicano Attitudes Toward Birth Control." *Imágenes de la Chicana* 1 (n.d.).

Flores, Rosalie. "The New Chicana and Machismo." *Regeneración* 2, no. 4 (1974): 55–56.

Fraire-Aldava, Eugene. "A Study of Ironic Tone and Meaning: Octavio Romano's 'Goodbye Revolution, Hello Slum': A Study of Ironic Tone and Meaning." *Aztlán* 3, no. 1 (1972): 165–169.

Funk, R. D. "Foundation Aiding Militants." *Evening Outlook,* March 24, 1970.

Furet, Francois. *Interpreting the French Revolution.* Translated by Elborg Forster. Cambridge: Cambridge University Press, 1981.

Galicia, H. Homero. "Chicanos and Schools: A Perspective for Chicano Alternative Educational Situations." In *Chicano Alternative Education,* 1–16. Hayward, Calif.: Southwest Network, 1973.

Gallegos y Chávez, Ester. "The Northern New Mexican Woman: A Changing Silhouette." In *The Chicanos: As We See Ourselves,* edited by Arnulfo D. Trejo, 67–79. Tucson: University of Arizona Press, 1979.

Gándara, Patricia. "Passing Through the Eye of the Needle: High-Achieving Chicanas." *Hispanic Journal of Behavioral Sciences* 4, no. 2 (1982): 167–179.

García, Alma M. "The Development of Chicana Feminist Discourse, 1970–1980." *Gender and Society* 3, no. 2 (1989): 217–238.

———. "El feminismo chicano: Un panorama histórico." *Fem* 10, no. 4 (1986): 23–24.

———. "Introduction." In *Chicana Feminist Thought: The Basic Historical Writings,* edited by Alma M. García, 1–16. New York: Routledge, 1997.

———. "Studying Chicanas: Bringing Women into the Frame of Chicano Studies." In *Chicana Voices: Intersections of Class, Race, and Gender,* edited by Teresa Córdova et al., 19–29. Colorado Springs: National Association for Chicano Studies Publication, 1986.

Garcia, E. "The Chicana." *¡Es Tiempo!* 2, no. 2 (1972): 10.

García-Acevedo, María Rosa. "Return to Aztlán: Mexico's Policies toward Chicanos/as." In *Chicanas/Chicanos at the Crossroads: Social, Economic, and Political Change,* edited by David R. Maciel and Isidro D. Ortiz, 130–155. Tucson: University of Arizona Press, 1996.

García-Camarillo, Mia. "Equal Rights Amendment." *Caracol* 3, no. 3 (1976): 8–9.

———, and Susana de la Torre. "Mujeres en el movimiento: Platica de la mujeres de Caracol." *Caracol* 3, no. 1 (1976): 10–11.

Garcia, Elena H. "Chicana Consciousness: A New Perspective, a New Hope." In *La mujer-en pie de lucha,* edited by Dorindo Moreno. San Francisco: Espina de Norte Publications, 1973.

Garcia, F. Chris. "Orientations of Mexican American and Anglo Children Toward the U.S. Political Community." *Social Science Quarterly* 53, no. 4 (1973): 814–829.

——. "The Political Socialization of Mexican Americans: A Comparison of the Orientations of Mexican American and Anglo Children with Regard to Their Support of the American Political System." Ph.D. dissertation, University of California at Davis, 1972.

——, ed. *La Causa Politica: A Chicano Politics Reader.* Notre Dame, Ill.: University of Notre Dame Press, 1974.

García, Gilberto. "Beyond the Adelita Image: Women Scholars in the National Association for Chicano Studies, 1972–1992." *Perspectives in Mexican American Studies* 5 (1995): 35–61.

García, Ignacio M. *Chicanismo: The Forging of a Militant Ethos Among Mexican Americans.* Tucson: University of Arizona Press, 1997.

——. "Juncture in the Road: Chicano Studies Since 'El Plan de Santa Bárbara.'" In *Chicanas/Chicanos at the Crossroads: Social, Economic, and Political Change,* edited by David R. Maciel and Isidro D. Ortiz, 181–203. Tucson: University of Arizona Press, 1996.

——. *United We Win: The Rise and Fall of La Raza Unida Party.* Tucson: University of Arizona, 1989.

García, Jorge. "Background Paper." In *A Symposium on Chicano Studies Part II: Foundations for Action.* Los Angeles: National Association for Chicano Studies, Southern California FOCO, 1987.

García, Juan Castañon. "Teatro Chicano and the Analysis of Sacred Symbols: Towards a Chicano World-View in the Social Sciences." *El Grito del Sol* 3, no. 1 (1978): 37–49.

Garcia, Mario T. "The Chicano University." In *Ghosts in the Barrio: Issues in Bilingual-Bicultural Education,* edited by Ralph Poblano, 349–356. San Rafael, Calif.: Leswing Press, 1973.

——. *Desert Immigrants: The Mexicans of El Paso, 1880–1920.* New Haven, Conn.: Yale University Press, 1981.

——. "Internal Colonialism and the Chicano." *La Luz* 3, no. 8 (1974): 27–28.

——. "Introduction: Chicano Studies in the 1980s." In *History, Culture, and Society: Chicano Studies in the 1980s,* edited by Mario García, et al., 7–10. Ypsilanti, Mich.: Bilingual Press, 1983.

——. "José Vasconcelos and La Raza." *El Grito* 2, no. 4 (1969): 49–51.

——. *Memories of Chicano History: The Life and Narrative of Bert Corona.* Berkeley: University of California Press, 1994.

Garcia, Philip. "Chicano Unemployment in the Seventies." *La Red/The Net* 32 (1980): 2–3.

García, Richard. "Creating a Consciousness, Memories, and Expectations: The Burden of Octavio Romano." In *Chicano Discourse: Selected Conference Proceedings of the National Association for Chicano Studies,* edited by Tatcho Mindiola Jr. and Emilio Zamora, 6–31. Houston, Tex.: Mexican American Studies Program, 1992.

Garcia, Velia. "La Chicana and Women's Liberation." *La Gente de Aztlán* 1, no. 6 (1971): 7, 10.

Garza, Hisauro Alvarado. "Nationalism, Consciousness, and Social Change: Chicano Intellectuals in the United States ." Ph.D. dissertation, University of California at Berkeley, 1984.

Garza, Hisauro. "Origins and Evolution of an Alternative Scholarship and Scholarly Organization." In *Chicano Discourse: Selected Conference Proceedings of the National Association for Chicano Studies*, edited by Tatcho Mindiola Jr. and Emilio Zamora, 40–50. Houston, Tex.: Mexican American Studies Program, 1992.

Gilabert, César. *El Habito de la Utopia: Análisis del Imaginario Sociopolítico en el Movimiento Estudiantil de México, 1968*. Mexico City, Mex.: Instituto de Investigaciones, 1993.

Giroux, Henry A., and Peter McLaren. "Paulo Freire, Postmodernism, and the Utopian Imagination: A Blochian Reading." In *Not Yet: Reconsidering Ernst Bloch*, edited by Jamie Owen Daniel and Tom Moylan, 138–162. London: Verso, 1997.

Gomez, Anna Nieto, and J. Anthony Vasquez. *The Needs of the Chicano on the College Campus*. Washington, D.C.: U.S. Department of Health, Education and Welfare, 1969.

Gómez-Quiñones, Juan. *Chicano Politics: Reality and Promise 1940–1990*. Albuquerque: University of New Mexico Press, 1990.

———. "Critique on the National Question, Self-Determination, and Nationalism," *Latin American Perspectives* 9, no. 2 (1982): 62–83.

———. *Development of the Mexican Working Class North of the Rio Bravo*. Los Angeles: UCLA Chicano Studies Research Center, 1982.

———. "The First Steps: Chicano Labor Conflict and Organizing, 1900–1920." *Aztlán* 3, no. 1 (1972): 13–49.

———. *Mexican Students Por La Raza: The Chicano Student Movement in Southern California, 1967–1977*. Santa Barbara, Calif.: Editorial La Causa, 1978.

———. "Questions Within Women's Historiography." In *Between Borders: Essays on Mexican/Chicana History*, edited by Adelaida R. Del Castillo, 87–97. Encino, Calif.: Floricanto Press, 1990.

———. *Sembradores, Ricardo Flores Magon y el Partido Liberal Mexicano: A Eulogy and Critique*. Los Angeles: University of California, Chicano Studies Center, 1977.

———. "Toward a Perspective on Chicano History," *Aztlán* 2, no. 2 (Fall 1971): 1–49.

———. "To Leave to Hope or Chance: Propositions on Chicano Studies, 1974." In *Parameters of Institutional Change: Chicano Experiences in Education*, edited by the Southwest Network, 153–166. Hayward, Calif.: Southwest Network, 1974.

———. "On Culture." *Revista Chicano-Riquena* 5, no. 2 (1977): 290–308.

Gonzales, Juanita Helena. "Sex Role Stereotypes." *La Luz* 1, no. 9 (1973): 20–21.

Gonzáles, Rodolfo "Corky." *Message to Aztlán: Selected Writings.* Houston, Tex.: Are Público Press, 2001.

Gonzales, Sylvia Alicia. "The Chicana in Literature." *La Luz* 1, no. 9 (1973): 51–53.

———. "The Chicana Perspective: A Design for Self-Awarness." In *The Chicanos: As We See Ourselves,* edited by Arnulfo D. Trejo, 81–99. Tucson: University of Arizona Press, 1979.

———. "Congress of InterAmerican Women Writers—An Overview." *De Colores* 3, no. 3 (1977): 8–15.

———. "The Latina Feminist: Where We've Been, Where We're Going." *Nuestro* 5, no. 6 (1981): 45–47.

———. "Organizations." *La Luz* 8, no. 4 (1979): 14–15.

———. "Toward a Feminist Pedagogy for Chicana Self-Actualization." *Frontiers* 5, no. 2 (1980): 48–51.

Gonzales, Sylvia Alicia, and David Sandoval. "Introduction." In *A Symposium on Chicano Studies.* Los Angeles: National Association for Chicano Studies, Southern California FOCO, 1987.

Gonzalez, Deena. *Refusing the Favor: The Spanish-Mexican Women of Santa Fe, 1820–1880.* Oxford: Oxford University Press, 1999.

Gonzalez, Deena, Teresa McKenna, and Emma Perez. "Background Paper on Chicana and Chicano Studies." In *A Symposium on Chicano Studies Part II: Foundations for Action.* Los Angeles: National Association for Chicano Studies, Southern California FOCO, 1987.

Gonzalez, Gilbert G. "A Critique of the Internal Colony Model," *Latin American Perspectives* 1 (1974): 154–161.

Gonzalez, Josue. "The Status of Bilingual Education Today: Un vistazo y un repaso." *NABE* 2, no. 1 (1978): 13–20.

Grebler, Leo, Joan W. Moore, and Ralph C. Guzman. *The Mexican American People: The Nation's Second Largest Minority.* New York: Free Press, 1970.

Greisch, Jean. "The Face and Reading: Immediacy and Mediation." In *Re-Reading Levinas,* edited by Robert Bernasconi and Simon Critchley, 67–82. Bloomington: Indiana University Press, 1991.

Guerra, Manuel H. "What Are the Objectives of Chicano Studies?" *Epoca* 1, no. 2 (1971): 8–12.

Guide to Chicano Studies Departments, Programs, and Centers. Los Angeles: UCLA Chicano Studies Center, 1975.

Gutiérrez, Armando, and Herbert Hirsch. "The Militant Challenge to the American Ethos: 'Chicanos' and 'Mexican Americans.'" *Social Science Quarterly* 53, no. 4 (1973): 830–845.

Gutiérrez, Félix. "Spanish-Language Radio and Chicano Internal Colonialism." Ph.D. dissertation, Stanford University, 1976.

Gutiérrez-Jones, Carl. *Rethinking the Borderlands: Between Chicano Culture and Legal Discourse*. Berkeley: University of California Press, 1995.

Gutiérrez, José Angel. *The Making of a Chicano Militant: Lessons from Cristal*. Madison: University of Wisconsin Press, 1998.

Gutierrez, Ramon A. "Community, Patriarchy, and Individualism: The Politics of Chicano History and the Dream of Equality." *American Quarterly* 45, no. 1 (1993): 44–72.

Guzman, Ralph. "Politics and Policies of the Mexican-American Community." In *Minority Group Politics: A Reader,* edited by Stephen J. Herzog, 192–198. New York: Holt, Rinehart and Winston, 1971.

Haro, Carlos Manuel. *Criticisms of Traditional Postsecondary School Admissions Criteria: A Search for Alternatives*. Occasional Papers no.1, Los Angeles: UCLA Chicano Studies Center Publications, 1978.

———, ed. *The Bakke Decision: A Question of Chicano Access to Higher Education*. Document No. 4. Los Angeles: Chicano Studies Center, nd.

Haro, Carlos, and Rosa Martinez Cruz. "Coalition Formed to Oppose Bakke." *El Mirlo* 4, no. 1 and 2 (1976): 1–3.

Hayes-Bautista, David Emmett. "Becoming Chicano: A "Dis-Assimilation" Theory of Transformation of Ethnic Identity." Ph.D. dissertation, University of California at San Francisco, 1974.

Hernández, Carrol A., ed. *Chicanos: Social and Psychological Perspectives*. 2nd ed. St. Louis, Mo.: C.V. Mosley Co., 1976.

Hernández, Deluvina. "La Raza Satellite System," *Aztlán* 1, no. 1 (1970): 13–36.

———. *Mexican American Challenge to a Sacred Cow*. Los Angeles: Chicano Studies Center, 1970.

Hernandez, Francisco Javier. "Schools for Mexicans—A Case Study of a Chicano School." Ph.D. dissertation, Stanford University, 1982.

Hernandez, Isabel. "Una ideologia." *Inside the Beast* 1, no. 13 (1973): 43–45.

Hernández, José, Leo Estrada, and David Alvírez. "Census Data and the Problem of Conceptually Defining the Mexican American Population." *Social Science Quarterly* 53, no. 4 (1973): 671–687.

Hernandez, Norma G. *Reality and Goal Orientation: A Model for Research on Mexican Americans*. Renato Rosaldo Lecture Series Monograph, vol. 3. 1987.

Hernandez, Patricia. "Lives of Chicana Activists: The Chicano Student Movement (A Case Study)." In *Mexican Women in the United States: Struggles Past and Present,* edited by Magdalena Mora and Adelaida R. Del Castillo, 17–25. Los Angeles: Chicano Studies Research Center Publications, 1980.

Hernández-Chávez, Eduardo. "Meaningful Bilingual Bicultural Education: A Fairytale." *NABE* 1, no. 3 (1977): 49–54.

———, Andrew D. Cohen, and Anthony F. Beltramo. *El leguaje de los Chicanos.* Arlington, Va.: Center for Applied Linguistics, 1975.

Herrera-Sobek, María. "Metodos útiles para la enseñanza del acento ortográfico español." *NABE* 3, no. 1 (1978): 65–72.

Hobsbawm, Eric, and Terence Ranger, eds. *The Invention of Tradition.* Cambridge: Cambrige University Press, 1983.

Horkheimer, Max. "The Authoritarian State." *Telos* 15 (1973): 3–20.

———. *Eclipse of Reason.* New York: Seaburg Press, 1974.

Horkheimer, Max, and Theodor W. Adorno. *Dialectic of Enlightenment.* New York: Seabury Press, 1972.

"Interview with Octavio Paz." *Raza de Bronce* 1, no. 3 (1973): 5, 12.

Jacoby, Russell. *The End of Utopia: Politics and Culture in an Age of Apathy.* New York: Basic Books, 1999.

Johnson, Henry Sioux, and William J. Hernández-M. *Educating the Mexican American.* Valley Forge: Hudson Press, 1970.

Juárez, Nicandro F. "José Vasconcelos and La Raza Cósmica." *Aztlán* 3, no.1 (1972): 51–82.

Kanellos, Nicolás. "Meditaciones: De Flores y de Cantos." *Revista Chicano-Riqueña* 5, no. 4 (1978): 1.

Kelley, Robin D. G. *Freedom Dreams: The Black Radical Imagination.* Boston: Beacon Press, 2002.

Kellner, Douglas. "Ernst Bloch, Utopia, and Ideology Critique." In *Not Yet: Reconsidering Ernst Bloch,* edited by Jamie Owen Daniel and Tom Moylan, 80–95. London: Verso, 1997.

Klor de Alva, J. Jorge. "Being, Solitude, and Susceptibility in Mexican Thought: From Adler to Marx in Thirty-five Years." *El Grito del Sol* 2, no. 4 (1977): 39–67.

———. "California Chicano Literature and Pre-Columbian Motifs: Foil and Fetish." *Confluencia* 1, no. 2 (1986): 18–26.

———. "Chicano Philosophy." In *Chicano Literature: A Reference Guide,* edited by Julio A. Martinez and Francisco A. Lomelí, 148–161. Westport, Conn.: Greenwood Press, 1985.

———. "Critique of National Character vs. Universality in Chicana Poetry." *De Colores* 3, no. 3 (1977): 20–24.

———. "Gabino Barreda and Chicano Thought." *Aztlán* 14, no. 2 (1983): 343–358.

———. *Introduction to Mexican Philosophy.* N.p: n.d.

"La Causa." *La Raza* 2, no. 4 (1969): n.p.

La Comision Femenil Mexicana Nacional, Inc. "Chicana Service Action Center." *Regeneración* 2, no. 3 (1973): 6–7.

"La Conferencia de Mujeres por La Raza." In *Profile in the Mexican American Woman,* edited by Martha Cotera. Austin, Tex.: National Educational Laboratory Publishers, Inc., 1976.

La Coronela. "Cultural Nationalism: A Fight for Survival." *Chicano Student Movement* 2, no. 2 (1969): 3.

"La Raza Council on Higher Education." *El Popo* 5, no. 1 (1972): 6–7.

"La Raza Nueva," *Bronce Magazine* 1, no. 4 (1969): 16.

Levinas, Emmanuel. *Ethics and Infinity.* Pittsburgh, Pa.: Duquesne University Press, 1985.

———. "Ethics as First Philosophy." In *The Levinas Reader,* edited by Seán Hand, 75–87. Oxford: Blackwell Publishers, 1989.

———. "Martin Heidegger and Ontology." *Diacritics* 26, no. 1 (1996): 11–32.

———. *Otherwise Than Being or Beyond Essence.* Pittsburgh, Pa.: Duquesne University Press, 1998.

———. *Totality and Infinity.* Pittsburgh, Pa.: Duquesne University Press, 1969.

Levitas, Ruth. "Educated Hope: Ernst Bloch on Abstract and Concrete Utopia." In *Not Yet: Reconsidering Ernst Bloch,* edited by Jamie Owen Daniel and Tom Moylan, 65–79. London: Verso, 1997.

Levy, Ze'ev. "Utopia and Reality in the Philosophy of Ernst Bloch." In *Not Yet: Reconsidering Ernst Bloch,* edited by Jamie Owen Daniel and Tom Moylan, 175–185. London: Verso, 1997.

Limón, José. "Agringado Joking in Texas Mexican Society: Folklore and Differential Identity." In *New Directions in Chicano Scholarship,* edited by Ricardo Romo and Raymund Paredes, 33–50. Santa Barbara: UCSB Center for Chicano Studies, 1984.

———. "The Expressive Culture of a Chicano Student Group at the University of Texas at Austin, 1967–1975." Ph.D. dissertation, University of Texas at Austin, 1978.

Limón, José E. "Western Marxism and Folklore: A Critical Introduction." *Journal of American Folklore* 96, no. 379 (1983): 34–52.

Lizárraga, Sylvia S. "Observaciones acerca de la crítica literaria chicana." *Revista Chicano-Riqueña* 10, no. 4 (1982): 55–64.

Lloyd, Rees, and Peter Montague. "Ford and La Raza: "They Stole Our Land and Gave Us Powdered Milk." *Ramparts* 9, no. 3 (1970): 10–18.

Longauex y Vásquez, Enriqueta. "Soy Chicana Primero." *El Cuaderno* 1, no. 1 (1971): 17–22.

———. "Third World Women Meet." *El Grito del Norte* 4, no. 1 (1973).

———. "The Woman of La Raza." In *The Barrio: A Chicano Anthology,* edited by Luis Omar Salinas and Lillian Faderman, 20–24. San Francisco: Canfield Press, 1973.

López, Manuel I. "The Role of the Chicano Student in the Chicano Studies Program." *Epoca* 1, no. 2 (1971): 13–17.

Lopez, Ronald W., and Darryl D. Enos. *Chicanos and Public Higher Education in California*. Sacramento, Calif.: Joint Committee on the Master Plan for Higher Education, 1972.

Lopez, Ronald W., Arturo Madrid-Barela, and Reynaldo Flores Macías. *Chicanos in Higher Education: Status and Issues*. Los Angeles: Chicano Studies Center Publications, 1976.

Lopez Saenz, Lionila. "Machismo, No! Igualdad, Si!" *La Luz* 1, no. 2 (1972): 19–24.

López, Sonia A. "The Role of the Chicana Within the Student Movement." In *Essay on La Mujer*, edited by Rosaura Sánchez and Rosa Martinez Cruz, 16–29. Los Angeles: UCLA Chicano Studies Center, 1977.

López y Rivas, Gilberto. *The Chicanos: Life and Struggles of the Mexican Minority in the United States*. New York: Monthly Review Press, 1973.

Lorde, Audre. "The Master's Tools Will Never Dismantle the Master's House." In *Sister Outsider: Essays and Speeches*, edited by Audre Lorde, 110–113. Freedom, N.Y.: Crossing Press, 1984.

———. "The Master's Tools Will Never Dismantle the Master's House." In *This Bridge Called My Back: Writings by Radical Women of Color*, edited by Cherríe Moraga and Gloria Anzaldúa, 98–101. New York: Kitchen Table, 1981.

Lucero, Marcela C. "Resources for the Chicana Feminist Scholar." In *For Alma Mater: Theory and Practice in Feminist Scholarship*, edited by Paula A. Treichler, Cheris Kramarae, and Beth Stafford, 393–401. Urbana: University of Illinois Press, 1985.

Lugones, María. "Hablando cara a cara/Speaking Face to Face: An Exploration of Ethnocentric Racism." In *Making Face, Making Soul/Haciendo Caras: Creative and Critical Perspectives by Women of Color*, edited by Gloria Anzaldúa, 46–54. San Francisco: Aunt Lute Foundation Books, 1990.

———. *Pilgrimages/Pererinajes: Theorizing Coalition Against Multiple Oppressions*. Lanham, Md.: Rowman and Littlefield Publishers, Inc., 2003.

———. "Playfulness, 'World'-Travelling, and Loving Perception." In *Making Face, Making Soul/Haciendo Caras: Creative and Critical Perspectives by Women of Color*, edited by Gloria Anzaldúa, 390–402. San Francisco: Aunt Lute Books, 1990.

———. "Purity, Impurity, and Separation." *Signs: Journal of Women in Culture and Society* 19, no. 2 (1994): 458–479.

Machado, Manuel A. *Listen Chicano!: An Informal History of the Mexican-American*. Chicago: Nelson-Hall, 1978.

Macías, Reynaldo Flores. "Schooling of Chicanos in a Bilingual, Cultural Relevant Context." In *Parameters of Institutional Change: Chicano Experiences in Education*, edited by the Southwest Network, 109–134. Hayward, Calif.: Southwest Network of the Study Commission on the Undergraduate Education of Teachers, 1974.

————, ed. *Perspectivas en Chicano Studies*. Los Angeles: Chicano Studies Center, 1977.

Macías, Reynaldo, Juan Gómez-Quiñones, and Raymond Castro. "Objectives of Chicano Studies." *Epoca* 1, no. 2 (1971): 31–34.

Macías, Reynaldo Flores, Carolyn Webb de Macías, and William De La Torre. *Educación Alternativa: On the Development of Chicano Bilingual Schools.* Hayward, Calif.: Southwest Network, n.d.

Macías, Ysidro. "The Chicano Movement." In *Pain and Promise: The Chicano Today,* edited by Edward Simmen, 137–143. New York: Mentor Books, 1972.

Macias, Ysidro R. "The Ultimate Pendejada." In *Contemporary Chicano Theatre,* edited by Roberto S. Garza, 135–164. Notre Dame, Ill.: University of Notre Dame, 1976.

Maciel, David R. "Introduccion bibliográfica a la historia intellectual de México." *Aztlán* 3, no. 1 (1972): 83–132.

Madrigal, Reyes Rachel. "La Chicana and the Movement: Ideology and Identity." Ph.D. dissertation, Claremont Graduate University, 1977.

"MALCS Declaration." In *Chicana Critical Issues,* edited by Normal Alarcón et al. Berkeley, Calif.: Third Woman Press, 1993.

Maldonado, Carlos S. *Colegio Cesar Chavez, 1973–1983: A Chicano Struggle for Educational Self-Determination.* New York: Garland Press, 2000.

Maldonado-Torres, Nelson. Against War: Views from the Underside of Modernity. Durham: Duke University Press, 2008.

Mangold, M., ed. *La Causa Chicana: The Movement for Justice.* New York: Family Service Association of America, 1972.

Manuel, Frank E., and Fritzie P. Manuel. *Utopian Thought in the Western World.* Cambridge: Harvard University Press, 1979.

Marcuse, Herbert. *An Essay on Liberation.* Boston: Beacon Press, 1969.

————. "Repressive Tolerance." In *A Critique of Pure Tolerance,* edited by Robert Paul Wolff, Barrington Moore Jr., Herbert Marcuse, 95–137. Boston: Beacon Press, 1969.

Mares, Antonio. "El Coyote: Between Two Cultures." *El Cuaderno* 2, no. 1 (1972): 20–23.

Mares, E.A. "Introduction." *El Cuaderno* 3, no. 1 (1973): 1–2.

————. "The Fiesta of Life: Impressions of Paulo Freire." *El Cuaderno* 3, no. 2 (1974): 5–16.

————. "Myth and Reality: Observations on American Myths and the Myth of Aztlán." *El Cuaderno* 3, no. 1 (1973): 35–50.

Margolis, Eric, ed. *Hidden Curricula in Higher Education.* New York: Routledge, 2001.

Marin, Christine. *A Spokesman of the Mexican American Movement.* San Francisco: R and E Research Associates, 1977.

Mariscal, George. *Brown-Eyed Children of the Sun: Lessons from the Chicano Movement, 1965–1975.* Albuquerque: University of New Mexico Press, 2005.

Marrufo, Boqui. "What Is Carnalismo?" *La Enchilada* 1, no. 1(1975): 1–2.

Martinez, Elizabeth. "'*Chingón* Politics' Dies Hard: Reflections on the First Chicano Activist Reunion." In *Living Chicana Theory,* edited by Carl Trujillo, 123–135. Berkeley, Calif.: Third Woman Press, 1998.

———. "Viva La Chicana and All Brave Women of La Causa." *El Grito del Norte* 4, no. 4–5 (1971): a–b.

Martinez, Elizabeth, and Ed McCaughan. "Chicanas and Mexicanas Within a Transnational Working Class." In *Between Borders: Essays on Mexican/ Chicana History,* edited by Adelaida R. Del Castillo, 31–60. Encino, Calif.: Floricanto Press, 1990.

Martinez, Max. "The Necessity for Chicano Literary Critics." *Caracol* 2, no. 9 (1976): 18–19.

Martinez, Oscar. "Manifest Mexicanism." *Con Safos* 1, no. 3 (1969): 34–35.

Martinez, Samuel C., and Hijos de Sol staff. *Hijos del Sol: An Approach to Raza Community Mental Health.* Oakland, Calif.: Casa del Sol, 1981.

Martinez, Samuel C., and Roberto Vargas. *Razalogía: Community Learning for a New Society.* Oakland, Calif.: Razagente Assoc., 1984.

Martinez, Thomas. "Chicanismo." *Epoca* 1, no. 2 (1971): 35–39.

Martinez, Thomas M. *Chicanismo.* Santa Barbara, Calif.: Chicano Studies Institute, 1970.

Matsuda, Gema. "La Chicana Organizes: The Comisión Femenil Mexicana in Perspective." *Regeneración* 2, no. 4 (1974): 25–27.

Maymi, Carmen. "Fighting to Open the Doors to Opportunity." *Agenda* 4 (1974): 8–10.

McClintock, Anne. *Imperial Leather: Race, Gender, and Sexuality in the Colonial Contest.* London: Routledge, 1995.

McLaren, Peter. *Schooling as a Ritual Performance: Towards a Political Economy of Educational Symbols and Gestures.* London: Routledge and Kegan Paul, 1986.

MEChA. "Chicano Studies Accused of Fostering Male Chauvinism." In *La mujer-en pie de lucha,* edited by Dorindo Moreno. San Francisco: Espina de Norte Publications, 1973.

Medina, Cecilia. "Chicanas Live in Aztlán Also." In *Ghosts in the Barrio: Issues in Bilingual-Bicultural Education,* edited by Ralph Poblano, 151–152. San Rafael, Calif.: Leswing Press, 1973.

Medina, Celia. *Chicanos, Existentialism and the Human Condition.* San Jose, Calif.: Marfel Associates, 1974.

Melville, Margarita B. "Ethnicity: An Analysis of Its Dynamism and Variability Focusing on the Mexican/Anglo/Mexican American Interface." *American Ethnologist* 10, no. 2 (1983): 272–289.

————. "Introduction." In *Twice a Minority: Mexican American Women,* edited by Margarita B. Melville, 1–16. St. Louis, Mo.: C.V. Mosby Co., 1980.

————. "Mexican Women Adapt to Migration." *International Migration Review* 12, no. 2 (1978): 225–235.

Merod, Jim. *The Political Responsibility of the Critic.* Cornell, N.Y.: Cornell University Press, 1987.

"Mexican American Cultural Center and Aztlán—Chicano Journal of the Social Sciences and the Arts." *Aztlán* 1, no. 1 (1970): vi.

Mindiola, Anastacio "Tatcho," Jr. "Introduction." In *Occupied America: A Chicano History Symposium,* edited by Rodolfo Acuña, 5–8. Monograph Series No. 3. Houston, Tex.: Mexican American Studies 1982.

————. "Marxism and the Chicano Movement: Preliminary Remarks." In *Perspectivas en Chicano Studies,* edited by Reynaldo Flores Macías, 179–186. Los Angeles: UCLA Chicano Studies Center, 1977.

Minjares, Valerie. "Chicanos for Political Unity." *Si Se Puede* 1, no. 4 (1975): 2, 11.

Mirandé, Alfredo. "The Chicano Family: A Reanalysis of Conflicting Views." *Journal of Marriage and the Family* 38, no. 4 (1977): 747–756.

————. "Chicano Sociology: A New Paradigm for Social Science." *Pacific Sociological Review* 21, no. 3 (1978): 293–312.

————. "Introduction." *De Colores* 6, no. 1–2 (1982): 1–6.

————. "A Reinterpretation of Male Dominance in the Chicano Family." *The Family Coordinator* 28, no. 4 (1979): 473–479.

————. "Research/Curriculum in Chicano Studies." In *A Symposium on Chicano Studies Part II: Foundations for Action.* Los Angeles: National Association for Chicano Studies, Southern California FOCO, 1987.

————. "Sociology of Chicanos or Chicano Sociology? A Critical Assessment of Emergent Paradigms." *Pacific Sociological Review* 25, no. 4 (1982): 495–508.

Mirandé, Alfredo, and Evangelina Enríquez. *La Chicana: The Mexican-American Woman.* Chicago: University of Chicano Press, 1979.

Mireles, Irma. "La mujer en la communidad: Ayer, hoy, y siempre." *Caracol* 2, no. 11 (1976): 4, 11.

Molina, Maria Luisa. "Papusa" and "Fragmentations: Meditations on Separatism." *Signs: Journal of Women in Culture and Society* 19, no. 2 (1994): 449–457.

Molina de Pick, Gracia. "Reflexiones Sobre El Feminismo y La Raza." *Regeneración* 2, no. 4 (1974): 33–34.

————. "Reflexiones Sobre El Feminismo y La Raza." *La Luz* 1, no. 4 (1972): 58.

Montejano, David. "Frustrated Apartheid: Race, Repression, and Capitalist Agriculture in South Texas, 1920–1930." In *The World System of Capitalism: Past and Present,* edited by Walter Goldfrank, 131–168. Beverly Hills, Calif.: Sage Publications, 1979.

————. "Is Texas Bigger Than the World-System? A Critique from a Provincial Point of View." *Review* 4, no. 3 (1981): 597–628.

Montiel, Miguel. "The Social Science Myth of the Mexican American Family." *El Grito: A Journal of Contemporary Mexican-American Thought* 3, no. 4 (1970): 56–64.

Moore, Joan W., and Alfredo Cuéllar. *Mexican Americans.* Englewood Cliffs, N.J.: Prentice-Hall, Inc., 1970.

Mora, Magdalena. "The Tolteca Strike: Mexican Women and the Struggle for Union Representation." In *Mexican Immigrant Workers in the U.S.,* edited by Antonio Rios-Bustamante, 111–117. Los Angeles: CSRC Publications, 1981.

Moraga, Cherríe. "Between the Lines: On Culture, Class, and Homophobia." In *This Bridge Called My Back: Writings by Radical Women of Color,* edited by Cherríe Moraga and Gloria Anzaldúa, 105–106. New York: Kitchen Table, 1981.

————. "Entering the Lives of Others: Theory in the Flesh." In *This Bridge Called My Back: Writings by Radical Women of Color,* edited by Cherríe Moraga and Gloria Anzaldúa, 85–90. New York: Kitchen Table, 1981.

————. "La Güera." In *This Bridge Called My Back: Writings by Radical Women of Color,* edited by Cherríe Moraga and Gloria Anzaldúa, 27–34. New York: Kitchen Table, 1981.

————. "Preface." In *This Bridge Called My Back: Writings by Radical Women of Color,* edited by Cherríe Moraga and Gloria Anzaldúa, xiii–xix. New York: Kitchen Table, 1981.

Moraga, Cherríe, and Gloria Anzaldua, eds. *This Bridge Called My Back: Writings by Radical Women of Color.* New York: Kitchen Table, 1981.

Morales, Armando. *Ando Sangrando: A Study of Mexican American—Police Conflict.* La Puente, Calif.: Perspectiva Publications, 1972.

————. "A Study of Mexican American Perceptions of Law Enforcement Policies and practices in East Los Angeles." Ph.D. dissertation, University of Southern California, 1972.

Morales, Aurora Levins. "' . . . And Even Fidel Can't Change That.'" In *This Bridge Called My Back: Writings by Radical Women of Color,* edited by Cherríe Moraga and Gloria Anzaldúa, 53–56. New York: Kitchen Table, 1981.

Morales, Rosita. "La mujer todavia impotente." *Hijas de Cuauhtémoc* 1 (1971): 4.

Moreno, Dorinda. *La mujer es la tierra; La tierra da vida.* Berkeley, Calif.: Casa Editorial, 1975.

Moreno Gladden, Dorinda. "Political Education Workshop." *Hijas de Cuauhtémoc* 2 (1971): 3.

Moreno, Raul. "Quieren ser hombres?" In *La mujer-en pie de lucha,* edited by Dorindo Moreno. San Francisco: Espina de Norte Publications, 1973.

Moschkovich, Judit. "'—But I Know You, American Woman.'" In *This Bridge Called My Back: Writings by Radical Women of Color,* edited by Cherríe Moraga and Gloria Anzaldúa. 79–84. New York: Kitchen Table, 1981.

Moya, Paula M. "Chicana Feminism and Postmodernist Theory." *Signs: Journal of Women in Culture and Society* 26, no. 2 (2001): 441–484.

Mujeres en Marcha. *Chicanas in the 80's: Unsettled Issues.* Berkeley, Calif.: Chicano Studies Library Publications, 1983.

Muñoz, Carlos. "The Development of Chicano Studies, 1968–1981." In *Chicano Studies: A Multidisciplinary Approach,* edited by Eugene E. García, Francisco A. Lomelí, and Isidro D. Ortiz, 5–18. New York: Teachers College Press, 1984.

———. "On the Nature and Cause of Tension in the Chicano Community: A Critical Analysis." *Aztlán* 1, no. 2 (1970): 99–100.

———. "Politics and the Chicano: On the Status of the Literature." *Aztlán: Chicano Journal of the Social Sciences and Arts* 5, no. 1–2 (1974): 1–7.

———. "The State of the Art in the Study of Chicano Politics." In *Chicanos and the Social Sciences: A Decade of Research and Development (1970–1980),* edited by Isidro D. Ortiz, 47–58. Santa Barbara: UCSB Center for Chicano Studies, 1983.

———. "Toward a Chicano Perspective of Political Analysis." *Aztlán* 1, no. 2 (1970): 15–26.

Muñoz, Carlos, Jr. "The Politics of Chicano Urban Protest: A Model of Political Analysis." Ph.D. dissertation, Claremont Graduate School, 1973.

———. "The Politics of Educational Change in East Los Angeles." In *Mexican American and Educational Change,* edited by Alfred Castaneda et al. New York: Arno Press, 1974.

———. "The Politics of Protest and Chicano Liberation: A Case Study of Repression and Cooptation." *Aztlán* 5, No. 1–2 (1974): 119–141.

———. "The Quest for Paradigm: The Development of Chicano Studies and Intellectuals." In *History, Culture, and Society: Chicano Studies in the 1980s,* edited by Mario García et al., 19–36. Ypsilanti, Mich.: Bilingual Press, 1983.

———. *Youth, Identity, Power: The Chicano Movement.* London: Verso, 1989.

Murguía, Edward. *Assimilation, Colonization, and the Mexican American People.* Austin, Tex.: Center for Mexican American Studies, University of Texas, 1975.

National Association for Chicano Studies. "Preamble." In *Chicano Studies: Critical Connection Between Research and Community,* edited by Teresa Córdova, i. Albuquerque, N.Mex.: National Association for Chicano Studies, 1992.

"National Chicanas Conference." *La Verdad* 29 (1971): 15–17.

"National Chicano Political Conference." In *Profile in the Mexican American Woman,* edited by Martha Cotera. Austin, Tex.: National Educational Laboratory Publishers, Inc., 1976.

Nava, Yolanda M. "The Chicana and Employment: Needs Analysis and Recommendations for Legislation." *Regeneración* 2, no. 3 (1973): 7–9.

Navar, Isabelle. "La Mexicana." *Agenda* 4 (1974): 3–5.

———. "La Mexicana: An Image of Strength." *Regeneración* 2, no. 4 (1974): 4–6.

Navarro, Armando. *Mexican American Youth Organization: Avant-Garde of the Chicano Movement in Texas*. Austin: University of Texas Press, 1995.

Navarro, Joseph. "The Condition of Mexican-American History." *Journal of Mexican American History* 1, no. 1 (1970): 25–52.

Nieto, Consuelo. "The Chicana and the Women's Rights Movement: A Perspective." *Civil Rights Digest* 6, no. 3 (1974): 10–11.

NietoGomez de Lazarin, Anna. "Chicana Feminism." *Caracol* 2, no. 5 (1976): 3–5.

———. "Chicana Identity." *Regeneración* 1, no. 10 (1971): 9.

———. "The Chicana Perspectives for Education." *Encuentro Femenil* 1, no. 1 (1973): 34–61.

———. "Chicanas in the Labor Force." *Encuentro Femenil* 1, no. 2 (1974): 28–33.

———. "Employment Discrimination: How Chicanos Can Combat It." *Somos* 2, no. 7 (1979): 34–35, 40.

———. "La Femenista." *Encuentro Femenil* 1, no. 2 (1974): 34–47.

———. "Madres por Justicia." *Encuentro Femenil* 1, no. 1 (1973): 12–19.

———. "Un Proposito Para Estudios Femeniles De La Chicana." *Regeneración* 2, no. 4 (1975): 31–32

Nogales, Luis. "Chicanismo and Education: Building a Better World." *Chicanismo* 1, no. 6 (1970): n.p.

"Nota preliminary." *Revista Chicano-Riqueña* 1, no. 1 (1973): i.

Novoa, Bruce. *Chicano Poetry: A Response to Chaos*. Austin: University of Texas Press, 1982.

———. "El Estraño e increible caso de la misteriosa desaparición del Profesor K." *Caracol* 3, no. 12 (1977): 12–14.

Nuñez, Rene, and Raoul Contreras. "Principles and Foundations of Chicano Studies: Chicano Organization on University Campuses." In *A Symposium on Chicano Studies Part II: Foundations for Action*. Los Angeles: National Association for Chicano Studies, Southern California FOCO, 1987.

———. "Principles and Foundations of Chicano Studies: Chicano Organization on University Campuses in California." In *Chicano Discourse: Selected Conference Proceedings of the National Association for Chicano Studies*, edited by Tatcho Mindiola Jr. and Emilio Zamora, 32–39. Houston, Tex.: Mexican American Studies Program, 1992.

Oeste, Marcia. "Mujeres Arriba y Adelante." *La Luz* 1, no. 2 (1972): 39–40.

Ojeda, Raul Hinojosa. "International Class Politics of Capital and Labor Flows: Towards a Framework for Praxis." In *The New Nomads: From Immigrant*

Labor to Transnational Working Class, edited by Marlene Dixon and Susanne Jonas, 67–80. San Francisco: Synthesis Publications, 1982.

Olguin, Rick Alan. "The Politics of Criticism as a Criticism of Politics: The Mutual Concerns of Ethnic Studies and Political Theory." Ph.D. dissertation, Stanford University, 1986.

Olivarez, Elizabeth. "Women's Rights and the Mexican American Women." *Regeneración* 2, no. 4 (1974): 40–42.

Olveira, Annette. *MALDEF: Diez Años.* N.p., n.d.

Orange County Brown Berets. "The Adelitas Role en el movimiento." *Hijas de Cuauhtémoc* 1 (1971): 10.

Ordonez, Elizabeth J. "Narrative Texts by Ethnic Women: Rereading the Past, Reshaping the Future." *MELUS* 9, no. 3 (1982): 19–28.

Orendain, Melanie. "Sexual Taboo y La Cultura?" *Imágenes de la Chicana* 1 (n.d.).

Ornelas, Charles. "Book Review of *The Mexican-American People: The Nation's Second Largest Minority.*" *El Grito* 4, no. 4 (1971): 12–20.

Ornelas, Charles, Charles Brazil Ramirez, and Fernando V. Padilla. *Decolonizing the Interpretation of the Chicano Political Experience.* Los Angeles: UCLA Chicano Studies Center, 1975.

Oropeza, Lorena. "Introduction." In *Enriqueta Vasquez and the Chicano Movement: Writings from El Grito del Norte,* edited by Lorena Oropeza and Dionne Espinoza. Houston, Tex.: Arte Publico Press, 2006.

———. *Raza Si! Guerra no! Chicano Protest and Patriotism During the Viet Nam War Era.* Berkeley: University of California Press, 2005.

Orozco, Cynthia. "Sexism in Chicano Studies and the Community." In *Chicana Voices: Intersections of Class, Race, and Gender,* edited by Teresa Córdova et al., 11–18. Colorado Springs: National Association for Chicano Studies Publication, 1986.

Ortega, Carlos F. "Introduction: Chicano Studies as a Discipline." In *Chicano Studies: Survey and Analysis,* edited by Dennis J. Bixler-Márquez et al. Dubuque, Iowa: Kendall/Hunt Publishing Co., 1997.

Ortega y Gasset, José. "La superioridad Anglo-Sajona vista." *Con Safos* 1, no. 3 (1969): 19–20.

Ortego, Philip D. "Backgrounds of Mexican American Literature." Ph.D. dissertation, University of New Mexico, 1971.

———. "Chicano Education: Status Quo? Reform? Revolution." In *Ghosts in the Barrio: Issues in Bilingual-Bicultural Education,* edited by Ralph Poblano. San Rafael, Calif.: Leswing Press, 1973.

———. *Montezuma's Children.* N.p.: Amerex Press, 1971.

Ortiz, Flora Ida. "The Distribution of Mexican American Women in School Organizations." *Hispanic Journal of Behavioral Sciences* 4, no. 2 (1982): 181–198.

Ortiz, Isidro D. "Foreword." In *Chicanos and the Social Sciences: A Decade of Research and Development (1970–1980)*, edited by Isidro D. Ortiz. Santa Barbara, Calif.: UCSB Center for Chicano Studies, 1983.

———. "The Rearguarders Thesis and Latina Elites: A Case Study." *Perspectives in Mexican American Studies* 5 (1995): 171–195.

Ortiz, John. "On Ideological Conflicts." *Regeneración* 2, no. 1 (1971): 17–18.

Padilla, Amado M. "Editorial." *Hispanic Journal of Behavioral Sciences* 1, no. 1 (1979): 1–3.

———. "Notes on the History of Hispanic Psychology." *Hispanic Journal of Behavioral Sciences* 2, no. 2 (1980): 109–128.

———. "Psychological Research and the Mexican American." In *La Causa Chicana: The Movement for Justice,* edited by M. Mangold, 65–77. New York: Family Service Association of America, 1972.

Padilla, Genaro M. *My History, Not Yours: The Formation of Mexican American Autobiography.* Madison: University of Wisconsin Press, 1993.

Padilla, Raymond V. "Apuntes para la documentación de la cultura chicana." *El Grito* 5, no. 2 (1971–1972): 3–46.

———. "Chicano Studies at the University of California, Berkeley: En busca del campus y la comunidad." Ph.D. dissertation, University of California at Berkeley, 1974).

———. *Chicano Studies Revisited: Still in Search of the Campus and the Community.* El Paso: University of Texas at El Paso, 1987.

———. "Chicano Studies Revisited: Still in Search of the Campus and the Community." In *A Symposium on Chicano Studies Part II: Foundations for Action.* Los Angeles: National Association for Chicano Studies, Southern California FOCO, 1987.

———. "A Critique of Pittian History." *El Grito* 6, no. 1 (1972): 3–44.

———. "Freireismo and Chicanizaje." *El Grito* 6, no. 4 (1973): 71–84.

———. "Transformacion Chicana; Chicano Transformation; Transformasion Xikana." *NABE* 1, no. 1 (1976): 73–85.

———. "Transformational Education: A Chicano Pedagogy of Reconstruction." *Bilingual Resources* 2, no. 3 (1979): 2–8.

Pardo, Mary S. *Mexican American Women Activists: Identity and Resistance in Two Los Angeles Communities.* Philadelphia, Pa.: Temple University Press, 1998.

Paredes, Américo. "Folk Medicine and the Intercultural Jest." In *Spanish-Speaking People in the United States: Proceeding of the 1968 Annual Spring Meeting of the American Ethnological Society,* edited by June Helm. Seattle: University of Washington Press, 1968.

———. "On Ethnographic Work Among Minority Groups." In *New Directions in Chicano Scholarship,* edited by Ricardo Romo and Raymund Paredes, 1–32. Santa Barbara, Calif.: UCSB Center for Chicano Studies, 1984.

———. *A Texas-Mexican Cancionero: Folksongs of the Lower Border.* 1976; reprint, Austin: University of Texas Press, 1995.

———. *"With His Pistol in His Hand": A Border Ballad and Its Hero.* Austin: University of Texas Press, 1958.

———, ed. *Humanidad: Essays in Honor of George I. Sánchez.* Los Angeles: UCLA Chicano Studies Center, 1977.

Paz, Octavio. *The Labyrinth of Solitude.* Translation by Lysander Kemp, Tara Milos, Rachel Philips Belash. New York: Grove Press, Inc., 1985.

———. *The Other Mexico: Critique of the Pyramid.* New York: Grover Press, Inc., 1972.

Peñalosa, Fernando. "The Changing Mexican-American in Southern California." *Sociology and Social Research* 51, no. 4 (1967): 405–417.

———. "Recent Changes Among the Chicanos." *Sociology and Social Research* 55, no. 1 (1970): 47–52.

———. "Sociolinguistic Theory and the Chicano Community." *Aztlán* 6, no. 1 (1975): 1–11.

———. "Toward an Operational Definition of Mexican-American." *Aztlán* 1, no. 1 (1970): 1–12.

"Pensamiento Serpentino: A Cultural Trampa or Is the Teatro Campesino Campesino." *La Gente de Aztlán* 5, no. 1 (1974): 5, 14.

Peralta Aguilar, Linda. "Unequal Opportunity and the Chicana." *Regeneración* 2, no. 4 (1974): 45–46.

Pérez, Emma. *The Decolonial Imaginary: Writing Chicanas into History.* Bloomington: Indiana University Press, 1999.

Poblano, Ralph. "Introduction." In *Ghosts in the Barrio: Issues in Bilingual-Bicultural Education,* edited by Ralph Poblano. San Rafael, Calif.: Leswing Press, 1973.

———, ed. *Ghosts in the Barrio: Issues in Bilingual-Bicultural Education.* San Rafael, Calif.: Leswing Press, 1973.

Poblete, Juan, ed. *Critical Latin American and Latino Studies.* Minneapolis: Minnesota University Press, 2003.

Porath, Don. "Chicanos and Existentialism." *De Colores* 1, no. 2 (1974): 6–30.

"Preface." *Encuentro Femenil* 1, no. 1 (1973): n.p.

Racho, Suzan, et al. "Houston Chicana Conference." *La Gente de Aztlán* 1, no. 6 (1971): 6–7.

Ramirez, Manuel, III. "Cognitive Styles and Cultural Democracy in Education." *Social Science Quarterly* 53, no. 4 (1973): 895–904.

Ramirez, Manuel, III, and Alfredo Castañeda. *Cultural Democracy, Bicognitive Development, and Education.* New York: Academic Press, 1974.

Ramos, Betsy. "A mi me dieron el talento." *Chilam Balam* 1, no. 3 (1972): 12–13.

Ramos, Reyes. "A Case in Point: An Ethnomethodological Study of a Poor Mexican American Family." *Social Science Quarterly* 53, no. 4 (1973): 905–919.

Ramos, Samuel. *Profile of Man and Culture in Mexico.* Translation by Peter G. Earle. Austin: University of Texas Press, 1962.

"Raza Unida Party Platform 1972." In *Profile in the Mexican American Woman,* edited by Martha Cotera. Austin, Tex.: National Educational Laboratory Publishers, Inc., 1976.

Rebolledo, Tey Diana. "The Maturing of Chicana Poetry: The Quiet Revolution of the 1980s." In *For Alma Mater: Theory and Practice in Feminist Scholarship,* edited by Paula A. Treichler, Cheris Kramarae, and Beth Stafford, 143–158. Urbana: University of Illinois Press, 1985.

Rendon, Armando. *Chicano Manifesto.* New York: Collier Books, 1971.

Report of the President's Task Force on Chicanos and the University of California. N.p.: 1975.

Reyna, José. "Raza Humor in Texas." *Revista Chicano-Riqueña* 4, no. 1 (1976): 27–33.

Reyna, José R. "Tejano Music as an Expression of Cultural Nationalism." *Revista Chicano-Riqueña* 4, no. 3 (1976): 37–41.

Reyna, José Reynaldo. "Mexican American Prose Narrative in Texas: The Jest and Anecdote." Ph.D. dissertation, UCLA, 1973.

Rincon, Bernice. "Chicanas on the Move." *Regeneración* 2, no. 4 (1974): 52.

———. "La Chicana." *Regeneración* 1, no. 10 (1971): 15–18.

———. "La Chicana: Her Role in the Past and Her Search for a New Role in the Future" *Regeneración* 2, no. 4 (1974): 36–39.

Rios, Sam. "An Approach to Action Anthropology: The Community Project, C.S.U.S." *El Grito del Sol* 3, no. 1 (1978): 51–65.

Rios-C., Herminio. "A Historical and Comparative Content and Linguistic Analysis of the Development of the Image of the Chicano in the Literature from 1804–1980 and Its Implications to Education." Ed.D. thesis, University of San Francisco, 1980.

Risco, Eliezer. "Before Universidad de Aztlán: Ethnic Studies at Fresno State College." In *Parameters of Institutional Change: Chicano Experiences in Education,* edited by the Southwest Network, 41–47. Hayward, Calif.: Southwest Network, 1974.

Rivera, Julius. *On Chicano Studies.* Chicano Studies Institute, 1970.

Robinson, Bea Vasquez. "Are We Racist? Are We Sexist?" *Agenda* (1976): 23–24.

Rochin, Refugio I. "The Short and Turbulent Life of Chicano Studies: A Preliminary Study of Emerging Program and Problems." *Social Science Quarterly* 53, no. 4 (1973): 884–894.

Rocco, Raymond. "The Chicano in the Social Sciences: Traditional Concepts, Myths, and Images." *Aztlán* 1, no. 2 (Fall 1970): 75–97.

———. "A Critical Perspective on the Study of Chicano Politics." *Western Political Quarterly* 30, no. 4 (1977): 558–573.

———. "Marginality and the Recovery of History: On Leopoldo Zea." *Canadian Journal of Political and Social Theory* 4, no. 3 (1981): 42–50.

———. "Positivism and Mexican Identity—Then and Now." *Aztlán* 14, no. 2 (1983): 359–371.

———. "Chicano Studies and Critical Political Theory." In *Chicano Studies: A Multidisciplinary Approach,* edited by Eugene E. García, Francisco A. Lomeli, and Isidrio D. Ortiz, 255–266. New York: Teachers College Press, 1984.

Rodarte, Irene. "Machismo vs Revolution." In *La mujer-en pie de lucha,* edited by Dorindo Moreno. San Francisco: Espina de Norte Publications, 1973.

Rodriguez, Germana Carmen. "Antonio Caso, Erich Fromm y el Chicano: Un estudio de ideologies." In *The Third Annual El Alma Chicana Symposium,* edited by Randall Jimenez, unpaginated. San Jose: California State University, Associated Students and Mexican-American Graduate Studies Department, 1973.

Rodríguez, Ileana, ed. *The Latin American Subaltern Studies Reader.* Durham, N.C.: Duke University Press, 2001.

Rodríguez, Juan. "Acercamiento a cuatro relatos de . . . *Y no se lo tragó la tierra.*" *Mester* 5, no. 1 (1974): 16–24.

———. "Donde Esta la onda?" *Revista Chicano-Riquena* 3, no. 3 (1975): 3–5.

———. "El desarrollo del cuento chicano: Del folklore al tenebroso mundo del yo." *Mester* 4, no. 1 (1973): 19–31.

———. "Temas y motivos de la literatura chicana." In *Festival Flor y Canto III,* edited by Arnold C. Vento et al., 162–168. Austin, Tex.: Pajarito Press, 1975.

———. "La búsqueda de identidad y sus motivos en la literatura chicana." In *The Identification and Analysis of Chicano Literature,* edited by Francisco Jimenez, 170–178. New York: Bilingual Press, 1979.

Rodriguez, Roberto. "Chicano Studies Pioneer Praised: Colleagues, Former Students Pay Tribute as Julian Samora Struggles with Terminal Illness." *Black Issues in Higher Education* 12, no. 16 (1995): 34.

Romanell, Patrick. *Making of the Mexican Mind.* Lincoln: University of Nebraska Press, 1952.

Romano-V., Octavio Ignacio. "The Anthropology and Sociology of the Mexican-American: The Distortion of Mexican-American History." *El Grito* 2, no. 1 (1968): 43–56.

———. Book Review of: *North From Mexico: The Spanish-Speaking People of the United States* [by Carey McWilliams]. *El Grito* 4, no. 1 (1969): 52–56.

———. "The Chosen One." *El Grito* 5, no. 1 (1972): 37–41.

———. "Constitutional Issues and the Rise of the Professional Class in the United States." *El Grito del Sol* 5, no. 2 (1980): 9–24.

———. "Don Pedrito Jaramillo: The Emergence of a Mexican-American Folk Saint." Ph.D. dissertation, University of California at Berkeley, 1963.

———. "Donship in a Mexican-American Community in Texas." *American Anthropologist* 62 (1960): 966–976.

———. *Geriatric Fu: My First Sixty-five Years in the United States.* Berkeley, Calif.: TQS Books, 1990.

———. "Goodbye Revolution—Hello Slum." *El Grito* 2, no. 1 (1968): 8–14.

———. "The Historical and Intellectual Presence of Mexican-Americans." *El Grito* 2, no. 2 (1969): 32–46.

———. "Introductory Comments." *El Grito* 5, no. 1 (1971): 6–8.

———. "Introduction." In *El Espejo The Mirror: Selected Chicano Literature,* edited by Octavio Ignacio Romano-V. Berkeley, Calif.: Quinto Sol Publications, 1972.

———. "Introduction." *El Grito* 2, no. 3 (1969): ii.

———. "Minorities, History, and the Cultural Mystique." *El Grito* 2, no. 1 (1967): 5–11.

———. "Mugre de la cancíon: A Play (Sin Fin) En Tres Actos." *El Grito* 4, no. 1 (1970): 50–55.

———. "Notes on the Modern State." *El Grito* 5, no. 1 (1971): 78–88.

———. "Plegaria." *El Grito* 4, no. 1 (1971): 62–63.

———. "Social Science, Objectivity, and the Chicanos." *El Grito* 4, no. 1 (1970): 4–16.

———. "Tonatiuh International—The First Year." *El Grito del Sol* 1, no. 4 (1976): 6–7.

———. "Un Telefono." *El Grito* 4, no. 1 (1971): 64–65.

———. "Yo no perdi nada . . ." *El Grito* 4, no. 1 (1971): 66.

Romano-V., Octavio Ignacio, and Herminio Rios C. "Quinto Sol and Chicano Publications: The First Five Years, 1967–1972." *El Grito* 5, no. 4 (1972): 3–11.

Romero, Mary. *Maid in the U.S.A.* New York: Routledge, 1992.

———. "Transformation of Culture through Appropriation." Ph.D. dissertation, University of Colorado, 1980.

Romo, Ricardo. "Reconstruction of Chicano History: Acuña's *Occupied America.*" In *Occupied America: A Chicano History Symposium,* edited by Rodolfo Acuña et al., 35–40. Monograph Series No. 3. Houston, Tex.: Mexican American Studies, 1982.

Romo, Ricardo, and Raymund Paredes, eds. *New Directions in Chicano Scholarship.* Santa Barbara, Calif.: UCSB Center for Chicano Studies, 1984.

Rosaldo, Renato. "Anthropological Perspectives on Chicanos, 1970–1980." In *Chicanos and the Social Sciences: A Decade of Research and Development (1970–1980),* edited by Isidro D. Ortiz, 59–84. Santa Barbara, Calif.: UCSB Center for Chicano Studies, 1983.

———. *Chicano Studies, 1970–1984.* Stanford, Calif.: Stanford Center for Chicano Research, 1985.

———. *Culture and Truth: The Remaking of Social Analysis.* Boston: Beacon Press, 1989.

Rosen, Ruth. *The World Split Open: How the Modern Women's Movement Changed America.* New York: Penguin Books, 2000.

Ross, Dorothy. *The Origins of American Social Science.* Cambridge: Cambridge University Press, 1991.

Rubalcava, Luis Alberto. "Assimilation Among Urban Chicanos: A Structural and Cultural Analysis." Ph.D. dissertation, University of Michigan, 1980.

Saavedra-Vela, Pilar. "Hispanic Women in Double Jeopardy." *Agenda* 7 no. 6 (1977): 4–7.

Sabagh, Georges, and David Lopez. "Religiosity and Fertility: The Case of Chicanas." *Social Forces* 59, no. 2 (1980): 431–439.

Sacramento Brown Beret. "Why a Brown Beret Formed or Emerged in the Southwest?" *La Causa* 1, no. 3 (1969): n.p.

Said, Edward. *The World, the Text, and the Critic.* Cambridge: Cambridge University Press, 1983.

Saldívar, José David. *Border Matters: Remapping American Cultural Studies.* Berkeley: University of California Press, 1997.

Saldívar, Ramón. *Chicano Narrative: The Dialectics of Difference.* Madison: University of Wisconsin Press, 1990.

———. "A Dialectic of Difference: Toward a Theory of the Chicano Novel." *MELUS* 6, no. 3 (1979): 73–92.

Saldívar-Hull, Sonia. *Feminism on the Border: Chicana Gender Politics and Literature.* Berkeley: University of California Press, 2000.

———. "Feminism on the Border: From Gender Politics to Geopolitics." In *Criticism in the Borderlands: Studies in Chicano Literature, Culture, and Ideology,* edited by Héctor Calderón and José David Saldívar, 203–220. Durham, N.C.: Duke University Press, 1991.

Salinas, Rodolfo. "Chicano Power: Pride and Prejudice." *Con Safos* 1, no. 3 (1969): 14.

Samora, Julian. *Los Mojados: The Wetback Story.* Notre Dame, Ill.: University of Notre Dame Press, 1971.

Samora, Julian, and Ernesto Galarza. "Research and Scholarly Activity." *Epoca* 1, no. 2 (1971): 51–54.

Samora, Julian, and Richard Lamanna. "Mexican-Americans in a Midwest Metropolis." In *Racial and Ethnic Relations,* 2nd ed., edited by Bernard E. Segal. New York: Thomas Y. Cromwell Company, 1972.

Samora, Julian, and Patricia Vandel Simon. *A History of the Mexican-American People.* Notre Dame, Ill.: University of Notre Dame, 1977.

Sanchez, Corinne. "Higher Education y La Chicana?" *Encuentro Femenil* 1, no. 1 (1973): 27–33.

Sánchez, Federico. "Raices Mexicanas." *El Grito del Sol* 1, no. 4 (1976): 75–87.

———. "Looking Back on Chicano Thought." *Con Safos* 8 (1972): 39–42.

Sánchez, Lionel. *La Raza Community and Chicano Studies.* Santa Barbara, Calif.: Chicano Studies Institute, 1970.

Sánchez, Paul. "Memoirs of a Chicano Administrator." In *Parameters of Institutional Change: Chicano Experiences in Education,* edited by the Southwest Network, 48–61. Hayward, Calif.: Southwest Network, 1974.

Sanchez, Rita. "Chicana Writer Breaking out of the Silence." *De Colores* 3, no. 3 (1977): 31–37.

———. "Imágenes de la Chicana." *Imágenes de la Chicana* 1 (n.d.).

Sánchez, Rosaura. "The Chicana Labor Force." In *Essay on La Mujer*, edited by Rosaura Sánchez and Rosa Martinez Cruz, 3–15. Los Angeles: UCLA Chicano Studies Center, 1977.

———. "Chicano Bilingualism." In *New Directions in Chicano Scholarship*, edited by Ricardo Romo and Raymund Paredes, 209–225. Santa Barbara: UCSB Center for Chicano Studies, 1984.

———. "La crítica marxista: popuesta para la crítica literaria chicana." *Revista Chicano-Riqueña* 8, no. 3 (1980): 93–96.

———. "Critique of Oral Language Assessment Instruments," *NABE* 1, no. 2 (1976): 120–127.

———. "La gramática transformacional y el estudio del español chicano." *Aztlán* 7, no. 1 (1977): 7–12.

———. "The History of Chicanas: A Proposal for a Materialist Perspective." In *Between Borders: Essays on Mexican/Chicana History*, edited by Adelaida R. Del Castillo, 1–29. Encino, Calif.: Floricanto Press, 1990.

———. *Telling Identities: The Californio testimonios*. Minneapolis: University of Minnesota Press, 1995.

Sandoval, Chela. "Feminism and Racism: A Report on the 1981 National Women's Studies Association Conference." In *Making Face, Making Soul/ Haciendo Caras: Creative and Critical Perspectives by Women of Color*, edited by Gloria Anzaldúa. San Francisco: Aunt Lute Foundation Books, 1990.

Saragoza, Alex. "The Significance of Recent Chicano-related Historical Writings: An Appraisal." *Ethnic Affairs* 1 (1987): 24–62.

Saragoza, Elvira. "La Mujer in the Chicano Movement." *Bronce* 1, no. 4 (1969): 13.

Schürmann, Reiner. "Concerning Philosophy in the United States." *Social Research* 61, no. 1 (1994): 89–114.

Scott, Joan Wallach. *Gender and the Politics of History*. New York: Columbia University Press, 1988.

Sedano, Michael V. "Chicanismo in Selected Poetry from the Chicano Movement, 1969–1972: A Rhetorical Study." Ph.D. dissertation, University of Southern California, 1980.

Segade, Gustavo V. "An Introduction to Floricanto." In *An Anthology of Chicano Literature*, edited by Alurista et al., 1–5. Los Angeles: University of California Press, 1976.

———. "Identity and Power: An Essay on the Politics of Culture and the Culture of Politics in Chicano Thought." *Aztlán* 9, no. 1 (1978): 85–92.

———. "Toward a Dialectic of Chicano Literature." *Mester* 4, no. 1 (1973): 4–5.

Segura, Andrés. "Continuidad de la tradición filosófica Nahuatl en la danza de concheros." *El Cuaderno* 3, no. 1 (1973): 16–33.

Segura, Denise A., and Beatriz M. Pesquera. "Beyond Indifference and Antipathy: The Chicana Movement and the Chicana Feminist Discourse." *Aztlán* 19, no. 2 (1988–1990): 69–92.

Sena-Rivera, Jaime. "Extended Kinship in the United States: Competing Models and the Case of la Familia Chicana." *Journal of Marriage and the Family* 41, no. 1 (1979): 121–129.

Servín, Manuel P., ed. *An Awakened Minority: The Mexican-Americans.* Beverly Hills, Calif.: Glencoe Press, 1970.

Sierra, Christine Marie. "The Political Transformation of a Minority Organization: The Council of La Raza, 1965–1980." Ph.D. dissertation, Stanford University, 1983.

Singh, Nikhil Pal. *Black Is a Country: Race and the Unfinished Struggle for Democracy.* Cambridge: Harvard University Press, 2004.

"Si, Se Puede." *Agenda* 1, no. 10 (1976): 3–11.

Skerry, Peter. *Mexican Americans: The Ambivalent Minority.* New York: Free Press, 1993.

Smith, Barbara, and Beverly Smith. "Across the Kitchen Table: A Sister-to-Sister Dialogue." In *This Bridge Called My Back: Writings by Radical Women of Color,* edited by Cherríe Moraga and Gloria Anzaldúa, 113–127. New York: Kitchen Table, 1981.

Soldatenko, Michael. "Constructing Chicana and Chicano Studies: 1993 UCLA Conscious Students of Color Protest." In *Latina/o Los Angeles: Global Transformation, Migrations, and Political Activism,* edited by Enrique C. Ochoa and Gilda Laura Ochoa. Tucson: University of Arizona Press, 2005.

———. "The Quincentenary of an Erasure: From Caliban to Hispanic." *Mexican Studies/Estudios Mexicanos* 13, no. 2 (1997): 385–421.

Solis, Arnaldo. "Chicano Mental Health: Introduction to Chicano Values." *Calmecac* (Summer 1980): 49–56.

———. "Chicano Values: Living in Balance." *Calmecac* (Spring 1982): 30–32.

———. "Chicano Values—Part III." *Calmecac* (Winter 1984): 16–20.

———. "Traditional Chicano Centering." *Calmecac* (Spring 1982): 18–19.

Sosa Riddell, Adaljiza. "Chicanas and El Movimiento." *Aztlán* 5, no. 1–2 (1974): 155–166.

Sosa Riddell, Adaljiza, and Robert Aguallo Jr. "A Case of Chicano Politics: Parlier, California." *Aztlán* 9, no. 1 (1979): 1–22.

Sotomayor, Marta. "La Década de la Mujer." *Agenda* 7, no. 6 (1977): 2.

Stanley, Liz. "Introduction." In *Feminist Praxis,* edited by Liz Stanley, 3–19. London: Routledge, 1990.

Stanley, Liz, and Sue Wise. *Breaking Out: Feminist Consciousness and Feminist Research.* London: Routledge and Kegan Paul, 1983.

———. "Method, Methodology, and Epistemology in Feminist Research Processes." In *Feminist Praxis,* edited by Liz Stanley, 20–60. London: Routledge, 1990.

"Symposium at Irvine." *La Gente de Aztlán* 4, no. 4 (1974): 4.

Tijerina, Reies López. *Mi lucha por la tierra.* Mexico City: Fondo de Cultura Económica, 1978.

———. *They Called Me "King Tiger": My Struggle for the Land Our Rights.* Houston, Tex.: Arte Público Press, 2000.

Tirado, Michael David. "The Mexican American Minority's Participation in Voluntary Associations." Ph.D. dissertation, Claremont Graduate School, 1970.

"To Think . . . To Act . . . Is to Be Alive." *Regeneración* 2, no. 3 (1973): 36.

Treviño, Jesús Salvador. *Eyewitness: A Filmmaker's Memoir of the Chicano Movement.* Houston, Tex.: Arte Público Press, 2001.

Trueba, Enrique T. "Issues and Problems in Bilingual Bicultural Education Today." *NABE* 1, no. 1 (1976): 11–19.

———. "The Meaning and Use of Context in Ethnographic Research: Implications for Validity." *NABE* 6, no. 2–3 (1981–1982): 21–34.

Trueba, Enrique T., and Pamela G. Wright. "On Ethnographic Studies and Multicultural Education." *NABE* 5, no. 2 (1980–1981): 29–56.

Trujillo Gaitan, Marcella. "The Dilemma of the Modern Chicana Artist and Critic." *Heresies* 2, no. 4 (1979): 5–10.

Trujillo, Marcela. "The Terminology of Machismo." *De Colores* 4, no. 3 (1978): 34–42.

"UCLA Chicanos Sit-In." *Centro* 3, no. 4 (1974): 2.

Ugarte, Sandra. "Philosophy Workshop." *Hijas de Cuauhtémoc* 2 (1971): 1–3.

Una Chicana. "Abajo con los machos." In *La mujer-en pie de lucha,* edited by Dorindo Moreno. San Francisco: Espina de Norte Publications, 1973.

Urista, Alberto. "Oscar Z. Acosta: In Context." Ph.D. dissertation, University of California at San Diego, 1983.

Vaca, Nicolás C. "The Black Phase." *El Grito* 2, no. 1 (1968): 40–48.

———. "The Comparative Study of Values in Five Cultures Project and the Theory of Value." *Aztlán* 12, no. 1 (1981): 89–120.

———. "Message to the People." *Quinto Sol Mexican-American Liberation Papers* 1 (1967): 1–8.

———. "The Mexican-American in the Social Sciences 1912–1970. Part I: 1912–1935." *El Grito* 3, no. 3 (1970): 3–24.

———. "The Mexican-American in the Social Sciences 1912–1970. Part II: 1936–1970." *El Grito* 4, no. 1 (1970): 17–51.

———. "The Negro Movement as an Anti-revolution." *El Grito* 2, no. 2 (1969): 61–70.

Vaca, Nick Corona. "Sociology Through Literature: The Case of the Mexican-American." Ph.D. dissertation, University of California at Berkeley, 1976.

Vaillancourt, Pauline Marie. *When Marxists Do Research*. New York: Green-woord Press, 1986.

Valadez, Senon. "In Search of a Perspective: An Apology Long Overdue." *El Grito del Sol* 3, no. 1 (1978): 67–73.

Valdez, Armando, Albert Camarrilo, and Tomás Almaguer. *The State of Chicano Research on Family, Labor, and Migration*. Stanford, Calif.: Stanford Center for Chicano Research, 1983.

Valdez, Luis. "The Tale of La Raza." In *The Chicanos: Mexican American Voices*, edited by Ed Ludwig and James Santibañez, 95–100. Baltimore, Md.: Penguin Books Inc., 1971.

———. "Notes on Chicano Theatre." *El Teatro* (1970): 5.

———. *Pensamiento serpentino: A Chicano Appraoch to the Theater of Reality*. N.p.: Cucaracha Publications, 1973.

Valerio, Anita. "It's In My Blood, My Face—My Mother's Voice, The Way I Sweat." In *This Bridge Called My Back: Writings by Radical Women of Color,* edited by Cherríe Moraga and Gloria Anzaldúa, 41–45. New York: Kitchen Table, 1981.

Vargas, Adrian. "Carnalismo." *Chilam Balam* 1, no. 3 (1972): 16–17.

Vargas, Roberto. *Provida Leadership: A Guide to Human/Social Transformation*. Oakland, Calif.: Razagente Assoc., 1985.

Vásquez, Carlos. "Women in the Chicano Movement." In *Mexican Women in the United States: Struggles Past and Present,* edited by Magdalena Mora and Adelaida R. Del Castillo, 27–28. Los Angeles: UCLA Chicano Studies Research Center, 1980.

Vasquez, Melba J. T. "Confronting Barriers to the Participation of Mexican American Women in Higher Education." *Hispanic Journal of Behavioral Sciences* 4, no. 2 (1982): 147–165.

Vásquez, Richard. "Chicano Studies: Sensitivity for Two Cultures." In *The Chicanos: Mexican American Voices,* edited by Ludwig and James Santibañez, 205–211. Baltimore, Md.: Penguin Books Inc., 1971.

Vázquez, Francisco H. "Aztec Epistemology." *El Grito* 5, no. 4 (1972): 74–79.

———. "Chicanology: A Postmodern Analysis of Meshicano Discourse." *Perspectives in Mexican American Studies* 3 (1992): 116–147.

———. "Chicano Studies and a Liberal Arts Education." *Somos* 1, no. 2 (1978): 36–37.

———. "Philosophy in Mexico: The Opium of the Intellectuals or a Prophetic Insight?" *Canadian Journal of Political and Social Theory* 4, no. 3 (1981): 27–41.

Veloz, Josefina Estrada. "Chicana Identity: Gender and Ethnicity." Ph.D. dissertation, New Mexico State University, 1981.

Vento, Arnold C. *Festival Flor y Canto II*. Austin, Tex.: Pajarito Press, 1975.

Vigil, Diego. "Marx and Chicano Anthropology." *El Grito* 3, no. 1 (1978): 19–34.

Vigil, Ernesto B. *The Crusade for Justice: Chicano Militancy and the Government's War on Dissent.* Madison: University of Wisconsin Press, 1999.

Vigil, James Diego. "Understanding the Chicano People: The Six C's Model of Sociocultural Change." *Campo Libre* 1, no. 2 (1981): 141–167.

Villarreal, Rosa Martha. "Existentialism and . . . y no se lo trago la tierra." *TQS Currents* 13, no. 5 (1996): n.p.

Votaw, Carmen Delgado. "Cultural Influences on Hispanic Feminism." *Agenda* 10, no. 1 (1980): 44–49.

Wagner, Nathaniel N., and Marsha J. Haug. *Chicanos: Social and Psychological Perspectives.* St. Louis, Mo.: C.V. Mosley Comp., 1971.

Weinstein, Michael, and Deena Weinstein. "The Problematic of Marginality in Mexican Philosophy." *Canadian Journal of Political and Social Theory* 4, no. 3 (1981): 21–26.

"Why a Chicano Party?" In *La Raza: Why a Chicano Party?,* edited by Roger Alvarado et al., 3–12. New York: Merit Pamphlet, 1970.

Williams, Raymond. "Base and Superstructure in Marxist Cultural Theory." *New Left Review* 82 (1973): 3–16.

———. "The Future of Cultural Studies." In *The Politics of Modernism: Against the New Conformists,* edited by Raymond Williams, 151–162. London: Verso, 1989.

———. *Marxism and Literature.* Oxford: Oxford University Press, 1977.

"Women Caucus Makes History." *Regeneración* 2, no. 3 (1973): 32.

Yamada, Mitsuye. "Asian Pacific American Women and Feminism." In *This Bridge Called My Back: Writings by Radical Women of Color,* edited by Cherríe Moraga and Gloria Anzaldúa, 71–75. New York: Kitchen Table, 1981.

———. "Invisibility Is an Unnatural Disaster: Reflections of an Asian American Woman." In *This Bridge Called My Back: Writings by Radical Women of Color,* edited by Cherríe Moraga and Gloria Anzaldúa, 71–75. New York: Kitchen Table, 1981.

Ybarra, Lea. "Empirical and Theoretical Developments in the Study of Chicano Families." In *The State of Chicano Research on Family, Labor, and Migration,* edited by Armando Valdez, Albert Camarrillo, and Tomás Almaguer, 91–110. Stanford, Calif.: Stanford Center for Chicano Research, 1983.

———. "When Wives Work: The Impact on the Chicano Family." *Journal of Marriage and the Family* 44, no. 1 (1982): 169–178.

Ybarra-Frausto, Tomás. "The Chicano Movement and the Emergence of a Chicano Poetic Consciousness." In *New Directions in Chicano Scholarship,* edited by Ricardo Romo and Raymund Paredes, 81–109. Santa Barbara: UCSB Center for Chicano Studies, 1984.

Zamora, Bernice. "The Chicana as a Literary Critic." *De Colores* 3, no. 3 (1977): 16–19.

———. "Editorial." *El Fuego de Aztlán* 3 (1977): 1–2.

———. "Our Truth, Our Voice." *El Fuego de Aztlán* 3 (1976–1977): 3.

Zamora, Carlos. "Humanismo y Praxis Artistica." *Mester* 4, no. 1 (1973): 3.

Zamora, Emilio. "Critical Comments on *Occupied America*." In *Occupied America: A Chicano History Symposium,* edited by Rodolfo Acuña et al., 41–47. Monograph Series No. 3. Houston, Tex.: Mexican American Studies, 1982.

Zavella, Patricia. "The Problematic Relationship of Feminism and Chicana Studies." *Women's Studies* 17, no. 1–2 (1989): 25–36.

———. *Women's Work and Chicano Families: Cannery Workers of the Santa Clara Valley.* Ithaca, N.Y.: Cornell University Press, 1987.

Index

Action research, 59, 110–12
Acuña, Rodolfo, 36–37, 51, 100, 121–22, 124, 125, 152, 178, 184–85
Aguilera Gómez, Manuel, 102
Alarcón, Justo, 90, 122, 123
Alarcón, Norma, 162–63
Alejandro, Franco, 41
Almaguer, Tomás, 51, 53, 170
Alternative institutions, 84–85
Alurista (Alberto Urista Heredia), 36, 73, 91
Alvarez, Rodolfo, 48
Amaro, Arturo, 82
Amaya, Abel, 100
anthropology, Chicano Studies and, 117–20
Anzaldúa, Gloria, 164, 166, 174, 175, 179–80, 184
Apodaca, Linda, 157
Aragón de Shepro, Theresa, 72
Arce, Carlos, 97–98, 121
Arellano, Estevan, 85–86
Armas, José, 77, 139
Arroyo, Luis, 124
Arvizu, Steven, 120
Atencio, Tomás, 85–86
Aztlán: Chicano Journal of the Social Sciences and the Arts, 13, 66, 97, 103, 170; formulation of Chicano Studies and, 46–57. See also International Journal of Chicano Studies Research

Baca Zinn, Maxime, 115–16, 152–53, 159, 161
Bakhtin, Mikhail, 19–20

Bakke decision, 101
Barreda, Gabino, 107, 108
Barrera, Elma, 140–41
Barrera, Mario, 51, 52–53, 110, 170
Basso, Sister Teresita, 82
Bernal, Esmeralda, 72
Bilingual Review, 57
The Bilingual Review/La Revista Bilingue, 103
Blackwell, Maylei, 145
Blea, Irene, 113
Bloch, Ernst, 18
Brazil Ramirez, Charles, 96
Bronner, Stephen Eric, 18
Brown Berets, 88, 144–45
Bruce-Novoa, Juan, 80
Burma, John H., 48

Cabán, Pedro, 177
Cadena, Gilbert, 117
Calderón, Héctor, 180
Camarillo, Albert, 96
Campo Libre: Journal of Chicano Studies, 97, 104
canon formation, Chicano Studies and, 102–11
Caracol, 57, 103
Cárdenas, Gilbert, 56–57
Carnalismo, 72, 74
Carranza, Elihu, 74–76, 84, 106, 171
Carta Abierta, 104
Casavantes, Edward, 48, 104
Caso, Alfonso, 107
Caso, Antonio, 82
Castañeda, Alfredo, 104, 114
Castañeda, Antonia, 163

Castañeda, Carlos, 47, 113
Castoriadis, Cornelius, 20
Castro, Raymond, 44–45, 48, 49, 97
Cervantes, Fred, 52
Chavarría, Jesús, 49, 50, 55, 124
Chávez, César, 15, 89
Chavez, Mauro, 76
Chicanas: criticism of movement and,
  173; cultural nationalism and, 133–
  34; *el movimento and,* 131–43; first
  National Chicana Conference and,
  136–42; intellectual production,
  151–61; loyalists and, 140; nation-
  alism and, 140; organizations, 160;
  overview of, 130–31; student move-
  ments and, 131–43
chicanismo, 39–40, 89; Perspectivist
  Chicano Studies and, 71–74; as
  philosophy, 74–78
Chicano Council in Higher Education
  (CCHE), 42
Chicano Law Review, 57
Chicanos(as): Chicano studies and, 3;
  indigenous heritage of, and literary
  and intellectual output, 91–92
Chicano student movements, 130–31
Chicano Studies, 75, 189n2; action
  research and, 110–12; activism of,
  173; anthropology and, 117–20;
  Aztlán and formulation of, 46–57;
  canon formation and, 102–11;
  Chicanos(as) and, 3; consolidation
  of, 128–29; contemporary, 174–75;
  curriculum, 35–37; empirics and,
  94; empirics and "good," 122;
  Empirical Chicano Studies as, 64–
  66; institutional support for, 127–
  28; institution building, 1975-1982,
  97–102; internationalization of,
  101–2; Marxism and, 123–24, 127;
  opposition and dominance of, 83–
  84; political science and, 120–21;
  research, 112–27; sociology and,
  116–17; student movement and, 3;
  success of, as academic project, 63;
  tension between advocacy and institutional demands and, 95–96. *See
  also* Empirical Chicano Studies;
  Perspectivist Chicano Studies

Ciaramelli, Fabio, 187
Cisneros, Victor, 124–25
community service, 86–87, 111
conferences, 59–60, 101
Con Safos, 57, 69
Contreras, Jesse, 42, 68
Córdova, Teresa, 160–61
Corona, Bert, 63
Cortes, Carlos, 49
Cota-Robles de Suarez, Cecilia, 153
Cotera, Martha, 131, 132, 149
Cruse, Harold, 66
Cruz, Sor Juana Inez de la, 145
Cuádraz, Gloria, 161
Cuéllar, Alfred, 66, 72–73, 82–83
Cuéllar, José B., 80, 112
cultural nationalism, 50–51; chicanas
  and, 133–34
curriculum, Chicano studies, 35–37

Davalos, Karen Mary, 23
Decierdo, Margarita, 161
*De Colores: Journal of Emerging
  Raza Philosophies,* 57
Del Castillo, Adelaida, 134, 142–43,
  145, 146
Doctrina de la raza, 77
D-Q University, 85, 204n135

Echeverría Alverez, Luis, 102
Eger, Ernestina, 80
El Alma Chicana Symposium, 82
*El Concilio Nacional de Estudios
  Chicanos,* 43–46
El Cuaderno, 57
*El Grito: A Journal of Contemporary
  Mexican-American Thought*
  (Romano), 13, 22–27, 97, 103,
  160, 169
El Grito del Sol, 57, 119–20
Elizondo, Sergio, 44, 110
el movimento, 3, 6; chicanas and,
  131–43
El Plan de Santa Barbara, 13, 27–31,
  64, 94–95, 169–70; formation of
  Empirical Chicano Studies and,
  39–43
Empirical Chicano Studies, 6–8, 38–
  39, 46; alternative variants and, 83;

Aztlán and, 170; as Chicano Studies, 64–66; Chicano Studies as, 64–66; formation of, 39–43; founding of, 31–33; summary of, 171–72. *See also* Chicano Studies
empirics, 38–39; control of Chicano Studies and, 94; "good" Chicano Studies and, 122
Encurentro Feminil, 57, 145–46, 160
Enos, Darryl, 40
Enríquez, Evangelina, 122–23, 155–56
Essentialism, Perspectivist Chicano Studies and, 88–92
Estrada, Leobardo, 111, 121

Fanon, Franz, 123
feminism, Chicana, 143–51, 177, 182. *See also* Chicanas
Fleck, Ludwik, 32
Flores, Estevan, 116–17, 125, 126–27
Flores, Francesca, 132, 137–38
Flores, Guillermo, 110
Flores Cabellero, Romeo, 102
Flores Magón brothers, 107
Ford Foundation, 99, 100
Freire, Paulo, 76, 123, 150
Fromm, Erich, 82

Galarza, Ernesto, 47, 63, 110, 113
García, Alma, 130–31, 132, 133, 143–44
Garcia, Elena, 134
Garcia, F. Chris, 120–21
García, Ignacio, 40, 102, 113, 178
García, Jorge, 178
García, Mario, 95, 122, 176
Garcia, Velia, 138–39, 140
Garza, Hisauro, 60–61
Gilabert, César, 17
Giroux, Henry, 18
Gómez-Quiñones, Juan, 29, 39, 44–45, 48, 49, 51, 53, 61–62, 95–96, 97, 105–7, 124, 125, 157–58
Gonzales, Rodolfo "Corky," 15, 89, 133
Gonzales, Sylvia, 108, 123, 149–50
González, Deena, 161, 177
Grebler, Leo, 33, 48

Guerra, Manuel, 43
Gutiérrez, José Angel, 63, 102
Gutierrez, Ramon, 145
Gutiérrez-Jones, Carl, 180, 181–82
Guzman, Ralph C., 33, 48

Hayes-Bautista, David, 92
Heredia, Alberto Urista (Alurista), 36, 73, 91
Hernández, Duluvina, 33–35, 46–47, 80, 170
Hernandez, Norma G., 112–13
Herstories, Chicana, 143–47
higher education, Chicanos in, 61
Hijas de Cuauhtémoc, 137, 144, 145, 146, 160
Hill Collins, Patricia, 174
Hinojosa, Rolando, 123
Hispanic Journal of Behavior Sciences, 104
historical research, Chicano, 123; Marxism and, 125–27
Hitch, Charles J., 61–62, 128
Horkheimer, Max, 19, 172
Houston Conference. *See* National Chicana Conference in Houston
Howton, David R., 103
Husserl, Edmund, 185

interdisciplinarity, 54–55
internal colonial model, 51–54, 112, 125
International Journal of Chicano Studies Research, 55. *See also Aztlán: Chicano Journal of the Social Sciences and the Arts*

Jacoby, Russell, 16–17
Journal of Mexican-American Studies, 57
journals, 103–4; Chicana, 160; Chicana perspectives in, 160; feminist, 145–46. *See also specific journal*

Klor de Alva, Jorge, 107–9
knowledge, 3–4

La Academia de la Nueva Raza, 85
La Cosecha, 160

La Palabra: Revista de Literatura Chicana, Comadre, 160
La Raz Unida Party, 63–64
La Revista Bilingue/The Bilingual Review, 103
Levinas, Emmanuel, 185–87, 188
Levins Morales, Aurora, 164
Levy, Ze'ev, 20
Limón, José, 119, 125–26
literary criticism, Chicano, 78, 122–23
Lizárraga, Sylvia S., 122
Lloyd, Rees, 63
Longauex y Vásquez, Enriqueta, 132, 135–36, 139–40
Lopez, Josefina, 143
Lopez, Ronald, 40, 42
López, Sonia, 132
López Portillo, José, 102
López Tijerina, Reies, 15, 102
Lorde, Audre, 165–66, 179
Lugones, María, 10, 77

Macías, Reynaldo, 44–45, 48, 49, 97
Maciel, David R., 68
Madrid, Arturo, 61, 99
Maize: Cuadernos de Arte y Literatura Xicana, 103
Manuel, Frank, 16
Manuel, Fritzie, 16
Marcuse, Herbert, 18
Mares, E. A., 76–77, 90
Martí, Oscar, 108
Martinez, Donato, 67–68
Martínez, Elizabeth, 132, 134
Martinez, Max, 123
Martinez, Olga, 132
Martinez, Samuel C., 87
Martinez, Thomas, 71
Marxism: Chicano historical research and, 125–27; Chicano Studies and, 123–25, 127; feminist studies and, 158
Matsuda, Gema, 145
McCaughan, Ed, 134
McKenna, Teresa, 177
McLaren, Peter, 17, 18
McWilliams, Carey, 25

Medina, Celia, 71, 108
Mejia Briscoe, Lori, 132
Melville, Margarita, 152
Mexican American activists, 5–6
Mexican American Youth Organization, 63
Mindiola, Anastacio "Tatcho," Jr., 125
Mirandé, Alfredo, 115–16, 155–56
Movimiento Estudiantil Chicano de Aztlán (MEChA), 61
Molina de Pick, Gracia, 154–55
Montague, Peter, 63
Moore, Joan W., 33, 48
Morales, Rosita, 144
Mujeres Activas en Letras y Cambio Social (MALCS), 160
Mujeres en Marcha, 160
Muñoz, Carlos, Jr., 14–15, 29, 40–41, 49–50, 52, 53–54, 56, 60, 82, 112, 113, 170, 176–77
Muñoz, Rosalio, 110
Murguía, Edward, 48

National Association for Chicano Studies (NACS), 57–64, 84, 100–101, 160, 171
National Association of Chicano Social Scientists, 100
National Chicana Conference in Houston, Chicanas and, 136–42
National Chicano Commission of Higher Education, 98–99, 99, 171
National Council of La Raza, 63
nationalism, Chicanas and, 140
Navar, Isabelle, 154
Nazareth, Peter, 123
NietoGomez, Anna, 132, 134, 136, 140–41, 146–51, 156
Novoa, Juan Bruce, 122, 123
Nuñez, Rene, 28

Olguin, Rick, 6
organized research units (ORUs), 62
Ornelas, Charles, 51, 96
Orozco, Cynthia, 136, 146
Ortega, Carlos, 41, 56
Ortega y Gasset, José, 68, 69, 79, 88, 170

Ortego, Philip, 123
Ortiz, Isidro, 102

Padilla, Amado, 48, 92, 104, 121
Padilla, Fernando V., 96
Padilla, Genaro, 180
Padilla, Raymond, 30, 33–35, 80, 98, 169–70, 193n113
Paredes, Américo, 113, 117–18, 123
Paz, Octavio, 24, 68, 77, 170
Peñalosa, Fernando, 46–47, 56
Perez, Emma, 177, 182
Perspectivist Chicano Studies, 6–8; as academic project, 78–84; break up of, 84; chicanismo and, 71–74; essentialism and, 88–92; evaporation of, 93; introduction to, 67–70; self-consciousness and, 92; summary of, 170–71. See also Chicano Studies
Pitt, Leonard, 33
Policy research, 111
Political science, Chicano Studies and, 120–21
Porath, Dan, 88–89, 108
Portillo, Estela, 160

Quantitative research, 48
Quinto Sol collective, 13, 22–23

Race, 4–5
Ramírez, Manuel, III, 104, 114
Ramos, Reyes, 82
Ramos, Samuel, 68, 170
la raza cósmica, 107
Razalogía, 87, 89
Regeneración, 57
Rendon, Armando, 63, 156
la resolana, 86
Revista Chicano-Riqueña, 57, 103
Reyna, José R., 122
Rincon, Bernice, 141, 155
Rios-C., Herminio, 122
Risco, Eliezer, 84–85
Rivera, Julius, 43, 47
Rivera, Tomás, 79, 123
Rocco, Raymond, 54, 80–81
Rochin, Refugio, 65–66
Rodriguez, Germana Carmen, 82

Rodríguez, Juan, 78–80, 104, 123
Romanell, Patrick, 68–69
Romano, Octavio I., 13, 22–27, 80, 83, 84, 88, 119
Rosaldo, Renato, 118, 119, 180, 181
Ross, Dorothy, 4

Saldívar, José David, 117, 180
Saldívar, Ramón, 123, 180
Saldívar-Hull, Sonia, 158
Samora, Julian, 110, 113–14, 118
Sanchez, Corinne, 146–47
Sánchez, Federico, 108, 109–10
Sánchez, George I., 47, 113
Sánchez, Paul, 61, 84
Sanchez, Ricardo, 123
Sanchez, Rita, 162–63
Sánchez, Rosaura, 122, 156–57, 180
Santos, Robert, 121
Saragoza, Alex, 124–25
Sedano, Michael, 78
Segade, Gustavo, 78
self-consciousness, Perspectivist Chicano Studies and, 92
Sena-Rivera, Jaime, 47, 57
Servín, Manuel P., 48
Shepro, Aragón de, 106, 113
Singh, Nikhil Pal, 5
Smith, Barbara, 165
Smith, Beverly, 165
social responsibility, 77
sociology, Chicano Studies and, 116–17
Solis, Arnaldo, 89–90
Sommers, Joseph, 123
Sosa Riddell, Adaljiza, 154
Southwest Council of La Raza, 63
Stanley, Liz, 180–81
student movements: in California, 14–22; Chicanos and, 131–43; Chicano studies and, 3

Tejidos, 57, 104
Terrazas Acevedo, Jorge, 62–63, 71
Third Women, 160, 162
This Bridge Called My Back, 163–67, 174, 175–83, 179–80

thought collectives, 32
thought styles, 32
Tienda, Marta, 121
Treviño, Jesús, 91
Trujillo, Marcela, 163

UCLA Mexican American Culture
  Center, 49
Utopia, 16–21

Vaca, Nick, 23, 70, 84, 119
Valdez, Luis, 91
Valizzan, Lupe, 132
Vargas, Robert, 72, 89
Vargas, Roberto, 87

Vasconcelos, José, 69, 107
Vázquez, Francisco, 69, 91
Vialpando, Geralda, 110
Vidal, Mirta, 132

Williams, Raymond, 8–9

Ybarra, Lea, 153
Ybarra-Frausto, Tomás, 122

Zamora, Bernice, 123
Zamora, Carlos, 78
Zavella, Patricia, 161
Zea, Leopoldo, 81, 107

About the Author

Michael Soldatenko is Professor and Chair of Chicano Studies at California State University, Los Angeles. His recent work has explored the development of Chicano(a) studies as well as campus politics in the United States and Mexico in the 1960s and 1970s. His recent essays include "México 68: La imaginación al poder," *Latin American Perspectives* 32 (2005); "Constructing Chicana and Chicano Studies: 1993 UCLA Conscious Students of Color Protest," in *Latina/o Los Angeles: Global Transformation, Migrations and Political Activism*, edited by Enrique C. Ochoa and Gilda Laura Ochoa (Tucson: University of Arizona Press, 2005); "The Mexican Student Movements: Los Angeles and Mexico City, 1968," *Latino Studies* 1, no. 2 (2003); and "How Chicano Studies Joined the Curriculum: Radicalism and the Hidden Curriculum in Higher Education," in *Hidden Curricula in Higher Education*, edited by Eric Margolis (New York: Routledge, 2001).

www.ingramcontent.com/pod-product-compliance
Lightning Source LLC
Chambersburg PA
CBHW021854020426
42334CB00013B/330